The
WoodenBoat Index
Issues 1-100

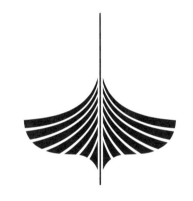

Compiled by Anne Bray

Assistant
Cynthia Curtis

Library of Congress Cataloging-in-Publication Data

Bray, Anne.
The woodenboat index : issues 1-100 / compiled by Anne Bray.
p.   cm.
ISBN 0-937822-22-1 : $12.95
1. Woodenboat—Indexes. 2. Boatbuilding—Periodicals—Indexes.
3. Boats and boating—Periodicals—Indexes.   I. Title.
VM320.W66 1991 Suppl.
623.8'207— dc20   91-27114
CIP

WoodenBoat magazine is published bimonthly and is available by subscription or at
the newsstand. For information regarding the magazine, write to:

WoodenBoat
P.O. Box 78
Brooklin, Maine 04616

Published by WoodenBoat Publications, Brooklin, Maine 04616

The
WoodenBoat Index
Issues 1-100

Compiled by Anne Bray

Assistant
Cynthia Curtis

Copy Editing
Jane Crosen

Proofreading
Beata Gray

Design
Olga Lange

Design Assistance
Sandy Cohen

Cover photograph
Ken Woisard

Welcome to our Index to the first 100 issues of *WoodenBoat* magazine, spanning a period of nearly 17 years. We are pleased and proud to be able to offer this comprehensive reference tool, which is the culmination of months of careful effort. We believe that *WoodenBoat* contains a great deal of original and timeless material, and that collectively, the issues constitute a unique and valuable resource. We also recognize, of course, that access to this material becomes much more complex as we continue to publish these issues. Because we are committed to making the back issues accessible to readers, we want also to ensure that they can be utilized to their full potential. This Index should make it much easier.

Our first Index covered 36 issues, the next (at ten years) covered 60, and a supplement included 18 more. We have long looked forward to being able to offer one single volume in which so many issues could be included. The result should easily and effectively aid both simple and complex information searches.

The Index was developed and compiled by Anne Bray, who, with the assistance of Cynthia Curtis, manages the research library at WoodenBoat, where virtually every question regarding editorial material ends up. The Index is a creation, therefore, inspired by the needs of readers and researchers. It is designed to be practical, to streamline the research process, whether it be on planking methods, modern yacht designers and builders, or the history of yachts and boats. We are deeply committed to making every issue of *WoodenBoat* valuable to our readers, and this Index is an expression of that mission. We hope that it serves its purpose well.

—*Jon Wilson, Editor*
WoodenBoat *magazine*

How to Use This Index

example:

A & T Marine Services, builder:
 NAJA 30 kit boats, 38:84
Abbott, Ken, author:
 "Out of My Class," 12:40
Abeking and Rasmussen, builder (Germany):
 Concordia yawl, 67:100, 68:70, 80:64
 12-Meter-class boats, 68:40
Abel, Kenneth, author and illustrator:
 "The Narrowboats of Great Britain," 41:98
ABILITY (Scottish fishing vessel):
 comments, photo, 62:68
ABLE (cutter):
 comments, detail photo, 69:104
 comments, photo, 76:60
ABRAHAM RYDBERG (four-masted bark):
 comments, photo, 87:56
Abramson, Dean, photographer:
 "Carroll Lowell Comes in from
 the Cold," 70:84
A-cat class:
 history, photos, 62:60
A-cat class, MARY ANN:
 history, photo, 62:60

Annotation in two forms:
 Description
 Title (in quotes)

Reference information:
 Issue 62, page 60

NOTE: Page reference always refers to first page of
 article in which subject appears.

 For author and title, refer to the contents
 pages of this index, which start on page 94.

1

A & T Marine Services, builder:
NAJA 30 kit boats, 38:84

Abbott, Ken, author:
"Out of My Class," 12:40

Abeking and Rasmussen, builder (Germany):
Concordia yawl, 67:100, 68:70, 80:64
12-Meter-class boats, 68:40

Abel, Kenneth, author and illustrator:
"The Narrowboats of Great Britain," 41:98

ABILITY (Scottish fishing vessel):
comments, photo, 62:68

ABLE (cutter):
comments, detail photo, 69:104
comments, photo, 76:60

ABRAHAM RYDBERG (four-masted bark):
comments, photo, 87:56

Abramson, Dean, photographer:
"Carroll Lowell Comes in from the Cold,"
70:84

A-cat class:
history, photos, 62:60

A-cat class, MARY ANN:
history, photo, 62:60

A-cat class, SPY:
history, photo, 62:60

A-cat class, WASP:
history, photo, 62:60

Accommodation plan:
comments by Joel White, 75:111

ACE (speedboat):
design and construction commentary,
photos, 45:77

Acetone:
hazards of use, 93:86

a.c.f. (American Car & Foundry), builder:
association with Walter McInnis, 53:38

a.c.f. 41 (power cruiser):
comments, plans, 53:38

Ackerman, Edward (Ned):
comments, 31:18, 33:2, 33:20

Ackerman, Edward (Ned), author:
"Rediscovering Hackmatack," 9:44

Acorn class, LITTLE JOSIE:
history, owner's comments, photo, plans,
30:46

Acorn skiff (sailing skiff):
advice on painting for decoration, 93:42
building commentary, photos, plans, 56:60
comments, photo, 70:74

ACTIV (Danish topsail schooner):
comments, photo, 85:64

ACTIVE (pilot gig):
comments, plan, 25:28

ACTIVE (schooner):
account of passage from Rhode Island to
England, photos, 7:20
charter of, 42:82

ADAGIO (Barnegat Bay sneakbox):
rebuilding, 47:102

Adair, D.C.:
letter on marine plywood, 57:8

Adams, Charles Francis, III:
profile, photo, 85:74

Adams, Fred and Donald, builders:
Alexandria Bay boats, 49:58

Adams, Kenny, builder:
construction methods, 73:86

Adams, Michael, author:
"A Decade of Legendary 12s," 68:40

Adams, William G.:
letter on Honduras dugout canoe, 77:6

Adamson, Dayna, author:
"JOY is a Wooden Boat," 17:69

A. Dauphinee & Sons:
profile, 94:64

ADELAIDE II (New York 30):
history, 35:20

Adhesives:
commentary by Aimé Ontario Fraser, 92:23
commentary by John Pazereskis, 19:46
commentary by Gerald Schindler, 4:47
comments by John Guzzwell, 84:64
comments by George I. (Sonny) Hodgdon,
Jr., 59:88
comments by Frank Prothero, 48:30
for quick-and-dirty rowboat repairs, 93:29
for sparmaking, 15:64
properties of glues, glueability of woods,
44:133
See also Aerolite glue, Arabol, Bedding
compounds, Detco, Dexeze, Epoxy,
Isocyanate resins, Resorcinol, Shellac,
Sikaflex, 3M 5200, Travaco, Unibond,
Weldwood glue

Adirondack guideboat:
boat school project, harvesting ribs for,
photos, 59:64
comments, photos, 3:2
construction commentary, photos, plans,
18:55
cover photo/Rosine and Peter Lemon, 18:0

Adirondack Museum (NY):
boat types at, 29:102
comments, 6:24, 18:55

Adkins, Jan, author:
"The Vineyard Triangle," 33:30
reviewer of *The Art of Knotting and Splicing*
(book), 28:95

Adkins, Jan, illustrator:
"Cordage," 22:16
"Cordage: Camel Hitch," 30:18
"Cordage: Cleopatra's Eye Splice," 24:20
"Cordage: Netting," 27:18
"Cordage: On Knots," 17:38
"Cordage: Slings," 28:18
"Cordage: The Manila Marriage," 25:18
"Cordage: True Lovers' Knots," 23:20
"Cordage: Turk's Head," 19:17
"Don't Give Up the Ship," 26:24
"Shovels and Pails: An Antipodal
Instructional Recalled," 60:120
"The Elements of Seamanship: Keeping
the Water Out," 40:38
"The Elements of Seamanship: Keeping
from Hitting Anything," 41:42
"The Elements of Seamanship: Keeping
Her Going," 42:38
"They Go Like the Wind," 31:42

ADRENALIN (Formula 40 class):
comments, photos, 84:48

cover photo/Christian Février, 87:0
design and construction, history, photos,
plans, 87:66

A.D. Story Shipyard, builder:
history, photo, 61:32

Advanced Sharpie (yawl):
comments, plan, 92:42

ADVENT (schooner):
comments, photo, 51:40

ADVENTURE (schooner):
log of cruise, photo, 39:32

ADVENTURESS (Crowninshield schooner):
history, photos, use as sail training vessel,
90:94

Adze:
Borneo/description, illustrations, 30:93
comments, 24:76, 36:53
for building Haisla dugout canoe, 69:64

Aeolus Boats, builder:
description of boats, 37:36

AERIEL (cutter):
designs/McCurdy and Rhodes, 100:108

Aerolite glue:
comments by John Pazereskis, 19:46
comments by Gerald Schindler, 4:47
for transom repair to Pacemaker 30, 16:20
for wedge-seam construction, 98:82

Aesthetics in boat design:
comments by Art Paine, 99:48
comments by Joel White, 75:111
comments by Jon Wilson, 28:62

AFRICA (cutter):
designs/William Garden, 64:98

Africa, Kit, builder:
construction methods for canoe yawl
LA MOUETTE, 75:62

Africa, Spike, author:
"Cordage: Barrel Sling," 29:18
"Cordage: Cleopatra's Eye Splice," 24:20
"Cordage: English Bag Knot," 20:18
"Cordage: Masthead Knot," 21:16
"Cordage: Netting," 27:18
"Cordage: Purchase," 22:16
"Cordage: Reef Knot," 18:19
"Cordage: Slings," 28:18
"Cordage: The Manila Marriage," 25:18
"Cordage: The Monkey Fist," 26:20
"Cordage: True Lovers' Knots," 23:20
"Cordage: Turk's Head," 19:17
"On Knots," 17:38

African dhow:
construction commentary, history, photos,
46:88

African dhow, NAWALILKHIL:
a passage on, 46:88

African dugout canoe:
history, photos, 40:78

African mahogany:
comments, 10:35

Afrormosia (wood):
comments, 10:35

A.H. Moody & Son, builder:
sloop TORETTA, 22:46

AIDA (spidsgatter):
comments, photos, 78:50

AÏDA (yawl):
cover photo/Sherry Streeter, 60:0
winter layup, 30:54

AIMÉE (Friendship sloop):
comments, 2:15

Ainsworth, W.L., author:
reviewer of *On the Hawser: A Tugboat Album*
(book), 42:114

Air-drying lumber:
techniques, 9:31, 10:39, 67:76
theory and technique for stacking, 66:92
See also Wood, for boatbuilding
AIRFORCE (cutter):
account of sinking, 75:22
comments, detail photos, 99:48
design and construction commentary,
photos, 68:72
editorial by Jon Wilson, 73:2
letter by Walter Greene, 70:1
Airolite canoes: (*See* Geodesic Airolites)
Air pollution:
comments by Richard Jagels, 80:108
Ajeman, Bob:
letter on bonding, 67:7
Ajootian, Fred, author:
"Pouring the Lead Keel," 15:70
"Setting Up," 14:38
letter on bevels, 15:12
ALACRAN (sharpie ketch):
design compared to sharpie EGRET,
reefing technique, 59:36
Alaska limit seiner:
cover photo/Joe Upton, 37:0
history, photos, plans, 37:31
Alaska limit seiner, TINY ROY II:
comments, plans, 37:31
Alaska packer:
history, photos, 36:66
Alaska yellow cedar:
comments, 24:100
letter by Molly Kemp and Nick Olmsted,
78:6
ALBACORE III (power cruiser):
designs/Eldredge-McInnis, Inc., 93:128
Albee, Chip:
letter on wood harvesting, 11:4
ALCYONE (schooner):
comments, photo, 48:30
cover photo/Neil Rabinowitz, 82:0
Alden, John G., designer:
association with Walter McInnis, 54:34
comments, 2:15, 6:14, 7:17, 41:78
profile, 32:66
schooner HALF MOON, 93:52
schooner VOYAGER, 33:90
yawl ISLA TROTHE, 52:92
yawl ROYONO, 1.4
See also Designs, Alden, John G.
Alder saplings, use:
construction of River Boyne coracle, 79:17
ALERION III (sloop):
as related to Bermuda dinghy CONTEST,
57:42
bow chock design for, 30:84
comments, 33:50
ALERT (Bolger sloop):
comments, photo, 92:42
ALERT (Wylie sloop):
design commentary, photo, 63:56
letter by Taylor Chambers, 64:7
Alexander, Michael, photographer:
cover photo/ketch FRI, 22:0
Alexandria Bay boats:
builder of, photos, 48:66
comments, photos, 49:58
Alexis, Javance, builder (Grenada):
comments, 50:106
Alford, Michael:
comments on historic vessel reproduction,
96:64

delineator of sharpie sloop IDIE, 13:68
**Alford, Michael, and Charles McNeil,
authors:**
"Sailing the Carolina Sharpie IDIE," 13:68
ALFREDA (A-scow):
comments, 39:123
ALICE (power cruiser):
design commentary, plans, 97:92
ALICE (sloop):
comments, photo, 91:92
Allen, Bob, author:
"Seattle's Center for Wooden Boats," 90:72
Allen, Tim, author:
"Building Louvered Doors," 94:84
Allen, Tim, builder:
technique/dovetails, 98:89
Allyn, Robert C., delineator:
Danish lifeboat for JOSEPH CONRAD,
43:72
schooner L.A. DUNTON, 6:44
ALMA (scow schooner):
comments, 38:36
comments, photo, 61:88, 72:60
cover photo/Harry Dring, 3:0
history, photo, plan, 3:8
ALOHA (launch):
photos, repair comments, 95:82
Alpha-Beachcomber dory:
history, photos, 36:78
owner's comments, photos, 36:83
ALPHARD (ketch):
comments, photo, 49:44
ALTA C (fishing schooner):
comments, photo, 87:56
letter by Stanley T. Spicer, 88:11
ALTAIR (schooner):
comments, photo, 90:84
cover photo/Patrick Roach, 90:0
ALTAMAR (Cal 32 class):
comments, photos, plans, 83:38
Aluminum:
for boatbuilding, 10:43
ALVIN CLARK (schooner):
account of last voyage, plans, 52:52
history, 52:66
history, photos, 52:59
letter on, 54:5
AMANDA F. LEWIS (pungy schooner):
comments, painting, photos, 45:56
AMARETTO (sardine carrier):
as bait boat, photos, 58:60
AMARYLLIS (catamaran):
history, performance, 23:63, 23:64
AMARYLLIS II (catamaran):
comments, 91:38
comments, photo, 84:34
AMAZON (brigantine):
history, painting, 6:60
AMBASSADRESS (schooner):
comments, photo, 91:92
AMBERJACK (schooner):
racing, 13:82
AMERICA (schooner):
how to build her half model, painting,
photos, plans, 54:67
AMERICA (Swampscott dory):
comments, photo, 61:52
American Car & Foundry: (*See* a.c.f.
[American Car & Foundry], builder)
American Power Boat Association (APBA):
comments, 80:32
AMERICAN STAR (pulling boat):
comments, photo, 40:30

AMERICA's Cup:
account of PURITAN–GENESTA match,
71:52
comments, 56:102
comments by James W. Brown, 92:34
comments by Olin F. Stephens II, 98:50
correspondence/N.G. Herreshoff and
W.P. Stephens, 100:70
designs by Edward Burgess, 41:26
history of 12-Meter-class boats, 68:40
J-boats, 46:30
profile of Charles Francis Adams III, 85:74
12-Meter, ENDLESS SUMMER (ex-DAME
PATTIE), 18:32
Amesbury skiff:
comments, photo, 27:26
AMIGO (yawl):
comments, photo, 42:82
AMIGO MIO (power cruiser):
comments, plans, 50:31
AMORITA (Cal 32 class):
comments, photo, plans, 83:38
AMORITA (New York 30):
comments, history, 35:20
Amphibi-Con class:
advice on painting for decoration, 93:42
design commentary, plan, 61:42
Amphibi-Con class, FLISK:
comments, photo, 61:42
Amphibi-ette class:
design commentary, photo, plan, 61:42
AMTEC (Formula 40 class):
comments, photo, 92:34
Amundsen, Adolf, builder:
Whitehall pulling boats, 16:15
Amundsen, Ole, builder:
sloop PHYLLIS, 16:17
Amundsen, Roald:
comments, 85:44
Anchor chain scrubber:
product review by Daniel Porter, 93:116
Anchor chock:
comments, detail photo, 74:80
Anchors:
anchoring methods, 19:16, 27:74, 36:18,
43:50, 58:82
comments, 43:50
comments, detail photos, 65:52, 69:104
Ancient Mariners' Yesteryear Regatta (CA):
comments, photos, 65:76
Anderheggen, Peter, author:
"Learning to Build in Wood," 42:100
Andersen, Doug, author:
"Custom Sawmilling," 51:106
"Native vs. Imported Lumber," 70:38
"Perfectly Seasoned: Air-Drying Your
Lumber, Part I," 66:92
"Perfectly Seasoned: Air-Drying Your
Lumber, Part II," 67:76
Andersen, Ring, builder (Denmark):
Danish ketch FRI, 87:36
Anderson, Fletcher, author:
"Championships for Struer," 82:44
letter on canoe paddling, 56:6
Anderson, Hans (Pop), builder:
scow schooners, 3:8
Andrews, Alexis, photographer:
"Classics for Charter," 91:50
Andrews, C.H. (Bob), author:
"Before You Let Her Go," 30:46
Andrews, Chris, designer:
research vessel NISMIME, 30:20

Andrews, Clifton, author and photographer:
"A Lucky Break," 18:82
Andrews, Dudley, builder:
comments, 37:80
ANDRILLOT (cutter):
comments, plan, 24:32
ANDURIL (sloop):
comments, 23:25
Angelique (wood):
comments, 10:35
letter on its characteristics, 25:7
ANGELITA (Eight-Meter):
cold-molded hull repair, 60:76
comments, photo, plans, 83:38
history, photos, plan, rebuilding of (as
Olympic contender), 59:40
Angelwing rig:
letter by Tom Godfrey, 63:7
Angler's Loop:
cordage technique, 72:40
**Anglia Marine Group Training Assoc.
(England):**
comments, 42:97
ANNA KAY (catamaran):
comments, photo, 69:76
**ANNA KRISTINA (Norwegian sailing
freighter):**
restoration comments, photo, 73:96
ANNA ROSA (Norwegian sailing freighter):
comments, photo, 73:96
ANNE M (Monterey Clipper fishing boat):
comments, photo, 18:28
ANNE MARGRETHE (Danish ketch): (*See*
FRI [Danish ketch])
ANN FRANCES (Friendship sloop):
comments, photo, 29:61
ANNIE (St. Lawrence River skiff):
comments, plans, 21:26
construction commentary, plans, 20:48
ANNIE (yawl):
comments, 43:84
construction commentary, photos, 41:78
cover photo/Benjamin Mendlowitz, 41:0
ANNIE CHRISTENSON (steam schooner):
comments, photo, 61:100
Ansel, Willits, author:
"A Ship's Boat for the JOSEPH CONRAD,"
43:72
"The Repair and Replacement of Stems,"
39:97
ANTARES (motorsailer):
comments, 29:38
comments, photo, 28:20
Antigua charter fleet:
comments, photos, 91:50
Antique/classic boat cruise:
Florida antique boat cruise/Ann and Mike
Matheson, 90:78
Antique/classic boat shows:
Lake Tahoe Concours d'Élégance, 62:74
Thousand Islands Museum, 2:66
letter by Robert Melrose, 63:4
Antique/classic powerboat clubs:
list of, 77:79
Antique nautical instruments:
comments, 5:41
AN TRI VREUR (6.63-Meter sloop):
comments, photo, 85:64
ANZAC (motorsailer):
design commentary, photo, plan, 29:38
APACHE (New York 32):
history, 73:42

APHRODITE (commuter):
comments, photos, 94:74
APHRODITE (Plymouth lobsterboat):
comments, 1:65
Apitong (wood):
comments, 10:35
APPLEDORE I (schooner):
comments, photo, 76:36
APPLEDORE II (schooner):
comments, photo, 76:36
APPLEDORE III (schooner):
design and construction commentary,
history, photos, rig design, 76:36
Appledore Pod (pulling boat):
construction commentary, photo, 47:40
**Apprenticeshop of the Maine Maritime
Museum (ME):**
builder of Delaware Ducker, 48:96
builder of Tancook whaler VERNON
LANGILLE, 31:18, 58:82
comments, 71:44
philosophy, program, 4:31
Apprenticing:
comments by Ahoi Mench, 55:88
comments by Barry C. Nelson, 43:56
comments by Frank Prothero, 48:30
comments by Dean Stephens, 42:30
editorial by Jon Wilson, 42:2
in England, 6:20
letter on North Country Community
College (NY), 40:9
philosophy of the Apprenticeshop of the
Maine Maritime Museum, 4:31
AQUILA (cutter):
comments, photo, 32:36
AQUILA (New York 30):
comments, photo, 43:91
AQUILA (sloop):
comments, plans, 62:36
Arab dhow:
comments, photos, 40:78
Arabol (adhesive):
comments, 13:60, 14:64
for deck canvas repair, 25:89
product review by Dean Stephens, 91:110
ARAMINTA (ketch):
comments, photos, 56:38
ARBELLA (yawl):
comments, photo, 51:40
photo caption correction, 52:12
Archaeology, nautical:
ALVIN CLARK (schooner)/history,
photos, 52:59
ATOCHA/letter by John T. Dorwin, 71:7
ATOCHA/underwater archaeology
account, 68:56
Athenian trireme/reconstruction comments, photos, plans, 75:48
letter by John McClain, 72:5
letter by Kenneth R. Pott, 69:5
letters by Nicholas Dean, 70:7, 72:6
Ronson ship/archaeologist account, 63:96
Ronson ship/history, 63:101
Royal Ship of Cheops, history and restoration, 38:28
Archer, Colin, designer (Norway):
comments, 20:38, 46:30, 47:46, 51:133
comments, photo, 91:92
Norwegian polar exploration ship FRAM,
85:44
profile, 20:35
Archer, Jimmy:
on diesel engines, 54:108

Arctic Tern sloop:
comments, photos, plans, 85:52
AREOI (catamaran):
drawing of, 30:20
ARETE (Rozinante ketch):
design, performance commentary, photo,
plans, rig, 26:40
ARGONAUTA (cutter):
comments, drawing, 77:34
ARIA (Buzzards Bay 25):
comments, photos, 38:71, 43:94
ARIEL (Rozinante ketch):
comments, 26:40
ARLINE (power cruiser):
keel replacement, photos, 18:82
Armstrong, Thomas:
letter on projection lofting, 52:10
Arnold, Lester J.:
comments, 100:58
ARROW (commuter):
comments, photo, 94:74
Arstey, G.:
letter on spiling and bevel book, 16:13
Art: (*See* Maritime art)
Artese, Joseph:
interior designer of sloop WHITEFIN,
57:80
letter on sloop WHITEFIN, 58:7
ARUNDEL (Newfoundland trap skiff):
design and construction commentary,
origins of, photos, plans, 26:76
Arundel Shipyard, Inc., builder:
yawl ANNIE, 41:78
Asa Thomson skiff:
advice on painting for decoration, 93:42
design and construction commentary,
photos, plans, 29:50
A-scow class:
history, photo, plans, 39:123
A-scow class, ALFREDA:
comments, 39:123
ASGAARD II (brigantine):
comments, photo, 50:70
Ash (wood):
for boatbuilding, 9:31
for construction of E.M. White guide
canoe, 67:54
for construction of canoe paddle, 67:44
Ashby, Craig, builder:
cat-ketch SHEARWATER, 59:48
Ashcroft, Herbert J., builder (England):
comments, 27:78
Ashcroft planking system:
comments, 4:17
described, 27:78
for Rangeley Lake boat/R.R. Richards,
8:50
letter on, 4:10
ASHUMET (sloop):
comments, photo, 37:42
ASPENET (21' Knockabout class):
history, photos, plans, 7:17
letter on, 10:5
**Association of Fans of Old Fishing Boats
(Poland):**
commentary by Aleksander Celarek, 89:84
ATHENA (ketch):
charter of, 42:82
Athenian trireme:
reconstruction comments, photo, plans,
75:44
Atkin, John, designer:
ketch SYLTU, 12:14

review of plans catalog, 93:118
skiff, 6:6
See also Designs, Atkin, John
Atkin, William, designer:
comments, 47:46, 51:40, 79:64
power skiff BAGADUCE, 87:90
skiff RATION; 87:90
sloop BOSWELL, 27:47
sloop PHYLLIS, 16:17
Atkinson, Bob, author and photographer:
"As Old as the Dory," 18:71
Atkinson Travelers guide canoe:
comments, photos, plans, 96:80
Atlantic Challenge:
comments, 71:44
Atlantic 53 (Huckins power cruiser):
comments, photos, plans, 57:102
AT LAST (motorsailer):
design commentary, photo, plan, 29:38
ATOCHA (treasure ship):
letter by John T. Dorwin, 71:7
underwater archaeology account, 68:56
ATTU (halibut schooner):
comments, photo, 16:63
Atwater, William C., designer:
Indian class, 21:21
AUDUBON (cat rig):
comments, plans, 29:20
AUGUST MOON (ketch):
comments, photo, 20:80
Au Sable River boats:
design and construction commentary,
photo, 5:6
Austin Boat Shop, builder:
Penguin class, 27:94
Australia, designer: (*See* Morrison, Len)
Australia, maritime museum: (*See* Sydney
Maritime Museum)
Australia, watercraft: (*See* AUSTRALIA II [12-
Meter], Cadet dinghy, ENA [steam yacht])
Australia, wood:
annotated list, 95:102
commentary by Richard Jagels, 46:131,
47:123, 54:120, 91:118, 96:104
letter by Tim and Pauline Carr, 88:10
AUSTRALIA II (12-Meter):
comments on keel design, 62:36, 66:124
Autoboat, MERCEDES U.S.A.:
comments, plan, 79:92
AutoEXPAND (computer software):
lines-expansion program/sea kayak
QUEEN CHARLOTTE, 79:84
AVENGER (Bahamian sloop):
cover photo/Mark Silveira, 26:0
AVENGER (International 14 class):
history, photo, plan, 20:84
AVENGER (MCM class):
painting, 58:90
Awnings:
design for small craft, 34:86
Axe, use:
construction of Haisla dugout canoe, 69:64
construction of Panamanian dugout canoe,
74:27
construction of canoe paddle, 67:44
A-YA-SHE (Sid Skiff):
comments, photo, 40:88
AYESHA (yawl):
comments, detail photo, 69:104
Ayling, E.A., and Sons, Ltd.:
methods for oar building, 23:47

BABBOON (40' class):
history, photo, 48:58
Babbs, John, author:
"The McKenzie River Drift Boat," 52:80
Baber, William S., designer: (*See* Designs,
Baber, William S.)
BABY BOOTLEGGER (speedboat):
history, photos, plans, restoration commentary, 60:84
Backbone:
about frame sockets/Bud McIntosh, 34:66
assembly technique/Fred Ajootian, 14:38
assembly technique/Beetle Cat class, 51:99
assembly technique/ultralight-
displacement craft, 90:108
compiling lumber list/20' sloop/Joel
White, 87:46
deadwood construction/Bud McIntosh,
38:95
Dynel-and-epoxy overlay/Owens cutter,
61:104
fitting tailfeathers/Bud McIntosh, 35:56
illustrated glossary, 60:115
rabbeting technique for Whitehall/Bob
Baker, 45:108
rabbeting technique/Bud McIntosh, 33:66,
34:66, 35:56
setting-up technique/Fred Ajootian, 14:38
setting-up technique/Sam Manning, 99:94
setting-up technique/Bud McIntosh, 15:74,
35:56
See also Ballast keel, Keel construction,
Stem construction, Sternpost
Backrest:
comments, detail photo, 70:82, 76:70
Concordia yawl/comments, detail photos,
67:100
for sailing canoe, 37:57
for small rowing craft, 27:86
Badham, Michael, author:
"Good Sense and Seamanship," 34:51
"Lindsay Lord's POT O'GOLD," 48:38
"Other Ways," 44:117
"Strip Planking: Where Did It Come
From?", 57:55
"The International Boatbuilding Center,"
42:96
on maritime preservation, 41:36
BAGATELLE (Buzzards Bay 25' class):
compared to fiberglass version, 60:52
BAGATRIX:
a fantasy in fiberglass, 60:52
Bagley-Nunes Boatworks, builder:
comments, 50:31
Bahamian smack, UNITY B:
cover photo/Mark Silveira, 26:0
construction comments, history, sailing

techniques, photos, 81:34
cover photo/Benjamin Mendlowitz, 81:0
cover photo/Mark Silveira, 26:0
Bailer:
design for a leather one, 34:86
Bailey, L.D., author:
"Homebuilder's Project: Bill Page's
NELLIE," 1:20
Bain, Alfred:
profile, photo, 81:34
Baird, Mike, author:
"Coming of Age," 47:80
letter on Thistle class, 50:4
Bait boat operation:
aboard AMARETTO, 58:60
Baker, A.J., author:
"Degradation of Wood by Products of
Metal Corrosion," 3:18
Baker, A.W., and Jennifer Buckley, authors:
"Simplicity, Skiffs, and Sharpies," 66:48
**Baker, Robert H. (Bob), Jennifer Buckley,
and Kevin Dwyer, authors:**
"PEGGOTTY," 23:39
Baker, Robert H. (Bob), author:
"How to Build PICCOLO: Part I," 36:44
"How to Build PICCOLO: Part II," 37:57
"Keep it Simple," 32:32
letter on Westport skiff, 33:5
Baker, Robert H. (Bob), designer/builder:
catboat PEGGOTTY, 23:39
construction methods for flat-bottomed
skiffs and sharpies, 66:48
eulogy by Jon Wilson, 55:2
rabbeting techniques for Whitehall, 45:108
sailing canoe PICCOLO, 36:44, 37:57
sailing dinghy NELLIE, 1:20
Westport skiff, 32:29
Baker, William A., author:
"The Original Knockabouts: NANCY and
JANE," 8:62
"Welcome on Board," 26:36
on historic vessel reproduction, 96:64
Baker, William A., designer:
obituary by Maynard Bray, 44:78
pinnace DOVE, 26:30, 26:36
See also Designs, Baker, William A.
Balbin, Paul:
WoodenBoat School/Miskito (Honduras)
Indians project, 88:76
Balboa 26 (sloop):
comments, plan, 76:60
BALCLUTHA (square-rigger):
comments, 61:88
Baldwin, J., author:
"A Look Inside China," 49:108
Baldwin, Mark, author and photographer:
"Boatbuilding in Grenada," 50:106
letter on boatbuilding in Grenada, 51:10
Baldwin, Robert:
letter on Controversy 36 BOOMERANG,
63:4
letter on MCM class, 83:8
Ballast, inside:
on schooner CORONET, 32:20
replacing of, on sloop IOLAIRE, 3:59
Ballast bag:
design of, 34:86
Ballast keel:
casting techniques/Richard F. Remsen,
89:52
design comments/Henry Scheel, 62:36
epoxy fairing technique/Ted Hugger,
94:35

Ballast keel (*continued*)
for Biscayne Bay 14 daysailer, 98:28
letter on pouring lead, 80:6
method of attaching/Bud McIntosh, 33:66, 37:89
method of pouring lead/Fred Ajootian, 15:70
method of pouring lead/Brooklin Boat Yard, 49:97
method of pouring lead/James L. Meriam, 63:106
patternmaking for/Thomas MacNaughton, 24:68
patternmaking for/Bud McIntosh, 36:53
underwater salvage of, 2:28
Ballentine, Steve, builder:
comments, 41:84
repair of planking on yawl TIGRIS, 53:109
restoration of Herreshoff 12½ class, 56:93, 57:93
Ballin, designer:
wooden steam freighters, 40:94
BALOCCARE (power launch):
comments, photo, 52:86
Balough, William D.:
letter on Thistle class, 49:9
Balsa/hardwood composite: (*See* DuraKore)
Baltic trader: (*See* ACTIV [Danish topsail schooner], DEFENDER [trading ketch], FRI [Danish ketch], LINDØ [schooner])
Baltimore clipper: (*See* PILGRIM [schooner], PRIDE OF BALTIMORE [schooner], PRIDE OF BALTIMORE II [schooner])
Baman, Donald, builder:
construction methods for Maine cruise schooner JANET MAY, 63:74
BAMBINO (sloop):
comments, photo, 43:92
BANAMH AIGHSTIR (Scottish fishing vessel):
comments, photo, 62:68
Bancroft, Dennison and Margie, authors:
"The Bancroft Tapes," 7:31
Bandmill: (*See* Ross Bandmill Portable Sawmill)
Bandsaws:
building of, 45:33
sharpening method, 48:44
BANFIELD (Coast Guard lifeboat):
comments, photo, 65:76
Bangor Packet (rowing wherry):
cover photo/Benjamin Mendlowitz, 52:0
designs/Joel White, 52:122
Banks dory:
builder of, construction commentary, photos, 18:71
construction commentary, photos, plans, 19:32
Banks fisherman (schooner):
builders of (Story shipyard), comments, photos, 61:32
evolution of, 32:66
photo essay/Art Hanson, 87:56
racing history, 13:82, 56:102
Banks fisherman, BLUENOSE:
photos, racing history, 13:82, 56:102
Banks fisherman, BLUENOSE II:
letters on, 58:7, 59:9
Banks fisherman, ELSIE:
racing history, 56:102

Banks fisherman, GERTRUDE L. THEBAUD:
photo, racing history, 56:102
Banks fisherman, L.A. DUNTON:
comments, photos, 39:97
history, photos, plans, restoration, 6:44
Banks fisherman, PURITAN:
racing history, 56:102
BANSHEE (40' class):
history, photo, 48:58
Bantry Bay gig, LIBERTÉ:
comments, photo, 71:44
BANZAI (New York 30):
comments, photo, 35:20
Barbados fishing craft:
builder, 9:52
Barge: (*See* Spritsail barge, Thames sailing barge)
Bar Harbor 31' class:
comments, photo, 84:34
construction commentary, list of boats in class, plans, 45:68
Bar Harbor 31' class, DESPERATE LARK:
cover photo/Benjamin Mendlowitz, 84:0
history, photo, 45:68
Bar Harbor 31' class, INDIAN:
comments, 45:68
Bark: (*See* ABRAHAM RYDBERG [four-masted bark], CHARLES W. MORGAN [whaleship], KAIULANI)
Barkentine: (*See* GAZELA PHILADELPHIA, REGINA MARIS)
Barlow, Peter, author and photographer:
"Mystic: Small Craft Workshop," 5:24
Barmonde, Peter, author:
"Because They're the Best," 23:48
BARNACLE IV (Energy 48):
design and construction commentary, photo, 47:40
Barnard, Bruce, builder:
comments, 60:84
Barnard, William Lambert, author:
"From Knockabout to Yawl," 6:14
"The Cape Cod Catboat," 3:51
"The Maine Sloop," 2:15
"The Plymouth Lobsterboats," 1:65
Barnegat Bay A-cat:
builders, history, photos, 62:60
Barnegat Bay A-cat, MARY ANN:
history, photo, 62:60
Barnegat Bay A-cat, SPY:
history, photo, 62:60
Barnegat Bay A-cat, WASP:
history, photo, 62:60
Barnegat Bay sneakbox:
comments, 68:25
design and construction commentary, history, photos, 47:102
designs/Glen-L Marine, 61:124
history, performance commentary, photos, plans, 20:23
letter on, 48:10
list of builders, 68:25
Barnegat Bay sneakbox, ADAGIO:
rebuilding, 47:102
Barnegat Bay sneakbox, CENTENNIAL REPUBLIC:
comments, plans, 20:23, 70:104
Barnes, John, photographer:
cover photo/barkentine REGINA MARIS, 11:0
BARNSWALLOW (sloop):
comments, detail photos, plan, 74:80

Barr, Charlie:
comments, photo, 85:74
Barrett, Charles W., builder:
Rangeley Lake boats, 39:26
Barry, James P.:
on Mackinaw boats, 45:100
Barteau, Roy, builder:
comments, 76:60
Bartender (powerboat):
designs/George Calkins, 76:101
Barter, Fred:
caulking methods of, 17:32
Basque racing sculls:
history, photos, 40:52
Bassboat (power launch):
designs/Eldredge-McInnis, 12:68
history, plans, 54:34
Bassett, Ken, author:
reviewer of *Speedboat* (book), 87:105
Bassett, Ken, author and photographer:
"A Contemporary Planking Technique," 96:87
Bassett, Ken, builder:
profile, 54:82
Bassholmen Museum (Sweden):
comments, 58:48
BAT (Q-boat):
comments, photos, 85:74
Batavia of Kungsor, builder (Sweden):
Folkboat, 10:30
Bateau: (*See* Caddo Lake bateau, ISAAC McCASLIN, McInnis bateau [rowing craft], OTTER)
Bateau-type rowing skiff, RANDANDY:
history, racing, photo, 66:23
Bates Vocational-Technical Institute (WA):
boatbuilding program, 42:100
comments, 89:44
letter on, 44:9
Bath Marine Museum: (*See* Maine Maritime Museum)
Båtlodd (boatbuilding tool):
description of, 23:80
Battened sail:
commentary by Iain Oughtred, 77:44
comments by Tom Clark, 64:34
comments by Fritz Seyfarth, 64:34
letter by Robin Lincoln and Brion Toss, 66:7
Batten-seam construction: (*See* Planking, batten-seam)
Batteries:
commentary by Nigel Calder, 99:41
commentary by Jerry Kirschenbaum, 34:72, 35:69
commentary by Lloyd's Register of Shipping, 3:31
Baumgarden, Craig:
comments on maintenance, 100:38
Bausch, Carl, builder:
profile, photo, 54:74
Bavelas, Alex, author:
"Three Views of the SAANICH BEAGLE," 12:70
Bay Area Marine Institute (CA):
boatbuilding program, 42:100
builder of Monomoy surfboats, 44:90
comments, 31:18
Bayless, Allan, author:
"Leeboards," 22:71
B-class Frostbite dinghy: (*See* Frostbite dinghy, B-class)

Beachcomber dory: (*See* Alpha-Beachcomber dory)

Beach, David, designer: (*See* Designs, Beach, David)

Beams, cabintop:
construction commentary/Jon Wilson, 20:52
crown pattern for, fitting of/Bud McIntosh, 42:43

Beam shelf:
installation of/Bud McIntosh, 41:91

Bear class, San Francisco:
cover photo/Jay Daniel, 50:0
history, photos, 50:34

Beard, Tom, designer: (*See* Designs, Beard, Tom)

Bear Mountain Canoe Co., builder:
strip canoes, 31:58

Beaton, David, builder:
Barnegat Bay sneakbox, 47:102

Beaton, Lachlan (Lolly), builder:
Barnegat Bay A-cats, 62:60

Beauvais, Walter, designer:
iceboats, 39:88

BEAVER (Sonder boat):
comments, 73:32

Becksvoort, Christian, author:
"The Bandmill," 62:110

Bedding compounds:
applications of, 2:64, 11:36, 15:26, 20:52, 30:74, 49:89
comments by Giffy Full, 27:40
comments by Frank Prothero, 48:30
comments by Jim Richardson, 24:52
comments by Jon Wilson, 28:76
for quick-and-dirty rowboat repairs, 93:29
for transom replacement/Concordia 33 FREE SPIRIT, 99:28
painting technique before application, 93:70
See also Adhesives, Canvak, Detco, Dolfinite, Polysulfide, Roofing tar, Shellac, Sikaflex, Thiokol, 3M 5200, Travaco

Beebe, Doug, builder:
sloop WHITEFIN, 57:80

Beebe, Robert P., designer:
comments, 90:56
See also Designs, Beebe, Robert P.

Beech, Bob, photographer:
cover photo/three-fathom sharpie, 67:0

Beeston, Diane, photographer:
cover photo/schooner BRIGADOON, 88:0

Beetle Cat class:
construction commentary, 21:72
cover photo/Benjamin Mendlowitz, 30:0
fitting and bending frames, photos, 53:101
keel and transom construction, photos, 51:99
stem and centerboard trunk installation, photos, 52:107

Beken of Cowes, photographer:
cover photo/backbone assembly, Clare Lallow Yard, 6:0

Belaying pins:
construction method, illustrations, 83:116

BELISARIUS (yawl):
comments, photo, 43:91

Belize:
boatbuilding, dugout canoe, 40:78

Bell, Tim, builder (British Columbia):
wedge-seam construction technique, 98:82

Bell Woodworking, builder (England):
kit boats, 39:69

Belt frames:
peapod/Jimmy Steele, 77:74

Bemis, Alan, author:
"CIRRUS: A Treasure from Herreshoff," 34:42
eulogy for, 99:2

BEN ALLEN (motorsailer):
design commentary, photo, 29:38

Bending wood: (*See* Fire-bending, Steam-bending)

Benedict, Norman S.:
on boat plans and the public domain, 48:105

Benford, Jay R., author:
"SUNRISE," 3:61

Benford, Jay R., designer:
review of plans catalog, 93:118
See also Benford Design Group, designers; Designs, Benford, Jay R.

Benford Design Group, designers:
review of *Small Craft Plans* (book), 98:97

Benjamin, Don, author:
"Buying a Runabout," 77:79
letter on *BUC Used Boat Price Guide*, 79:8

Benjamin, Nat, builder:
profile, photo, 95:70
reframing technique for schooner VOYAGER, 69:94
restoration of Vineyard Haven 15, 47:86

Benjamin, S.G.W., author:
"The Weather's Every CAPRICE," 62:88

Benjamin River Marine, builder:
repair of Winter Harbor 21 class, 93:76

Benneche, Kristian:
letter on bosun's chair, 72:6

Bennet, John S.:
letter on removal of rivets, 73:8

Bennett, Ernestine:
profile, photo, 90:94

Benson, F., and R. Hopkinson, authors:
"Wooden Tall Ship GAZELA PRIMEIRO," 11:24

Benson, Tom:
letter by John Mecray, 79:8

Benton, Nicholas (Nick), author:
"Docking a Schooner Under Sail," 17:26
on maritime preservation, 41:36
on swaged terminal inspections, 81:75

Bentzen, Ivor, builder (Norway):
yawl BLUE MOON, 2:58

Bequia sloop, NELLYROSE:
owner's comments, photos, 68:29

Bergeson, Lloyd:
owner of New York 30 COCKATOO II, 35:27

Bergeson, Lloyd, author:
"Folkboats Revisted," 10:30
letter on gaff rigs, 98:6
letter on New York 30 COCKATOO II, 37:7

Berg, Georg, designer (Denmark):
spidsgatters, 78:50

Bermuda fitted dinghy:
design and construction commentary, history, photos, plans, 57:42

Bermuda fitted dinghy, CONTEST:
comments, photo, plans, 57:42

Bermuda fitted dinghy, SPIRIT OF BERMUDA:
comments, 57:42

Bermuda fitted dinghy, VICTORY III:
comments, 57:42

Bermuda Maritime Museum (Bermuda):
comments, 57:42

Bermudian rig:
commentary by Iain Oughtred, 77:44
comments by Colin Palmer, 92:76
letter by Colin Palmer, 94:6

Bernard, William, designer:
comments, 38:64

Bernhard, Nicolaas Adrianus, builder (Netherlands):
Dutch boeier, 27:32

Bernhardt, R.D.:
letter on toxic effects of epoxy and isocyanate, 59:6

Berryman, Eric:
on maritime preservation, 38:36, 41:36

Berths:
Concordia yawl/comments, detail photos, 67:100
design for, 30:86
folding canvas/comments, detail photo, 74:80

"Best Boat" (single scull):
designs/Uffa Fox, 54:130

BETSY (21′ class):
history, photos, 1:58, 4:25

Bevel book:
letters on, 15:12, 16:13
use of, 13:50

Beveling, dutchmen (graving pieces):
technique/Maynard Bray, 78:84

Beveling, frames:
New York 50 class repair, 58:107
outboard runabout Downeaster 18, 73:67
schooner SPIRIT OF MASSACHUSETTS, 82:48

Beveling, planks:
carvel/commentary on plank curvature/Ed McClave, 100:31
carvel/for Catspaw dinghy/Joel White, 27:63
carvel/for Herreshoff 12½/Steve Ballentine, 57:93
carvel/for Maine lobsterboat/Royal Lowell, 16:39
carvel/technique/Bud McIntosh, 18:38
carvel/transom replacement/FREE SPIRIT (Concordia 33)/Brion Rieff, 99:28
lapstrake/for Adirondack guideboat/Howard Ford, 18:55
lapstrake/for Grand Banks dory/Jan Zimmermann, 19:32
lapstrake/for Norwegian pram/Arne Emil Christensen, Jr., 49:28
lapstrake/for pulling boats/Shew & Burnham, 77:76
lapstrake/for sailing canoe PICCOLO/Bob Baker, 36:44
plywood lapstrake/for ultralight canoe/Tom Hill, 54:74
plywood lapstrake/for Acorn skiff/Iain Oughtred, 56:60
plywood lapstrake/for Nutshell pram/Joel White, 60:100
plywood lapstrake/technique/Kenneth G. Mobert, 43:44
strip/for Bear Mountain Canoe/Ted Moores, 31:58
strip/for Hampton boat/Dick Pulsifer, 57:50
strip/for kayak/Curtis Rindlaub, 57:60

Bevel rule:
designed by Joe Trumbly, 89:44

Biddle, Virginia, author:
"A Proper Lady," 68:80
"A SAGA," 49:74
Bielinski, Jon, author:
"San Francisco's Oldest Rowing Clubs,"
40:46
"The People's Timber," 45:46
"The Shipwrights' Co-op: A Report from
the Inside," 34:38
letter on Jeremy Fischer-Smith, 41:9
Bierig, David:
letter on Huckins PT 69, 57:7
Biggs, David:
letter on brush spinners, 92:4
BIG KEX (power cruiser):
design commentary, 56:48
BIHANIC (Breton working craft):
comments, photo, 85:64
Bilge pump:
design for, 23:44
Bilge stringers:
construction comments by Ed McClave,
68:87
BILL OF RIGHTS (schooner):
comments, photo, 43:92
Biloxi schooner:
history, photos, plans, 37:80
Biloxi schooner, CURTIS FOUNTAIN:
comments, 37:80
Biloxi schooner, JULIA DELACRUZ:
comments, photo, 37:80
Biloxi schooner, MARY FOSTER:
comments, 37:80
Biloxi schooner, MARY MARGARET:
history, 37:80
Binney, Arthur, designer:
comments, 72:44
Birchbark canoe:
building commentary, photos, 36:36
construction methods for Henri
Vaillancourt canoe, 87:80
BIRDWATCHER (cat rig):
comments, plan, 86:76
Birney, Robert, photographer:
cover photo/Eight-Meter-class sloops, 32:0
Birra, G. Francis, author:
"Keeping Up with LINDØ," 42:92
Biscayne Bay 14 daysailer:
advice on painting for decoration, 93:42
how-to-build series, photos, plans, 96:24,
97:31, 98:28
Bissell, Frank:
comments, 97:86
Bitt, bowsprit:
comments, detail photo, 66:90
Bitumastic:
as deck-covering adhesive, 25:89
Bjørkedal, Sigur, builder (Norway):
replica of Viking Age merchant ship, 68:19
Bjørkedal boats:
construction methods, photos, use, 95:38
Black, Paul, illustrator:
"Clear Morning," 32:40
Black, Richard, designer:
critique of cat-ketch SHEARWATER
design, 59:48
BLACK ADDER (Merlin Rocket):
comments, photo, 58:100
Blackburn, Howard:
profile/painting, photos, 61:52
BLACK DIAMOND (sardine carrier):
comments, 59:70

BLACKFISH (schooner):
comments, plans, 62:36
Blackford, Charles Minor, author:
"Opinion: To Whom We Should Pay
Honor," 11:10
"The Flatness Issue," 16:26
BLACK HAWK (schooner):
comments, photo, plan, 28:20
Blackistone, Bruce Edward:
letter on historic vessel reproduction, 98:4
BLACK KNIGHT (power cruiser):
comments, photo, 53:38
interior arrangement, photos, plans, 93:52
BLACK MAGIC (outboard cruiser):
design commentary, photo, plans, 30:96
Blacksmith:
profile of Vernon Walters, 94:64
Blacksmithing:
techniques and equipment, 50:46
Black walnut:
comments by Richard Jagels, 72:105
Blackwater sailing canoe:
comments, photo, 70:74
Blaisdell, builder:
Malabar Jr., 65:56
Blake, Bryan, builder:
Core Sound sharpie TORTUGA, 35:76
Blake, D.W., author:
"Sassafras," 80:82
Blake, Maxwell, designer: (*See* Designs,
Blake, Maxwell)
Blanchard, Harold, builder:
canoes, 54:74
Blanchard, Norman C., builder:
profile, photo, 94:54
Blanchard, Norman J., builder:
profile, 94:54
Blanchard Boat Company, builder:
profile, photos, 94:54
Blanchard Knockabout:
comments, photo, plans, 94:54
Blanchard 36 Standardized Cruiser:
comments, photos, 94:62
comments, photos, plans, 94:54
See also MER-NA (Blanchard 36
Standardized Cruiser)
BLANCHE RING (dragger):
comments, 79:48
Blandford, Percy W., author and illustrator:
"English River Skiffs," 30:36
"Fitting the Bottom Plywood Panel," 28:80
Blaney, Roy, builder:
ketch CALYPSO, 32:103
profile, 32:36
Blatchford, John, author:
reviewer of *The Annapolis Book of Seamanship*
(book), 90:138
Blindhiem, Dale, photographer:
cover photo/DISCOVERY's launch, 89:0
Block Island cowhorn:
history, photos, plans, 22:22
Block Island cowhorn, GLORY ANNA II:
comments, photos, 22:22
rudder design, 32:76
stem replacement, 39:97
Blocks:
built by A. Dauphinee & Sons, 94:64
Blocks, handy billy:
how to build, 41:58
letters on, 42:10
Blocks, wooden and metal:
construction commentary, illustrations,
83:93

Blocks, wood-shell:
letters on, 53:6, 53:7
maintenance procedures, 50:67
BLOODHOUND (cutter):
comments, photo, 90:84
BLOODHOUND (yawl):
comments, photo, 59:96
BLOODSTONE (pinky):
racing of, 58:52
Bloom, Mary, photographer:
"The Stevens Family: A Nova Scotia
Tradition," 34:26
BLUEBILL (motorsailer):
comments, photo, 28:29, 29:38
BLUEFISH (motorsailer):
comments, plan, 28:20
BLUEGILL (sailing skiff):
designs/Steve Redmond, 72:98
BLUE HERON (motoryacht):
comments, photo, 94:54
BLUE JACKET (cutter):
designs/Uffa Fox, 59:116
BLUE JACKET (motorsailer):
comments, plan, 28:20
Blue Jay class:
construction commentary, history, photos,
plans, 15:42
BLUE MOON (yawl):
designs/Thomas Gillmer, 2:58
BLUENOSE (fishing schooner):
comments, photo, 56:102, 87:56
racing history, 13:82, 56:102
BLUENOSE II (fishing schooner):
letter on, 58:9, 59:9
BLUE SEA III (ketch):
comments, plans, 75:34
BLUE STAR (ketch):
design and construction commentary,
photos, plans, 43:76
BLUE STAR (trawler-yacht):
comments, plans, 75:34
Blumensaadt, Eric:
letter on warship NIAGARA, 98:4
BOADICEA (English smack):
history, performance, photos, plan, 36:20
Board, R.W.V., author:
"The Once and Future FOXY," 59:96
Boarding ladder:
detail photo, comments, 70:82
how to build, illustrations, 84:91
Boardman, Edwin, designer:
comments, 36:78
Boardsails:
commentary by Iain Oughtred, 78:66
Boatbuilders: (*See* Builder profiles)
Boatbuilding:
advice from R.D. Culler, 21:10
advice on basic techniques/Gordon Linen,
10:13
comments by John Gardner, 40:30
comments by Frank Prothero, 48:30
comments by Dean Stephens, 42:30
conference on, 17:3
estimating construction costs, 7:36
philosophy of R.D. Culler, 4:4
standards/comments by Paul Lipke, 34:32
standards, craftsmanship studies/Jon
Wilson, 22:2, 24:2, 26:53, 27:57, 28:59,
29:89, 30:89, 31:79, 32:88
See also Safety precautions
Boatbuilding industry:
comments by Philip C. Bolger, 61:38
comments by Paul Lipke, 34:32

comments by Kenneth C. Mobert, 74:25
comments by Bruce Northrup, 63:11
comments by Jon Wilson, 19:62
editorial by Jon Wilson, 75:2, 85:2, 97:2
letter by Dexter Cooper, 64:9

Boatbuilding industry, England:
comments by Peter Spectre, 70:74
letter by Richard Franklin-Pierce, 64:8

Boatbuilding school directory:
comments, 42:100

Boatbuilding schools: (*See* Anglia Marine
Group Training Assoc. [England],
Apprenticeshop of the Maine Maritime
Museum [ME], Bates Vocational-Technical
Institute [WA], Bay Area Marine Institute
[CA], Cape Fear Technical Institute [NC],
Center for Wooden Boats [WA],
Chesapeake Academy of Traditional
Boatbuilding [VA], Duck Trap
Woodworking [ME], Graves Boatbuilding
School [MA], International Boatbuilding
Training Center [England], Landing
School of Boatbuilding & Design [ME],
Lowestoft College of Further Education
[England], Maine Marine Vocational
Center [ME], Mystic Seaport Museum
[CT], Northwest School of Wooden
Boatbuilding [WA], Norfolk School of
Boatbuilding [VA], North Country
Community College [NY], Phoenix
Boatshop Cooperative [MA], Pioneer
Marine School [NY], Project Seal [MA],
Saltdal Videregående Skole [Norway], Salt
Boatbuilding School [ME], Seattle
Community College [WA], Southampton
Boatbuilding School [England], Thousand
Islands Shipyard Museum [NY], Town
Marine Museum [NY], Wooden Boat
Center [CA], WoodenBoat School [ME])

Boatbuilding, Third World: (*See* Third World
boatbuilding)

Boatbuilding wood: (*See* Wood, for boatbuilding)

Boat covers:
boatyard and sailmakers' recommendations, materials and frames, 54:92
design by Maynard Bray, 24:44
design by Paul Bryant, 48:91
letter on Canvak, 57:8
materials and frames for, 13:33

Boat cradles:
comments by Jon Wilson, 12:59
construction comments with drawings/
Maynard Bray, 69:86
design by Paul Bryant, 48:91
for storing and shipping boats/ Dan
MacNaughton, 18:51

Boathooks:
compared, design comments, photos, 71:25
design for, 34:86

Boathouse:
design, 34:86, 48:74
See also Boatshops

**Boat Organization for Preservation of
Traditional Norwegian Boat Types**
comments, 28:36

Boat ownership:
comments by Jon Wilson, 58:2, 64:2, 66:2,
69:2, 95:2

Boat plans: (*See* Plans for boatbuilding)

Boat plans catalogs:
review by Mike O'Brien, 89:112, 93:118,
96:98

Boatshops:
Pete Culler's workshop, photos, 27:81
Pete Culler's workshop, photos, plans,
28:83
Harold Payson's workshop, photos, 85:27

Boat shows:
1988/commentary by Mary Lou Dietrich,
82:34
See also Ancient Mariners' Yesteryear
Regatta [CA], Antique/classic boat
shows, Classic yacht regatta, Douarnenez
88 [boat show, France], Foxy's Wooden
Boat Regatta [B.V.I.], Lake Tahoe,
Concours d'Élégance [CA], Museum of
Yachting's Classic Yacht Regatta [RI],
Old Time Barnegat Bay Decoy &
Gunning Show [NJ], Victoria Classic Boat
Festival [BC], Wooden Boat Festival [WA],
Wooden Boat Show [RI])

Boatyard directory:
for Northwestern United States, 33:81

Boatyard hazards: (*See* Safety precautions)

Bob Cat (catboat):
designs/Winthrop L. Warner, 36:94

Bobrow, Jill, author:
"For a Keg of Rum," 2:8

BOC Challenge:
letter by Dick Cross, 69:5
See also AIRFORCE (cutter)

Boeier, PHOENIX:
design and construction, performance,
photos, plan, rig, 27:32

Boettcher, Norman, designer: (*See* Designs,
Boettcher, Norman)

Bohannon, Jerold D.:
letter on marine insurance, 70:4

BOLD WATER (cutter):
cold-molded hull repair, 60:76

Bolger, Philip C., author:
"A Ghost That Only We Could See," 75:72
"Brad Story: The New Generation," 61:38
"Designs: ALICE: An Echo from a Time of
Innocence," 97:92
"Forest Belle," 66:38
"L. Francis Herreshoff, Part I," 55:32
"L. Francis Herreshoff, Part II," 56:38
"Six Cruising Scenarios," 86:76
letter on plywood butt blocks, 67:5
reviewer of *John Alden and His Yacht Designs*
(book), 56:128

Bolger, Philip C., designer:
Cartopper construction model, 85:36,
86:29
Cartopper dinghy, 87:29, 88:31
comments, 54:82
comments on sprit rig, 89:30
cruising boat designs/comments, plans,
86:76
Forest Belle yawl, 66:38
Gloucester Light Dory, 41:63, 42:44, 43:96
Instant Boats, 7:64
profile, photos, 92:42
sharpies, 25:36
yawl MOCCASIN, 18:20

Bolger Cartopper (construction model):
how to build, photos, 86:29
tools and materials for building, photos,
plans, 85:36

Bolger Cartopper dinghy:
comments, photos, plans, 85:36
comments, plan, 86:76
design commentary, 85:38

how-to-build series, photos, 87:29, 88:31
See also Designs, Bolger, Philip C.

Bolts:
defined and illustrated, 81:82

Bombigher, Daniel J., designer (France):
letter on beach cruiser/sharpie Miss
Simplette, 76:6
profile, photo, 71:74
See also Designs, Bombigher, Daniel

Bon, E.H., author and photographer:
"The Dutch Boeier," 27:32

Bonavita, Fred, author:
"Boatbuilders by Degrees," 20:33
reviewer of *Dream Ships* (book), 12:78

Bonding systems:
commentary by Jerry Kirschenbaum, 23:30,
24:78, 25:61
commentary by Lloyd's Register of
Shipping, 2:24
commentary by Ed McClave, 65:114, 93:94
comments by George Cadwalader, 41:84,
70:23
letter by Bob Ajeman, 67:7
letter by Stephen Olson, 95:7

Bonfigli, Michael:
WoodenBoat School/Miskito (Honduras)
Indians project, 88:76

Book reviews: (*See* Reviews [book])

Boom bale:
forging of, 50:46

BOOMERANG (Controversy 36):
letter by Robert Baldwin, 63:4

Boom jaws:
design by William Garden, 59:100

Boone, Jim, author:
"Against the Flow," 72:84

Booth, Oliver, designer:
iceboats, 14:26

Booth, Tom, designer (England):
Merlin Rockets, 58:100

Borisenko, Jim, author and photographer:
"Yukon Practicalities," 91:34

Borneo adze:
described, 30:93

Boston, Howard, designer:
comments, 32:93

Boston Boatbuilding Skill Shop (MA):
boatbuilding program, 42:100

BOSTON FLOATING HOSPITAL (steamer):
comments, photo, 73:32

Boston Whaler:
comments, 43:40
design comments by Llewellyn Howland
III, 60:52

Bosun's chair:
critiques, 70:92
letter by Kristian Benneche, 72:6
letter by Brion Toss, 72:9
procedures for going aloft, 70:92

BOSWELL (sloop):
owner's comments, photos, plans, 27:47

Bot cezowy (Polish fishing craft):
comments, plans, 89:80

Bot kôn (Polish fishing craft):
comments, plans, 89:80

Botting, Sam, builder (Ontario):
Dispro boats, 55:68

Bottom paint analysis:
MICRON 22 critique, 46:66
SHARKSKIN critique, 46:66

Bottom planking: (*See* Planking, bottom)

Bot żakowy (Polish fishing craft):
comments, photos, plans, 89:80
Bouchal, Gerald, author:
"Surfing Sea Bright Style," 17:29
Boudreau, Peter, builder:
PRIDE OF BALTIMORE II, 96:50
profile, photo, 96:58
Bouffier, Elzeard:
on woodlot management, 27:22
BOUNDING HOME (schooner):
comments, photo, 65:76
BOUNTY (ketch):
design commentary, photo, 56:38
designs/L. Francis Herreshoff, 89:114
Bounty ketch (modified), LA FILLE D'OR:
design, construction, performance,
photos, plans, 67:82
Bow chocks:
for sloop ALERION III, 30:84
Bowden, Hal:
comments on maintenance, 100:38
Bowden, Herb:
comments, 73:32
BOWDITCH (schooner): (see NATHANIEL BOWDITCH)
BOWDOIN (schooner):
comments, photos, 28:20
history, photos, plans, 47:30
Bowie, Phil, author:
"A Flair for Raging Inlets," 17:23
Bowker, Francis E., author:
letter on schooner JOHN F. LEAVITT, 34:5
Bowknot:
technique, 72:40
Bow profile:
comments by Joel White, 75:111
Bowsprit bitt:
detail photo, comments, 66:90
Boyle, Robert H.:
letter on Hudson River Fishermen's
Association, 62:7
Boynton, Lee, illustrator:
"Roy Blaney Knows What's Right," 32:36
Braatz, Ernest:
letter on surveys, 74:6
Bradley, Dick:
comments, 60:41
Bradley, Sonny, builder:
Koa canoe, 59:80
Brady, John:
letter on GAZELA PRIMEIRO, 46:5
Bragg, Caleb:
comments, 60:84
BRAINSTORM (sloop-rigged lobsterboat):
comments, photo, 69:42
BRANKSOME (steam yacht):
comments, photo, 98:66
Brannon, Charlie:
letter on historic vessel reproduction, 99:4
Brashier Bros., builder:
comments, 37:80
Bray, Anne, photographer:
"Building the Nutshell Pram," 60:100
"Live Oaking Today," 46:80
"New Life for Old Decks," 66:64
"Renewing TARNE's Keel, Part I," 49:97
"Renewing TARNE's Keel, Part II," 50:59
"Steam-Bending an Oak Coaming, 44:86
Bray, Anne and Maynard, authors:
"Quick Steps to Spring Painting, Part I,"
63:87
"Quick Steps to Spring Painting, Part II,"
64:58

letter on solvent for cleaning brushes, 65:6
Bray, Kathy, author:
reviewer of *Finishing* (book), 64:106
Bray, Kathy, illustrator:
"A Cold-Molded Rejuvenation," 52:92
"A Leak-Proof Hatch for the Foredeck,"
87:112
"A Matter of Detail," 75:76
"A Matter of Detail: Fitting a Dutchman,"
78:84
"Bending Rangeley Stems at Mystic
Seaport," 33:74
"Building a Hollow Mast," 91:25
"California's Ancient Canoe," 35:82
"Deck Care," 77:60
"Double-Sawn Framing," 82:48
"Extending the Life of a Skiff," 32:57
"How to Build a Double Paddle," 37:67
"In My View: The Battenless Mainsail,"
64:34
"Making Belaying Pins," 83:116
"Making a Wooden Cleat," 82:33
"Other Ways: Boat Rollers, Bailers,
Boathouses, etc." 34:86
"Other Ways: Fixing a Leaky Shaftlog,"
40:102
"Other Ways: Picking Up Through Plastic,"
35:95
"Other Ways: Shifting Leeboards," 38:98
"Painting for Decoration," 93:42
"Plank Curvature," 100:31
"Replacing Planks," 80:56
"Scarfs and Butts," 86:109
"Set Work: A Show of Force," 85:99
"Sprit Rig Basics," 89:30
"Teak on Teak," 72:53
"The Concordia Yawls," 80:64
"The Repair and Replacement of Stems,"
39:97
"The Weather Side of Gaff Rig," 53:48
"To Stop a Leak," 84:44
"Trailers & Cradles, Planks & Rollers,"
69:86
"Whipping WHIPPET Into Shape," 93:76
Bray, Maynard, author:
"A Brighter Future," 96:73
"A Dove for St. Mary's," 26:30
"A Matter of Detail," 65:52, 66:90, 68:70,
69:104, 70:82, 71:92, 74:80, 75:76, 76:70,
90:66
"A Matter of Detail: Stems and
Breasthooks," 25:52
"A Matter of Detail: The Concordia Yawl,"
67:100
"A Matter of Detail: Fitting a Dutchman,"
78:84
"A Plywood Lapstrake Classic," 56:60
"A Schedule for Maintaining Your Wooden
Boat," 75:30
"Acquisition is Just the Beginning," 38:40
"Alfred Bain and the UNITY B," 81:34
"Bienvenue à Douarnenez 88," 85:64
"Building the Biscayne Bay 14, Part I," 96:24
"Building the Biscayne Bay 14, Part II,"
97:31
"Building the Biscayne Bay 14, Part III,"
98:28
"Building the Nutshell Pram," 60:100
"Building YOREL's Transom," 95:67
"California Schoonerman," 70:42
"Class without Flash," 95:60
"Cold-Molded Overlay," 61:104
"Damaged Planks: Their Repair and

Replacement," 53:109
"Deck Care," 77:60
"Designs: 17' Rover Class Sloop," 28:97
"Designs: Three Concordia Cruisers,"
48:126
"Designs: Three Crowninshield
Knockabouts," 37:116
"Heydeys at Herreshoff's," 84:34
"Improving the Building Process," 77:74
"Keeping a Wooden Hull from Drying
Out," 54:88
"Lapstrake Methods," 77:76
"Live Oaking Today," 46:80
"Looking Good Again: A Refinishing
Story," 40:56
"Making Your Boat Tight Again," 57:112
"Obituary: William Avery Baker
Remembered," 44:78
"Other Ways," 67:30
"PAULINE, A Working Sardine Carrier,"
59:74
"Painting for Decoration," 93:42
"Places to Go: Museums with Small Boats
to See," 29:102
"Planking the MORGAN," 36:98
"Product Review: T & L Screw Extractors,"
93:117
"Renewing TARNE's Keel, Part I," 49:97
"Renewing TARNE's Keel, Part II," 50:59
"Restoration of a 12½-Footer, Part I," 56:93
"Restoration of a 12½-Footer, Part II," 57:93
"Sonny Hodgdon's Half Models," 33:41
"The Concordia Yawls," 80:64
"The Foundry in Use," 73:24
"The Genius of N.G. Herreshoff," 33:50
"The Incredible Herreshoff Dugout,"
14:54
"The Modern Wooden Navy," 58:90
"The New York 32s," 73:42
"The Whitehall Backbone," 45:108
"Traditional Teak Grates," 62:53
"Trailers & Cradles, Planks & Rollers,"
69:86
"Two Views of the Bar Harbor 31s," 45:68
"Understanding a Novi Boat," 45:88
"Ways and Means at Riverside Boat Yard,"
48:91
"Whipping WHIPPET Into Shape," 93:76
"Winter Layup Afloat," 30:54
on Bermuda fitted dinghy CONTEST,
57:42
on Fishers Island 31-footers, 34:42
on Swedish kåg, 58:48
on catboat PEGGOTTY, 23:39
on construction details of CORONET,
32:20
on planking ultralight canoes, 54:74
on steaming planks and forging, 53:52
reviewer of *Boatowner's Sheet Anchor* (book),
21:92
Bray, Maynard, author and illustrator:
"Matter of Detail: Bow Chocks," 30:84
"Matter of Detail: Keels," 28:56
"Matter of Detail: Rudders," 32:76
"Matter of Detail: Rudders and Tillers,"
31:84
"Matter of Detail: Seat Knees," 26:80
"Matter of Detail: Stern Sheets," 27:86
"Matter of Detail: Toe-Rails," 29:94
"The Better Canvas Cover," 24:44
Bray, Maynard, author and photographer:
"Name in Gold, Hail in Black," 99:54

Bray, Maynard, illustrator:
"L. Francis Herreshoff, Part II," 56:38
Bray, Maynard, photographer:
"LADY JEANNE," 37:72
Bray, Maynard and Kathy, authors:
"Bungs," 80:63
Bray, Maynard and Nathanael, authors:
"The Fishing Ports of Portugal," 72:80
Bray, Maynard, and Pete Smyth, authors:
"On the Hunt," 76:44
Bray, Maynard, Jerry Kirschenbaum, and Jon Wilson, authors:
"William Hand: Evolution of an Architect, Part II," 29:38
Bray, Maynard, Meg Davis Maiden, and Paul Stubing, authors:
"From Sail to Power: The Evolution of the Noank Lobsterboat," 69:42
Brazil, Bahia:
boatbuilding commentary by John Sarsfield, 66:84
Breasthook:
design and construction/Maynard Bray, 25:52
installation/Bud McIntosh, 41:91
installation in Biscayne Bay 14, 97:31
installation in Catspaw dinghy, 28:64
installation in Grand Banks dory, 19:32
installation in sailing canoe PICCOLO, 37:57
installation in Yankee Tender, 31:71
Breeze, Richard:
letter on Chinese maritime source material, 71:8
Breiby, John:
letter on lapstrake planking, 77:4
Breitenback, John C.:
letter on apprenticeship program, 40:9
BRENDA (yawl):
comments, photo, 84:34
Brendze, Art, author:
"ANNIE," 41:78
Brener, Roland:
owner of Eight-Meter REALITY, 34:20
Brener, Roland, author:
"REALITY: What a Concept," 34:24
Brennan, Peter J.:
letter on historic vessel reproduction, 97:6
Brenne, Harald P., builder (Norway):
at Norwegian boatbuilding school, 23:80
clamp designs of, 29:67
Brenne clamp:
design for, 29:67
Brewer, Edward S. (Ted), designer:
sharpies, 25:36
See also Brewer, Wallstrom and Associates, Inc.; Designs, Brewer, Edward S.
Brewer, Malcolm, builder:
comments, 37:2
letter on, 50:10
profile, 49:51, 49:53
profile, photo, 49:44
schooner SILVERHEELS, 1:32
Brewer, Wallstrom and Associates, Inc., designer:
comments, 12:44
See also Designs, Brewer, Wallstrom and Assoc., Inc.
Brewer 39 (sloop):
designs/Edward S. (Ted) Brewer, 26:96
BRIGADOON (schooner):
cover photo/Diane Beeston, 88:0

Brigantine: (See AMAZON, MARY CELESTE, VARUA)
Briggs, Bert, builder:
comments, 66:48
Briggs, Daniel, builder:
cold-molded hull repair, 60:76
Briggs, Jerry, builder:
Colorado River dories, 15:47
Brightwork: (See Interior brightwork, Varnishing)
BRILLIANT (schooner):
comments, photo, 2:8, 65:76, 98:50
Bristol Bay Boat, Columbia River Gillnetter:
history, photos, 22:27
Bristol boats:
comments, 100:70
Bristol Channel pilot cutter, HIRTA:
sailing techniques, photo, 71:60
British Columbia, builders: (See Bell, Tim; Brown, Gregory; Bruigom, George; Farrell, Allen; Gartside, Paul; Jespersen, Bent; McQueen, George; Nyce, Tom; Trenholme, Bill; Wayland Marine)
British Columbia, designers: (See Burns, Byron; Garden, William)
British Columbia, boat shows: (See Victoria Classic Boat Festival)
Brokerage business:
letter by William Page, 61:6
Bronze floors and knees:
construction and installation in cutter TALEISIN, 51:72
floors/design of George F. Lawley & Son, 26:80
Bronze strapping:
comments by Bud McIntosh, 84:44
Brooklin Boat Yard, builder:
Catspaw dinghy, 26:48, 27:63, 28:64
ketch DOVEKIE, 5:55, 7:31
Nutshell pram, 60:100
power cruiser LADY JEANNE, 37:72
repair of ketch TARNE, 49:97, 50:59
rowing wherry BANGOR PACKET, 52:122
Yankee Tender skiff, 30:74, 31:71
Brooks, David, author and photographer:
"Building the Wayfarer Dinghy Kit," 51:88
Broom, Michael, author and photographer:
"Dudley Davidson's Secrets," 39:50
Brouwer, Norman:
on maritime preservation, 38:36
Brown, Gregory, builder (British Columbia):
Whitehall LILY, 53:86
Brown, James W. (Jim), author:
"Able to Go: The Boats of John Guzzwell," 84:64
"Modern Multihulls, Part I," 91:38
"Modern Multihulls, Part II," 92:34
"Plank-on-Frame Dugouts," 88:76
letter on Third World boatbuilding, 43:4
reviewer of The Cruising Multihull (book), 98:98
Brown, James W. (Jim), author and photographer:
"Building a Proper Icebox," 99:74
"Crooked Drawers," 98:89
"Knock on Wood, Part I: Plight of the Canoe People," 40:78
"Knock on Wood, Part II: The Laminated Dugout Caper," 41:50
"Knock on Wood, Part III: Windwagons of the Future," 42:66
Brown, James W. (Jim), designer/builder:
comments, 83:58

letter on epoxy, 66:5
multihulls, 41:50, 42:66, 54:56
profile, photo, 69:76
Brown, James W. (Jim), photographer:
cover photo/catamaran VAKA BUSI, 69:0
cover photo/proa KAURI, 83:0
Brown, James W. (Jim), John Marples, and Dick Newick, authors:
"Bagging the GULL, Part I," 64:83
"Bagging the GULL, Part II," 65:97
Brown, Jim P., author:
"Havilah Hawkins," 88:60
"Henry Scheel," 62:36
"Save It!," 60:76
"WHITEFIN," 57:80
Brown, Polly, author and photographer:
"An Adventure in Antiques," 90:78
Brown, Polly, photographer:
cover photo/trimaran ROGUE WAVE, 23:0
Brown, Roger, builder (England):
steam launch, 13:76
Brown, Russell, designer:
profile, 83:58
Brown, Sandy, photographer:
"Interior Arrangements," 93:52
cover photo/yawl COTTON BLOSSOM IV, 38:0
Brown, Tom, author:
"Sam Devlin," 85:52
Brown, Woody:
comments, 91:38
Brownell hydraulic trailer:
comments, photo, 69:86
BROWN SUGAR (sloop):
design and construction commentary, photos, 30:50
BRUCE (International 14 class):
construction commentary, photos, plans, 20:87
Bruce, Ian, author:
"Hot-Weather Varnishing," 76:22
Bruce, Ian, author and illustrator:
"A Leak-Proof Hatch for the Foredeck," 87:112
Bruigom, George, builder (British Columbia):
profile, 19:76
Bruin, Bill, photographer:
cover photo/Harvey Gamage, 13:0
Brundage, Kip, photographer:
cover photo/dock scene, 71:0
Bruning, Leslie, author:
"The Venetian Gondola," 15:21
BRUNSWICK LION (St. John River boat):
construction commentary, history, photos, plans, 15:34
Brushes: (See Paintbrush)
Bryant, Paul, author:
"Fitting Out: A Guide to Getting Her Ready Again," 93:36
Bryant, Paul, builder:
cradle design of, photo, 69:86
disc-sanding technique, 63:87
on boat covers, 54:92
on methods of storing boats, 48:91
on paint primers, 46:66
refinishing techniques, 40:56
BRYONY (cutter):
comments, photos, 62:82
BUCKAROO (motorsailer):
design commentary, photo, plan, 29:38
Buckhout, Jacob, builder and designer:
iceboats, 14:26

Buckley, Jennifer, author:
"Canvas and Other Winter Cover Stories,"
54:92
"Fitting Out in the Fall," 72:25
"Gatherings," 34:60
"Holding Fast: Sonny Hodgdon on Glues,"
59:88
"The Finishing Touch," 46:66
"Wooden Yachts Earning Their Keep,"
42:82
reviewer of *Mystic Seaport Museum Watercraft*
(book), 31:94
Buckley, Jennifer, and A.W. Baker, authors:
"Simplicity, Skiffs, and Sharpies," 66:48
**Buckley, Jennifer, Kevin Dwyer, and Bob
Baker, authors:**
"PEGGOTY," 23:39
Bucknell, Barry, designer (England):
Mirror dinghy, 23:88
BUC Used Boat Price Guide:
letter by Don Benjamin, 79:8
letter by Boyd Mefferd, 79:7
Buehler, George, author:
"Opinions: Wood as a Boatbuilding
Material," 5:32
Buehler, George, author and photographer:
"A Look at JUNO After 12 Years," 79:64
Buehler, George, designer:
review of plans catalog, 89:112
BUFFLEHEAD (cutter):
comments, photo, 51:40
Bugeye, JENNY NORMAN:
builder, construction commentary, photos,
65:32
Bugeye-rigged sharpie:
design commentary, plan, 36:62
Builder profiles:
A.D. Story Shipyard, 61:32
Bassett, Ken, 54:82
Bausch, Carl, 54:74
Benjamin, Nat, 95:70
Blanchard Boat Company, 94:54
Blaney, Roy, 32:36
Boudreau, Peter, 96:58
Brewer, Malcolm, 49:44, 49:51, 49:53
Brown, James W. (Jim), 69:76
Bruigom, George, 19:76
Burnham, Cecil, 77:70
Bush, Fabian (England), 70:74
Calhoun, Dale, 82:19
Carpenter, Vic and Hazel, 45:50
Chantiers Navals de l'Estérel (France),
39:44
Clark, John, 98:74
Clarke, Dick, 65:90
Crosby, Eddie, 34:82
Cunningham, Bruce, 20:58
Cutts, Edmund A., 78:30
Day, Arno, 63:38
Devlin, Sam, 85:52
Dodge, Duffy, 92:28
Edwards, Mark (England), 74:54
Fahey, Mick, 67:38
Farrell, Allen, 67:19
Fife, William (Scotland), 90:84
Freebody, Peter (England), 57:72
Frost, William (Pappy), 70:84
Gannon, Ross, 95:70
Gardner, John, 40:30, 90:36
Gartolda, Tehamo (Panama), 74:27
Goetz, Eric, 23:25
Goodall, C.A. (Tony), (England), 86:70
Grunwald, Bill, 37:36

Guzzwell, John, 84:64
Hickman, Albert, 100:46,
Hill, Tom, 54:74
Huckins, Frank Pembroke, 56:48, 57:102
Johnson, Forest E., 86:44
Lange, Bob, 77:34
Lowell, Carroll, 70:84
Luzier, George, 66:56
Lyman Boat Works, 82:60, 82:68
Mason, Mark, 60:84,
Matthews, Scott J., 38:114
McCarthy, Lucy, 79:22
McIntosh, David C. (Bud), 51:40
Mench, Ahoi, 55:88
Mills, Clark, 36:73
Monfort, Platt, 76:72
Moores, Ted, 31:58
Morgan, Bill, 71:82
Nimphius, Ferdinand (Red), 25:42
Norton, Joe, 86:52
Nunes, Antonio, 50:31
Odell, Jim, 27:26
Payson, Harold H. (Dynamite), 85:27
Pocock, Stan, 21:36
Prothero, Bob, 62:82
Prothero, Frank, 48:30
Pulsifer, Dick, 57:50
Richardson, James B., 65:32
Rowsell, Spud (England), 58:100
Sano, Ichiro (Japan), 80:50, 80:54
Shew, Dick, 77:70
Sloan, Bob, 70:42
Smith, Everett, 65:66
Smith, Herb, 76:36
Smith, Melbourne, 78:76
Staudacher, Jon, 80:24
Stauter, Lawrence, 72:90
Steele, Jimmy, 77:70
Stelmok, Jerry, 67:54
Stephens, Dean, 42:30
Stevens, David, 34:26
Story, Arthur Dana, 61:32
Story, Brad, 61:38
Story, Dana, 61:38
Stulen, Chip, 95:38
Sturges, Ed, 54:74
Tamm, Bror, 46:30
Telesmanick, Leo, 21:72
Thomson, Asa, 29:50
Trumbly, Joe, 89:44
Tyrell, Jack (Ireland), 50:70
Vaillancourt, Henri, 87:80
Watts, Simon, 73:60
White, Chris, 54:56
Wilbur, Jack, 69:48
See also Model building
Bulkheads:
bevels for, 13:50
fitting method/Bud McIntosh, 43:61
installation in Biscayne Bay 14 daysailer,
97:31
raised panels/how to build/Arch Davis,
99:86
scribing method (jogglestick), 39:106
Bulwarks:
construction method/Bud McIntosh, 67:91
fastening of, 13:65
Bungs:
commentary/Maynard Bray, 80:63
commentary/Ed McClave, 55:43
commentary/Bud McIntosh, 55:107
comments/Ed McClave, 93:70
letter by Gavin Watson, 84:5

letter by Roger Yonkin, 82:6
letter by Peter S. Zimmerman, 81:5
method of removing/W. Lyman Phillips,
9:24
teak deck overlay repair, 72:53
Bunyan, Dick, builder:
Hooper Bay kayak, 58:74
Burckmyer, Peter A., author:
"The Hudson's Hardwater Heritage,"
14:26
Burckmyer, Peter A., photographer:
cover photo/iceboat COLD WAVE, 14:0
Burgess, Edward, designer:
comments, 37:42, 41:26, 43:64, 44:24,
46:30, 72:44, 85:74
40'-class sloops, 48:58, 49:66
profile, 71:52
Burgess, John T.:
letter on Landing School of Boatbuilding
& Design, 76:7
Burgess, W. Starling, designer:
brigantine VARUA, 65:44
comments, 37:42, 46:30
fishing schooners, 56:102
profile, 71:52, 72:44, 73:32, 74:42
12-Meter-class boats, 68:40
**Burgess and Packard, designers and
builders:**
history, 72:44, 73:32
Winter Harbor 21 class (builder), 93:76
Burke, John G., author:
"Designs: 16' V-Bottomed Cat for Mr.
Hagan," 55:122
"Designs: 45' She-Pungy for Captain Eddie
Crosby," 55:122
"Eddie Crosby's Last Boat," 34:82
reviewer of *The Boatwright's Companion*
(book), 74:109
Burke, John G., builder:
construction technique for oars, 71:28
BURMA (motorsailer):
comments, photos, 97:76
cover photo/Benjamin Mendlowitz, 97:0
design and construction comments, photo,
97:86
gold leafing technique, photos, 99:54
Burn, Michael, author:
"Albert Strange and the Canoe Yawl
SHEILA," 64:49
Burnham, Cecil, builder:
profile, photo, 77:70
Burns, Byron, designer (British Columbia):
comments, 46:114
Burns, Chuck, author:
"SKIDOO: Designer's Comments," 51:85
Burns, Chuck, designer:
Burns 30 class, SKIDOO, 51:80, 51:83,
51:85
cutter TOPAZ, 26:70
Burns, M.J., illustrator:
"The Weather's Every CAPRICE," 62:88
Burns 30, SKIDOO:
design and construction commentary,
photos, plans, 51:80
design and construction commentary,
photos, 51:85
performance commentary, photos, 51:83
Burt, Erford, designer:
Vineyard Haven 15, 47:86
Burtis Boat Works, builder:
Penguin class, 27:94

Burtner, Evers, author:
"Swampscott Dories: Three of My Own,"
36:83
Burundi canoe:
comments, photo, 69:76
Bush, Fabian, builder (England):
profile, photo, 70:74
Bush, Guy, builder (Nova Scotia):
Cape Island boats, 46:42
Bush Island boat:
evolution from sail to power, history,
photos, 46:42
letter on, 47:7
Bushnell, David, designer:
6' submarine TURTLE, 21:74
BUT & BEN (schooner):
comments, photos, 60:96
Butler, Farnham, designer and builder:
profile, 61:42
Butler, John R., author:
"A Different Kind of Love," 19:48
Butler, Marya, illustrator:
"The Borneo Adze: Sulu Boatbuilding
Tool," 30:93
Butler, Paul, author:
"The Borneo Adze: Sulu Boatbuilding
Tool," 30:93
Butt blocks:
belt frames/peapods/Jimmy Steele, 77:74
commentary by Ed McClave, 67:23
commentary by Lyman Phillips, 21:66
commentary by Michael Podmaniczky,
66:45
comments by Bud McIntosh, 18:38
comments by Bill Modrell, 15:7
installation in ketch CARRIE L/Skip
Zahniser, 42:74
letter by Phil Bolger, 67:5
letter by Michael Podmanizcky, 69:11
repair of carvel planking, 80:56
repair of lapstrake powerboats, 71:38
repair of schooner VOYAGER, 69:94
Buying a wooden boat:
advice from professional surveyors and
a broker, 60:62
comments by Dick Sciuto, 2:71, 3:69, 4:70
guide for antique and classic runabouts,
77:79
guide for self survey, 89:22
letter by Don Benjamin, 79:8
letter by William Page, 61:6
letter on BUC Used Boat Price Guide, 79:7
See also Surveying
Buzzards Bay 12½-class:
comments, photo, 84:34
rebuilding by Steve Ballentine, 56:93, 57:93
refinishing by Paul Bryant, 40:56
rudder detail, 32:76
Buzzards Bay 25'-class, ARIA:
comments, photo, 38:71, 43:94
Buzzards Bay 25'-class, BAGATELLE:
compared to fiberglass version, 60:52
Buzzards Bay 30'-class:
comments, photos, 39:76
Buzzards Bay 30'-class, MASHNEE:
comments, photo, 43:91, 65:76
Byerley, Jolyon, author:
"Classics for Charter," 91:50

Cabin interior:
interior arrangements, 93:52
mock-up technique for 36' cold-molded
cutter/Val Haigh, 84:29
Cabin launch:
design comments, photos, 36:108
See also CHEROKEE, COMET
Cabin lockers:
construction method, drawings/Aldren
Watson, 76:89, 77:87
Cabin sole:
construction method, drawings/Aldren
Watson, 81:65, 82:75
Cabin trunk:
construction technique/Bud McIntosh,
42:53
letter on camber of cabintop, 22:6
rebuilding the cabintop/Jon Wilson, 20:52
recanvasing/International One-Design,
22:74
recanvasing/Jon Wilson, 22:72
seam repair/Jon Wilson, 24:100
CACHELOT (Dispro launch):
comments, photo, 55:68
Cackler (outboard garvey):
comments, photos, plans, 85:52
designs/Sam Devlin, 91:96
Caddell, John B., II:
comments, 95:60
Caddell's Drydock:
copper sheathing of GAZELA PHILA-
DELPHIA, 74:19
Caddo Lake bateau:
builders, construction methods, origins,
photos, plans, 62:44
Cadet class:
comments, photo, 74:64
Cadet dinghy:
construction commentary, history, photos,
plans, 52:100
letter on, 55:9
Cadet dinghy, KITTIWAKE III:
history, photos, 52:100
Cadwalader, George, author:
"A Cautionary Tale Continued," 70:23
"Auxiliary Power: Views from Experience,
Living with Diesel," 54:106
"Building a Cheap Boat Shelter," 48:74
"GAUNTLET: A Cautionary Tale," 41:84
"Screws, Tubes & Doohickeys," 81:82
Cahill, Pat, author:
"Whitehall to Windward," 24:58
Cahill, Tim, author:
"Good Guys in Outlaw Boats," 73:86
letter on Mark and Chris Lavin, 75:6

Cahoon, Rick, author:
"The Long Oars of Pete Culler," 71:28
Cain, Scott, builder:
repair/sloop WHITE WINGS, 23:50, 24:72
Caiques:
design commentary, photos, 21:42
Calahan, H.A.:
comments on New York 32 class, 73:42
Calder, Nigel, author:
"A Trouble-Free DC System," 99:41
Calhoun, Dale, builder:
comments, photo, 82:19
CALICO JACK (skipjack):
designs/Joseph Gregory, 79:106
California laurel (wood):
for boatbuilding, 35:45, 43:120
letter on use of, 41:7
CALIFORNIAN (schooner):
comments, photo, 78:76
CALISTO V. CANELLI (power cruiser):
designs/John Atkin, 28:99
Calkins, George, designer: (See Designs,
Calkins, George)
Cal 32 class:
history, photos, plans, 83:38
Cal 32 class, ALTAMAR:
comments, photos, plans, 83:38
Cal 32 class, AMORITA:
comments, photo, plans, 83:38
Cal 32 class, ESCAPE:
comments, photo, plans, 83:38
Cal 32 class, TEMPEST:
comments, photo, plans, 83:38
Calvert Marine Museum (MD):
boats at, 29:102
CALYPSO (ketch):
designs/Thomas Gillmer, 32:102
Camber Craft, builder:
sailing pram TULIP, kit boat, 39:69
Camden class:
designs/B.B. Crowninshield, 37:116
Camden Shipbuilding Corp., builder:
boats built by Malcolm Brewer, 49:53
schooner SILVERHEELS, 1:32
Campbell, Robert J., author:
"I Didn't Know I Couldn't Do It," 21:49
CAMPERNELL (pilot gig):
comments, photo, 25:28
Camper & Nicholson, builders (England):
comments, 15:29
Eight-Meter REALITY, 34:20
12-Meter-class boats, 68:40
Campion, Chris:
letter on marine insurance, 68:5
Camp Skiff (outboard cruiser):
designs/Howard I. Chapelle, 82:108
Canadian pine:
comments by Richard Jagels, 70:101
Canal boat (narrowboat):
design and construction commentary,
drawing, history, plans, 41:98
C & B Marine, builder:
cold-molded boats, 26:70
restoration of Eight-Meter sloop ANGE-
LITA, 59:40
CANARD (cat rig):
comments, photo, 61:38
CANDID GYPSY (power cruiser):
designs/A.G. Skidmore, 17:46
Candleholder:
comments, detail photo, 65:52
CANIM (power cruiser):
comments, photo, 65:76

Cannell, Jennifer, photographer:
cover photo/sloop WHITEFIN, 57:0
Canoe, double-paddle:
design commentary by Mike O'Brien, photos, plans, 90:56
designs/L.F. Herreshoff, 19:83, 60:140
Canoe, double-paddle, Chumash tomol:
design and construction commentary, history, photos, plans, 35:82
Canoe, double-paddle, Herreshoff dugout:
construction commentary, photo, plans, 14:54
Canoe, double-paddle, Old Town stripper:
kit boat, 38:84
Canoe, double-paddle, Rob Roy:
comments, photo, 55:88
comments, plan, 70:104
Canoe, double-paddle, ultralight:
builders of, planking technique of Tom Hill, 54:74
Canoe, double-paddle, Wee Lassie:
how to build, photos, plans, 100:92
Canoe, power, VOYAGEUR:
comments, photo, 67:38
Canoe, sailing:
designs/Ned Costello (delineator), 20:89
rig design for, 22:33
Canoe, sailing, African Sesse:
design and construction commentary, history, photos, 40:78
Canoe, sailing, Blackwater:
comments, photo, 70:74
Canoe, sailing, Burgess and Packard design:
comments, plan, 73:32
Canoe, sailing, Chesapeake log:
construction commentary, history, photos, 6:26
Canoe, sailing, Cruising class:
history, photos, 24:90
Canoe, sailing, MacGregor:
designs/Iain Oughtred, 84:106
Canoe, sailing, Micronesian paopao:
design and construction, history, performance, photos, 31:42
Canoe, sailing, PICCOLO:
how to build, photos, plans, 36:44, 37:57
Canoe, sailing, Polynesian:
design and construction commentary, history, plans, 19:25
Canoe, sailing, TWILITE:
builder of, comments, photos, 65:66
Canoe, sailing, Willits:
construction commentary, history, photos, 55:82
Canoe, sailing, YAKABOO:
letter by John Martsolf, 82:5
Canoe, single-paddle, Bear Mountain Canoe (strip):
construction commentary, photos, 31:58
Canoe, single-paddle, Burundi dugout:
comments, photo, 69:76
Canoe, single-paddle, E.H. Gerrish (wood-and-canvas):
repair techniques/Rollin Thurlow, 78:56, 79:72
Canoe, single-paddle, E.M. White guide (wood-and-canvas):
builder of, construction comments, photos, 67:54
cover photo/Garrett Conover, 78:0
Canoe, single-paddle, expedition canoe:
selecting and using, 96:80

Canoe, single-paddle, Haisla dugout:
construction method, photos, 69:64
Canoe, single-paddle, Hawaiian koa log canoe:
construction commentary, history, photos, 59:80
Canoe, single-paddle, Honduran dugout:
letter by William G. Adams, 77:6
use in La Mosquitia, Honduras, 88:76
Canoe, single-paddle, MacKenzie bark canoe:
building commentary, photo, 36:36
Canoe, single-paddle, Mexican dugout:
construction commentary, photos, 20:61
Canoe, single-paddle, Olympic contenders:
comments by John Hanson, 13:34
Canoe, single-paddle, Panamanian dugout:
Kuna dugout construction, history, sailing techniques, 97:62
construction commentary, photos, 74:27
Canoe, single-paddle, plywood RANDOM SCOOT:
building from a kit, photos, 31:50
essay on theft of, 53:66
Canoe, single-paddle, Snowshoe (Geodesic Airolite):
construction commentary, photos, 76:77
Canoe, single-paddle, Tanganyika Liftnet canoe:
comments, plans, 42:66
plans, 41:50
Canoe, single-paddle, Vaillancourt bark canoe:
construction methods, photos, 87:80
Canoe paddle:
building instructions for double paddle, photos, 37:67
comments, plan, 57:60
construction method/Alexandra Conover, plans, 67:44
Canoe paddling:
attempted by an old salt, 6:43
letter on technique, 56:6
technique of Alexandra Conover, 55:79
Canoe pole:
building instructions, 49:40
Canoe poling:
history and technique, 49:40
Canoe repair:
technique of Jim Emmett, 25:22
wood-and-canvas repair/Rollin Thurlow, 78:56, 79:72
wood-and-canvas repair/Jerry Stelmok, 79:77
wood-and-canvas technique/Jerry Stelmok, 29:68
wood-and-canvas technique/George D. Orr, Jr., 35:94
Canoe yawl:
designs/Charles Wittholz, 56:130
Canoe yawl, CHERUB II:
comments, plans, 64:49
Canoe yawl, CLOUD:
comments, photo, plans, 64:49
Canoe yawl, EEL:
comments, plans, 75:62
Canoe yawl, ISOBEL:
construction commentary, photos, plans, 97:70
Canoe yawl, LA MOUETTE:
construction commentary, photo, 75:62
sailing critique, 75:69

Canoe yawl, ROZINANTE:
design, photos, plans, rig, 26:40
Canoe yawl, SHEILA:
construction and rig commentary, history, photos, plans, 64:49
Canoe yawl, SNIKERSNEE:
comments, photo, 100:70
Canoe yawl, WENDA:
designs/Albert Strange, 80:102
Canoe yawl, Windswept:
designs/Ted Brewer Yacht Designs, 63:116
Cant frames:
for pinnace DOVE, 26:30
Cantiere Motonautico Serenella, builder (Italy):
construction methods, history, 52:86
letter on, 54:9
Canvak:
letter on use, 57:8
Canvas:
patching techniques/wood-and-canvas canoes, 79:72
waterproofing technique/Harold Gates, 79:17
Canvasback, SALLY MAY:
comments, photo, 95:70
Canvas-covered decks:
comments/Biscayne Bay 14 daysailer, 98:28
letter on technique, 25:8
maintenance and repair/Maynard Bray, 64:58, 77:60
materials and technique/Jon Wilson, 22:72
materials and technique/International One-Design, 22:74
materials and technique/SEA BIRD yawl, 43:38
repair using Arabol, 25:89
repair using Dexeze, 13:60
repair/Giffy Full, 27:40
repair/Ed McClave, 75:89
technique/H. Rosenfeld, 14:64
technique/Ed McClave, 75:89
Canvas-covered hulls:
technique for River Boyne coracle, 79:17
technique for canoes/Jerry Stelmok, 29:68, 79:77
technique for canoes/George D. Orr, 35:94
Canvas doghouse:
comments, detail photos, 67:100
Canvas preservative:
Cuprinol, 22:94
Canvaswork, techniques for:
cringles, 32:49
ditty bag construction, 31:30, 32:49
grommet, 32:49, 55:114
herringbone stitch, 37:95
sail details, 32:49
seizing hanks, 35:80
sewing a patch, 36:86
sewing reef nettles, 38:100
Canvaswork, tools for:
comments, 31:30
CAPALL (hooker):
photo, 50:74
Cape Cod catboat:
advice on painting for decoration, 93:42
design and construction commentary, history, photo, 3:51
designs/Brewer, Wallstrom and Assoc., Inc., 20:91
rudder and tiller design for, 31:84

Cape Cod Shipbuilding Company, builder:
comments, 47:46
CAPE COD (steamer):
comments, photo, 61:32
Cape Fear Technical Institute (NC):
boatbuilding program, 42:100
CAPE HORN (troller):
comments, photo, 38:78
Cape Island boat:
evolution from sail to power, history,
photos, 46:42
letter on, 47:7
CAPRICE (pilot schooner):
account of voyage, 62:88
CAPRICE (Six-Meter class):
comments, photo, 83:38
CAPTAIN WALRUS (cutter):
designs/William Garden, 64:98
CAPT. R.D. CULLER (scow schooner):
design and construction commentary,
plans, 30:42
CARA MIA (New York 30):
history, 35:20
restoration comments, 35:30
Caravello, Joe, author:
"Ferdinand Nimphius: Making Wood Work
in the Midwest," 25:42
"RUBY's Bloom," 25:48
Carbon fiber:
characteristics and applications, 25:76
comments, 16:29, 59:48
for Formula 40 ADRENALIN, 87:66
for Ultralight-displacement boat MAGIC
CARPET, 90:108
Cardboard dory model: (*See* Dory, Banks)
CARDHU (sloop):
comments, plan, 24:24
CARDINAL VERTUE (cutter):
history, 24:32
Carey, George, author:
"DYON," 64:40
Carey, J.B., author:
"BROWN SUGAR: 7,600 Pounds of Pure
Power," 30:50
Cargo schooner: (*See* JOHN F. LEAVITT,
VERNON LANGILLE)
Cargo ship, wooden freighters for WWI:
design and construction commentary,
history, photos, 40:94
Caribbean boatbuilding:
Grenada fishing craft, 50:106
letters on, 51:10, 52:6
CARIBE MONIQUE (power cruiser):
charter of, 42:82
CARIBOU (power cruiser):
electrical system, 32:79
photo, 27:40
Carlisle, Johan, builder:
comments, 44:90
CARL J (dragger):
comments, photo, 75:34
CARL M. LARKIN (Monomoy surfboat):
comments, drawing, 77:34
Carnell, David W.:
letter on professional tools, 69:7
Carney, Walter, builder:
Cape Cod catboats, 3:51
CAROL (sloop):
designs/C.W. Paine, 39:132
Carolina sharpie, IDIE:
history, photos, plans, specifications, 13:68
Carolina skiff:
construction commentary, photos, 6:6

Carpenter, Vic, builder (Ontario):
comments, 45:2
construction methods, 45:50, 46:82
speedboat ERA, 50:52
**Carpenter, Vic and Hazel, builders
(Ontario):**
profile, 45:50
Carr, James, author:
"FRAM: The Ultimate Ice Ship," 85:44
Carr, J. Revell, author:
"Our Thanks to John Gardner," 90:36
comments on maritime preservation, 41:36
comments on Rosenfeld photo collection,
90:46
Carr, Tim and Pauline:
letter on Australian boatbuilding woods,
88:10
profile, photos, 86:36
CARRANDON (power fishing craft):
comments, photo, 50:70
CARRIE L (ketch):
building commentary, photo, 42:74
Carroll, R.P.:
comments, 100:70
Carryaway boat:
comments, photos, 58:52
letter by Glen Leland, 62:9
Carter, Dick, designer:
sloop CHRISTINE, 56:86
Carter, Grace B., author:
"The Return of the Sailing Peapod," 1:42
Carter, John, author:
"Swampscott Dories: Work or Pleasure,"
36:78
Carter, Richard F., author:
"Taken Easy," 8:7
Cartopper dinghy: (*See* Bolger Cartopper
[construction model], Bolger Cartopper
dinghy)
Carucci, Mitch, photographer:
"The Great South Bay Scooters," 92:52
cover photo/Great South Bay Scooter, 92:0
Carvel planking: (*See* Planking, carvel)
Casey, Franc, author:
reviewer of *Wooden Boat Restoration & Repair*
(book), 100:120
Cassidy, Ernie, author:
"Sprit Rig Basics," 89:30
CASTALIA (steam launch):
design and construction commentary,
photos, 15:29
Casting:
comments by Stephen Olsen, 46:52
lead keels/Richard Remsen, 89:52
patternmaking for ballast keel/Bud
McIntosh, 36:53
patternmaking for hardware/Michael
Podmaniczky, 39:58
small-boat hardware, photos, 73:24
Casuarina (wood):
for boatbuilding, 47:123
Catalpa (wood):
characteristics, 43:120
Catamaran:
commentary by Jim Brown, 42:66, 69:76,
91:38,
commentary by Nathanael G. Herreshoff,
23:64
designs by James Wharram, 23:77
Catamaran, AMARYLLIS:
history, performance critique by N.G.
Herreshoff, 23:64

Catamaran, AMARYLLIS II:
comments, 91:38
comments, photo, 84:34
Catamaran, ANNA KAY:
comments, photo, 69:76
Catamaran, EARTHLIGHT:
design and construction commentary,
photos, 23:77
Catamaran, LAZY SUSAN:
design and construction commentary,
plans, 42:66
Catamaran, Malibu Outrigger class:
design commentary, photos, plans, 33:86
Catamaran, Pahi AREOI:
design commentary, plans, 30:20
Catamaran, Pahi CAPTAIN COOK:
design commentary, plans, 30:20
Catamaran, SAILSKI:
photo, 55:32
Catamaran, Shark:
design and construction commentary,
history, photos, 69:29
Catamaran, STRIDER:
designs/Richard and Lilian Woods, 73:106
letter by Richard and Lilian Woods, 74:7
Catamaran, TARANTELLA:
performance critique by N.G. Herreshoff,
23:64
Catamaran, TAULUA:
design and construction commentary,
voyage, photos, 72:70
Catamaran, Tornado class:
Olympic contender, plan, 13:34
history, photo, 25:98
kit boat, 38:84
Catamaran, VAKA BUSI:
comments, photo 69:76
Catboat:
designs/Brewer, Wallstrom and Assoc.,
Inc., 20:91
designs/R.D. (Pete) Culler, 55:122
designs/Paul R. Kotzebue, 50:130
designs/Winthrop Warner, 36:94
Catboat, Beetle Cat:
construction commentary, 21:72
fitting and bending frames, photos, 53:101
keel and transom construction, photos,
51:99
stem and centerboard trunk installation,
photos, 52:107
Catboat, BOB CAT:
designs/Winthrop Warner, 36:94
Catboat, Cape Cod:
design and construction commentary,
history, photos, 3:51
designs/Brewer, Wallstrom and Assoc.,
Inc., 20:91
rudder and tiller design for, 31:84
Catboat, FRANCES:
designs/Wilton Crosby, 62:96
Catboat, GRACIE:
comments, photo, 3:51
Catboat, KATHERINE:
designs/Paul R. Kotzebue, 50:130
Catboat, MAB:
comments, photo, 91:92
Catboat, PANDORA:
cold-molded hull repair, photo, 60:76
Catboat, PEGGOTTY:
construction commentary, photo, plans,
23:39
Catboat, PRUDENCE:
comments, photo, 32:36

Catboat, SCAT:
cruising in Maine, 24:64
Catboat, Sun Cat:
design commentary, 36:73
CATCH ONE (Prowler power craft):
comments, photo, 86:44
C.A. THAYER (schooner):
comments, photos, 38:36, 61:88, 72:60
Cat-ketch: (*See* ARUNDEL [Newfoundland
trap skiff]; Block Island cowhorn; Crotch
Island pinky; Designs, Baker, William A.;
Designs, Bolger, Philip C.; Designs, Culler,
R.D. (Pete); Designs, Garden, William;
Designs, Paine, C.W.; Designs, Pittaway,
Rob; Designs, Zimmer, Nelson; EAST HUE
AND CRY; Egret sharpie; GOLDENEYE;
JUNIPER; Kingston lobsterboat; LIGHT-
FOOT; Mackinaw boat; MIST; Norwalk
Island sharpie; Plymouth lobsterboats;
ROBIN; SAILSKI; SHEARWATER)
Cat rig: (*See* Acorn skiff [sailing skiff];
AUDUBON; Barnegat Bay A-cat; Barnegat
Bay sneakbox; Beetle Cat class; BIRD-
WATCHER; CANARD; Catboat; Catspaw
dinghy [Herreshoff Columbia model];
Columbia River gillnetter; Cruising Class
sailing canoe; Delaware ducker; DRAGON-
FLY 15 [trimaran]; H-14 [sailing dinghy];
International 14 class; Moth class; New
Haven sharpie; North Haven dinghy;
Penguin class; San Francisco Pelican class;
Sid Skiff [sailing dinghy]; TELKKÄ
[Swedish ship's boat]; Turnabout class)
Cat-schooner: (*See* BRUNSWICK LION [St
John River boat]; ITATAE; SIB [trimaran];
TELKKÄ [Swedish ship's boat])
**Catspaw dinghy (Herreshoff Columbia
model):**
how to build, photos, plans, 26:48, 27:63,
28:64
Cat-yawl: (*See* Chebacco 20; CLARA;
COQUINA; Designs, Bolger, Philip C.;
Designs, Costello, Ned; MICRO; RESOLU-
TION)
Caulking:
comments, 2:64
letter on wood for mallets, 18:7
letters on, 17:6, 38:9
repair technique/Maynard Bray, 57:112
repair technique/Clarence Dirks, 22:94
technique for Catspaw dinghy, 28:64
technique for Danish ketch FRI, 87:36
technique for pinnace DOVE, 26:30
technique for underwater repair, 4:30,
57:66
technique/Fred Barter, 17:32
technique/Clarence Dirks, 24:40
technique/Sam Manning, 16:47
technique/Bud McIntosh, 46:103, 55:107
technique/Bill Modrell, 13:85
technique/Joel White, 37:86
See also Seams
Caulking compounds:
for lapstrake planking/Walter J. Simmons,
92:90
for quick-and-dirty rowboat repairs, 93:29
types and application techniques/Aimé
Ontario Fraser, 92:23
See also Seam compounds
CCA (wood preservative):
comments by Richard Jagels, 73:108,
76:115, 89:106

CECELIA J (schooner):
design commentary, history, photos, 53:38
Cecil, Owen, author and photographer:
"Chip Stulen, Boatbuilder," 95:38
Cedar:
species for boatbuilding, 9:31
Cedar, Alaska yellow:
comments, 24:100
letter by Molly Kemp and Nick Olmsted,
78:6
Cedar, incense (wood):
for boatbuilding, 42:123
Cedar, Northern white:
for E.M. White guide canoe, 67:54
for flat-bottomed skiff or sharpie, 66:48
Cedar, Port Orford:
for planking, outboard boat TROUT
UNLIMITED, 64:70
for planking, sloop MELE KAI, 64:92
for planking, trawler-yacht NORDSØ, 74:74
Cedar, Spanish:
comments, 10:35, 30:94, 36:89
Cedar, white:
comments, 33:72
for birchbark canoe, 87:80
for planking, 16:39, 28:64
letter on, 32:9
Cedar boatboards:
comments on by R.D. (Pete) Culler, 3:68
for decking/Biscayne Bay 14 daysailer,
98:28
Ceiling:
illustrated glossary, 60:115
installation technique/Bud McIntosh,
47:69
Celarek, Aleksander, author:
"Traditional Boats in Poland Today," 89:84
Celarek, Aleksander, author and illustrator:
"The Smaller Boats of Kaszuby," 89:80
Celarek, Aleksander, illustrator:
"Boats of the Polish Coast," 89:74
Celebrity class, SEOLADAIR:
photos, rebuilding commentary, 22:61
CELT (Alpha-Beachcomber dory):
comments, photo, 36:78
**CENTENNIAL REPUBLIC (Barnegat Bay
sneakbox):**
comments, plans, 20:23, 70:104
Centerboard:
construction method/Bud McIntosh, 78:41
for Biscayne Bay 14 daysailer, 98:28
for Whitehall pulling boat, 24:58
letter on lead-pouring technique, 80:6
maintenance for skipjack FLORA, 9:50
Centerboard trunks:
Beetle Cat, 52:107
Biscayne Bay 14 daysailer, 97:31
Catspaw dinghy (Herreshoff Columbia
model), 27:63, 28:64
comments, detail photo, 65:52
comments on antifouling/Mike O'Brien,
80:85
construction method/Bud McIntosh, 78:41
Center for Adirondack Studies (NY):
boatbuilding program, 42:100
Center for Wood Arts (CA):
boatbuilding program, 42:100
Center for Wooden Boats (WA):
boatbuilding program, 42:100
boats at, 29:102
history, 24:36
history, photos, 90:72

Center, Robert, designer:
comments, 41:26
CERO (sportfisherman):
comments, plan, 54:34
Chadwick, John, Jr., builder:
sneakboxes, 47:102
Chainplates:
comments, detail photo, 69:104
for Biscayne Bay 14 daysailer, 98:28
Chainsaw, use:
construction of Haisla dugout canoe, 69:64
Chainsaw milling:
equipment for, technique/Bob Darr, 37:98
equipment for, technique/Will Malloff,
50:38
frames for Adirondack guideboat, 59:64
knees produced by, technique/Frank
Morse, 30:66
Chaisson, George L., builder:
cutter CORINEUS/comments, 85:21
dories, 36:83
CHALLENGE (schooner):
letter on, 54:5
CHALLENGER (Peterson 41):
cover photo/Neil Rabinowitz, 100:0
Chamberlain, William, builder/designer:
Alpha-Beachcomber dory, 36:78
dories, 38:83
Chamberlain dory skiff:
comments, photo, 73:60
Chamberlin, Carl, illustrator:
"Oarlocks on Your Own," 73:21
Chamberlin, E.H., author:
"RHIANNON," 8:18
Chambers, Taylor M., author:
"Hot Ideas for Cold-Molded Boats," 63:56
"SKIDOO," 51:80
"SKIDOO: Swift and Sensitive," 51:83
letter on sloop ALERT, 64:7
Chameleon dinghy (nesting dinghy):
designs/Danny Greene, 99:116
Chandler, Bob, author:
"The Ancient and Versatile Vlet," 52:75
**Chantiers Navals de l'Estérel, builder
(France):**
construction methods of French military
craft, 39:44
Chapelle, Howard I.:
association with John Gardner, 40:30
comments, 1:8, 5:12, 5:44, 13:61, 33:33,
36:62, 52:59, 97:52
comments about Essex-built fishing
schooners, 61:32
comments on by Bud McIntosh, 51:40
delineator of New England working sloop,
58:116
designer profile, photos, 84:76
developer of National Watercraft
Collection, 77:21
letter by Harry Sucher, 85:7
obituary, 5:1
on carryaway boats, 58:52
on Mackinaw boats, 45:100
on sharpies, 3:24, 56:76
on strip planking, 57:50
on Tancook whaler, 58:82
pinky schooner RELIANCE, 18:46
sharpies, 25:36
See also Designs, Chapelle, Howard I.
Chapin, E. Barton, III, author:
"Paintbrush Care," 99:104
letter on transom repair, 100:4

Chapman, Fredrik Henrik, designer:
Swedish ship's boat TELKKÄ, 60:68
CHARETTE II (iceboat):
comments, plans, 39:88
CHARIS II (multihull):
comments, photo, 92:34
Charles, Alden, photographer:
cover photo/trimaran JUNIPER, 54:0
CHARLES COOPER (square-rigger):
comments, photo, 38:36, 38:45
CHARLES W. MORGAN (whaleship):
comments, 38:36, 41:36, 46:80
cover photo/Benjamin Mendlowitz, 36:0
planking technique, photos, 36:98
Charley Noble (smokestack):
design for, 49:86
CHARLOTTE (launch):
comments, plan, 75:34
Chartering:
Baltic Trader LINDØ, 42:92
Friendship sloop RED JACKET, 11:65
10-Meter sloop GRACIL, 91:56
wooden boats in the Caribbean, 91:50
wooden boats in the Virgin Islands, 42:82
Chart Kit:
comments by Jon Wilson, 83:86
letter by James G. Owen, 86:5
Chase, Irvin, designer:
Elco 26, 13:26
Chason, Don, builder:
sportfishing boats, 76:44
Chebacco 20 (cat-yawl):
comments, photo, 61:38
Cheek, Vernon, photographer:
cover photo/cutter SYRINX, 63:0
CHEERIO (Eight-Meter):
racing incident, 60:41
Cheever, David:
letter on Bud McIntosh, 52:7
Cheney, Tod, author:
"AIRFORCE," 68:72
"In the Wake of a High: The Creation and
Demise of AIRFORCE," 75:22
Cheniers, builder:
Mackinaw boat, 45:100
Cheops Royal Ship:
history, photos, plans, restoration commentary, 38:28
CHEROKEE (cabin launch):
history, photos, restoration comments, 61:100
letter by Bob Harris, 62:7
CHERUB II (canoe yawl):
comments, plans, 64:49
CHESAPEAKE (yawl):
chartering, 42:82
Chesapeake Academy of Traditional Boatbuilding (VA):
boatbuilding program, 14:34
comments, 13:5
Chesapeake Bay bugeye, JENNY NORMAN:
builder, construction commentary, photos, 65:32
Chesapeake Bay crabbing skiff:
design and construction commentary, plans, 69:100
Chesapeake Bay log canoe:
construction commentary, history, photos, 6:26
Chesapeake Bay Maritime Museum (MD):
boats at, 29:102
comments, 48:86

Chesapeake Bay outboard skiff:
comments, 67:117
Chesapeake Bay pungy, RUBEN DE CLOUX:
designs/Bruce Northrup, 68:110
Chesapeake Bay pungy schooner:
history, photos, plans, 45:56
Chesapeake Bay skiff:
comments, plans, 84:76
Chesapeake Bay skipjack:
designs/Charles Coad, 19:82
Chesapeake Bay skipjack, CALICO JACK:
designs/Joseph Gregory, 79:106
Chesapeake Bay skipjack, FLORA:
centerboard repair, 9:50
Chesapeake Bay skipjack, SIGSBEE:
photos, racing, 3:34
Chesapeake Bay skipjack, STANLEY NORMAN:
photos, restoration commentary, 35:62
CHESTER L. PIKE (sardine carrier):
comments, 59:70
CHEWINK III (Massachusetts Bay 21):
comments, photo, 72:44
Chicago Maritime Society:
comments, 63:8
CHIMO (speed launch):
comments, 50:52
China: (See Chinese boatbuilding, Chinese junk, Chinese lugsail, Chinese maritime tradition)
CHINA CLOUD (Chinese junk):
construction, design, performance commentary, photos, 67:19
Chincoteague scow:
construction commentary, photos, 49:81
Chine boats:
design and construction comments/ George Buehler, 79:64
Chinese boatbuilding:
commentary on construction methods, photos, 49:108
fire-bending of wood, photos, 44:104
Chinese junk:
design and construction commentary, history, photos, 66:76
Chinese junk, CHINA CLOUD:
construction, design, performance commentary, photos, 67:19
Chinese junk, MING HAI:
history, photos, 16:35
Chinese lugsail:
commentary by Iain Oughtred, 78:66
comments by Colin Palmer, 92:76
letter by Colin Palmer, 94:6
Chinese maritime tradition:
letter by Richard Breeze, 71:8
letter by Matthew Walker, 67:5
Chines, steam-bent:
outboard runabout Downeaster 18, 73:67
Chipman, Craig
letter on Melbourne Smith, 79:5
CHIPS (P class):
comments, photo, 74:42
CHIQUITA (40' class):
history, photos, 48:58
Chisel, Japanese:
critique, 72:21
Chisel, thonging:
use in leatherworking, 68:64
CHLOE (speedboat):
comments, photo, 62:74

Chock, bow:
for sloop ALERION III, 30:84
Chock, bulwark:
making a pattern for, 39:58
Choy, Rudy, designer:
comments, 91:38
Chris-Craft Constellation:
design commentary, photo, plans, 32:100
Chris-Craft Corporation, builder:
Chris-Craft Constellation, 32:100
Chris-Craft Family Cruiser, 39:119
Chris-Craft Ranger 23, 27:96
Chris-Craft Riviera, 96:87
Chris-Craft Streamline Cruiser, 39:119
Chris-Craft 23, 21:96
runabouts, 10:53
Chris-Craft Family Cruiser (power cruiser):
construction commentary, history, photo, 39:119
Chris-Craft Ranger 23 (power cruiser):
design commentary, photo, plans, 27:96
Chris-Craft Riviera:
replanking, photos, 96:87
Chris-Craft Streamline (power cruiser):
construction commentary, history, photo, 39:119
Chris-Craft 23 (power cruiser):
design and construction commentary, photos, plans, 21:96
CHRISTABEL (power cruiser):
comments, photo, 12:66
Christensen, Arne Emil, Jr., author:
"A Viking Ship to Sail the World," 68:19
"Building a Norwegian Pram," 49:28
"Sure Eye and Steady Hand," 28:39
comments, 28:36
reviewer of Colin Archer and the Seaworthy Double-Ender (book), 32:86
reviewer of Hooper Bay Kayak Construction (book), 45:115
CHRISTINE (sloop):
construction commentary, photos, racing of, 56:86
CHRISTMAS (cutter):
comments, photo, 74:42
CHRISTOPHER COLUMBUS (sloop):
comments, photo, 61:52
Chudleigh, Tom, builder (England):
pilot gigs, 25:28
Chumash tomol (canoe):
design and construction commentary, history, photos, plans, 35:82
Church, Jesse Wells, builder:
Mackinaw boats, 45:100
Churchill, Eton F., author:
letter on Ghosts of Cape Horn (film), 46:9
reviewer of Ghosts of Cape Horn (film), 45:29
Churchill, Owen:
comments, 59:40
CIGARETTE (commuter):
comments, photo, 94:74
CIMBA (Pacific proa):
comments, photos, plans, 83:58
CINDERELLA (cutter):
comments, photo, 91:92
Circular saw:
method of sharpening/Harold Payson, 48:44
CIRRUS (Fishers Island 31):
history, photos, plans, rig conversion, 34:42
plywood-and-Dynel deck overlay, photos, 66:64

CITY OF HELENA (steamboat):
comments, photo, 64:64
Clamp:
cement form/comments, 24:76
critique of clamps by Adjustable Clamp Co., 1:77
critique of clamps by Wetzler Clamp Co., 1:77, 2:70
critique/Jon Wilson, 12:42
Norwegian finger/how to build, 24:77, 29:67
product review by Daniel Porter, 93:120
spar/design of John Marsland, 15:60
spar/design of Bud McIntosh, 60:125
spar/design of Lin and Larry Pardey, 15:64
various types discussed/Sam Manning, 99:94
various types discussed/W.J. Simmons, 12:62
Clamp and shelf construction:
comments by Joel White, 63:116
Clapham, Thomas, designer:
comments, 100:70
sharpies, 25:36
Clapp, George, author and photographer:
"Transom Repair," 16:20
CLARA (cat-yawl):
comments, 51:72
comments, photo, 84:34, 100:70
CLARA (cutter):
comments, photo, 41:26, 90:84
Clare, David, photographer:
"The Steam Yacht ENA," 90:102
Clare Lallow Yard (England): (*See* Lallow, Clare, builder)
CLAREL (iceboat):
comments, 38:64
Clark, Ephraim C.S.:
letter on epoxy, 34:10
Clark, James F.:
letter on wood for caulking mallets, 18:7
Clark, John, builder:
profile, photo, 98:74
wedge-seam construction techniques, 98:82
Clark, Martyn J.:
letter on historic vessel reproduction, 98:4
Clark, Robert, designer (England):
sloop TORETTA, 22:46
Clark, Russell, author:
"The Cutter Craze," 41:26
"The History of Small Yacht Design, Part I: SCHEMER," 37:42
Clark, Tom:
comments about battenless mainsails, 64:34
letter on marine hardware, 33:5
on boat cover materials, 54:92
reviewer of *The Shape of Speed* (video), 80:93
Clark-Craft, builder:
Quintet 6 kit boat, 39:69
Clarke, Dick, builder:
profile, photo, 65:90
Class A Frostbite dinghy:
comments, plans, 75:34
Classic Boat Festival: (*See* Victoria Classic Boat Festival, British Columbia)
Classic yacht regatta:
commentary, photos, 38:71, 43:92
preparations for racing, 95:55
See also Museum of Yachting's Classic Yacht Regatta (RI)
CLAUS EILEEN (Danish seiner):
comments, photo, 88:40

CLAUS SORENSEN (Danish seiner):
comments, photos, 88:40
Cleat:
construction method, illustrations, 82:33
design for, by Gil Stratton, 14:14
Cleaving:
technique, 72:70
Clemans, Robert:
letter on vacuum bagging, 45:11
Clench nails:
installation for planks and frames/small craft, 26:28
installation for sailing canoe PICCOLO, 36:44
letter on, 28:7
removal from lapstrake planking, 92:90
Clench rings, bronze:
use on cutter TALEISIN, 51:72
Cleverly, Richard:
letter on Eva Hollmann's design, 7:3
Clipper ship, CUTTY SARK:
comments, photo, 38:36, 46:54
Clipper ship, SEA WITCH:
comments, painting, 78:76
CLOUD (canoe yawl):
comments, photo, plans, 64:49
Coad, Charles E., designer: (*See* Designs, Coad, Charles E.)
Coaming:
replacing on Herreshoff 12½/Steve Ballentine, 57:93
steam-bending technique/Joel White, 44:86
COASTER (schooner):
photo, racing, 13:79
COASTER I (schooner):
comments, 1:30
COASTER III (schooner):
as example of half-model building, 33:41
comments, 1:30
Coast Guard lifeboat, BANFIELD:
comments, photo, 65:76
Coast Guard, U.S.:
letter on boardings, 91:6
small-craft regulations, 3:1, 6:65, 50:16
vessel design by Walter McInnis, 53:38, 54:34
Coates, John:
comments about Athenian trireme, 75:48
Coble, Paul:
advice on refastening, 80:85
Cobles:
comments, photo, 69:86
design and construction, history, photos, 86:70
design and construction, history, photos, plan, use, 86:58
Cochran, Barbara, author:
"Ideas: Leaks Are Lousy," 13:60
Cochran, Drayton:
association with Walter McInnis, 54:34
COCKATOO (Folkboat):
history, photo, plans, 10:30
COCKATOO II (New York 30):
comments, 35:20
letter on, 37:7
performance of, 35:27
Cockpit:
comments, detail photo, 74:80
design and construction/Bud McIntosh, 46:103 illustrated glossary, 60:115
scuppers/installation, 14:81

COFFEE GRINDER (sloop):
construction commentary, photo, 46:82
Coffin, Donna, illustrator:
"ISH-TY-IQUE," 31:48
Coffin, Edward, builder:
Friendship sloop RAY OF HOPE, 53:48
Cogge ketch:
designs/William Garden, 87:119
Colcord, Lincoln, author:
"Hardtack's Running Moor," 50:96
Cold-molded hull construction:
BOC Challenger AIRFORCE, 68:72
building techniques/Allan Vaitses, 15:33
comments by Thomas MacNaughton, 4:17
comments by Jon Wilson, 26:70
comments by Tom Wylie, 63:56
compared to carvel, 44:90
Constant Camber technique/Jim Brown, 41:50
Constant Camber technique/John Marples, 44:99
Constant Camber technique/skiff GULL, 64:83, 65:97
Eight-Meter REALITY/Bent Jespersen, 34:20
Florida sportfishing boats, 76:44
GOLDEN DAZY/Gougeon Brothers, Inc., 16:29
letter on, 10:5
McCurdy and Rhodes cutter AERIEL, 100:108
modified Bounty ketch LA FILLE D'OR, 67:82
Monomoy surfboat/Bay Area Marine Institute, 44:90
power cruiser YOREL, 95:67
sailing dinghy Tender Ten/East Bay Boatworks, 22:77
scantling rules, 4:17
Shark catamaran, 69:29
Swede 55 VORTEX/Steve White, 100:84, 100:88
technique/John Guzzwell, 84:64
ultralight-displacement boat MAGIC CARPET, 90:108
utility outboard boat RIVERKEEPER, 61:72
vacuum bagging/John Marples, 44:99
veneer thickness, 17:86
See also Hot molding, Vacuum bagging
Cold-molded hull repair:
Alden yawl ISLA TROTHE/Rick Kotalac, 52:92
catboat PANDORA/Daniel Briggs, Molly's Cove Boatworks, 60:76
critique by professional builders, 52:92
critique/John Shortall III, 7:45
Eight-Meter sloop ANGELITA, 59:40
Falmouth Quay punt CURLEW, 86:36
letter on, 53:6
Luders 16-class SILHOUETTE/Steve White, 55:102
Nine-Meter TANGO II/Don Watson, Concordia Co., 60:76
Owens cutter FALCON/Bent Jespersen, 60:76, 61:104
power cruiser YAZOO/Daniel Briggs, Molly's Cove Boatworks, 60:76
techniques/Gougeon Brothers, Inc., 55:96
techniques/Reuel Parker, 89:92
techniques/Jim Watson, 55:96

COLD WAVE (iceboat):
    comments, photo, 38:64
    cover photo/Peter A. Burckmyer, 14:0
Cole, John N., author:
    "Winter," 2:57
Coleman, Dale Alan:
    letter on traditional sailmaking, 54:116
Coleman, Raymond:
    letter on Canvak, 57:8
COLIN ARCHER (ketch):
    construction commentary, photos, 20:38
Collemer, Elmer, builder:
    comments, 2:58, 60:134
Collins, Joseph William:
    profile, 77:21
Collins, Rex and Roy, builders (England):
    Falmouth oyster boats, 31:36
Colomby, Bo, author:
    "How the Legend Began," 20:82
Colonial shipbuilding:
    wood for, 58:120
Colorado River dory:
    cover photo/Walter Rist, 15:0
    design and construction commentary,
        performance, photos, 15:47
Colson, Herbert, builder:
    sardine carriers, 59:70
Colson, Ralph, builder:
    sardine carriers, 59:70
COLUMBIA (schooner):
    racing of, 13:82
COLUMBIA (12-Meter):
    comments, photo, 68:40
Columbia River gillnetter:
    history, photos, 22:27
COLUMBINE (cutter):
    comments, plan, 71:52
Combewright, Wayland, author and builder:
    "All for a Horse," 72:70
Comet class:
    history, photos, plan, 31:90
COMET (launch):
    comments, photo, 62:74
COMET (steamer):
    design commentary, photo, 3:49
COMET II (schooner):
    design and construction commentary,
        34:26
Commuter launch, KATOURA:
    comments, photo, plans, 52:40
Commuters:
    commentary by Philip C. Moore, 94:74
Companionway dropboards:
    construction method/Bud McIntosh, 67:91
Companionway ladder:
    detail photo, comments, 66:90
Companionway rails:
    construction method/Bud McIntosh, 67:91
Companionway sliding hatch cover:
    construction method/Bud McIntosh, 67:91
Composite construction:
    sloop GAUNTLET, 41:84
    10-Meter RAPIER, 3:71
    20-Square-Meter Tumlaren, 19:18
    yawl ROYONO, 1:4
Compounds, bedding: (See Bedding com-
    pounds)
Compton, Jesse, builder (Grenada):
    comments, 50:106
Compton, Leo, builder (Grenada):
    comments, 50:106
Computer software:
    AMBUSH and YACHT/product review by

Chris White, 87:108
    AutoEXPAND (lines-expansion program)/
        sea kayak QUEEN CHARLOTTE, 79:84
    comments on computer-aided yacht design
        by Ed McClave, 100:31
    letter on computer-aided yacht design by
        Andrew Davis, 99:8
Concept Marine, builder:
    cat-ketch SHEARWATER, 59:48
Conch fishing:
    technique, 81:34
Concordia Company, builder:
    Beetle Cat, 21:72, 51:99, 52:107, 53:101
    Concordia sloop-boat, 4:4, 29:98
    comments on by Bud McIntosh, 51:40
    recommendations for boat covers, 54:92
    repair of cold-molded hulls, 60:76
Concordia sloop-boat:
    comments, photos, 4:4
    design and construction commentary,
        photos, plans, 29:98
Concordia sloop-boat, FILSADAR:
    comments, photos, 55:88
Concordia 28 (sloop):
    designs/W.B. Harris, Concordia Co.,
        48:126
Concordia 28, SHAWNEE:
    design commentary, 48:126
Concordia 31 (sloop):
    designs/W.B. Harris, Concordia Co.,
        48:126
Concordia 31, LAUAN:
    comments, plan, 48:126
Concordia 31, STAR DUST:
    letter on, 50:8
    photo, 51:40
Concordia 33 (sloop):
    designs/W.B. Harris, Concordia Co.,
        48:126
Concordia 33, FREE SPIRIT:
    comments, photo, 48:126
    plywood-and-Dynel deck replacement,
        photos, 66:64
    transom replacement, letter on, 100:4
    transom replacement, photos, 99:28
Concordia yawl:
    construction, design, history, photos, plans,
        80:61
    editorial by Jon Wilson, 80:2
    model, photos, 97:52
    sailing techniques/Waldo Howland, 80:72
Concordia yawl, JAVA:
    history, painting, photo, 80:72
Concordia yawl, PARAMOUR:
    comments, photo, 43:92
Concordia yawl, SAFARI:
    comments, photo, 80:64
Concordia yawl, SEA HAWK:
    comments, photo, 80:64
Concordia yawl, SHIMAERA:
    comments, photo, 80:64
Concordia yawl, THISTLEDOWN:
    comments, detail photos, 67:100, 68:70
    comments, photo, 80:64
Concours d'Élégance, Lake Tahoe:
    boat show commentary by Peter Spectre,
        62:74
Condon, Albert, designer:
    New England draggers, 79:48
CONDOR (sloop):
    photos, 47:74
CONE (lobsterboat, power):
    comments, photo, 69:42

Conner, Dan, author:
    "Other Ways: Mast Protection," 42:27
Connor, Sam, builder:
    comments, 17:14
Conover, Alexandra:
    association with Mick Fahey, 67:38
    on canoe-paddling technique, 55:79
    technique for building canoe paddle, 67:44
Conover, Garrett:
    association with Mick Fahey, 67:38
Conover, Garrett, author:
    "The North Woods Canoe," 96:80
Conover, Garrett, photographer:
    cover photo/E.M. White canoe, 78:0
CONQUEROR (sardine carrier):
    comments, 59:70
Conrad, James H., and Thad Sitton, authors:
    "The Caddo Lake Bateau," 62:44
Conrad, Richard, author:
    "The San Francisco Pelican," 30:29
CONSEQUENCE (Controversy 30):
    comments, photo, 61:42
Consolidated Shipbuilding Corporation,
    builder:
    power cruiser LADY MONA, 22:57
Constant Camber:
    projects of Jim Brown, 69:76
    skiff GULL/Jim Brown and John Marples,
        64:83, 65:97
    technique/Jim Brown, 41:50, 42:66
    technique/John Marples, 44:99, 49:112
    technique/Chris White, 54:56
Constant Camber Boatworks, builder:
    SIB 32 kit boat, 39:69
Constellation (power cruiser):
    design commentary, photo, plans, 32:100
CONSTITUTION (frigate):
    comments, 46:76
    history, illustrations, photos, turnaround
        cruise, 83:32
Construction plan:
    comments by Joel White, 75:111
CONTEST (Bermuda fitted dinghy):
    comments, photo, plans, 57:42
CONTINENTAL (sardine carrier):
    comments, 59:70
Controversy class:
    design and construction commentary,
        photo, plans, 61:42
Controversy 26 class:
    design commentary, photo, plan, 61:42
Controversy 27 class:
    design commentary, plans, 61:42
Controversy 28 class:
    design commentary, plans, 61:42
Controversy 30 class:
    design commentary, photo, plans, 61:42
Controversy 30 class, CONSEQUENCE:
    comments, photo, 61:42
Controversy 36 class:
    design commentary, photo, plans, 61:42
Controversy 36 class, BOOMERANG:
    letter by Robert Baldwin, 63:4
Conway, John:
    letter on historic ship preservation, 68:7
Coolidge, Leigh, designer:
    Blanchard 36 Standardized Cruiser, 94:54
Cooney, Kit, builder:
    comments about Lyle Hess cutter, 76:60
Cooperatives, boatbuilding:
    Mellemværftet Shipyard, 84:58
    Sausalito Shipwrights' Co-op/history and
        guidelines, 34:36, 34:38

Cooper, Dexter:
letter on boatbuilding industry, 64:9
Copper sheathing:
cutter ISKRA/Frank Mulville, 67:35
GAZELA PHILADELPHIA/Steve Masone,
74:19
Coppola, Giancarlo, designer (Italy):
ketch FARMILY, 29:20
Copyright law, boat designs:
comments by John Gardner, 47:46
comments by Jon Wilson, 32:2, 47:2, 47:46
forum, 48:105
letter on, 49:5
COQUINA (cat-yawl):
comments, photo, 84:34
Coracle, River Boyne:
construction commentary, history, photos,
79:17
Cordage, techniques for:
Angler's Loop, 72:40
backsplices, 52:112
bag knot, 20:18
barrel sling, 29:18
bowknot, 72:40
camel hitch, 30:18
Cleopatra's Eye Splice, 24:20
constrictor (single and double) knot,
48:100, 72:40
cringles, 32:49
grommet, 32:49, 55:114
hitches, 39:102, 40:92, 48:100, 50:101
hitches, letter on, 32:5
Jug Sling, 20:18
lashing, 50:101
macramé, 18:19
Manila Marriage knot, 25:18
masthead knot, 21:16
Matthew Walker knot, 52:112
Monkey Fist knot, 26:20
netting, 27:18
reef knot, 18:19
seizing, 48:100
seizing hanks, 35:80
service, 48:100, 59:106
sheet bends, 53:96
slings, 25:18, 28:18
stopper knot, 52:112
transom knot, 72:40
Turk's Head hitches, 40:92
Turk's Head knot, 19:17, 32:49, 40:92,
72:40
Turquoise Turtle knot, 72:40
water knot, 23:20
whippings, 25:18, 52:112
See also Bosun's chair
Core Sound sharpie, TORTUGA:
design and construction commentary,
photos, plans, 35:76
CORINEUS (cutter)
history, photos, plans, 85:21
Corinthian (power cruiser):
designs/Glen-L Marine, 46:11
CORINTHIAN (scow sloop):
comments, 73:32
Corinthian 53 (power cruiser):
photo, 57:102
Corliss engine:
comments, photo, 81:21
Cormack, George A.:
comments, 100:70
Cornell, Skip:
on finish work, 46:66

Cornerposts, cabin:
construction technique/Bud McIntosh,
42:53
Cornish gig:
history, photos, plans, 25:28
Cornish gig, TESS:
comments, drawing, 77:34
CORONET (schooner):
design and construction commentary,
history, photos, plans, 32:20
painting, preservation, 39:76
Cosine Wherry (recreational shell):
design and construction commentary,
photo, plans, 100:100
Costello, Ned, delineator: (*See* Designs,
Costello, Ned, delineator)
COTTON BLOSSOM IV (yawl):
cover photo/Sandy Brown, 38:0
Cotton caulking, use:
deck seams, 77:60
Cottreau, Richard, builder:
comments, 40:17
Cotuit skiff (daysailer):
comments, photo, 99:48
Countertop fiddles:
comments, detail photo, 65:52
COUNTESS (commuter):
comments, photo, 28:20, 94:74
Covering boards:
construction/Bud McIntosh, 46:103
repair of, on sloop IOLAIRE, 13:65
Cowes steam launch:
design and construction, plans, 13:76
Cowhorn: (*See* Block Island cowhorn)
Crabbing skiff: (*See* Chesapeake Bay crabbing
skiff)
Crab Claw rig:
comments by Colin Palmer, 92:76
Crabtree, August, model builder:
profile, photo, 63:80
Cradles, for boats:
comments/Jon Wilson, 12:59
construction comments, drawings, 69:86
design for storing and shipping boats,
18:51
design/Paul Bryant, 48:91
letter on, 22:5
See also Grounding out, Poppets
Craftsmanship studies:
"Elements of Craftsmanship"/Jon Wilson,
26:53, 27:57, 28:59, 29:89, 30:89, 31:79,
32:88
Crampton, Bill, author:
"Irish Hookers," 50:74
reviewer of *The Evolution of the Wooden Ship*
(book), 90:136
Crane, Clinton, designer:
association with Walter McInnis, 52:40
comments, 54:34, 60:84
12-Meter-class boats, 68:40
Cresswell, Jeremy, author:
"Danish Seiners," 88:40
Cresswell, Jeremy, author and photographer:
"The Scottish Fishing Fleet," 62:68
Cringles:
making of, 32:49
Cristofani's Boat Works, builder:
comments, 21:49
Crocker, Samuel S., designer:
comments, 32:66, 60:115
comments on by Bud McIntosh, 51:40
sloop Sallee Rover, 87:46
See also Designs, Crocker, Samuel S.

Crockett Brothers Boat Yard:
on boat covers, 54:92
Crook timber:
guide for selecting, 40:120
Crosby, C.W. & H.S., builder:
Cape Cod catboats, 3:51
Crosby, Eddie, builder:
profile, 34:82
Crosby, H. Manley, designer:
Wianno Senior class/comments, 91:58
Crosby, William F., designer:
comments on Snipe class, 89:36
editorial by Jon Wilson, 89:2
Crosby, Wilton: (*See* Designs, Crosby, Wilton)
Crosen, Jane, illustrator:
"A Week Along the Thames," 74:54
"Alfred Bain and UNITY B," 81:34
"ISKRA Sails Down East," 53:90
"Rowing the Maine Coast," 47:52
"Sardine Carriers, Part I," 58:52
"The Art of Finding Your Way," 59:102
"The Janggolans of Madura," 77:52
"The Scottish Fishing Fleet," 62:68
Cross, Dick:
BOC Challenge (1986) account, 75:22
letter on BOC Challenge (1986), 69:5
profile, photo, 68:72
Cross, Michael, designer:
comments about cutter EMILY, 66:56
CROSSBOW II (proa):
comments, 14:7
Crosscut saw:
sharpening technique/Harold Payson,
47:91
Crotch Island pinky:
comments, photo, plans, 4:31
Crouch, George, designer:
comments, 48:66, 97:76
speedboat BABY BOOTLEGGER, 60:84
CROW (cutter):
designs/William Garden, 64:98
Crowell, Gary, photographer:
"Strip-Building a Double-Paddle Canoe,"
100:92
Crowley, Michael, author:
"Better With Age," 16:63
"Lapstrake Plank Repair," 71:38
"Preserving Norway's Sailing Freighters,"
73:96
"Sardine Carriers, Part I," 58:52
"Sardine Carriers, Part II," 59:70
Crowninshield, B.B., designer:
comments, 32:66
sloop GYPSY, 13:40
See also Designs, Crowninshield, B.B.
CRUISER (sandbagger):
comments, plan, 63:112
plan, 37:42
Cruising:
Arkansas, Buffalo River/bateau ISAAC
McCASLIN, 72:84
Caribbean/Tahiti ketch JOSEPHA, 8:36
chartering in the Caribbean, 91:50
cruising boat commentary and
designs/Philip Bolger, 86:76
cruising story by Maurice Griffiths, 91:89
cutter CORINEUS, 85:21
England/Swedish ship's boat, TELKKÄ,
60:68
England, Thames River/Thames River
skiff, 74:54
expedition canoe, 96:80
Florida/antique-boat cruise, 90:78

Florida/ketch MEADOWLARK, 38:58
loss of schooner TYEHEE, account of, 83:74
loss of schooner TYEHEE, letters on, 84:5
loss of schooner TYEHEE, navigation comments, 83:86, 83:88
Maine/Friendship sloop RED JACKET, 11:65
Maine/catboat SCAT, 24:64
Maine/peapod, 47:52
Maine/sloop KATY G, 11:62
Maine to Nova Scotia/cutter ISKRA, 53:90
Maine to Nova Scotia/peapod, 70:68
Nantucket/SEA BIRD yawl, 43:30
New Jersey/schooner LAZY JACK, 15:40
offshore/cutter ISKRA, 40:72
offshore/ketch DOVEKIE, 7:31
offshore/schooner ACTIVE, 7:20
offshore/SEA BIRD yawl, 44:32
offshore/yawl SCUD, 21:58
South Pacific/ketch MAYA, 9:16
Virginia to New York/sloop HIPPO-CAMPUS JR, 8:46
Cruising Class sailing canoe:
history, photos, 24:90
CRUISING CLUB (sloop):
comments, photo, 61:52
Crumlin-Pedersen, Ole:
comments, 11:15
C-STAR (singlehanded transatlantic race):
commentary by James W. (Jim) Brown, 91:38
Culfor Marine Ltd., builder (England):
steam launch, 13:76
Culler, R.D. (Pete), author:
"Ask the Pros: Pine Tar," 19:98
"Boatbuilding: The Philosophy of an Approach," 4:4
letter/advice to boatbuilders, 21:10
letter/Cuprinol for sails, 23:8
on Rushton canoes, 11:2
Culler, R.D. (Pete), designer/builder:
bateau-type rowing skiff RANDANDY, 66:23
comments, 27:26, 28:83, 55:88, 90:56
comments on sprit rig, 89:30
dollies for moving small boats, 69:86
eulogy for, 23:2
oar design, 71:28
on cedar boatboards, 3:68
on color schemes for commercial sailing vessels, 5:72
outboard launch MRS. JONES, 68:80
schooner JOHN F. LEAVITT, 31:18
scow schooner CAPT. R.D. CULLER, 30:42
sharpies, 25:36
Sharptown barge, 87:90
tools, workshop, 27:81
workshop, 28:83
See also Designs, Culler, R.D. (Pete)
Culzean Ship & Boatbuilding Company Limited, builder (Scotland):
cutter VAGRANT, 61:80
Cunliffe, Tom, author and photographer:
"Sailing a Bristol Channel Pilot Cutter," 71:60
Cunningham, Bruce, builder:
profile, 20:58
Cuprinol:
comments by Richard Jagels, 61:123
letter on, 23:8
use of, 11:70, 15:26, 18:94, 21:21, 21:58, 21:79, 22:94, 28:76, 29:68, 79:72

CURLEW (Falmouth Quay punt):
history, photos, plans, repair, 86:36
CURLEW (sloop):
letter on, 41:11
Curragh (Irish pulling boat):
design and construction commentary, history, photos, 10:25, 50:80
Curry, James M., author:
"Building a Traditional Sharpie Today," 1:8
"The Nearly Forgotten Art of Making Planes," 11:52
"The Traditional Sharpie: Performance Aspects," 3:24
Curry, James M., builder:
New Haven sharpie, 1:8, 2:32, 3:24
Curry, James M., photographer:
"Sharpie Update," 2:32
Curry, Manfred:
experiments with rig design, 78:66
Curtis, Edward:
on building sea kayaks, 58:74
CURTIS FOUNTAIN (Biloxi schooner):
comments, 37:80
CUSHING (torpedo boat):
comments, photo, 84:34
Custer, Jack, author:
"Building the Belles of the Western Rivers," 64:64
Cutter controversy:
comments by Russell Clark, 41:26
Cutter design:
commentary by Andrew Hepburn, 85:21
CUTTERHEAD (Blanchard 36 Standardized Cruiser):
comments, photo, plans, 94:54
cover photo/Neil Rabinowitz, 94:0
Cutters: (See ABLE, AERIEL, AFRICA, AIRFORCE, ANDRILLOT, AQUILA, ARGONAUTA, BLOODHOUND, BOLD WATER, BRYONY, BUFFLEHEAD, CAPTAIN WALRUS, CARDINAL VERTUE, CINDERELLA, CLARA, COLUMBINE, CONTENT, CORINEUS, CROW, CURLEW [Falmouth Quay punt], CYRELA, DRUMBEAT, DYARCHY, ELLY, ENTERPRISE, ETAIN, FALCON, FIONA, FOAM, HALLOWE'EN, HIRTA [Bristol Channel pilot cutter], HOBO, ISKRA, JOLIE BRISE, JUNO, KATOURA, KELPIE, KELPIE II, KLYSMA, LAPWING, LITTLE HOPE, MADCAP [Bristol Channel Pilot cutter], MADGE, MAID OF ENDOR, Maxwell Cutter, MIZPAH, MURIEL, NAVAHOE, NELLIE [Itchen cutter], NIGHTFALL, NIGHT RUNNER, NINGUI, NIRVANA, NYSSA, OCEAN BIRD, ORIVA, Oysterman 22, PACIFIC TRADER, PASTIME, PETREL, PRISM, PURITAN, RENEGADE, RONDINA, SASKIANNA, SAUK, SCHEMER, SERAFFYN, SHIRIS, SHONA, SOLWAY MAID, SPARKLE, STAR, SYRINX, TALEISIN, THAENO, THELMA IV, THISTLE, TREASURE, TRUCE, VAGRANT, VERTUE, VERTUE XXXV, VINDEX, WATER RAT, WHITE HEATHER, YARANA, YOLANDE)
Cutts, Edmund A., builder:
editorial by Jon Wilson 78:2
letter by William J. Hingst, 79:5
profile, photo, 78:30
Cutts and Case, Inc., builder:
history, photo, 78:30
on boat covers, 54:92

CUTTY SARK (clipper ship):
comments, photo, 46:54
comments, photo, 38:36
CYGNET (sloop):
comments, photo, 78:30
Cypress (wood):
Arizona/for boatbuilding, 42:123
comments, 33:72
comments by Richard Jagels, 66:109
species for boatbuilding, 9:31
use/Caddo Lake bateau, 62:44
CYRELA (cutter):
comments, photo, 8:67
CZAR (pilot gig):
photo, 25:28
CZARINNA (power yacht):
designs/William Garden, 96:112

Dacron sailcloth:
commentary by Robin Lincoln, 93:60
Dacron, use:
decking on recreational shell KINGFISHER, 62:103
Geodesic Airolites, 76:72, 76:77
DAGNY IV (Norwegian sailing freighter):
restoration comments, photo, 73:96
Dagwell, Charles, builder:
Mackinaw boat, 45:100
Dahl, Christian W., author and photographer:
"NORDSØ," 74:74
Dahlmer, Larry, builder:
interview by Myfanwy Phillips, 58:34
DAKINI (yawl):
designs/Philip Bolger, 92:96
Daly, Tom, builder (Ireland):
curraghs, 50:80
DAME PATTIE: (See ENDLESS SUMMER [12-Meter class])
DANAE (power cruiser):
comments, photo, 65:76
DANCING DRAGON (yawl):
comments, photo, 42:82
DANDELION (R-boat):
comments, photo, 85:74
Daniel, Jay, photographer:
cover photo/Bear class, 50:0
Danielson, Scott, author:
"The Wake in the Fjord," 28:42
Dark Harbor 12½ class:
designs/B.B. Crowninshield, 37:116
Dark Harbor 17½ class:
designs/B.B. Crowninshield, 37:116
Darling, Lois:
editorial/eulogy by Jon Wilson, 94:2
Darling, Lois, author:
"Ratty's Boat," 94:44

Darling, Lois, illustrator:
"Our Thanks to John Gardner," 90:36

Darrell, Bert, designer (Bermuda):
comments, 57:42

Darroch, Lynn, author:
"Importing Tropical Wood," 69:35
"The Education of a Young Boatbuilder," 55:88

Darr, Robert, author:
"Alternatives to the Lumberyard," 35:45
"Milling Your Own," 37:98
letter on California laurel, 41:7

DAUNTLESS (schooner):
comments, photo, 70:42

Dauphinee, Arthur:
profile, photo, 94:64

Dauphinee & Sons: (*See* A. Dauphinee & Sons)

Davidson, Dudley:
comments, 39:2
disc-sanding technique, 39:50
letter by Gerry Mygaard, 40:5

Davies, Tom and Stef, photographers:
cover photo/pouring lead, the Apprenticeshop, 4:0

Davis, Andrew, author:
"A New PRIDE for Baltimore," 96:50
"Double-Sawn Framing," 82:48
"Thomas Gillmer and the PRIDEs," 96:56
letter on boatbuilding in Grenada, 51:10
letter on use of computers in yacht design, 99:8
reviewer of *The Historic American Merchant Marine Survey* (book), 62:115

Davis, Arch, author:
"Building a Hollow Mast," 91:25
"Fairing," 94:29
letter on terms for cold-molded construction, 95:8
reviewer of *The New Cold-Molded Boatbuilding* (book), 95:118

Davis, Arch, author and illustrator:
"Making Laminated Frames," 97:44
"Raised Panels," 99:86

Davis, Charles G., designer:
comments, 37:42

Davis, Dennis, author and builder:
"Building the DK 13 Kayak," 70:56

Davis, Frank, designer: (*See* Designs, Davis, Frank ["Red"])

Davis, Gherardi, author:
"How It All Began," 35:32

Davis, Harry, builder:
Chumash tomol canoe, 35:82

Davis, Meg: (*See* Maiden, Meg Davis)

Davis, Richard O., designer:
association with William Hand, 29:38
motorsailers BURMA, HOLIDAY, SEER, 97:86
profile, drawing, 97:76

Davis, S. Owen, designer/builder:
sharpie, 36:62

Davis, Stanley O., author:
"The Old Man's SHARPIE," 36:62

Davis, Stephen L., author:
"A Quest for Perfection," 12:14
"NIGHT RUNNER and Her Master," 77:40
"Port Townsend's Bob Lange," 77:34

Davis, Stephen L., illustrator:
"Buying a Runabout," 77:79
BOC Challenger AIRFORCE, 68:72

Davis, Tony, builder:
association with Arno Day, 63:38

letter on Arno Day, 66:5

Day, Arno, author and illustrator:
"Lofting Curved, Raked Transoms," 98:41

Day, Arno, designer/builder:
comments, 79:22
letter by Tony Davis, 66:5
profile, photo, 63:38

Day, Frances and Frederick:
letter on, 46:5
owners of Bar Harbor 31 DESPERATE LARK, 45:68

Day, George, author:
"MAYA," 9:16
"To Each His Own," 16:66
"Voyaging in the Trade Winds: To Tahiti on JOSEPHA," 8:36
"Water Spider: The Shells of Joseph Garofalo," 21:40

Day, George, photographer:
cover photo/ketch JOSEPHA, 8:0

Day, Jane, author:
"Forest Timber: Who Has It? Who Gets It?", 29:82
"Harvesting Hackmatack Knees: A Conversation with Frank Morse," 30:66
"Lucy's Launch," 79:22
"Putting Down Roots: Your Own Woodlot," 35:50
"Replacing What You Use," 81:121
"Roy Blaney Knows What's Right," 32:36
"The Geodesic Airolites," 76:72
"The Masterful Work of Malcolm Brewer," 49:44
"The Return of Working Sail," 31:18
"WHITEHAWK Flies," 25:56

Day, Jane, author and photographer:
"Building by Eye in America," 49:36
"Every Inch a Riverman," 67:54
"George Kirby Jr. Paint Co.," 28:50
"Lowell's Boat Shop," 27:26

Day, Jim, builder:
on finish work, 46:66

Day, Rick:
letter on rig and hull performance, 94:4

Day, Thomas Fleming, author:
"Across the Atlantic in SEA BIRD," 44:32
"SEA BIRD," 43:26
"SEA BIRD as a Keel Craft," 43:35
"The Trying of SEA BIRD," 43:30

Day, Thomas Fleming, designer:
profile, 43:26

Dayton, Douglas M.:
on Third World timber supplies, 59:56

Deadwood:
building technique/Sam Manning, 99:94
building technique/Bud McIntosh, 38:95

DeAlteris, Roy, builder:
comments, 14:34

Dean, Jeff, author and photographer:
"Birchbark Canoes and a Different Drummer," 36:36

Dean, Nicholas, author:
"Manhattan's Mystery Merchant Ship: Her Discovery Today," 63:96
letters on nautical archaeology, 70:7, 72:6

Dean, Nicholas, photographer:
cover photo/Archer-designed CAPRI-CORNUS, 29:0

Deben Four-Tonner:
designs/Maxwell Blake, 8:67

DEBUTANTE III (iceboat):
comments, 38:64

Decay in wooden boats:
causes and prevention, 2:36, 11:36, 35:96, 52:118
letter on prevention, 43:9
types of, 34:91

Decay resistance of wood:
chemical modifications, 21:18
comments, 2:36
durability ratings, 54:120
mahoganies, lauans, 49:124
oaks, red and white, 1:48, 65:112
sapwood vs. heartwood, 20:20
See also Preservatives

Deckbeams:
compiling lumber list/20' sloop/Joel White, 87:46
installation and laminating technique/Bud McIntosh, 41:91, 42:53
installation and laminating technique/Jon Wilson, 20:52
outboard runabout Downeaster 18, 74:87

Deck canvasing:
comments/Biscayne Bay 14 class, 98:28
letter on technique, 25:8
maintenance and repair/Maynard Bray, 64:58, 77:60
repair/Ed McClave, 75:89
technique for International One-Design, 22:74
technique for SEA BIRD yawl, 43:38
technique/Giffy Full, 27:40
technique/Ed McClave, 75:89
technique/H. Rosenfeld, 14:64
technique/Jon Wilson, 22:72
use of Arabol, 25:89
use of Dexeze, 13:60

Deck construction:
Biscayne Bay 14 daysailer, 98:28
building technique/Bud McIntosh, 46:103
building technique/Skip Zahniser, 42:74
DK 13 kayak, 70:56
Downeaster 18 outboard runabout, 75:53
fairing technique/Arch Davis, 94:29
illustrated glossary, 60:115
KINGFISHER recreational shell, 62:103
See also Canvas-covered decks, Teak decks

Deck details:
photos, 47:74

Deck maintenance:
for tropical conditions, 83:48
teak and teak overlay/Maynard Bray, 64:58, 77:60

Deck repair:
comments by Donald Street, 25:89
Dynel-and-epoxy overlay technique/Owens cutter, 61:104
letters on materials, 30:6
plywood-and-Dynel deck replacement/Concordia 33, 66:64
plywood-and-Dynel overlay/Fishers Island 31, 66:64
plywood/Malabar Jr., 65:56
teak overlay/ketch ISABELLE, 72:53
technique/Giffy Full, 27:40

Deck survey:
guide for self-survey/Paul Lipke, 83:22

Deem, Marise, author:
"Overboard: A Wife's Tale," 80:21

DEFENDER (trading ketch):
history, photos, repair commentary, 92:62

DEFIANT (sportfishing launch):
photo, 66:56

De Gast, Robert, author:
"Documentation Primer," 8:44
Deininger, Madeleine, photographer:
"Building the KINGFISHER, Part I," 61:60
"Building the KINGFISHER, Part II," 62:103
Deks Olje:
critique, 46:66
letter on, 48:12
Delaware ducker:
design and construction commentary, 48:86
history, paintings, 48:78
performance commentary, photos, 48:83
Delaware ducker, GREENBRIAR:
plans, 48:86
Delaware ducker, JOSEF W:
cover photo/Benjamin Mendlowitz, 35:0
performance, 48:83
plans, 48:86
Denby, Jeanette, builder:
speedboat ACE, 45:77
Denmark, builder: (*See* Andersen, Ring)
Denmark, designers: (*See* Berg, Georg; Hansen, M.S.J.; Utzon, Aage)
Denmark, watercraft: (*See* ACTIV [Danish topsail schooner]; FRI [Danish ketch]; SEBBE ALS [Viking ship replica]; Seiners, Danish; Spidsgatters)
DENYCE (schooner):
photos, trunnels for, 3:44
DeRidder, Jane, author:
"The Boat as a Way of Life, CHINA CLOUD," 67:19
Design competition, WoodenBoat:
rules for, 20:57
winners, 29:20, 30:20
Designer profiles:
Alden, John G., 32:66
Archer, Colin (Norway), 20:35
Bolger, Philip, 92:42
Bombigher, Daniel J. (France), 71:74
Brown, Russell 83:58
Burgess, Edward (Ned), 71:52
Burgess, W. Starling, 71:52, 72:44, 73:32, 74:42
Butler, E. Farnham, 61:42
Chapelle, Howard I., 84:76
Davis, Richard O., 97:76
Day, Thomas Fleming, 43:26
Devlin, Sam, 85:52
Eldredge-McInnis, Inc., 52:40, 53:38, 54:34
Fife, William (Scotland), 90:84
Gardner, John, 40:30, 90:36
Giles, Laurent (Jack), (England), 24:24
Gillmer, Thomas C., 96:56
Griffiths, Maurice (England), 91:78
Hand, William, 28:20, 29:38
Hawkins, Havilah, 88:60
Hepburn, Andrew, 85:21
Herreshoff, L. Francis, 55:32, 56:38
Herreshoff, Nathanael G., 33:50
Hess, Lyle, 76:60
Holt, Jack (England), 74:64
Huckins, Frank Pembroke, 56:48, 57:102
Lawrence, Thomas (England), 14:31
Martin, Arthur, 47:40
Monfort, Platt, 76:72
Monk, Edwin, 10:70
Nunes, Ernie and Manuel, 50:31
Oughtred, Iain (England), 70:74
Pocock, George, 21:36
Potter, Nicholas, 83:38

Scheel, Henry, 62:36
Smith, Melbourne, 78:76
Stephens, Olin F., 98:50
Strange, Albert (England), 64:49
Trumbly, Joe, 89:44
Tyrell, Jack (Ireland), 50:70
Warner, Winthrop, 75:34
Wharram, James (England), 23:77
White, Chris, 54:56
Wylie, Tom, 63:56
Designs appearing in *WoodenBoat* **design section, listed by designer:**
Designs, Alden, John G.:
18' sloop, O-boat, 32:102, 42:128
21' double-ended sloop, 40:126
21' sloop, Indian class, 42:126
25' keel/centerboard sloop, 40:128
30' sloop, 42:127
30' sloop, Malabar Jr. class, 41:128
41' schooner MALABAR II, 41:127
Designs, Alford, Mike:
15' touring kayak Tursiops, 97:108
Designs, Atkin, John:
18'7" Hardangersjekte, 26:95
20'3" cutter MAID OF ENDOR, 22:89, 59:116
25'8" cutter, 30:100
27' power cruiser, 28:99
28' modified Friendship sloop, 1:72
Designs, Baber, William S.:
26' runabout, 22:88
Designs, Baker, William A.:
17' cat-ketch EAST HUE AND CRY, 9:60
Designs, Beach, David:
17' outboard cruiser, 23:93
25' power cruiser, 9:62
Designs, Beard, Tom:
26' dory cruiser, 33:102
49' power cruiser, 25:97
Designs, Beebe, Robert P.:
10'6" rowing and sailing tender, 45:110
50' power cruiser PASSAGEMAKER, 93:128
Designs, Benford, Jay R.:
18' pocket cruiser Iota, 94:110
30' ketch, sailing dory, 17:45
34' pinky ketch SUNRISE, 3:61
Designs, Blake, Maxwell:
22'5" cutter, Deben Four-Tonner CYRELA, 8:67
Designs, Boettcher, Norman:
51'9" cutter SAUK, 27:91
Designs, Bolger, Philip C.:
23'6" sharpie MARTHA JANE, 80:102
24'9" cat-yawl, 58:116
28' lobsterboat, 77:101
28' power cruiser ALICE, 97:92
34'6" yawl, 92:96
37' cat-ketch, 26:94
Designs, Bombigher, Daniel:
22'6" sharpie Miss Simplette, 74:96
Designs, Brewer, Edward S. (Ted):
26'4" canoe yawl, Windswept, 63:116
39'6" sloop, 26:96
42'3" cutter, 24:93
53'9" pinky schooner DOVE, 3:65
Designs, Brewer, Wallstrom and Assoc., Inc.:
21'7" Cape Cod catboat, 20:91
26' sloop, Eastport pinky, 18:89
Designs, Buehler, George:
35'6" cutter, 6:68
49' batwing schooner, 25:94
Designs, Calkins, George:
22'7" powerboat, Bartender, 76:101

Designs, Chapelle, Howard I.:
14'1" sharpie sailing skiff, 88:114
15'3" sailing peapod, 33:104
17'11" Camp Skiff (outboard cruiser), 82:108
18'10" outboard boat WATERMAN, 82:108
Designs, Coad, Charles E.:
28' skipjack, 19:82
Designs, Concordia Co.:
Concordia 28, 31, 33, 48:126
Designs, Costello, Ned, delineator:
14'6" sailing canoe, 20:89
Designs, Crocker, Samuel S.:
19'9" sloop or yawl, 62:100
Designs, Crosby, Wilton:
20'10" catboat FRANCES, 62:96
Designs, Crowninshield, B.B.:
20'2" Dark Harbor 12½, 37:116
25'10" Dark Harbor 17½, 37:116
28'3" Camden class, 37:116
Designs, Culler, R.D. (Pete):
16' catboat, 55:122
17' sailing skiff, 24:96
18'6" sailing skiff, 57:118
45' pungy schooner, 55:122
Designs, Davis, Frank (Red):
19' sailing dory, 27:92
See also Designs, King & Davis
Designs, Devlin, Sam:
14'4" stitch-and-glue garvey, 91:96
Designs, Dobler, Joseph:
15'6" skiff, 57:118
Designs, Dow, Eric:
15' and 20' outboard boats, 21:86
Designs, Eldredge-McInnis, Inc.:
24' bassboat, 12:68
45'2" power cruiser ALBACORE III, 93:128
Designs, Evans, Tim:
40'10" St. Lawrence yawl replica, 85:117
Designs, Farmer, Weston:
17'3" outboard cruiser SUN DANCE, 82:108
17'11" outboard cruiser TRUMPET, 82:108
Designs, Fenger, Frederic A.:
30' cargo sloop, 31:98
Designs, Fox, Uffa:
21' Itchen Ferry punt BLUE JACKET (delineator), 59:116
26' single scull, "Best Boat," 54:130
Designs, Frost, Edwin:
24'9" sharpie LAZY JACK, 54:130
31'5" ketch PATIENCE, 95:110
Designs, Garden, William:
24' cutter KELPIE, 64:98
25' cutter KELPIE II, 64:98
25'4" cutter AFRICA, 64:98
25'4" Cutter #4, 64:98
28'6" cutter CAPTAIN WALRUS, 64:98
29' schooner TOADSTOOL, 68:114
30' cat-ketch, 35:98
30'9" launch FALCON, 66:120
32' cutter, 60:134
33' schooner GLEAM, 68:114
33' schooner THEO G, 68:114
36' schooner, 46:114
36'6" cutter CROW, 64:98
36'7" power cruiser, 27:89
37' troller, 39:128
40' schooner RAIN BIRD, 68:114
49' schooner UNION JACK, 68:114
50' Cogge ketch, 87:119
58'6" diesel cruiser, 14:59

Designs, Garden, William (*continued*)
60′ sloop OCEANUS (original and new design), 81:106
62′ power yacht TLINGIT, 96:112
92′ 6″ power yacht CZARINNA, 96:112
Designs, Gardner, John:
plywood sneakbox, 61:124
Designs, Gartside, Paul:
15′ pulling boat, Flashboat, 86:94
15′ 3″ schooner, 86:94
21′ 10″ cutter, Oysterman 22, 36:92
Designs, Giles, Laurent, Ltd.:
32′ 6″ Keyhaven yawl, 63:116
Designs, Gillmer, Thomas C.:
23′ yawl BLUE MOON, 2:58
37′ gaff ketch, 32:102
Designs, Glen-L Marine:
12′ 5″ plywood sneakbox, 61:124
24′ power cruiser HERCULES, 18:88
33′ lobsterboat cruiser, 38:120
42′ power cruiser, trawler-yacht, 46:113
Designs, Gloux, Herve:
34′ 6″ schooner, 22:90
Designs, Goeller, Frederick:
12′ sailing dinghy, 25:95
Designs, Gougeon Brothers:
8′ sailing pram, 18:86
Designs, Greene, Danny:
10′ 4″ Chameleon dinghy (nesting dinghy), 99:116
Designs, Gregory, Joseph:
24′ 8″ Chesapeake Bay skipjack CALICO JACK, 79:106
Designs, Hack, Joseph H.:
36′ sloop, 65:104
Designs, Haddock, Roger:
28′ power scow, 30:98
Designs, Hamlin, Cyrus:
48′ 3″ yawl, Wanderer, 67:112
Designs, Hankinson, Ken:
25′ 3″ sloop, Ensenada 25, 59:114
Designs, Harris, W.B.:
Concordia 28, 31, 33, 48:126
Designs, Hendel, Geerd:
60′ 6″ sportfisherman PORPOISE, 61:127
Designs, Herreshoff, L. Francis:
13′ beach cruiser, 70:104
25′ ice yacht, 38:119
57′ 6″ Bounty ketch, 89:114
double-paddle canoe, 19:83, 60:140
Designs, Hess, Lyle:
cutters SYRINX and TALEISIN, 63:116
Designs, Hollmann, Eva:
41′ cutter, 5:38
Designs, Hunt, C. Raymond:
43′ 1″ 510-class sloop, 7:69
55′ 7″ power cruiser STING RAY V, 98:104
Designs, Kaufman and Ladd:
23′ Maxwell cutter, 21:84
Designs, Kaufman Design, Inc.:
15′ 7″ nesting dinghies, 99:116
Designs, King, Bruce P.:
20′ sloop, 27:90
50′ cutter SASKIANNA, 83:112
Designs, King & Davis:
9′ 7″ dinghy, 47:126
11′ 8″ sailing skiff, 47:126
15′ 8″ dory skiff, 47:126
Designs, Kirby, Bruce:
26′ 3″ Norwalk Island sharpie, 74:96
Designs, Kotzebue, Paul R.:
21′ catboat KATHERINE, 50:130
34′ cruising sloop TIFFANY JANE, 34:102

49′ cruising sloop, 43:128
Designs, Krogen, James S.:
44′ motorsailer, 39:130
Designs, Long, Roger:
21′ 6″ cruising sloop, 19:80
Designs, MacGregor, Charles G.:
26′ yawl, plywood Sea Bird, 50:132
Designs, MacNaughton, Tom:
30′ sloop, Voyager 30, 5:64
Designs, MacNeill, Robert F.:
25′ 9″ power cruiser, Weekender, 19:84
Designs, Marcus, Daniel:
13′ 8″ duckboat, 65:108
Designs, Marples, John R.:
26′ folding trimaran, 49:112
Designs, Marshall, Roger:
26′ 9″ sloop, 23:92
Designs, Martin, David P.:
26′ sportfisherman, 24:95
Designs, McCurdy and Rhodes:
39′ 4″ cutter AERIEL, 100:108
Designs, Mudie, Colin:
30′ 6″ power cruiser, 26:97
Designs, Northrup, Bruce:
54′ 9″ pungy schooner RUBEN DE CLOUX, 68:110
Designs, Oughtred, Iain:
12′ double-paddle sailing canoe, Wee Rob, 84:106
13′ 7″ sailing canoe, MacGregor, 84:106
22′ 2″ pocket cruiser, Gray Seal, 94:110
Designs, Paine, C.W.:
24′ cat-ketch, 21:82
24′ 4″ sloop CAROL, 39:132
26′ sloop FRANCES, 18:84
Designs, Perry, Robert:
41′ sloop, Noble 41, 5:33
Designs, Peterson, Douglas B.:
32′ 10″ sloop, Peterson 33, 11:76
Designs, Peterson, Murray G. & Assoc.:
6′ 8″ pram, 28:98
27′ sloop, 60:134
Designs, Pittaway, Rob:
18′ pulling boat ROBIN, 51:131
Designs, Rabl, S.S.:
14′-15′ flattie skiff, 57:118
Designs, Rafel Marine:
30′ sloop, Mair 30, 63:116
Designs, Redmond, Steve:
16′ sailing skiff BLUEGILL, 72:98
16′ sailing skiff WHISP, 72:98
Designs, Rhodes, Philip L.:
17′ Rover class, 28:97
30′ 8″ ketch DOGSTAR, 23:94
Designs, Scheel, Henry A.:
25′ daysailer SHEARWATER, 66:124
36′ 8″ sloop, Scheel 36, 49:114
Designs, Selmer-Larsen, Johan:
16′ sailing punt MYRA, 71:105
Designs, Skidmore, A.G.:
25′ power fishing craft GIRL FRIDAY, 11:73
29′ 6″ cutter HOBO, 20:92
34′ power cruiser, 17:46
Designs, Smith, Nathan:
39′ 2″ ultralight sloop, 70:110
Designs, Sparkman & Stephens:
35′ sloop, 34:104
Designs, Sprague, Scott:
24′ tug and utility boat, 43:126
39′ 2″ ultralight sloop, 70:110
Designs, Stadel, George:
20′ sloop TOM COD, 47:128

Designs, Stambaugh, Karl A.:
15′ sailing skiff, Windward 15, 88:114
Designs, Stephens, Robert W.:
19′ 1″ Garvey Workboat, 91:96
Designs, Strange, Albert:
24′ 9″ canoe yawl WENDA, 80:102
Designs, Strayer, Charles M.:
16′ schooner, Longsplice (nesting prams), 99:116
Designs, Tanton, Yves-Marie:
31′ 2″ sloop, Half-Tonner, 24:94
Designs, Tucker, Tom:
20′ 6″ sloop LYRA, 10:65
21′ sloop LYRA II, 31:97
Designs, Wahlman, Erik:
18′ Greenland-style kayak, 97:108
Designs, Wallstrom, Bob:
43′ 11″ cutter, 25:96
Designs, Warner, Winthrop:
17′ 5″ catboat BOB CAT, 36:94
28′ ketch, 4:66
Designs, Warwick & Associates:
24′ 6″ sloop, 22:86
Designs, White, Joel:
20′ rowing wherry BANGOR PACKET, 52:122
29′ 4″ double-ended sloop, 90:122
Designs, Williams, Fenwick C.:
24′ gaff yawl, 28:96
Designs, Wittholz, Charles:
26′ sloop or yawl, 56:130
34′ trawler-yacht, 15:72
49′ cutter, 78:106
Designs, Woods, Richard and Lilian:
24′ catamaran STRIDER, 73:106
Designs, Wycoff, Arthur R.:
25′ 9″ power cruiser, 20:94
71′ ketch, 36:93
Designs, Zimmer, Nelson:
18′ 8″ cat-ketch, Mackinaw boat, 23:90
21′ sloop, 58:114
21′ 3″ utility launch, 43:124
45′ cutter, 51:133
De Silva Boats, builder:
outboard racing speedboats, 80:32
DESPERATE LARK (Bar Harbor 31):
cover photo/Benjamin Mendlowitz, 84:0
history, photo, plans, 45:68
Detco (seam filler), use:
teak deck overlay repair, 72:53
Detels, Pamela, and Janet Harris, authors:
"The Blue Jay," 15:42
Detroit Aero marine engine:
photo, 30:59
Detroit Engine Works:
photo, restoration commentary, 30:59
DEUCE (yawl):
comments, 75:70, 75:72
Deveau, John, builder:
dolly for moving boats, 69:86
Development class:
comments, detail photo, 69:104
comments, photo, 84:34
Devlin, Sam, author:
"A Seaworthy Double-Ended Powerboat," 76:101
Devlin, Sam, designer/builder:
profile, photo, 85:52
review of plans catalog, 89:112
See also Designs, Devlin, Sam
DeWitt, James, designer:
Acorn class, 30:46

Dexeze (adhesive):
use for deck canvas repair, 13:60
Dhow, African:
construction commentary, history, photos, 46:88
passage on NAWALILKHIL, 46:88
Dhow, Arab:
comments, photos, 40:78
DIABLESSE (ketch):
history, photos, plans, rig commentary, 81:52
Diamond class:
comments, photo, 74:64
Dick, Les:
owner of trading ketch DEFENDER/ comments, photo, 92:62
DICTATOR (Friendship sloop):
comments, photo, 29:61
Diddikai ketch, CARRIE L:
building commentary, photos, 42:74
Didham, Charles, builder:
sloop BROWN SUGAR, 30:50
Diesel engines:
compared to gasoline, maintenance of, 54:106
engine layup routine, 72:25
installation and operation, 54:108
Dietrich, Mary Lou, author:
"Festival Fever," 82:34
"Gearing Up for Safety," 79:41
"Product Review: Women's Work Gloves," 80:93
DILEMMA (sloop):
comments, 37:42
comments, plan, 41:26
Dillion, D.W. (Dave), delineator:
Bermuda dinghy CONTEST, 57:42
Delaware ducker, 48:86
North Shore dory, 36:82
Nutshell pram, 60:100
rowing wherry, Bangor Packet, 52:122
sailing peapod, 33:104
schooner AMERICA model, 54:67
schooner BOWDOIN, 47:30
sharpie-ketch EGRET, 56:76
skiff, Martha's Tender, 45:92, 46:94, 47:58
speedboat BABY BOOTLEGGER, 60:84
Tancook whaler VERNON LANGILLE, 58:82
yawl SEA BIRD, 43:30
Dinghy: (*See* INTERMEZZO; Lawley yacht tender; Peapods; Pram; Sailing dinghies; Skiff, Acorn; Whitehall pulling boats)
Dinghy Cruising Association:
comments, 70:68
DINGUS (sailing dinghy):
comments, photo, 65:76
Dion, Elmer, builder:
repair of yawl ROYONO, 1:4
Dipping lugsail:
commentary by Iain Oughtred, 73:80
comments by Colin Palmer, 92:76
sailing technique/English cobles, 86:58
Dirks, Clarence, author:
"Ask the Pros: Caulking," 22:94
"Getting the Feel of Caulking," 24:40
Disappearing Propeller Boat Co., builder (Ontario):
Dispro boats, history of, 55:68
DISCOVERY's launch:
comments, photos, plans, 89:86
cover photo/Dale Blindhiem, 89:0
environmental work, Puget Sound, 89:89

Disc sanding:
letter by Daniel MacNaughton, 95:4
technique for Wee Lassie canoe/Henry McCarthy, 100:92
technique/Paul Bryant, 40:56
technique/Dudley Davidson, 39:50
techniques for topsides, 63:87
DISPATCH (power launch):
comments, photo, 56:38
Displacement-to-length ratio (D/L):
comments by Joel White, 75:111
explained, 59:114
Dispro (Disappearing Propeller Boat):
cover photo/Tim Smutz, 55:0
history, photos, plans, 55:68
Disston handsaws:
comments, 70:31
history, 47:91
Ditchburn, builder:
comments, 50:52
Ditty bag:
how to make, 31:30, 32:49
Dividers:
product review, 100:124
DJINN (motorsailer):
comments, photo, 98:50
DK 13 kayak:
construction methods, photos, plans, 70:56
materials and tools list, 71:8
DN-class iceboat:
builder, design and construction commentary, history, photos, 86:52
comments, photos, 14:7
cover photo/Neal Mishler, 86:0
design commentary, photos, 39:88
history, photos, plan, 32:93
kit boat, 38:84
Dobler, Joseph, designer:
comments, 57:118
See also Designs, Dobler, Joseph
Docking under sail:
in schooner ST. MARGARET, 17:26
Documentation:
for pleasure boats, 9:2
procedure discussed/Robert de Gast, 8:44
Dodge, Lawrence (Duffy), builder:
comments on Malcolm Brewer, 49:44
profile, 92:28
Dodington, Paul, author:
"The Greatest Little Motorboat Afloat," 55:68
Doghouse, canvas:
comments, detail photos, 67:100
DOG STAR (ketch):
designs/Philip L. Rhodes, 23:94
Dolfinite (bedding compound), use:
comments, 99:66
construction of sloop MELE KAI, 63:106, 64:92
repair of fantail launch, 63:48
Dolley, John, illustrator:
"When the Keel Drops Off," 2:28
DOLLY (steam yacht):
comments, photo, plan, 98:66
DOLORES (lobsterboat, power):
comments, photo, 69:42
DOLPHIN (Newport 29):
comments, photo, 43:92
Donnan, Tad, author:
"The Longboats of Pitcairn Island," 13:22
DON QUIXOTE (schooner):
comments, photo, 70:42

Doors, louvered:
construction technique/Tim Allen, photos, 94:84
Doors, raised panels:
construction technique/Arch Davis, photos, plans, 99:86
Dorade ventilator:
detail photo, comments, 66:90
DORADE (yawl):
comments, photo, plan, 98:50
DOROTHY B (schooner):
comments, photo, 32:66
DOROTHY G (schooner):
design commentary, history, photo, 53:38
Dorwin, John T.:
letter on ATOCHA (treasure ship), 71:7
Dory, Aeolus:
comments, photo, 37:36
Dory, Alpha-Beachcomber:
history, photos, 36:78
owner's comments, photos, 36:83
Dory, Amesbury:
construction commentary, photos, 27:26
Dory, Banks:
construction commentary, 18:71
construction commentary, plans, 19:32
construction commentary, plans for card-board model, 90:63
Dory, Colorado River:
cover photo/Walter Rist, 15:0
design and construction commentary, performance, photos, 15:47
Dory, Gloucester Light:
how to build, photos, plans, 41:63
how to build, photos, 42:44, 43:96
Dory, John:
comments, photo, 70:74
Dory, North Shore:
photo, plans, 36:82
Dory, Opheim:
design and construction commentary, photos, 43:40
Dory, power:
designs/Tom Beard, 33:102
Dory, sailing:
designs/Jay R. Benford, 17:45
designs/Frank Davis, 27:92
Dory skiff:
designs from Lowell Boat Shop, 18:71
designs/King & Davis, 47:126
Dory skiff, Chamberlain:
comments, photo, 73:60
Dory, St. Pierre, EMME:
owner's comments, photos, 35:41
Dory, St. Pierre type:
owner's comments, photos, 2:52
Dory, Swampscott:
comments, photo, 61:52
construction commentary/George I. (Sonny) Hodgdon, 51:50
history, plans, 36:78
photo, plans, 36:82
Douarnenez 88 (boat show, France):
comments, photo essay, 85:64
DOUBLE EAGLE (sardine carrier):
comments, 59:70
DOUBLE EAGLE (schooner):
comments, photo, 70:42
Double paddle:
how to build, 57:60
how to build, photos, 37:67
Double-paddle canoe: (*See* Canoe, double-paddle)

Double planking: (*See* Planking, double)

Doucette, Herman and Roy, builders (Nova Scotia):
Grand Manan lobsterboat, 45:88

Douglas, Bob:
comments on builders Gannon and Benjamin, 95:70

Douglas-fir:
comments, 68:103
for hollow mast/Arch Davis, 91:25
for sharpie TERESA, 80:44

Douglass, Gordon (Sandy), designer:
Thistle class, 29:106, 47:80

Doulhit, Jim, author:
"The Monterey Clipper," 18:28

DOVE (pinky schooner):
designs/Edward S. Brewer, 3:65

DOVE (pinnace):
comments, 24:52, 96:64
construction commentary, photos, 26:30, 26:36

DOVEKIE (ketch):
account of passage, 7:31
photo essay of construction and launching, 5:55

Dovetail construction method:
for drawers/Tim Allen, 98:89
for skylights/Duffy Dodge, 92:28

Dow, Barbara Stacey, photographer:
"Building the Biscayne Bay 14, Part I," 96:24
"Building the Biscayne Bay 14, Part II," 97:31
"Building the Biscayne Bay 14, Part III," 98:28

Dow, Eric, author:
"The Schooner AMERICA: How to Build Her Half Model," 54:67

Dow, Eric, builder:
Biscayne Bay 14 daysailer, 96:24, 97:31, 98:28

Dow, Eric, designer: (*See* Designs, Dow, Eric)

Dowd, John and Beatrice, authors:
"Folding Boats at Sea," 53:80

Dowley, Brian, author and photographer:
"The Vineyard Haven 15," 47:86

Dowley, Brian, photographer:
"The Tradition of Burnside St.," 23:25

Downeaster 18 (outboard runabout):
comments by Jon Wilson, 73:67
construction methods, photos, plans, 73:67, 74:87, 75:53
design comments by Charles Wittholz, 73:77

DOXY (spidsgatter):
comments, photos, 78:50

Dragger:
future of wooden hulls, 69:54

Dragger, CARL J:
comments, photo, 75:34

Dragger, LITTLE FLOWER:
cover photo/Peter Prybot, 79:0

Dragger, New England:
construction, history, photos, plans, 79:48

Dragger, STAR:
comments, photo, 69:48

Dragger, ST. PETER:
operation of, photos, 69:54

DRAGONFLY 15 (trimaran):
comments, plan, 54:56

Drake, Mary Maynard, author:
"Jack Wilbur and the Return of the Noank Boats," 69:48

"Modelmaker Lloyd McCaffery," 73:52
"Off to Far Places," 76:36
"The Hackmatack Schooner JANET MAY," 63:74
reviewer of *Voyage to Understanding* (video), 78:90

Drange, Ole, builder (Norway):
Oselver boats, 28:42

Drascombe lugger (yawl):
design and construction commentary, photos, 26:73

Drawers:
dovetail construction method/Tim Allen, 98:89

Dreissigacker, Peter and Dick, designers:
comments, 54:82

DREOILIN (Galway hooker):
owner's comments, 96:36

Drift boat, McKenzie River:
construction commentary, history, photos, 52:80
letter on, 53:8

Drills, power:
critique of battery-powered drills, 82:100
critique of professional vs. consumer models, 68:35

Dring, Harry:
association with Karl Kortum, photo, 72:60
comments, 13:43, 14:45
letter by Debbie Kielb, 63:6
on maritime preservation, 38:36
on scow schooner ALMA, 3:8
profile, painting, photo, 61:88

Dring, Harry, photographer:
cover photo/scow schooner ALMA, 3:0

Drinker, Pemberton H., author:
"Sneakbox," 20:23
"Spiling the Garboard," 13:56
"They Go Like the Wind," 31:42
letter on sneakbox, 48:10

Driscoll, Terry:
profile, 46:2, 60:44

Driscoll Custom Boats, builder:
comments, 20:27

Dropboards, companionway:
construction method/Bud McIntosh, 67:91

DRUMBEAT (cutter):
designs/Charles Wittholz, 78:106

DRUSILLA (40′ class):
comments, photo, 41:26

Drying out of wooden hulls:
causes and prevention of, 54:88
letter on prevention of, 55:6

Duckboat, MERGANSER:
designs/Daniel Marcus, 65:108

Ducker: (*See* Delaware ducker)

Duck Trap Woodworking (ME):
boatbuilding program, 42:100

Duclon family, builders:
Alexandria Bay boats, 48:66

Dufrene, Emile, builder:
Lafitte Skiff, 14:74

Duggan, C. Herrick, designer (Canada):
A-scow, 39:123
comments, 37:42

Duggleby, Tony, author:
"The Scavenger's Art," 76:29

Dugout canoe, African Sesse:
design and construction commentary, history, photos, 40:78

Dugout canoe, Haisla:
construction method, photos, 69:64

Dugout canoe, Hawaiian koa:
construction commentary, history, photos, 59:80

Dugout canoe, Herreshoff design:
construction commentary, photo, plans, 14:54

Dugout canoe, Honduran:
letter by William G. Adams, 77:6
use in La Mosquitia, Honduras, 88:76

Dugout canoe, Kuna:
construction, history, sailing, 97:62

Dugout canoe, Mexican:
construction commentary, photos, 20:61

Dugout canoe, Panamanian piragua:
construction commentary, photos, 74:27

Duke, Bob, author:
reviewer of *Bahamas Video Cruise Guide* (video), 84:101
reviewer of *The Great Lakes, Volume I:* (video), 84:101
reviewer of *The Keys Video Cruising Guide* (video), 84:101
reviewer of *Virgin Islands Video Cruise Guide* (video), 84:101

Duncan, D.G., George Englerth, and T.C. Scheffer, authors:
"A Technical Comparison of Red and White Oaks," 1:48

Dungan, Mary, C., author:
"The Vanishing Craft of the Nile," 33:61

Dunn, Michael J.:
letter on schooner BLUENOSE II, 59:9

Dunphy, Paul, author:
"Ireland's Jack Tyrell," 50:70

Dunsford, Peter, designer:
15′ 6″ daysailer, 29:20

DUNTON, L.A. (schooner): (*See* L.A. DUNTON)

Duradon sailcloth:
commentary by Robin Lincoln, 93:60

DuraKore (balsa/hardwood composite):
product review by Mike O'Brien, 79:93

Durham, Bill, author:
"In My View: Wooden Boat Immigrants," 56:122
"The Last Boom: Wooden Shipbuilding in World War I," 40:94
letter on engine noise and power, 67:7
letter on small-scale models, 99:4
on maritime preservation, 41:36

Dutch boeier, PHOENIX:
design, construction, performance, and rig commentary, photos, plans, 27:32

Dutchman (graving piece):
fitting technique/Maynard Bray, 78:84
fitting technique/Brion Rieff, 99:28

Dwyer, Kevin, Jennifer Buckley, and Bob Baker, authors:
"PEGGOTTY," 23:39

DYARCHY (cutter):
comments, photo, plans, 24:24

Dyer, William, builder:
comments, 27:94

Dynel, use:
cold-molded hull overlay/Owens cutter FALCON, 61:104
deck/outboard runabout Downeaster 18, 75:53
for hull sheathing, 17:54
plywood deck overlay/Fishers Island 31, 66:64
plywood deck replacement/Concordia 33, 66:64

DYON (sloop):
history, photo, plans, 64:40
DYRAFJELD (Norwegian sailing freighter):
restoration comments, photos, 73:96
Dyson, George, author:
reviewer of *The Skin Boats of Saint Lawrence Island, Alaska* (book), 90:140
Dziubinski, Michael, author and illustrator:
"Removing Rusted Keelbolts," 89:105

EAGLE (dragger):
comments, photo, 79:48
EAGLE (fembøring):
comments, photo, 71:44
EAGLE (lobsterboat, sloop):
comments, photo, 69:42
EAGLE (schooner):
comments, photo, 48:91
cover photo/Benjamin Mendlowitz, 40:0
EAGLET (Massachusetts Bay 21):
comments, photo, plan, 72:44
Eakins, Thomas, illustrator:
"Delaware Ducker: Why the Ducker Today?", 48:86
"The Delaware Ducker: A Brief History," 48:78
EARTHLIGHT (catamaran):
design and construction commentary, photos, 23:77
Easom Boat Works, builder:
Acorn class, 30:46
East Bay Boatworks, builder:
Tender Ten, 22:77
EAST HUE AND CRY (cat-ketch):
designs/William Avery Baker, 9:60
Eastman, David, author:
"Classic Cruisers: BLACK MAGIC, Outboard Cruiser," 30:96
"Classic Cruisers: Chris-Craft Ranger 23," 27:96
"Classic Cruisers: Chris-Craft 23," 21:96
"Classic Cruisers: Elco Cruiser 42," 33:100
"Classic Cruisers: Elco Cruisette," 26:90
"Classic Cruisers: Elco 26," 24:98
"Classic Cruisers: 42′ Constellation," 32:100
"Classic Cruisers: Gar Wood Overniter," 34:100
"Classic Cruisers: GO-SUM, A 1908 Knock-Down Cruiser," 40:117
"Classic Cruisers: Huckins Sportsman 36," 35:92
"Classic Cruisers: Matthews 42′ DCFB," 31:92
"Classic Cruisers: 1934 Chris 24," 39:119
"Classic Cruisers: Pacemaker Day Boat," 23:96
"Classic Cruisers: Penbo 'Sardine Carrier' Yacht," 37:112

"Classic Cruisers: Richardson 31′ Sedan," 22:92
"Classic Cruisers: Some 1913 Cabin Launches," 36:108
"Classic Cruisers: The First Richardson Cruisabout," 28:92
"Classic Cruisers: The Matthews 38′ Twin-Cabin Cruiser," 38:114
"Classic Cruisers: The Prototype Cruisabout," 29:101
"Classic Cruisers: Wheeler 34," 25:102
"Preservation and the Richardson Boat Owners Association," 35:37
letter on Huckins Hull No. 1, 58:9
reviewer of *The Real Runabouts* (book), 25:104
Eastport pinky:
designs/Brewer, Wallstrom and Assoc., Inc., 18:89
Eastport pinky, Lubec boat:
lofting of, 12:44
EASTWARD (Friendship sloop):
comments, photo, 2:22
EASTWARD (schooner):
comments, photos, 53:38
Eastward Ho! class:
comments, plan, 53:38
East/West Custom Boats, builder:
comments, 47:40
Ebbutt, Peter, designer:
sloop CHRISTINE, 56:86
ECHO (steamboat):
design, construction commentary, photos, 67:70
Echo Bay Boats:
designs/13′8″ duckboat, 65:108
Eckert, Gerald, photographer:
"The Bear Mountain Canoes," 31:58
Eckhoff, Gus, builder:
restoration of sloop HIPPOCAMPUS JR, 6:55
Eddy, Robert H., Jr.:
profile (modelmaker), photo, 97:52
Edge-joint gluing techniques:
compared to spline joints/Michael Podmaniczky, 59:93
Edge-setting:
letter by Bent Thygeson, 87:7
technique/Bud McIntosh, 85:99
EDITH JANE (Mackinaw boat):
history, photo, 45:100
Editorials: (*See* Phillips, W. Lyman; Spectre, Peter H.; Wilson, Jon)
EDNA (21′ class):
history, photos, 1:58, 4:25
EDWARD M (sardine carrier):
letter by Charles Stackpole, 62:8
Edwards, Mark, builder (England):
profile, photo, 74:54
Edwards, Morry, author:
"Dream-Boat Man," 76:60
"Sons of the Fleet," 69:54
"The Fisherman's Sea Tractor," 79:48
"3 of a Kind: Tim, Pauline, and CURLEW," 86:36
reviewer of *Men's Lives: The Surfmen and Baymen of the South Fork* (book), 73:112
Edwards, Morry, author and photographer:
"Out of the Delta," 72:90
cover photo/Stauter-built boats, 72:0

EEL (canoe yawl):
comments, plans, 75:62
Egg Harbor 31 (power cruiser):
comments, plan, 92:42
Egret sharpie:
advice on painting for decoration, 93:42
Egret sharpie, EGRET:
comments by Jon Wilson, 56:2
comments, photo, 71:94
design and construction commentary, owner's comments, photos, plans, 56:76
design compared to sharpie ALACRAN, 59:36
Egret sharpie, GRIMALKIN:
design and construction commentary, performance, photos, plans, 71:94
letter by Graham Ero, 73:10
Egypt, Royal Ship of Cheops:
history, museum, photo, plans, restoration commentary, 38:28
Egypt, working craft:
history, photos, 33:61
E.H. Gerrish canoe (wood-and-canvas):
repair techniques/Rollin Thurlow, 78:56, 79:72
Ehrhorn, Jack, author:
"The Essence of Lofting: A West Coast View," 12:43
Eide, John, author and photographer:
"The Moliceiros of Aveiro Lagoon," 95:48
Eight-Meter class:
cover photo/Robert Birney, 32:0
Eight-Meter class, ANGELITA:
as Olympic contender, history, photos, plan, rebuilding, 59:40
cold-molded hull repair, 60:76
comments, photo, plans, 83:38
Eight-Meter class, CHEERIO:
racing, 60:41
Eight-Meter class, REALITY:
cold-molded hull construction, photos, 34:20
Eight-Meter class, YUCCA:
comments, photo, 83:38
EILEEN (sloop):
comments, photo, 90:84
EIRA (Folkboat):
deck repair, 15:26
Ekki (wood):
comments, 10:35
Elco (Electric Launch Company), builder:
Elco Cruisette 34, 26:90
Elco 26, 24:98
Elco 42, 33:100
power cruiser MEADOWLARK, 25:24
power cruisers VINTAGE ROSE and WHITE RABBIT, 13:26
Elco Cruisette 34 (power cruiser):
design commentary, photo, 26:90
Elco 26 (power cruiser):
history, photo, 24:98
Elco 42 (power cruiser):
design and construction commentary, photo, plans, 33:100
Eldjarn, Gunnar, and Bjørn Skauge, authors:
"A Norwegian Boatbuilding School," 23:80
Eldredge, Albert, designer:
association with Walter McInnis, 53:38, 54:34
Eldredge, Ned:
letter on harvesting boat lumber, 30:7
Eldredge-McInnis, Inc., designer:
comments, 95:60

Eldredge-McInnis, Inc., (*continued*)
history, 52:40, 53:38, 54:34
power cruiser BLACK KNIGHT, 93:52
Richardson Cruisabout, 28:92, 29:101
ELECTRA (sloop):
comments, photo, 84:34
Electrical systems:
commentary by George Cadwalader, 41:84, 70:23
commentary by Nigel Calder, 99:41
commentary by Jerry Kirschenbaum, 24:78
commentary by Lloyd's Register of Shipping, 2:24
commentary by Ed McClave, 65:114, 93:94
letter by Bob Ajeman, 67:7
letter by Stephen Olson, 95:7
load calculations, 32:79
See also Batteries, Bonding systems
Electric foundry:
construction methods, plans, using, 73:21
Electric Launch Company, builder: (*See* Elco [Electric Launch Company], builder)
Electrolysis:
commentary by A.J. Baker, 3:18
commentary by George Cadwalader, 70:23
commentary by Jerry Kirschenbaum, 23:30, 24:78, 25:61
commentary by Lloyd's Register of Shipping, 2:24
commentary by Ed McClave, 55:43, 65:114, 93:94
effect on sloop GAUNTLET, 41:84
effect on sloop ROYONO, 1:4
letter by Bob Ajeman, 67:7
See also Bonding systems
ELEUTHERA (sloop):
comments, photo, 6:20
EL HADJ (sloop):
comments, photo, 85:64
Eliasson, Rolf, designer (Sweden):
49′ 10″ sloop, 29:20
ELI D. HOYLE (wooden freighter):
comments, 40:94
ELISSA (square-rigger):
comments, 38:36
ELIZABETH SILSBEE (fishing schooner):
comments, photo, plans, 73:32
ELLEN IVY (Tancook schooner):
construction commentary, photos, plans, 5:44, 7:56
Elliot, John:
director of International Boatbuilding Training Center, 42:96
Elliot, John and Douglas, builders (England):
Drascombe boats, 26:73
Elliott, Douglas, author and photographer:
"One Mahogany Log," 20:61
Elliott, Jennifer: (*See* Buckley, Jennifer, author)
Ellis, Herbert, builder:
Rangeley Lake boats, 39:26
Ellison, Ben:
WoodenBoat School/Miskito (Honduras) Indians project, 88:76
Ellison, Ben, author:
" 'Glass vs. Wood," 100:38
ELLY (cutter):
comments, photo, 89:64
cover photo/William Gilkerson, 58:0
history, painting, photos, plans, rebuilding commentary, 58:40
Elm (wood):
characteristics of, 43:120

ELMAC (sloop):
comments, plans, 53:38
EL PLACIDA (sardine carrier):
comments, photo, 59:70
Elsaesser, Armin E., III, author:
"Sailing the PRIDE," 44:72
on historic vessel reproduction, 96:64
ELSIE (fishing schooner):
comments, photo, 32:66
racing history, 56:102
Elvidge, Ed, photographer:
cover photo/sardine carrier JOYCE MARIE, 59:0
Emberá Indians, builders:
Panamanian dugout canoe, 74:27
Emergency Fleet, WWI (wooden freighters):
history, photos, plans, 40:94
EMILY (cutter):
design and construction commentary, photos, plans, 66:56
Emlen, George, author and photographer:
"Conversation with a Master Caulker," 17:32
EMME (St. Pierre dory):
owner's comments, photos, 35:41
Emmer, Seth, author and photographer:
"Watertight!: A Simple Teak Deck," 15:26
Emmett, Jim, author:
"A 'Thwartships Double Berth," 30:86
"Ever Try Finishing Off From a Float?" 17:41
"Mast Making: Start From Scratch," 15:58
"New Life for an Old Canoe," 25:22
"Save a Cotton Plant," 17:40
"The Care and Feeding of Teak Decks," 11:70
"Wintering on the Chesapeake," 32:62
Emmett, Jim, author and illustrator:
"Lofting Aids," 20:68
Emmons, Elbridge G., builder:
Swampscott dory, 36:78
Emmons, Gerry, builder:
Swampscott dory, 36:83
E.M. White canoe (wood-and-canvas):
builder of, construction comments, photos, 67:54
comments, photos, 96:80
cover photo/Garrett Conover, 78:0
ENA (steam yacht):
history, photos, plans, restoration, 90:102
ENDEAVOUR (motorsailer):
galvanic corrosion, 23:30
owner's comments, photos, plan, 28:29
ENDLESS SUMMER (12-Meter class):
comments, 98:82
design and construction commentary, photos, plans, racing, 18:32
ENDYMION (staysail schooner):
comments, photo, plan, 83:38
Energy 48, BARNACLE IV (power cruiser):
design and construction commentary, photos, plan, 47:40
Engines:
advice for fitting out, 93:36
cooling and exhaust systems, power-train alignment, ventilation, 69:22
Corliss engine/comments, photo, 81:21
diesel and gasoline/compared, maintenance, 54:106
fittings/fuel pump to tank, 81:82
installation and operation, 54:108
layup routine, 72:25
letter on transmission coupling, 71:5

maintenance, 54:101
maintenance, use of unleaded gas, 91:70
one-lunger/reference sources, restoration commentary, 30:59
opinions on use, 4:64
surveying guide, 77:79
England, boatbuilding industry:
comments by Peter H. Spectre, 70:74
letter by Richard Franklin-Pierce, 64:8
England, boatbuilding schools: (*See* International Boatbuilding Training Center, Southampton Boatbuilding School)
England, builders: (*See* A.H. Moody & Son; Ashcroft, Herbert J.; Bell Woodworking; Brown, Roger; Bush, Fabian; Camper & Nicholson; Chudleigh, Tom; Collins, Rex and Roy; Culfor Marine Ltd.; Edwards, Mark; Elliot, John and Douglas; Freebody, Peter; Goodall, C.A. [Tony]; Granta Boats Ltd.; Harris, "Hardwood"; Hinks, Alan; Hinks, Joseph; Holt, Arthur; Houlton Boatworks; Kimber, Harold; Lallow, Clare; Machin Knight & Sons Ltd.; Peters, Frank; Rowsell, Spud; Souter, Wilfred; Whisstock's Boatyard; Williamson, James)
England, designers: (*See* Booth, Tom; Bucknell, Barry; Clark, Robert; Designs, Blake, Maxwell; Fox, Uffa; Giles, Laurent [Jack]; Holmes, George; Holt, Jack; Jones, Martin; Kemp, Dixon; Lawrence, Thomas; Macalpine-Downie, J.R.; Milne, Peter; Morrison, Philip; Mudie, Colin; Nicholson, Charles; Oughtred, Iain; Paxton, Roland; Proctor, Ian; Sheppard, Fred; Strange, Albert; Watkinson, John; Wharram, James)
England, Liverpool:
comments by Peter H. Spectre, 66:35
England, maritime museums:
guide to, 46:54
See also Essex Shipbuilding Museum, Exeter Maritime Museum, Merseyside Maritime Museum, National Maritime Museum, Poole Maritime Museum, St. Katherine's Dock, Windermere Steamboat Museum
England, watercraft: (*See* Acorn skiff [sailing skiff]; BOADICEA [smack]; Bristol Channel pilot cutter, HIRTA; Cobles; Cowes steam launch; Drascombe lugger [yawl]; Falmouth Quay punt; Falmouth oyster boat; Fireball class; FOUDROYANT [frigate]; FOXY [sailing dinghy]; HMS WARRIOR; ISKRA [cutter]; Itchen Ferry cutter, BLUE JACKET; JOLIE BRISE [pilot cutter]; LIZZIE ANNIE [Essex smack]; Merlin Rocket class; Mirror class; Narrowboat [canal boat]; PEGGY [schooner]; Pilot gig; River skiff, English; Spritsail barge; SUNBEAM [smack]; Thames River skiff; TORETTA [sloop]; Vertue class; Wayfarer dinghy)
England, woodcarvers: (*See* Gaches, Norman; Whitehead, Jack)
Englerth, George, T.C. Scheffer, and C.G. Duncan, authors:
"A Technical Comparison of Red and White Oaks," 1:48
Enoe, Alwyn, builder (Grenada):
comments, 50:106
Ensenada 25:
design/Ken Hankinson, 59:114
ENTERPRISE (cutter):
comments, photo, 64:49

Enterprise class:
comments, photo, 74:64
Environmental patrol craft: (*See*
DISCOVERY's launch, RIVERKEEPER
[utility outboard launch])
Environmental Protection Agency:
on sealers for wood preservatives, 61:123
Epoxy:
as a filler for repair, 62:113, 82:117
as sealer under varnish, 99:66
commentary by Aimé Ontario Fraser,
84:48
commentary by George I. (Sonny)
Hodgdon, Jr., 59:88
commentary by John Pazereskis, 19:46
commentary by Gerald Schindler, 4:47
comments by John Guzzwell, 84:64
comments by Ferdinand Nimphius, 25:42
comments by Jim Richardson, 24:52
critique, 16:29
for Ashcroft construction, 8:50
for BOC Challenger AIRFORCE, 68:72
for Biscayne Bay 14 daysailer, 98:28
for bungs, 29:77
for Chris-Craft Riviera repair, 96:87
for cold-molded construction/Reuel
Parker, 89:92
for cold-molded hull overlay/Owens cutter
FALCON, 61:104
for cold-molded overlay/Falmouth Quay
punt CURLEW, 86:36
for Constant Camber construction, 41:50
for Constant Camber construction/skiff
GULL, 64:83, 65:97
for DN-class iceboat, 86:52
for Energy 48 (power cruiser), 47:40
for final hull and keel fairing, 94:35
for fitting a dutchman, 78:84
for hull repair, 55:96
for hull sheathing, 17:54, 60:76
for icebox construction, 99:74
for laminating frames, 97:44
for modified Bounty ketch LA FILLE
D'OR, 67:82
for Nutshell pram, 60:100
for offshore raceboat JESSE JAMES, 73:86
for outboard runabout Downeaster 18,
75:53
for plywood deck replacement/Concordia
33 FREE SPIRIT, 66:64
for recreational shell KINGFISHER, 61:60
for sharpie TERESA, 80:44
for sloop GOLDEN DAZY, 16:29
for sparmaking, 15:60
for stitch-and-glue construction, 85:52
for strip canoes, 31:58
for strip-planked kayak, 57:60
for Swede 55 VORTEX, 100:84
for Thistle hull, 47:80, 49:9
for transom construction/power cruiser
YOREL, 95:67
for transom replacement/Concordia 33
FREE SPIRIT, 99:28
for trimaran ADRENALIN, 87:66
for Wayfarer dinghy kit, 51:88
for Wee Lassie double-paddle canoe,
100:92
letter by Jim Brown, 66:5
letters on use, 14:89, 21:12, 34:10
letters on WEST System, 27:6
toxic effects, letters on, 24:9, 59:6, 85:6
toxic potential, 62:113

toxic potential, safeguards for use, 59:48,
79:34
Epoxy undercoater:
product review by David Roberts, 99:112
EPPLETON HALL (paddlewheel tug):
comments, photo, 72:60
ERA (speedboat):
construction commentary, photos, 50:52
Erickson, Beth, photographer:
"Chainsaw Lumbermaking: Natural Knees,"
50:38
Erickson, John, author:
"SAM WISE: A Skiff for All Seasons," 29:56
Ericson, Henry, builder (Sweden):
yawl SAGA, 49:74
Erikson, Gustav:
letter by Ed Yeomans, 73:10
Erikson, John, and Herb Yates, authors:
"The Columbia River Gillnetter," 22:27
Erismann, Martin, delineator:
Block Island cowhorn, 22:22
Ero, Anne Clark, photographer:
"Building the Downeaster 18, Part I," 73:67
"Building the Downeaster 18, Part II,"
74:87
"Building the Downeaster 18, Part III,"
75:53
Ero, Graham, author and builder:
"Building the Downeaster 18, Part I," 73:67
"Building the Downeaster 18, Part II,"
74:87
"Building the Downeaster 18, Part III,"
75:53
letter on Egret sharpie GRIMALKIN, 73:10
Ero, Graham, builder:
construction methods for Egret sharpie
GRIMALKIN, 71:94
ESCAPADE (yawl):
comments, photo, 38:75
ESCAPE (Cal 32 class):
comments, photo, plans, 83:38
Espave (wild cashew), wood:
for Panamanian dugout canoe, 74:27
Essays and fiction:
"A Different Kind of Love"/Robert Butler,
19:48
"A Rowboat for Our Times"/John P. Wiley,
Jr., 85:95
"Clear Morning"/Heidi Landecker, 32:40
"Consider the Peapod"/Clinton Trow-
bridge, 17:61
"Cousin Sam's Friendship Sloop"/Earle
Westcott, 7:8
"DREOLIN"/John Seymour, 96:36
"Good Sense and Seamanship"/Michael
Badham, 34:51
"Money to Spare"/Julius Johnson, 17:66
"Old John's Kicker"/Joe Richards, 9:22
"On the Road to Quality"/Paul Lipke,
34:32
"Opinions: Is Symmetry a Lost
Word?"/Richard Olofsson, 6:71
"Out of My Class"/Ken Abbott, 12:30
"Overboard: A Wife's Tale"/Marise Deem,
80:21
"Railboat"/Bill Vaughn, 95:34
"Rough Water Over the Sands"/Maurice
Griffiths, 91:89
"Shovels and Pails: An Antipodal
Instructional Recalled"/Ross Norgrove,
60:120
"The Old Building"/John Garber, 9:47
"The Rowboat"/John Garber, 10:48

"The Singular Beauty of Wooden
Boats"/Llewellyn Howland III, 60:52
"The Stuff Dreams Are Made Of"/Karen R.
Jackson, 86:13
"The Theft of RANDOM SCOOT"/David
Kendall, 53:66
"The Vineyard Triangle"/Jan Adkins, 33:30
"To Err Is Human, To Admit Divine"/Fritz
Seyfarth, 60:41
"To Whom We Should Pay
Honor"/Charles Blackford, 11:10
"What Good Is Wood?"/David Keith, 10:43
"Why Aren't Heads Called Tails?"/Bob
Leve, 46:49
"Winter"/John Cole, 2:57
Essex Shipbuilding Museum (England):
comments, 12:9
ESTELLA (Friendship sloop):
cover photo/Jan Lee, 19:0
Esterly, Diana Eames, author:
"The Swampscott Dory—Hodgdon Style,"
51:50
Estes, Charlie, builder:
Alexandria Bay boats, 48:66
ETAIN (cutter):
comments, plans, 24:24
Eucalyptus (wood):
characteristics, 43:76, 47:123
comments by James W. (Jim) Brown, 41:50
comments by Robert Darr, 35:45
comments by Richard Jagels, 46:131,
70:101
EUGENIA (steam yacht):
comments, photo, 84:34
European woods:
comments by Richard Jagels, 71:111
EVA H (sardine carrier):
comments, 59:70
Evans, Lewis, author:
"St. Lawrence Yawls," 8:58
Evans, Tim, designer: (*See* Designs, Evans,
Tim)
EVENING STAR (yawl):
racing of, 13:79
Even Keel Boat Shop, builder:
history, 70:84
Eventide (sloop):
comments, plans, 91:78
Everett Canoe and Guideboat Works,
builder:
sailing canoe TWILITE, 65:66
EXCALIBUR (ketch):
model, photos, 97:52
Excalibur Leisure Skills Center (NY):
letter by Leo McCarthy, 62:7
Exeter Maritime Museum (England):
comments, 46:54
letter on, 48:12
EXPRESS (power cruiser):
comments, photo, 50:70
Express cruiser, SLY MONGOOSE:
brief history, 54:34
Express cruiser, THUNDERBIRD:
comments, photos, 62:74
cover photo/Benjamin Mendlowitz, 62:0
Express cruisers:
by Huckins Yacht Corp., 56:48
by Walter McInnis, 52:40
Eyemouth Boatbuilding Co., builder
(Scotland):
fishing craft, 62:68

Faering:
Bjørkedal boats/construction methods, photos, use, 95:38
comments, photos, plans, 28:36, 28:39
comments, plans, 23:80
Faering Design:
comments, 95:38
Fahey, Francis (Mick), builder:
profile, photos, 67:38
FAIRFA (power cruiser):
comments, photo, 57:102
Fairform Flyer (power cruiser):
design commentary, photo, 56:48
Fairing, hull:
technique for Biscayne Bay 14 daysailer/Eric Dow, 98:28
technique of Scott Cain, 94:72
technique of Arch Davis, 94:29
technique of Ted Hugger, 94:35
technique of Bud McIntosh, 55:107
See also Disc sanding
FALCON (launch):
designs/William Garden, 66:120
FALCON (lobsterboat, power):
comments, photo, 69:42
FALCON (New York 32):
letter by Mike Sloan, 74:7
FALCON (Owens cutter):
cold-molded hull repair, photos, 60:76, 61:104
Falkland Islands:
resting place for historic ship relics, 38:36
Fallon, Jack, author:
"Tuning Up with Jack Fallon," 91:67
Falmouth oyster boat:
comments, photos, 17:63
design and construction commentary, photos, plans, 31:36
Falmouth Quay punt:
CURLEW/history, photos, plans, repair, 86:36
design commentary, history, 63:116
FANNY DUNKER (Class A Frostbite dinghy:
comments, plans, 75:34
Fantail launch:
repair commentary, photos, 63:48
FANTASY (power cruiser):
comments, photo, 17:63
Farley, Ed, builder:
restoration of skipjack STANLEY NORMAN, 35:62
Farmer, Weston, author:
"POOR RICHARD," 20:76
"Understanding a Boat Plan," 21:30
Farmer, Weston, designer:
association with Elco, 33:100

letter on, 43:8
power launch POOR RICHARD, 20:76
See also Designs, Farmer, Weston
FARMILY (ketch):
design commentary, plans, 29:20
Farrell, Allen, builder (British Columbia):
comments, 20:80, 20:82
letter by John Summers, 68:5
profile, photos, 67:19
Fastenings:
comments by R.D. Culler, 15:7
comments by Richard Jagels, 45:115
comments by Frank Prothero, 48:30
comments by Robert Steward, 47:11
corrosion of, 3:18, 23:30, 24:78, 41:84, 55:43
corrosion of, preventive maintenance, 29:77
defined and illustrated, 81:82
for butt block, 67:23
for carvel planking repair, 80:56
for quick-and-dirty rowboat repair, 93:29
for transom replacement, 99:28
letters on galvanized steel type, 56:6
maintenance (iron) for tropical conditions/Allen Taube, 83:48
plastic/product review by Lyle Rupert, 99:110
refastening technique/Ed McClave, 55:43
refastening technique/L.E. Nicholson, 12:30
refastening technique/L.E. Nicholson, letters on, 14:9, 16:9
removal, for lapstrake planking repair/Walter J. Simmons, 92:90
See also Clench nails, Keelbolts, Lashing, Rivets, Staples, Tacks, Trunnels, Wood screws
Fastening schedule:
outboard runabout Downeaster 18, 74:87
Fatty Knees sailing dinghy:
comments, plans, 76:60
Fatula, George, builder:
advice on safety gear and procedures, 79:41
on finish work, 46:66
Favazza, Vito and Joe:
comments on future for wooden hulls for fishing boats, 69:54
FAVONIA (power cruiser):
designs/Colin Mudie, 26:97
FAWN (power launch):
cover photo/Robert Pittaway, 2:0
Fayard, Rudolph, builder:
comments, 37:80
FEARLESS (schooner):
history, photo, 32:66
Featherston, George, author:
"The English Coble," 86:58
FEDERALIST (toy ship):
comments, photo, 78:76
FEINTING WIZDUMB (Thistle class):
photos, rebuilding commentary, 47:80
FELISI (ketch):
comments, photo, 75:34
Felt, Irish:
use of, 13:85
Felucca replica, MATILDA D:
comments, photo, 42:30
construction commentary, drawings, history, 13:45
drawings, performance, plans, 14:45
Fembøring, EAGLE:
comments, photo, 71:44

Fenderboard:
comments, 99:66
Fender for small craft:
comments, detail photo, 76:70
Fenger, Frederic A., designer:
main-trysail rig comments, profile, photo, 81:52
See also Designs, Fenger, Frederic A.
FERDINAND (iceboat):
comments, photo, 39:88
Ferris, designer:
wooden freighters, 40:94
Ferrocement:
as a boatbuilding material, 10:43
Ferry: (*See* Steamboat, river; Volsunga II)
Fetesoff, Barbara, author:
"San Francisco's ALMA," 3:8
Février, Christian, photographer:
cover photo/Formula 40, ADRENALIN, 87:0
cover photo/Windermere Steamboat Museum, 98:0
letter on French-designed multihulls, 92:4
Fewtrell, Richard:
on maritime preservation, 38:36
Fiberglass:
as a boatbuilding material, 10:43
for Bolger Cartopper dinghy, 88:31
for bottom sheathing/classic speedboats, 65:90
for hull sheathing, 17:54, 19:94
for hull sheathing/Gloucester Light Dory, 43:96
for hull sheathing/Martha's Tender, 47:58
for hull sheathing/strip canoes, 31:58
for hull sheathing/strip kayak, 57:60
for hull sheathing/Wee Lassie double-paddle canoe, 100:92
for offshore raceboat JESSE JAMES, 73:86
for teak deck overlay repair/ketch ISABELLE, 72:53
survey of yard managers/wood vs. fiberglass, 100:38
Fiction: (*See* Essays and fiction)
FIDDLERS' GREEN (schooner):
comments, 9:44, 31:18
Field, Hale, designer:
comments, 76:60
Fife, William, I, designer/builder (Scotland):
profile, photo, 90:84
Fife, William, II, designer/builder (Scotland):
profile, photo, 90:84
Fife, William, III (Jr.), designer/builder (Scotland):
comments, 43:91
cutter CLARA, 41:26
cutter VAGRANT, 61:80
40′ class MINERVA, 49:66
ketch ISABELLE, 72:53
profile, photo, 90:84
Figureheads:
building and carving, for HMS WARRIOR, photos, 56:68
Fillers:
for wood-and-canvas canoe, 79:77
for wood rot, 62:113
See also Epoxy, Putty, Seam compounds
Film:
letter on *Ghosts of Cape Horn*, 46:9

review of *Ghosts of Cape Horn*, 45:29
See also Videos
FILSADAR (Concordia sloop-boat):
comments, photos, 55:88
FINAL FLING (speedboat):
comments, photos, 71:82
Financing for wooden boats:
commentary by Steve Henkel, 74:35
Finishes:
oil-type/interior brightwork technique, 83:66
removal technique/Rebecca Wittman, 81:88
See also Linseed oil, Painting techniques, Tung oil, Varnishing
FINISTERRE (yawl):
comments, photo, plan, 98:50
FIONA (cutter):
comments, photo, 90:84
Fireball class:
history, photos, 22:83
Firebending:
as an alternative to steam-bending, 44:104
Fireboat, MATTHEW J. BOYLE:
comments, photo, 53:38
FIREFLY (recreational pulling boat):
comments, photos, 54:82
First aid:
commentary by Mitchell K. Ross, M.D., 96:74
letter by David M. Goldenberg, M.D., 98:4
Fischer-Smith, Jeremy:
letter by Jon Bielinski, 41:9
Fish, Bob, designer:
comments, 43:64
Fisher, Bill, photographer:
cover photo/schooner MARY DAY, 39:0
Fisher, Mel:
ATOCHA project, 68:56
Fishers Island 23′ class:
construction commentary, photo, 33:50
Fishers Island 31′ class:
comments, photo, 84:34
history, listing of boats, 34:42
Fishers Island 31′ class, CIRRUS:
history, photos, plans, 34:42
plywood-and-Dynel deck overlay, photos, 66:64
Fishing craft:
future of wooden hulls, 69:54
of Portugal/photo essay, 72:80
of Scotland, 62:68
origins and development of New England draggers, 79:48
See also African dugout canoe; Alaska limit seiner; Alaska packer; ALTA C (fishing schooner); ANNE M (Monterey Clipper fishing boat); ATTU (halibut schooner); BANAMH AIGHSTIR (Scottish fishing vessel); Banks dory; Banks fisherman (schooner); Barbados fishing craft; Bassboat (power launch); Biloxi schooner; Block Island cowhorn; Bush Island boat; Caique; Cape Island boat; Chesapeake Bay skipjack; Chincoteague scow; Coble; Curragh (Irish pulling boat); Dragger; Falmouth oyster boat; Fly-fisherman, TROUT UNLIMITED; Gillnetters, (power and sail); Gloucester fishing schooner; Grand Manan lobster-boat; Grenada, builders and fishing craft; Halibut schooner; Harkers Island skiff (power); Galway hooker; Lafitte skiff;

Lincolnville wherry; Lobsterboat; Mackinaw boat; Maine lobsterboat; Maine sloop-boat; Monterey clipper; New Haven sharpie; Norwegian sailing freighters; Novi boat; Plymouth lobsterboat; Pomeranka (Polish fishing craft); Púcan (Irish fishing craft); Pungy schooner; Sardine carrier; Scotland, watercraft; Seiners, Danish; Sportfishing boats of Florida; Sportfisherman; Troller; UNITY B (Bahamian smack)
FISH TRUCK (proa):
comments, plan, 54:56
Fitting out: (*See* Maintenance)
Fitting-out fever:
comments by Jon Wilson, 51:2
Fitzgerald & Lee, builder:
Alexandria Bay boats, 49:58
510 class:
designs/C. Raymond Hunt, 7:69
Flag halyard belay:
comments, detail photo, 76:70
Flags, signal:
editorial by Jon Wilson, 67:2
Flashboat (pulling boat):
designs/Paul Gartside, 86:94
Fleming, Alfred (Bill), designer:
Elco power cruisers, 26:90, 33:100
Fletcher, Leon, author:
"Bill Grunwald: 26 Different Boats to Order," 37:36
FLICK (Amphibi-Con):
comments, photo, 61:42
Flintstone sanding machine:
comments, photo, 66:56
FLIRT (sloop):
deck recanvasing, 14:64
Float for hauling boat:
undecked pontoon for getting a keel into shallows, 36:96
Floorboards:
construction method, 75:76
construction method/outboard runabout Downeaster 18, 75:53
Floor timbers:
an analysis/D.M. Street, 19:72
bedding of/Jon Wilson, 28:76
compiling lumber list/20′ sloop/Joel White, 87:46
fastening technique/Bill Modrell, 16:70
in Biscayne Bay 14 daysailer/Eric Dow, 97:31
replacement technique/Paul Stubing, 35:30
various types described/Bud McIntosh, 44:43
Floor timbers, bronze:
construction and installation on cutter TALEISIN, 51:72
FLORA (skipjack):
centerboard maintenance, 9:50
Florida antique-boat cruise:
commentary by Polly Brown, 90:78
Florida sportfishing boats:
builders, design and construction commentary, photos, 76:44
FLOTSAM (power launch):
comments, plan, 24:24
Flounder Bay Lumber:
description of, 43:104
product review by Leslee Jaquette, 99:107
Flowers, Ralph, builder:
sloop FLIRT, 14:64

Fly-fisherman, TROUT UNLIMITED:
cover photo/Marty Loken, 64:0
design and construction commentary, photos, 64:70
FLYING CLOUD (motorsailer):
design commentary, plan, 29:38
Flying Dutchman class:
Olympic contender, photo, plans, 13:34
FLYING FIFTY (motorsailer):
charter of, 42:82
FOAM (cutter):
comments, plans, 64:98
Fogman, Jeff, builder:
on woodlot management, 35:50
Folding kayak, Klepper:
design and construction commentary, photos, use, 53:75, 53:80
Folding kayak, Nautiraid:
comments, 53:80
Foley, James P., author:
"Searching for EDNA's Past," 1:58
Foley, Robert, photographer:
cover photo/schooner LINDØ, 16:0
Folkboat class, COCKATOO:
history, photos, plans, 10:30
Folkboat class, EIRA:
deck repair, photos, 15:26
Folkboat class, LORRAINE:
comments, photo, 65:76
Folkboat class, STELLA:
modification of, photos, 5:67
Forbes, J. & G., Co., builder (Scotland):
comments on, 62:68
Ford, Frederick S., Jr., author:
"STAR: A Designer's Own Boat," 54:114
Ford, Howard, author:
"The Adirondack Guideboat," 18:55
Foreign: (*See* International)
Forest Belle yawl:
design, construction, and rig commentary, plans, 66:38
Forest E. Johnson Boat Works:
history, photos, 86:44
Forest Service, U.S.:
as a wood source, 45:46
Forging:
a boom balc, 50:16
ironwork for schooner HERITAGE, 53:52
See also Hardware
Formaldehyde:
in adhesives/toxic effects, 59:111
Formula 40 class, ADRENALIN:
comments, photos, 84:48
cover photo/Christian Février, 87:0
design and construction, history, photos, plans, 87:66
Formula 40 class, AMTEC:
comments, photo, 92:34
Forrest, Jim, builder:
speedboat ACE, 45:77
FORTUNE (schooner):
comments, photo, 38:71, 95:55
40′ class:
design commentary, history, photos, 41:26
design commentary, history, photos, plans, 48:58
design commentary, history, listing of boats, 49:66
40′ class, BABBOON:
history, photo, 48:58
40′ class, BANSHEE:
history, photo, 48:58

40′ class, CHIQUITA:
history, photo, 48:58
40′ class, DRUSILLA:
comments, photo, 41:26
40′ class, GORILLA:
history, photo, 49:66
40′ class, GOSSOON:
comments, photo, 71:52, 85:74
comments, photo, plan, 41:26
history, photo, 49:66
40′ class, HELEN:
history, photo, 49:66
40′ class, LIRIS:
history, photo, 49:66
40′ class, MARIQUITA:
history, photo, 49:66
40′ class, MINERVA:
history, 41:26
history, photo, 49:66
40′ class, NYMPH:
history, photo, plan, 48:58
40′ class, PAPOOSE:
comments, 85:74
history, photo, plan, 41:26
history, plan, 48:58
40′ class, TOMAHAWK:
history, 49:66
40′ class, VERENA:
history, photo, 49:66
40′ class, WASP:
comments, 41:26
40′ class, XARA:
history, photo, 48:58
46′ class, GLORIANA:
comments, 100:70
comments, photos, plan, 41:26
history, 4:25
history, photos, 49:66
Fossey, Joe, author:
"The Greatest Little Motorboat Afloat,"
55:68
Foss, John, builder:
schooner HERITAGE, 53:52
Foster, Dave, builder:
at the Apprenticeshop, 4:31
Foster, Greg, builder:
sixern, 71:44
Foster, Ray, photographer:
"The Hands of August Crabtree," 63:80
Fostle, D.W., author:
"The Boatbuilders of Alexandria Bay
Part I," 48:66
"The Boatbuilders of Alexandria Bay,
Part II," 49:58
FOUDROYANT (frigate):
history, photo, 22:42
Foundry: (*See* Lunenburg Foundry)
Foundry, electric:
how to build, plans, using, 73:21
Fowler, Lindsay A., author and photographer:
"Easy Does It!", 22:30
Fox, Uffa, author:
"Designs: The 'BEST BOAT'—A 26′ Single
Scull in Plywood," 54:130
Fox, Uffa, designer (England):
comments, 58:100
International 14 class, 20:84
sailing dinghy FOXY, 59:96
See also Designs, Fox, Uffa
FOXY (sailing dinghy):
construction commentary, history, photos,
plans, 59:96

Foxy's Wooden Boat Regatta (B.V.I.):
comments, photos, 65:76
FRAM (Norwegian polar exploration ship):
history, museum photos, plans, 85:44
Frame repair:
commentary by Ed McClave, 68:87
for cold-molded construction/Reuel
Parker, 89:92
laminating technique/Scott Cain, 23:50
laminating technique/Daniel
MacNaughton, 99:63
laminating technique/Robert Vespa, 51:59
letter on laminating by Ed McClave, 60:5
technique of Steve Ballentine/Herreshoff
12½, 56:93
technique of Steve Ballentine/yawl
TIGRIS, 53:109
technique of Benjamin River Marine/
Winter Harbor 21 class, 93:76, 93:84
technique of Gannon and Benjamin/
schooner VOYAGER, 69:94
technique of Ulf Henrikson/motor launch,
47:109
technique of Ed McClave/New York 50
SPARTAN, 58:107
technique of Keith Quarrier/St. Lawrence
skiff, 32:57
technique of Jerry Stelmok/wood-canvas
canoe, 29:68
technique of Paul Stubing/New York 30,
35:30
technique of Rollin Thurlow/E.H. Gerrish
canoe, 78:56
Frames, cant:
for pinnace DOVE, 26:30
Frames, double-sawn:
technique of Andy Davis/schooner SPIRIT
OF MASSACHUSETTS, 82:48
Frames, hot air-bent:
technique of Ulf Henrikson/motor launch
repair, 47:109
Frames, laminated:
letters on reframing, 60:5
technique of Scott Cain/sloop WHITE
WINGS, 23:50
technique of Arch Davis, 97:44
technique of Harold Ford/Adirondack
guideboat, 18:55
technique of John Gardner/McInnis
bateau, 51:66
technique of George I. Hodgdon Jr./
Swampscott dory, 51:50
technique of Daniel MacNaughton, 99:63
technique of Peterson Builders/MCM
class, 58:90
technique of Robert Vespa/sloop RONDO,
51:59
technique of Joel White/Nutshell pram,
60:100
Frames, sawn:
chainsaw milling for Adirondack guideboat, 59:64
comments by Frank Prothero, 48:30
technique for Bolger Cartopper dinghy,
87:29
technique for ketch CARRIE L, 42:74
technique for outboard runabout
Downeaster 18, 73:67
technique for Portuguese moliceiros, 95:48
technique for Yankee Tender skiff, 31:71
Frames, steam-bent:
compiling lumber list/20′ sloop/Joel
White, 87:46

technique for Nova Scotia lobsterboat,
45:88
technique of Bob Baker/lapstrake canoe
PICCOLO, 37:57
technique of Steve Ballentine/Herreshoff
12½, 56:93
technique of David Kubiak/Kodiak kayak,
58:68
technique of Tom MacKenzie/birchbark
canoe, 36:36
technique of Ed McClave/New York 50,
58:107
technique of Bud McIntosh, 15:74, 34:66
technique of James Meriam/sloop MELE
KAI, 63:106
technique of William Southworth/
Whitehall, 5:12
technique of Ray Speck/canoe yawl
LA MOUETTE, 75:62
technique of Jimmy Steele/peapods, 77:74
technique of Paul Stubing/New York 30,
35:30
technique of Leo Telesmanick/Beetle Cat,
53:101
technique of Joel White/Catspaw dinghy,
27:63
techniques for singlehanded boatbuild-
ing/Sam Manning, 99:94
Frame templates:
outboard runabout Downeaster 18, 73:67
France, builders: (*See* Chantiers Naval de
l'Estérel; Jolly, Jean)
France, designers: (*See* Bombigher, Daniel J.;
Langevin, Sylvester; Mauric, André)
France, military craft:
Chantiers Navals du l'Estérel, 39:44
France, watercraft: (*See* Douarnenez '88
[boat show]; Pilot cutter, JOLIE BRISE)
FRANCES (catboat):
designs/Wilton Crosby, 62:96
FRANCES (sloop):
designs/C.W. Paine, 18:84
Franklin, Lynn, author:
"Paddling Like an Ancient," 55:79
"Poling a Canoe," 49:40
Franklin-Pierce, Richard:
letter on boatbuilding industry (England),
64:8
Fraser, Aimé Ontario, author:
"Epoxy," 84:48
"Goops & Goos: Keeping the Water Out,"
92:23
"Product Review: Battery-Powered Tools,"
82:100
**FRATERNITÉ (French officers' barge
replica):**
comments, photo, 85:64
Fred, R.H.:
letter on mine countermeasure (MCM)
ships, 61:9
FREDONIA (schooner):
comments, plans, 84:76
Freeboard height:
comments by Joel White, 75:111
Freebody, Peter, builder (England):
profile, 57:72
**FREELANCE, ex-PIQUANT (power
launch):**
design commentary, photo, 56:38
history, 40:94
FREE SPIRIT (Concordia 33):
comments, 58:2
cover photo/Sherry Streeter, 60:0

designs/W.B. Harris (Concordia Co.), 48:126

plywood-and-Dynel deck replacement, photos, 66:64

transom replacement, letter on, 100:4

transom replacement, photos, 99:28

Freight canoe, VOYAGEUR:
comments, photo, 67:38

Freighter, WWI Emergency Fleet (1917-1920):
history, photos, plans, 40:94

FRENCH, LEWIS R. (schooner): (*See* LEWIS R. FRENCH)

Frese, Frederic, builder:
6′ submarine, 21:74

FRI (Danish ketch):
construction comments, history, photos, 87:36

cover photo/Michael Alexander, 22:0

planking repair, 44:104

FRIENDSHIP (R-class sloop):
comments, photo, 83:38

Friendship sloop:
designs/John Atkin, 1:72

essay on, "Cousin Sam's Friendship Sloop," 7:8

kit boat/McKie Roth, Jr., 39:69

Friendship sloop, AIMÉE:
comments, 2:15

Friendship sloop, ANNE FRANCES:
comments, photo, 29:61

Friendship sloop, DICTATOR:
comments, photo, 29:61

Friendship sloop, EASTWARD:
comments, photo, 2:22

Friendship sloop, ESTELLA A:
cover photo/Jan Lee, 19:0

Friendship sloop, GLADIATOR:
cold-molded hull repair, 60:76

Friendship sloop, Maine sloop-boat:
design and rig commentary, history, plans, 2:15

Friendship sloop, OLLIE:
comments, photo, 29:61

Friendship sloop, PRINCESS:
history, 1:11

Friendship sloop, RAY OF HOPE:
rerigging, 53:48

Friendship sloop, RED JACKET:
charter and performance, photos, 11:65

Friendship sloop, SARAH MEAD:
racing, 29:64

Friendship sloop, SKIMMER:
construction commentary, photos, 8:53

Friendship sloop, TANNIS:
comments, photo, 29:61

Friendship Sloop Days:
racing account, 2:22, 29:61, 29:64

Frigate: (*See* FOUDROYANT, TRINCOMA-LEE, USS CONSTITUTION)

Friolet, Gerard, builder (New Brunswick):
St. John River boat, 15:34

FRITZ (iceboat):
design commentary, history, 38:64

FROG PRINCESS (sloop):
designs/Bruce I. King, 27:90

Frost, Edwin, author:
"A Real Charley Noble," 49:86

"Designs: LAZY JACK, A Keel Sharpie," 54:130

"The Sounding Pole," 15:40

Frost, Edwin, author and illustrator:
"A Little Ship—LAZY JACK," 19:70

"A Wooden Bilge Pump," 23:44

"Designs: PATIENCE," 95:110

Frost, Edwin, designer: (*See* Designs, Frost, Edwin)

Frost, George, builder:
trading ketch DEFENDER, 92:62

Frost, William (Pappy), builder:
profile, 70:84

Frostbite dinghy, Class A:
comments, plans, 75:34

Frostbite dinghy, Class B:
comments, photos, plans, 83:38

Fryer, Doug:
profile, photo, 77:40

Full, Giffy:
advice on buying a wooden boat, 60:62

letter on surveying, 14:8

on maintenance procedures, 27:40

surveying methods, 26:57

Fuller, Benjamin A.G., author:
"Maritime Museum Highlights," 59:32

"News from the International Congress of Maritime Museums," 63:8

"Other Ways," 34:86

"Other Ways: Shifting Leeboards," 38:98

"The Delaware Ducker: A Brief History," 48:78

"The Delaware Ducker: The Ducker in Use," 48:83

comments on Howard I. Chapelle, 84:76

on sculling techniques, 100:60

reviewer of *Small Wooden Boats of the Atlantic* (book), 97:97

Funk, Linda, illustrator:
"Importing Tropical Wood," 69:35

Furtaw, Clay, author:
"The Professional Difference," 68:35

Gaches, Norman:
profile (woodcarver), 56:68

Gaff jaws:
illustration/Iain Oughtred, 75:80

proportions for/William Garden, 59:100

Gaff rig:
commentary by Iain Oughtred, 74:100, 75:80

letter by Lloyd Bergeson, 98:6

reefing techniques, 30:16

sailing techniques, 71:60

tuning techniques, 53:48

Gaff Yacht Society (Sweden):
comments, 13:5

GALATEA (Nereia ketch):
cover photo/Benjamin Mendlowitz, 56:0

Galbraith, Frank, builder:
Caddo Lake bateau, 62:44

Gallows frame:
comments, detail photo, 74:80

Galvanic corrosion: (*See* Electrolysis)

Galvanized steel:
commentary by Larry Montgomery, 82:27

Galway hooker:
history, photos, 50:74

Galway hooker, CAPALL:
comments, photo, 50:74

Galway hooker, DREOILIN:
owner's comments, 96:36

Galway hooker, HUNTER:
design and construction commentary, history, photo, 10:25

Galway hooker, 'MERICAN MOR:
construction commentary, history, photos, 50:74

Galway hooker, MORNING STAR:
comments, photo, 50:74, 85:64

Gamage, Harvey, builder:
cover photo/Bill Bruin, 13:0

New England draggers, 79:48

obituary, 13:38

schooner APPLEDORE II, 76:36

Gamble, Dale, photographer:
"LILY—A Boat Lover's Dream," 53:86

"Toad's Landing," 60:96

cover photo/Whitehall LILY, 53:0

GANNET (dragger):
comments, photo, 79:48

Gannon, Ross, builder:
profile, photo, 95:70

reframing technique/schooner VOYAGER, 69:94

Garber, John, author:
"The KATY G," 11:62

"The Old Building," 9:47

"The Rowboat," 10:48

Garden, William, author:
"A Diesel Cruiser," 14:59

"Ask the Pros: Seam Feathers," 17:86

"Designs: A Form of Therapy," 64:98

"Designs: FALCON: A Gentleman's Launch," 66:120

"Designs: Hooked on Schooners," 68:114

"Designs: 29′ Double-Ended Sloop," 90:122

"Designs: 30′ Cat-Ketch," 35:98

"The Right Jaws for Your Gaff and Boom," 59:100

"Toad's Landing," 60:96

letter on epoxy, plane-making, 14:89

on carvel planking, 3:71

reviewer of *Wood, Water & Light* (book), 87:107

Garden, William, designer:
cat-ketch MIST, schooners BUT & BEN and TOADSTOOL, 60:96

cat-schooner ITATAE, 93:52

comments, 35:98

designs compared to Murray Peterson's, 60:134

ketch RESOLUTE, 8:7

on wedge-seam construction, 98:82

sharpies, 25:36

sloop SAANICH BEAGLE, 12:70

See also Designs, Garden, William

Gardner, John, author:
"Marine Museums: Obligations and Objectives," 6:34

"The Modified McInnis Bateau," 51:66

"Traditional Boatbuilders' Tools," 1:14

"Whose Right? Boat Plans and the Public Domain," 47:46

Gardner, John, (*continued*)
on George Stadel, Jr., 47:128
on origins of strip planking, 57:55
reviewer of *Working Boats of Britain: Their Shape and Purpose* (book), 55:118
reviewer of *Wooden Planes and Cabinet Scrapers* (video), 72:103

Gardner, John, delineator:
Lawley yacht tender, 50:88

Gardner, John, designer/builder:
comments, 36:78, 77:70, 94:44
comments about boatyard hazards, 79:34
comments, photos, 11:52
letter by Robert M. Hallett, 41:7
profile, photos, 40:30
Swampscott dory, 51:50
tribute to, painting, 90:36
See also Designs, Gardner, John

Gardner, Robert, author:
"Bleeding Fastenings," 29:77

Gardner, William, designer:
40′-class yachts, 49:66

Garland, Joseph E., author:
"Substance to the Legend, Mystery to the Man," 61:52
"The Race It Blew and Others," 56:102

Garlington, Richard, builder:
sportfishing boats, 76:44

Garofalo, Joseph, builder:
racing shells, 21:40

Gartolda, Tehamo, builder (Panama):
profile, 74:27

Gartside, Paul, builder/designer (British Columbia):
launch FALCON, 66:120
See also Designs, Gartside, Paul

Garvey, CACKLER:
comments, photos, plans, 85:52
designs/Sam Devlin, 91:96

Garvey Workboat:
designs/Robert W. Stephens, 91:96

Garvie, William C., builder:
repair of sloop RONDO, 51:59

Gar Wood, Inc., builder:
Gar Wood Overniter, 34:100
runabouts, 10:53

Gar Wood Overniter (power cruiser):
design and construction commentary, photos, plans, 34:100

Gasoline engines:
compared to diesels, maintenance of, 54:101, 54:106
engine layup routine, 72:25
engine systems checkup, 69:22
letter about fuels for engines, 83:6
restoration commentary, 30:59

Gath, Charlie, builder:
replanking techniques, 96:87

GAUNTLET (sloop):
electrolytic deterioration, photos, repair, 41:84
repair critique, photos, 70:23

Gay, Reed, author:
"I'd Rather Be Sailing INTREPID," 1:80

GAZELA PHILADELPHIA (barkentine):
copper-sheathing process, photo, plan, 74:19

GAZELA PRIMEIRO (barkentine):
history, photos, plans, preservation and use, 11:24
history, photos, preservation, 44:62
letter on restoration, 46:5
See also GAZELA PHILADELPHIA

Geary, L.E. (Ted), designer:
association with Blanchard Boat Co., 94:54

Geary 18 class:
comments, 94:54

Gellatly, Michael, illustrator:
"Backyard Vacuum Bagging," 44:99
"Lofting by Numbers," 52:69
"Projection Lofting," 51:94
"The Burgess Legacy: The Early Years, Part I," 71:52
"The Handy Billy," 41:58
"The Singular Beauty of Wooden Boats," 60:52
"The Theft of RANDOM SCOOT," 53:66
"Tom Day and the SEA BIRD Yawl," 43:26
"Winter Reading: An Editor's Choice," 37:50

GeLu class:
comments, photo, 66:56

Gemini class:
construction commentary, photos, 12:24
cover photo/Michael Monahan, 12:0

GENESTA (sloop):
comments, 41:26, 71:52

GENNY W (power cruiser):
comments, photo, 61:38

Geodesic Airolites:
builder of, design and construction commentary, photos, 76:72
comments, 90:56
construction commentary, photos, 76:77

George Kirby Jr. Paint Co.:
history, 28:50

Georges River Boat Company, builder:
cutter SASKIANNA, 83:112

Germany, builder: (*See* Abeking and Rasmussen, Stulcken yard)

Germany, designer: (*See* Klepper, Johann)

Gerrard Bros., builder (Scotland):
fishing craft, 62:68

Gerrish canoe: (*See* E.H. Gerrish canoe)

Gerstel, David, author:
reviewer of *The American Coast Pilot* (book), 5:73

GERTRUDE L. THEBAUD (fishing schooner):
comments, photo, 61:32
photo, racing history, 56:102
racing history, 13:82

Getchell, David R., Sr., author:
"A Living from Small Boats?", 77:70
"Carroll Lowell Comes in from the Cold," 70:84
"Our Thanks to John Gardner," 90:36

Gibson, Gifford, author:
"Hardwater and Splinters: The Speed and Strength of the DN Iceboat," 86:52

Gibson, R. Dana, author:
"What Went Wrong," 83:88

Gig, Bantry Bay:
comments, photo, 71:44

Gig, Cornish:
history, photos, plans, 25:28

Gig, Cornish, TESS:
comments, drawings, 77:34

Gig, Pilot:
history, photos, plans, 25:28

Gilchrist, John H., author:
"Wreck at Cape Ann," 83:74

Giles, Albert W., author and builder:
"Steam Power, Fantail Stern," 67:70

Giles, Laurent (Jack), designer (England):
International 14 class, 20:84
profile, 24:24
Vertue class, 24:32
See also Designs, Giles, Laurent, Ltd.

Gilkerson, William T.:
on Dean Stephens, 42:30
profile, photo, 89:64

Gilkerson, William T., author and illustrator:
"ELLY: A Swedish Treasure in America," 58:40
"Ships Such as Those—MATILDA D, Part I," 13:43
"Ships Such as Those—MATILDA D, Part II," 14:45

Gilkerson, William T., illustrator:
"Aboard Old Ironsides," 83:32
"Give 'Em Hell, Harry," 61:88
"Hardtack's Running Moor," 50:96

Gilkerson, William T., photographer:
cover photo/cutter ELLY, 58:0

GILLCREST (tugboat):
cover photo/Stephen Hilson, 34:0

Gillmer, Thomas C., author:
"Designs: BLUE MOON Revisited," 2:58
"Howard Irving Chapelle," 5:1
"The Emergence of PRIDE, A Baltimore Clipper," 14:16

Gillmer, Thomas C., designer:
Baltimore clipper PRIDE OF BALTIMORE, 44:72
Baltimore clipper PRIDE OF BALTIMORE II, 96:50
ketch CALYPSO, 32:36
profile, photo, 96:56
See also Designs, Gillmer, Thomas C.

Gillnetters, power:
history, photos, use, 38:78

Gillnetters, sail:
history, photos, 22:27

Giono, Jean, author:
"The Man Who Planted Hope," 27:22

GIPSY JAC (ketch):
design and construction commentary, history, photos, 98:74

GIPSY MOTH III (sloop):
comments, photo, 50:70

GIRL FRIDAY (inshore fishing boat):
designs/A.G. Skidmore, 11:73

Git-Rot (wood preservative):
comments, 76:72

GLADIATOR (Friendship sloop):
cold-molded hull repair, 60:76

GLAD TIDINGS (pinky schooner):
comments, photo, plans, 84:76

GLEAM (schooner):
designs/William Garden, 68:114

GLEAM (12-Meter):
comments, 68:40
comments, photos, 38:75, 43:92

Glen-L Marine Designs:
comments, 90:56
review of plans catalog, 89:112
See also Designs, Glen-L Marine

Glidden, Marjory Downs:
letter on knockabout ASPENET, 10:5

GLOBE (storeship):
comments, plan, 78:76

GLORIANA (46′ class):
comments, 100:70
comments, photos, plan, 41:26
history, 4:25
history, photos, 49:66

GLORY ANNA II (Block Island cowhorn):
photos, plans, 22:22

photos, stem replacement, 39:97

Glossary:
illustrated, of wooden boat terms/ runabout IRENE, 77:79
illustrated, of wooden boat terms/yawl Sallee Rover, 60:115, 87:46

Gloucester fishing schooner:
builder of (Story Shipyard), comments, photos, 61:32
See also Banks fisherman (schooner)

Gloucester Light Dory:
comments, photo, plan, 92:42
how to build, photos, plans, 41:63
how to build, photos, 42:44, 43:96

Gloux, Herve, designer: (*See* Designs, Gloux, Herve)

Glover, J. Garrett, author:
"India's Teak Harvest," 32:42

Gloves, rubber:
advice for selecting and using, 79:41

Gloves, Womanswork:
product review, 80:93

Glues: (*See* Adhesives)

Gluing techniques:
advice from George I. (Sonny) Hodgdon, Jr., 59:88
for Constant Camber construction, 65:97
for edge-to-edge joints, 59:93
properties of oak, 65:112

Gockel, Paul, III, author:
"The Greatest Little Motorboat Afloat," 55:68

Godal, Jon:
comments on Norwegian lestabåt VARIN, 95:90

Goddard, David:
letter on Exeter Maritime Museum and cutter JOLIE BRISE, 48:12
on maritime preservation, 46:54

Goddard, David, photographer:
cover photo/Exeter Marine Museum craft, 46:0

Godfrey, Tom:
letter on angelwing rig for cat-ketch GOLDENEYE, 63:7

Goeller, Frederick, designer: (*See* Designs, Goeller, Frederick)

Goetz, Eric, builder:
profile, 23:25

Gold Cup race:
comments, 48:66, 60:84, 71:82, 73:32, 100:46

Golden, Richard, author:
"On Making a Beryllium-Copper Knife," 39:84

Goldenberg, David M.:
letter on first aid, 98:4

GOLDEN DAZY (sloop):
design and construction commentary, photos, 16:29

GOLDENEYE (cat-ketch):
comments, photo, 62:36
letter by Tom Godfrey, 63:7

GOLDEN GOOSE (sloop):
comments, photo, 45:50

Gold leafing:
technique, photos/Dave Gross, 99:54

Gomes, Charlie, builder:
Hampton boats, 57:50, 57:55

Gondola, Venetian:
design and construction commentary, photos, plans, 15:21

Goodale, Steve, builder:
pulling boat ROBIN, 51:131

Goodall, C.A. (Tony), builder (England):
profile, photo, 86:70

GOOD HOPE (sloop):
comments, photo, 91:50

Goodsell, Don, author:
"Designs: The Deben Four-Tonner," 8:67

Goodwin, Francis, author:
"Under Bare Poles," 68:50

Goodwin, Susan:
on boat cover materials, 54:92

GOOSANDER (motorsailer):
comments, plan, 28:20

Gooseneck fitting:
comments, illustrations, 91:25

Gordon, Joleen, author:
"The Basket Boat of Halifax Harbour," 79:17

GORILLA (40' class):
comments, photo, 49:66

GORM (Danish seiner):
comments, plans, 88:40

Gorski, Peter, illustrator:
"Do You Have a Moment?, He Asked," 66:35

Gorski, Richard (Dick), illustrator:
"Fo'c's'le," 61:11, 62:11, 63:13, 64:11, 65:11, 66:13, 67:11, 68:11, 70:9, 72:12, 73:14, 74:8, 75:10, 76:8, 77:8, 78:10, 79:9, 81:15, 82:13, 83:17, 84:14, 85:15, 87:17, 88:18, 89:19, 90:23, 91:8, 92:8, 93:10, 94:10, 95:10, 96:10, 97:16, 98:12, 99:9, 100:15
"MOCKINGULL: A Wing in the Water, a Wing in the Wind," 48:50

GOSSOON (40' class):
comments, photo, 71:52, 85:74
comments, photo, plan, 41:26
history, photo, 49:66

GOSSOON (motorsailer):
design commentary, plan, 29:38

GOSSOON (R-boat):
comments, photo, 85:74

GO-SUM (power cruiser):
design and construction commentary, photos, plans, 40:117

Goudy and Stevens, builder:
Thimble Island ferryboat VOLSUNGA II, 7:14

Gougeon, Jan, designer:
comments, 87:66

Gougeon, Meade, author:
"A Second Tri," 23:68
"Ask the Pros: Cold-Molded Veneers," 17:86
"GOLDEN DAZY: Revolution in Wood," 16:29
"Opinion: On Hydrodynamics, Structural Loads, Wood Fibers, & Beauty," 14:84
letter on toxic potential of epoxy, 24:9
letter on WEST System, 27:6
on epoxy, 16:27

Gougeon, Meade, designer:
comments, 87:66

Gougeon Brothers, Inc., builder:
DN iceboat, 32:93
epoxy testing, 84:48
Formula 40 ADRENALIN, 87:66
on cold molding, 55:96
sloop GOLDEN DAZY, 16:29
See also Designs, Gougeon Brothers

Government survey boat: (*See* USS SUISUN [power cruiser])

GP 14 class:
comments, plans, 74:64

Grabrails:
construction method/Bud McIntosh, 67:91

GRACIE (catboat):
photo, 3:51

GRACIL (10-Meter):
comments, photo, 91:56

Grand Banks dory: (*See* Banks dory)

Grand Banks fishing schooner: (*See* Banks fisherman [schooner])

Grand Craft (runabout):
cover photo/Steve Hilson, 44:0
design and construction commentary, photos, 44:80

Grandidier, Victor, author:
"CHRISTINE," 56:86

Grand Manan 45 (power cruiser):
comments, photo, 57:102

Grand Manan lobsterboat:
history, photos, use, 45:82

Grand Prix hydroplane:
Staudacher hydroplanes/comments, 80:24

Granta Boats Ltd., builder (England):
kit canoe, 31:50

Gratings, teak:
construction methods/Henry R. Hinckley Co., 62:53

GRATITUDE (coble):
comments, photos, 86:58

Graves, Garth, author:
"The Restoration of WHITE WINGS, Part I," 23:50
"The Restoration of WHITE WINGS, Part II," 24:72

Graves Boatbuilding School (MA):
program, 42:100

Graves Yacht Yard, builder:
International 210, 40:105

Graving piece: (*See* Dutchman)

Gray, Belford, builder:
skiff Martha's Tender, 45:92, 46:94, 47:58

Gray, Russell, builder:
schooner PILGRIM, 8:12

Gray Seal (pocket cruiser):
designs/Iain Oughtred, 94:110

GREAT HASTE (Massachusetts Bay 21):
comments, photo, 72:44

Great Lakes sharpie (sloop):
kit boat by Healy Boatworks, 38:84

GREAT REPUBLIC (sloop):
comments, photo, 61:52

Great South Bay Scooter:
cover photo/Mitch Carucci, 92:0
design and construction commentary, history, photos, plans, 92:52

GREAT WESTERN (sloop):
comments, photo, 61:52

Greavette, Tom, builder (Ontario):
Dispros, 55:68

Greavette Boat Co., builder (Ontario):
history, 55:68

Greavette Dispro (power launch):
history, 55:68

Greece, watercraft: (*See* Athenian trireme, Caiques)

Green, Gleason:
profile, 45:82

Green, Otis:
letter on Nova Scotia fishing boats, 47:5

Green, T.M., author and photographer:
"George Pocock Racing Shells, Inc.," 21:36

GREENBRIAR (Delaware ducker):
comments, plans, 48:86

Greene, Danny, designer: (*See* Designs, Greene, Danny)

Greene, Walter, builder:
BOC Challenger AIRFORCE, 68:72
letter on AIRFORCE, 70:4

Greenfield, Pete, author:
"The Falmouth Oyster Boats," 31:36

Greenheart (wood):
comments, 10:35, 59:56

Greenhill, Basil, author:
"TELKKÄ: A New Boat from the 18th Century," 60:68
on Howard I. Chapelle, 84:76
on maritime preservation, 46:54
on origins of strip planking, 57:55

Greer, Anne Lawrence, author:
"WHITE WINGS," 88:70

Greer, Jay, photographer:
"WHITE WINGS," 88:70

Gregersen's Boatshop, builder (Norway):
comments, 28:36

Gregory, Joseph, designer: (*See* Designs, Gregory, Joseph)

Gregson, Tony, author:
"Going It Alone in COMOX," 19:76

Grenada, builders and fishing craft:
boatbuilding techniques, construction commentary, photos, 50:106
letters on construction, 51:10

Grevillea (wood):
for boatbuilding, 47:123

Gribbins, Joseph, author:
reviewer of *Cats Conquer Offshore Racing: Big Seas '85* (video), 73:110
reviewer of *The Legend of Chris-Craft* (book), 87:110
reviewer of *Wood, Water & Light* (book), 87:107

Griffin, J.J., builder:
Columbia River gillnetter, 22:27

Griffiths, Maurice, author and illustrator:
"Rough Water Over the Sands," 91:89

Griffiths, Maurice, designer (England):
profile, 91:78

Griggs, Graeme, author:
"The Australian Cadet Dinghy," 52:100

GRIMALKIN (modified Egret sharpie):
design and construction commentary, photos, plans, sailing, 71:94
letter by Graham Ero, 73:10

Grobe, Kathleen, author:
"Winthrop Warner," 75:34

Grommet, rope:
letter on, 57:7
making of, 32:49, 55:114

Grommets, wire:
making of, 55:114

Groom, Winston, author:
"A Lineage of Craftsmanship," 78:30

Gross, Dave:
gold leafing technique, 99:54

Grounding out:
techniques/Paul Lipke, 70:52

Grunwald, Bill, builder:
profile, 37:36

Guardrail:
for Biscayne Bay 14 daysailer, 97:31

Guarea (wood):
comments, 10:35

Guideboat: (*See* Adirondack guideboat)

Guide canoe: (*See* E.M. White canoe)

Gulf Coast outboards:
Stauter Boat Works, 72:90

GULF STREAMER (trimaran):
comments, photo, 23:68

GULL (skiff):
construction methods, photos, plans, 65:97
how to build, photos, plans, 64:83

Gunter rig:
commentary by Iain Oughtred, 74:100
comments by Colin Palmer, 92:76
letter by Colin Palmer, 94:6

Guttmann, Hans Peter:
letter on electronic aids for navigating, 60:10

Guzzwell, John, builder:
profile, photos, 84:64

GYPSY (knockabout):
history, photos, plans, 13:40

Haase, Martin Rudy, author:
"DIABLESSE and Her Disputed Rig," 81:52

HABU (sportfishing boat):
comments, photo, 76:44

Hack, Joseph H., designer: (*See* Designs, Hack, Joseph H.)

Hacker, John L., designer:
association with Les Staudacher, 80:24
comments, 49:58, 71:82
runabout IRENE, 77:79
speedboat ACE, 45:77

Hacker Boat Company, builder:
construction methods, history, 71:82
runabouts, 10:53

Hackmatack (wood):
for boatbuilding, 9:31, 9:44
for Maine cruise schooner JANET MAY, 63:74
for schooner FIDDLERS' GREEN, 9:44
technique for harvesting knees/Frank Morse, 30:66
See also Larch (wood)

Hadley, Walter, author and photographer:
"Two Elcos," 13:26

Hagerty Marine Insurance:
interview with Steve Henkel, 81:29

Hahn, Walter, designer:
Florida sportfishing boats, 76:44

Haigh, Val, author:
"Mock It Up," 84:29

Haisla dugout canoe:
construction method, photos, 69:64

Haist, Paul, author:
"Projection Lofting," 51:94

Haitian small craft:
comments by Bill Durham, 56:122

HALAIA (motorsailer):
comments, plan, 28:20

HALCYON (sloop):
comments, plans, 75:34

Hale, Barbara M., author and photographer:
"Guideboats: From the Ground Up," 59:64

Halevi, Marcus, photographer:
"Double-Sawn Framing," 82:48

Halfhander (sloop):
comments, plans, 62:36

Half-model building:
how to build by lift method/George I. (Sonny) Hodgdon, Jr., 33:41
how to build schooner AMERICA/Eric Dow, 54:67

HALF MOON (Alden schooner):
interior arrangement, photos, plans, 93:52

Halibut schooner:
design and construction commentary, photo, plans, 16:63

Halibut schooner, ATTU:
comments, photo, 16:63

Hall, Christopher, author:
"The Restoration of the STANLEY NORMAN," 35:62

Hall, Phil, photographer:
"Traditional Teak Grates," 62:53

Hall Brothers, builder:
cabin launch CHEROKEE, 61:100

Hallett, Frank, builder:
sardine carriers, 58:52

Hallett, Robert N.:
letter on John Gardner, 41:7

HALLOWE'EN (cutter):
comments, photo, 90:81

Hambidge, Roger, builder:
comments, 6:44, 36:98

Hamburgh, Ray, author and illustrator:
"Before the Dream Fades," 33:33

Hamilton, Brooks W.:
letter on copyrighting of boat plans, 49:5

Hamlin, Cyrus, author:
"Ask the Pros: Strip Planking," 22:94

Hamlin, Cyrus, designer:
Hurricane Island pulling boat, 71:44
strip-planking technique, 61:42
See also Designs, Hamlin, Cyrus

Hampton boat (power launch):
construction commentary, photos, 57:50

Hampton Mariners' Museum (NC): (*See* North Carolina Maritime Museum)

HANAKEOKI (Hawaiian koa log canoe):
comments, 59:80

Hand, William H., Jr., designer:
association with Walter McInnis, 54:34
comments, 3:7, 4:30, 32:66, 97:76
motorsailer ENDEAVOUR, 28:29
profile, 28:20, 29:38
schooner BOWDOIN, 47:30

Handgrabs:
comments, detail photo, 65:52
construction method/Bud McIntosh, 67:91

Handsaws:
sharpening and rebuilding/Harold Payson, 47:91

Handsaws, Disston:
history, 47:91

Handy billy:
how to build, 41:58
letter on, 42:10

Hankins, Charles & Sons, builder:
Sea Bright skiff, 17:29

Hankins, Charles Edwin, builder:
power cruiser WILLOW, 18:26

Hankinson, Ken, designer:
letter on galvanized fastenings, 56:8
See also Ken Hankinson and Associates

Hanks, Consuelo Eames, illustrator:
"The Elements of Seamanship,
Part IV," 43:50
"The Elements of Seamanship,
Part V," 45:62

Hanley, C.C., builder:
Cape Cod catboats, 3:51
cutter ASHUMET, 37:42

Hanna, Jay:
profile (modelmaker), photo, 97:52

Hanna, Jay, author:
"Product Review: Choosing a Model Kit,"
85:109
"The Beauty of Construction Models,"
66:29
reviewer of *Carving Techniques and Projects*
(video), 83:97
reviewer of *To Build a Whaleboat: Historical
Notes and a Modelmaker's Guide* (book),
67:103

Hanna, John, designer:
ketch JOSEPHA, 8:36, 16:66

HANNIEL (steam yacht):
comments, plan, 71:52

Hansen, Art, author and photographer:
"Memories of a T-Wharfer," 87:56

Hansen, Gunnar, author:
"Friendship Sloop Days," 29:61

Hansen, M.S.J., designer (Denmark):
spidsgatter designs, 78:50

Hansen, Verner, builder (Norway):
comments, 28:36

Hanson, H.C., designer:
Alaska limit seiner, 37:31

Hanson, John and Vicki, authors:
"Antique Nautical Instruments," 5:41

Hanson, John K., Jr., author:
"Built to Win: Cruising Class Sailing
Canoes," 24:90
"Built to Win: DN Iceboat," 32:93
"Built to Win: International Fireball," 22:83
"Built to Win: International 14," 20:84
"Built to Win: International 210," 40:105
"Built to Win: Mirror Class Dinghy," 23:88
"Built to Win: The A-Scow," 39:123
"Built to Win: The Comet Class," 31:90
"Built to Win: The Malibu Outrigger,"
33:86
"Built to Win: The North Haven Dinghy,"
38:111
"Built to Win: Tornado Class," 25:98
"Built to Win: Turnabout Class," 36:105
"Chartering on a Smaller Scale," 91:56
"High Standards: Wooden Boats of the
Olympics," 13:34
"Kit Boats for the Eighties, Part I," 38:84
"Kit Boats for the Eighties, Part II," 39:69
"Open Boat Cruising," 24:102
reviewer of *Best of Uffa* (book), 29:108
reviewer of *Cruising in SERAFFYN* (book),
14:76
reviewer of *Dinghy Building* (book), 17:76
reviewer of *Ocean Crossing Wayfarer: To
Iceland and Norway in an Open Boat*
(book), 24:102
reviewer of *The Sea Bright Skiff and Other
Jersey Shore Boats* (book), 18:100
reviewer of *Uffa Fox: A Personal Biography*
(book), 29:108

HAPPY TIMES (speedboat):
comments, photos, 71:82

HARBINGER (ketch):
comments, photo, 91:50

Hardangersjekte:
designs/John Atkin, 26:95

Hardware:
casting technique/Richard Remsen, 73:24
comments by Stephen Olsen, 46:52
forging of a boom bale/Alan Scott, 50:46
forging of ironwork for schooner HER-
ITAGE/Doug Lee, 53:52
galvanizing techniques for/comments by
Larry Montgomery, 82:27
Lunenburg (Nova Scotia) manufacturers,
94:64
patternmaking procedures for
casting/Michael Podmaniczky, 39:58
product review of chandlers and manufac-
turers/Gary Weisenburger, 86:91
See also Gooseneck fitting, Seacocks

Hardy, Capt. Harold:
profile, 80:72

Hardy, David, author:
"A Strange Reincarnation," 97:70

Harkers Island skiff (power):
construction commentary, photos, 17:23

Harper, Jack, builder:
ketch PROSPECTOR, 44:108

Harrington, C.A. (Lyle), builder:
ketch SYLTU, 12:14

Harris, Bob:
letter on power launch CHEROKEE, 62:7

Harris, "Hardwood," builder (England):
sloop IOLAIRE, 2:48

Harris, Janet, and Pamela Detels, authors:
"The Blue Jay," 15:42

Harris, Wilder B., designer:
comments, 44:108, 46:30
See also Designs, Harris, W.B.

Hart, Kevin, author:
"In My View: Avoiding Product Liability
Suits," 57:39

Hart Nautical Museum, M.I.T. (MA):
comments, 29:38

Hartley, Carl, author:
"The Decay of Wood in Boats," 2:36

Hartsock, John A., author/designer:
"The Cosine Wherry," 100:100

Harvey, John, designer:
comments, 41:26

HARVEY GAMAGE (schooner):
comments, photo, 39:32

Haskins, Sturgis, author:
"ASPENET," 7:17
"Elusive Gypsy," 13:40
"Searching for EDNA's Past, Part II," 4:25

Hatch:
comments, detail photo, 69:104, 70:82

Hatch, companionway, sliding cover:
construction method/Bud McIntosh, 67:91

Hatch, Concordia yawl:
comments, detail photos, 67:100

Hatch, flat:
construction method/Bud McIntosh, 67:91

Hatch, foredeck:
design and construction, illustrations,
87:112

Hathaway, Carl, builder:
Adirondack guideboat, 59:64

HATTIE (Maine sloop-boat):
design and construction commentary,
plans, 2:15

Hauling boats: (*See* Moving boats)

Hawaiian Canoe Racing Association:
comments, 59:80

Hawaiian koa log canoe:
construction commentary, history, photos,
59:80

Hawkins, Havilah, author:
"Windmill Propulsion," 88:66

Hawkins, Havilah, designer/builder:
profile, photos, 88:60

Haxall, Bolling W., author:
"St. Lawrence Skiffs," 11:58

Haynes, Dean, builder:
Whitehall pulling boats, 16:15

HAZEL LEAH (sardine carrier):
comments, photo, 58:52

Hazell, Martin, author:
"Spritsail Barges," 38:88

Healy Boatworks, builder:
Great Lakes sharpie kit boat, 38:84

Hearing protection:
letter on, by Kenneth Hoffman, 81:7

Heartwood:
comments, 1:48, 2:36
discussed/Richard Jagels, 20:20

Heat gun:
technique for using/Rebecca Wittman,
81:88

Heating systems:
wood stoves for boats, 25:27, 31:25

Hecklinger, Frederick E.:
letter on maritime preservation, 47:9

Hegnauer, John R., author:
reviewer of *Blue Book of Coastal Vessels—
South Vietnam* (book), 86:89

HEIDI-GREG (Grand Manan lobsterboat):
comments, photo, 45:88

Heidt, Fred D.:
letter on bottom paint, 47:7

Heinman, Woody, designer:
McKenzie River drift boat, 52:80

Heisler, Ben, builder (Nova Scotia):
comments, 10:43

Heisler's Boat Yard, builder (Nova Scotia):
comments, 10:43

HELEK (Chumash tomol canoe):
construction commentary, photo, 95:82

HELEN (40' class):
comments, photo, 49:66

HELEN McCOLL (sardine carrier):
comments, photo, 59:70

Hendel, Geerd N., designer:
association with Malcolm Brewer, 49:51
comments on Malcolm Brewer, 49:44
See also Designs, Hendel, Geerd

**Henderson, John and Son, builder
(Scotland):**
comments, 7:5

Hengen, Willard, Jr. and Willard, Sr.:
profile, photo, 69:54

Henkel, Steve, author:
"A Niche in the Insurance Market," 81:29
"Charlie Wittholz, Yacht Designer," 73:77
"Financing Your Wooden Boat," 74:35
"Product Review: Solar Panels," 78:87

Henrikson, Ulf, author:
"Getting the Old Girl Back in Shape,"
47:109

Henrikson, Ulf, builder:
on hull shape and repair, 47:109

Henry B. Nevins, Inc., builder:
comments, 29:38, 97:76
New York 32 class, 73:42

Henry B. Nevins, Inc., builder (*continued*)
scantling rules of, 68:87
speedboat BABY BOOTLEGGER, 60:84
HENRY FORD (fishing schooner):
racing, 13:82
HENRY O. UNDERWOOD (sardine carrier):
comments, plans, 53:38, 59:70
Henry R. Hinckley Co., builder:
construction methods for teak gratings,
62:53
Hepburn, Andrew, designer:
profile, 85:21
HERCULES (power cruiser):
designs/Glen-L Marine, 18:88
Herd & MacKenzie, builder (Scotland):
Scottish fishing boats, 62:68
HERITAGE (schooner):
comments, 39:32
construction commentary, launching,
photos, plans, 53:52
Hernandez and Caldares, builder:
sloop WHITE WINGS, 23:50
Herreshoff, John Brown, builder:
comments, 100:70
comments, photo, 84:34
sloop SHADOW, 43:64
Herreshoff, L. Francis, designer:
association with W. Starling Burgess, 74:42
comments, 46:30, 47:40, 53:34, 98:74
comments about fishing schooners, 61:32
comments on, by Bud McIntosh, 51:40
designs of, letter on, 59:4
dugout canoe, 14:54
ketch DIDDIKAI, 42:74
ketch Meadow Lark, 25:36, 38:58
ketch Rozinante, 26:40
ketch TICONDEROGA, 25:56
on boatbuilders' tools, 1:14
on edge-gluing, 59:93
profile, 55:32, 56:38
sharpie, 25:36
sloop QUIET TUNE, 84:21
12-Meter class boats, 68:40
See also Designs, Herreshoff, L. Francis
Herreshoff, Nathanael G., author:
"The Catamaran Chronicle," 23:64
Herreshoff, Nathanael G., designer:
Bar Harbor 31' class, 45:68
Biscayne Bay 14 daysailer, 96:24, 97:31,
98:28
catamarans, 23:63, 23:64
Catspaw dinghy (Herreshoff Columbia
model), 26:48, 27:63, 28:64
comments, 19:72, 23:63, 32:66, 37:42,
41:26, 43:92, 46:30, 51:72, 54:34, 55:32,
57:42, 60:52
comments on, by Walter McInnis, 52:40
comments, photo, 84:34
correspondence with William P. Stephens,
photo, 100:70
design detail (metal knees), 63:116
design techniques, 45:68
Fishers Island 31' class CIRRUS, 34:42
40' class, 48:58
46' class, 49:66
New York 30' class, 35:20, 35:27, 35:35
profile, 33:50
sloop NEITH, 93:52
sloop SHADOW, 43:64, 44:24
12½' class, 40:56, 56:93, 57:93
Herreshoff 14 (H-14 sailing dinghy):
design commentary, 55:32

Herreshoff Manufacturing Co., builder:
Bar Harbor 31' class, 45:68
comments, 26:80, 29:94, 30:84, 31:84, 37:42
comments on, by Bror Tamm, 46:30
construction methods, 45:72
construction methods, history, 33:50
cradle design, photo, 69:86
Fishers Island 31' class CIRRUS, 34:42
history, photos, 84:34
New York 30' class, 35:20, 35:25, 35:27,
35:30, 35:32
scantling rules of, 68:87
12½' class, 40:56, 56:93, 57:93
yawl ROYONO, 1:4
Herreshoff Marine Museum (RI):
boat types at, 29:102
comments, 33:50
Herreshoff pram:
comments, photo, 73:60
Herreshoff Rendezvous:
1981 celebration/commentary, photos,
43:91
Herreshoff 12½' class:
comments, photo, 84:34
rebuilding by Steve Ballentine, 56:93, 57:93
refinishing by Paul Bryant, 40:56
rudder detail, 32:76
Herreshoff 28 (H-28 ketch):
comments, drawing, 56:38
Herringbone stitch:
technique for, 37:95
Hess, Lyle, designer:
cutter SYRINX, 63:38
cutter TALEISIN, 51:72
letter on *WoodenBoat* articles, 65:8
profile, photo, 76:60
See also Designs, Hess, Lyle
Hewson, Dana:
on finish work, 46:66
H-14 (sailing dinghy):
design commentary, 55:32
Hickman, Albert, designer:
profile, photo, 100:46
Hickman Sea Sleds:
design and construction commentary,
photos, plans, 100:46
design and construction comments,
photos, 100:58
Higgins and Gifford, builder:
21' class, 4:25
HILDA AND HELEN (dragger):
comments, 20:58
Hill, George, Jr., author:
"Rebuilding a Basket Case," 22:61
Hill, Tom, builder:
letter on Bud McIntosh, 52:7
planking methods for ultralight canoes,
54:74
Hill, Tom and Polly, authors:
reviewers of *The Wood & Canvas Canoe*
(book), 85:112
Hills Marine, photographer:
cover photo/Grand Craft runabout, 44:0
Hilson, Stephen, photographer:
cover photo/tugboat GILLCREST, 34:0
Hinckley, Henry R., Co., builder: (*See* Henry
R. Hinckley Co.)
Hingst, William J.:
letter on Ed Cutts, 79:5
Hinks, Alan, builder (England):
comments, 60:68
Hinks, Joseph, builder (England):
Swedish ship's boat TELKKÄ, 60:68

HIPPOCAMPUS JR (sloop):
cruise, 9:66
cruise, photo, 8:46
photos, repair commentary, 6:54
HIRTA (Bristol Channel pilot cutter):
sailing techniques, photos, 71:60
Hirte, Rebecca, photographer:
cover photo/Portuguese fishing craft, 33:0
Historic vessel reproduction:
commentary by Maynard Bray, 96:73
commentary by Peter H. Spectre, 72:60,
96:64, 96:72
editorial by Jon Wilson, 96:2
letter by Bruce Edward Blackistone, 98:4
letter by Eric Blumesaadt, 98:4
letter by Peter J. Brennan, 97:6
letter by Martyn J. Clark, 98:4
letter by Charles W. Smith, 99:4
letter by Peter Stanford, 97:4
Hitches:
comments, 39:102, 40:92, 48:100, 50:101
letter on, 32:5
HMS ROSE:
comments, 96:64
HMS TRINCOMALEE (frigate):
history, photos, 22:42
HMS VICTORY:
museum, photo, 46:54
HMS WARRIOR:
figurehead for/history, photo, 56:68
Hoagland, John:
letter on Weston Farmer, 43:8
Hoang, Hai and Van:
profile, photo, 69:54
Hoban, Art, builder:
Lyle Hess cutter, 76:60
Hobman, Robert J., author:
"The Creation of SIOLA TAU," 10:16
HOB NOB (yawl):
refastening, 12:30
HOBO (cutter):
designs/A.G. Skidmore, 20:92
Hobson, M.A., photographer:
"Stalking the Western Yew," 82:72
HOCI (motorsailer):
comments, plan, 97:76
design commentary, plan, 29:38
Hodgdon, George I., Jr. (Sonny), builder:
association with Malcolm Brewer, 49:44
construction method/power cruiser
YOREL, 71:92, 95:60
half models, 33:41
on gluing technique, 59:88
on origins of strip planking, 57:55
Swampscott dory, 51:50
transom construction/power cruiser
YOREL, 95:67
Hodgdon, George I., Jr. (Sonny), photographer:
"Building YOREL's Transom," 95:67
Hodgdon, Norman, builder:
comments, 34:104
Hodgdon, Tim, builder:
construction method/power cruiser
YOREL, 95:60
Hodgdon Bros., builder:
association with William Hand, 28:20
motorsailer ENDEAVOUR, 28:29
schooner BOWDOIN, 47:30
William Hand designs, 29:38
Hoes, Charles P.E.:
letter on toxicity of epoxy, 85:6

Hoffman, Kenneth A.:
letter on hearing protection, 81:7
Hoffman, Peter:
letter on angelique (wood), 25:7
Hoffmann, Frank:
comments, 52:59
Hole, W.J.:
comments, 94:54
HOLIDAY (motorsailer):
comments, photo, 97:76
design and construction comments,
photo, 97:86
Holland, Dennis, builder:
construction method/Baltimore clipper
PILGRIM, 64:76
Holland, Ron, designer:
sloop GOLDEN DAZY, 16:29
Holle, Beverly, author:
"The Block Island Cowhorn," 22:22
Holley, Anson, Sr., builder:
Biloxi schooners, 37:80
Hollingsworth, Bob, author:
"Other Ways: Let There Be Bandsaws,"
45:33
Hollister, Buell, author:
"Opinions: Power Corrupts," 4:64
Hollmann, Eva, author:
"My Ultimate Cruiser," 5:38
letter on cutter design, 7:3
Hollmann, Eva, designer: (*See* Designs,
Hollmann, Eva)
Holm, Ingrid, author and photographer:
"Boatbuilding in Morocco," 43:76
Holmes, Bill, author:
"Built to Win: Penguin Class," 27:94
Holmes, George, designer (England):
canoe yawl EEL, 75:62
Holness, J.W., author:
"Ashcroft's Simplex System," 27:78
"Exploring the Smacks of Itchen Ferry,"
14:22
"Winsome Waterwag," 19:67
Holness, J.W., delineator:
Waterwag class, 19:67
Holt, Arthur, builder (England):
association with Fabian Bush, 70:74
Holt, Jack, designer (England):
Mirror dinghy, 23:88
profile, photo, 74:64
Holt-Allen, builder:
kit boats, 39:69
Holzhauer, Charles, author:
"Henderson's Boatyard: Mallaig's
Tradition," 7:5
Homans, George Caspar, author:
"Sailing with Uncle Charlie," 85:74
Honduran dugout canoe:
letter by William G. Adams, 77:6
Honduras:
WoodenBoat School/Miskito Indians
project, photos, 88:76
Hooper Island sharpie:
comments, plan, 69:100
Hopkins, "Big John," photographer:
cover photo/schooner BILL OF RIGHTS,
20:0
**Hopkinson, Francis, and Richard Benson,
authors:**
"Wooden Tall Ship: GAZELA PRIMEIRO,"
11:24
Hoppen, Ed, builder:
Thunderbird class, 28:90

Horder, Garrett:
critique of cat-ketch MIST, 35:98
HORIZON (ketch):
cover photo/Benjamin Mendlowitz, 66:0
Hornet class:
comments, photo, 74:64
Hot molding:
techniques for, 55:96
Hough, designer:
wooden steam freighters, 40:94
**Houlton Boatworks, designer/builder
(England):**
Olympic Tornado kit boat, 38:84
Houseboat: (*See* Millie Hill)
**Howard Ship Yard and Dock Company,
builder:**
history, 64:64
Howell, Brian, builder:
comments, 84:21
Howes, Malcolm, author:
"The Wianno Senior," 91:58
Howland, A.C., builder:
Cape Cod catboats, 3:51
Howland, Llewellyn, III, author:
"A Farewell to Bror Tamm," 46:30
"Adventures in the Marine Arts Game,"
86:21
"America's Greatest Amateur Helmsman,"
85:74
"The Burgess Legacy: Part I," 71:52
"The Burgess Legacy: Part II," 72:44
"The Burgess Legacy: Part III," 73:32
"The Burgess Legacy: Part IV," 74:42
"The Singular Beauty of Wooden Boats,"
60:52
"Walter McInnis, Part I," 52:40
"Walter McInnis, Part II," 53:38
"Walter McInnis, Part III," 54:34
reviewer of *Great Yachts and Their Designers*
(book), 81:98
reviewer of *The Golden Pastime: A New
History of Yachting* (book), 75:101
reviewer of *William H. Webb: Shipbuilder*
(book), 100:119
Howland, Waldo:
comments, 80:64
comments on, by Bud McIntosh, 51:40
comments on Concordia yawls, 68:70
profile, 29:98
Howland, Waldo, author:
"JAVA, Father, and Capt. Hardy," 80:72
"Out of the Ashes: A Prospecting Tale,"
44:108
"The Alden Era," 32:66
"The Concordia Sloop-Boat," 29:98
letter on Ray Hunt, 82:8
on George Kirby Jr. Paint Co., 28:50
reviewer of *Schooner INTEGRITY* (book),
40:114
**Howorth, Peter C., author and photog-
rapher:**
"California's Ancient Canoe," 35:82
Hoy, John, builder:
sharpie ALACRAN, 59:36
Hoyt, Garry, designer:
comments, 92:34
H-28 (ketch):
comments, drawing, 56:38
Huckins, Frank Pembroke, designer/builder:
profile, 56:48, 57:102

**Huckins, Pembroke, and Nick Stowe,
authors:**
"The Huckins Yacht Corporation, Part I,"
56:48
Huckins Hull No. I:
design commentary, photos, 56:48
letter on, 58:9
Huckins Offshore 64 (power cruiser):
comments, photo, 56:48
Huckins power cruisers:
design and construction commentary,
history, photos, 35:92, 56:48, 57:102
Huckins PT boats:
design and construction commentary,
56:48
Huckins Yacht Corp., designer/builder:
history, 56:48, 57:102
Sportsman 36, 35:92
Hudson River Fishermen's Association:
environmental patrol craft, 61:72
letter by Robert H. Boyle, 62:7
Hudson River iceboats:
comments, 14:26, 38:64, 39:88
Hugger, Ted, author:
"Driving for Speed," 80:24
"Final Fairing," 94:35
"Warp Speed," 87:66
Hughes, Holly, author:
"The Willits Brothers' Canoes," 55:82
Hughs, Mariah, photographer:
"Building Louvered Doors," 94:84
Hughston, T.:
letter on grommets, 57:7
Hull, David A., author:
"Unity in Maritime Preservation," 44:70
Hull efficiency coefficient (HEC):
commentary by Colin Palmer, 92:76
letter by Colin Palmer, 94:6
Hull fittings: (*See* Through-hull fittings)
Hull form:
sailing performance commentary by Colin
Palmer, 92:76
Hull sheathing: (*See* Sheathing for wooden
hulls)
Humber Yawl Club (England):
comments, 64:49
Hunt, C. Raymond, designer:
comments, 7:69
letter by Waldo Howland, 82:8
International 210 class, 40:105
See also Designs, Hunt, C. Raymond
Hunt, Fitz, builder:
Alexandria Bay boats, 48:66
Hunt, Sammy, builder:
sneakboxes, 47:102
HUNTER (Galway hooker):
design and construction commentary,
performance, photo, 10:25
Huntington, L.D., Jr., builder:
SEA BIRD yawl, 43:26
HUNTRESS (New York 30):
comments, 35:20
letter on, 38:10
Huon pine:
durability of, 50:116
**Hurricane Island Outward Bound School
(ME):**
comments, 71:44
Hurricane Island pulling boat:
comments, photo, 71:44
Hutchinson Brothers, builder:
Alexandria Bay boats, 49:58

Hydraulic trailer, Brownell:
 comments, photo, 69:86
Hydroplane, TEMPO ALCOA:
 comments, photos, 80:24
Hydroplanes:
 Staudacher built/history, photos, racing,
  80:24
 outboard speedboat racing/history,
  photos, 80:32
Hylan, Doug, author:
 "A New Twist on Bending Frames," 93:84
Hyslop, John, designer:
 comments, 41:26, 43:64
 letter on, 51:6

IBIS (New York 30):
 history, 35:20
Iceboat:
 cover photo/Peter A. Burckmyer, 14:0
 designs/L.F. Herreshoff, 38:119
 history and development 1600–1930,
  photos, plans, 38:64
 history and development 1930–1980,
  photos, plans, 39:88
 See also CHARETTE II, CLAREL, COLD
  WAVE, DEBUTANTE III, DN class, FER-
  DINAND, FRITZ, Hudson River iceboats,
  ICICLE, JACK FROST, MARY B, Nite iceboat, NORTHWEST, Renegades,
  ROBERT SCOTT, Skeeter, WARRIOR II,
  WHIFF
Iceboat rigs:
 design commentary, plans, 38:64
Icebox:
 how to build, photos, plans/Jim Brown, 99:74
ICICLE (iceboat):
 comments, 14:26, 38:64
IDA MAE (sardine carrier):
 comments, photo, 59:70
Idem class:
 cover photo/Lyman W. Phillips, 9:0
 design and construction commentary,
  history, photos, 9:24
IDENEK (trimaran):
 comments, photo, 91:38
IDIE (Carolina sharpie):
 history, photo, plans, specifications, 13:68
IMAGINE (Malabar Jr.):
 repair commentary, photos, 65:56
IMELDA (motorsailer):
 design commentary, photo, 29:38
IMME GRAM (Viking ship replica):
 comments, photo, 11:15
IMOVA (power cruiser):
 comments, plan, 52:40
Importing procedures:
 tropical woods, 69:35

Imron (coating):
 use, 47:80
India:
 teak harvesting, 32:42
INDIAN (Bar Harbor 31):
 comments, photo, 45:68
INDIANA (steamboat):
 comments, photo, 64:64
Indian class (Alden):
 comments, 32:66
 designs/John Alden, 42:126
**Indian class, MONTAUK II (Cox &
 Stevens):**
 construction commentary, photos, plans,
  21:21
Indonesia, janggolans:
 design and construction commentary,
  photos, 77:52
Indonesia, Makassar ketch:
 construction commentary, photos, 14:66
Indonesia, perahu lambot, SIOLA TAU:
 design and construction commentary,
  photos, 10:16
INDUSTRY (commercial steamer):
 comments, photo, 90:84
Ingersoll, Gerald D., author:
 "Barbados Boatbuilding," 9:52
**Ingersoll, Gerald D., author and photog-
 rapher:**
 "Brunswick Lion," 15:34
Ingersoll, Stuart:
 comments on maintenance, 100:38
Insurance:
 product liability for boatbuilders, 57:39
Insurance, marine:
 commentary by Steve Henkel, 81:29
 commentary by A.T. Lyman, 72:28
 commentary by Matt Spaulding, 72:35
 commentary by Peter H. Spectre, 36:29
 editorial by Jon Wilson, 33:2, 68:2
 letter by Jerold D. Bohannon, 70:4
 letter by Chris Campion, 68:5
 letter by Andrew S. Low, 69:5
 letter by Skip Stevens, 70:8
Interior arrangements:
 commentary by Jon Wilson, photos, plans,
  93:52
Interior brightwork:
 application technique/Rebecca Wittman,
  83:66
INTERMEZZO (dinghy):
 builder, photos, 34:82
International: *See* African, Arab, Australia,
 Bahamian, Belize, Bequia, Brazil, British
 Columbia, Burundi, Caribbean, China,
 Denmark, Egypt, England, France,
 Germany, Greece, Grenada, Haitian,
 Honduras, Indonesia, India, Ireland, Italy,
 Japan, Kenyan, Mexico, New Zealand,
 Norway, Nova Scotia, Panama, Poland,
 Polynesia, Portugal, Scotland, Sweden
**International Boatbuilding Training Center
 (England):**
 program, 42:96
**International Congress of Maritime
 Museums:**
 news from/Benjamin Fuller, 63:8
International Fireball class:
 history, photos, 22:83
International Fishermen's Race:
 history, 13:82
International 14 class:
 history, photos, plan, 20:84

International 14 class, AVENGER:
 history, photo, plan, 20:84
International 14 class, BRUCE:
 construction commentary, photos, plan,
  20:87
International Moth class:
 history, photos, plans, 37:104
International Offshore Rule (IOR):
 commentary by Olin F. Stephens II, 98:50
International One-Design class:
 deck canvasing, 22:74
International Rule:
 comments, 68:40
International Tornado class:
 Olympic contender, plans, 13:34
 history, photo, 25:98
 kit boat, 38:84
International 210 class:
 history, photo, plans, 40:105
International Yacht Racing Union (IYRU):
 comments, 68:40
INTREPID (12-Meter):
 comments, 10:43
 comments, photo, plan, 98:50
 photo, 1:80
IOLAIRE (sloop):
 ballast replacement, 3:59
 deck maintenance, 25:89
 letter by Donald Street, Jr., 70:4
 owner's comments, photos, 2:48
 repairing bulwarks, 13:65
IONIA (ketch):
 comments, plans, 91:78
Iota (yawl):
 designs/Jay R. Benford, 94:110
IPBC (wood preservative):
 comments by Richard Jagels, 61:123
Ipil (wood):
 comments, 10:35
Ireland, builders: (*See* Daly, Tom; Mallon,
 Tom; Mons, Jackie; O'Ciobhain, Tomas;
 Sheahy, Danny; Tyrell, Jack)
Ireland, designers: (*See* Holland, Ron; Tyrell,
 Jack)
Ireland, watercraft: (*See* Curragh [Irish
 pulling boat], Galway hooker, Púcan [Irish
 fishing craft], River Boyne coracle)
IRENE (runabout):
 drawings, 77:79
Irish linen:
 use in copper sheathing process on
  GAZELA PHILADELPHIA, 74:19
Iroko (wood):
 comments, 10:35
 in repairing the cutter VAGRANT, 61:80
 in Shpountz 44-40, 71:74
 letter on, 47:9
Iron fastenings: *see* fastenings
ISAAC H. EVANS (schooner):
 comments, photo, 39:32
 letter on, 40:9
ISAAC McCASLIN (bateau):
 cruising Buffalo River, Arkansas, 72:84
ISABELLE (ketch):
 comments, photo, 38:71, 43:91
 teak deck overlay repair, photos, 72:53
ISH-TY-IQUE (sailing skiff):
 comments, 31:48
 cruising, Maine to Nova Scotia, 53:90
 cruising, offshore, 40:72
ISKRA (cutter):
 copper sheathing, photo, 67:35

design and construction commentary, performance, photos, 40:72

photos, voyaging, 53:90

ISLANDER (dragger):
comments, plan, 53:38

Island Falls Canoe Company, builder:
E.M. White canoe, 67:54

ISLAND RAVEN (power cruiser):
designs/William Garden, 27:89

ISLA TROTHE (yawl):
cold-molded hull repair, 52:92

ISOBEL (canoe yawl):
construction commentary, photos, plans, 97:70

Isocyanate resins:
letter on toxic effects of, 59:6

survey of, 48:123

ISTALENA (M class):
comments, photo, 55:32

Italy, builders: (*See* Cantiere Motonautico Serenella; Riva, Carol; Tramontin, Nedis)

Italy, designer: (*See* Coppola, Giancarlo)

Italy, watercraft: (*See* Gondola, Venetian; Motonautico launch; Riva speedboat; Venice, rowing craft)

ITATAE (cat-schooner):
interior arrangement, photos, plans, 93:52

Itchen boat, WILD ROSE:
comments, plans, 48:58

Itchen cutter, NELLIE:
comments, photo, 14:22

Itchen Ferry cutter, BLUE JACKET:
designs/Uffa Fox (delineator), 59:116

Itchen Ferry cutter, WONDER:
design and construction commentary, photos, plans, 14:22

Iversen, Jac N., designer (Sweden):
Folkboat, 10:30

Iwamoto, Gilbert, builder:
yawl UNICORN, 20:27

JACK FROST (iceboat):
comments, photo, 14:26

Jackson, Alice:
letter on Bob Sloan, 71:5

Jackson, Carl, author:
"Screws, Tubes & Doohickeys," 81:82

Jackson, David, author and builder:
"A Lasting Finish," 99:66

comments, 43:104

letter on trunnels, 46:5

on maintenance, 100:38

Jackson, Gifford, author and photographer:
"Something of My Own," 12:54

Jackson, Gifford, designer (New Zealand):
Marisol dinghy, 12:54

Jackson, Karen Roberts, author:
"The Stuff Dreams Are Made Of," 86:13

Jackson, Ralph, designer:
association with Winthrop Warner, 75:34

Jackson, Rick:
letter on maritime preservation, 53:9

JACOB PIKE (sardine carrier):
comments, 59:70

Jacobs, Sol:
comments, 79:48

Jacobson, Dwight E.:
letter on New York 30 HUNTRESS, 38:10

Jacobson, Joseph A., author:
"Joe Trumbly," 89:44

Jacques, Jack:
advice on surveying a wooden boat, 60:62

Jagels, Richard, author:
"A Call for Accurate Names," 70:101

"A Common Ancestry," 71:111

"A Mangled Tale," 51:121

"A Rosewood by Any Other Name," 36:89

"A Rosy Report, Fungus Amongus, and Worms?", 89:106

"A Trade Deficit in Pines," 83:107

"Acronym Update in Wood Products," 25:20

"Adapting New Strategies for Pine," 76:115

"Airborne Pollution and Forest Decline," 80:108

"Alternatives to Boycotting," 92:112

"Australian Woods," 46:131

"Bending Wood," 29:14

"Can the Pace Be Sustained?", 60:145

"Clear Boat Finishes," 26:22

"Clear Stock," 32:90

"Comparing Wood Species," 96:104

"Compression Wood in White Pine Planking," 88:100

"Correspondence from Down Under," 91:118

"Crook Timber," 40:120

"Defects or Gems—A Knotty Problem," 53:119

"Diary of a Shop Accident," 79:45

"Dimensional Instability," 33:72

"Distinguishing Mahogany from Substitutes," 55:120

"Drying Out," 23:22

"Forest Survival," 87:125

"Going to the Source" (book review), 75:99

"Growing Trees for Tomorrow's Boats," 81:117

"Growth Rate and Wood Properties," 39:115

"Health Hazards of Wood Additives," 59:111

"How Reliable Are Wood Durability Ratings?", 54:120

"Ignorance or Deception?", 41:123

"Improving Wood's Natural Durability," 31:88

"Isocyanate Resins for Woods," 48:123

"Joining Wood with Adhesives," 44:133

"Looking Behind the Grades," 20:20, 22:20

"Lumber Grading," 24:22

"Mildew, and Lots of It!", 100:128

"Modern Chemistry and the Wooden Boat," 21:18

"Mold, Sap Stain, and Preventing Decay," 35:96

"Paint Adhesion," 30:94

"Plantation Exotics: Considering the Alternatives," 97:104

"Plywood—An Engineered Wood Product," 56:125

"Plywood—Applications to Boatbuilding," 57:122

"Pressure-Treated Lumber Revisited," 85:121

"Pressure-Treated Timber," 28:94

"Rapid Lumber Drying for the Boatshop," 79:103

"Recycling a Renewable Resource," 93:134

"Saving a Pilot Cutter and Defining Silverballi," 73:108

"Sawmill Objectives," 38:108

"Scientific Names Are More Precise," 37:108

"Soothing the Conscience vs. Saving the Environment," 90:128

"Stabilizing and Preserving Wood," 82:117

"Summer-Built Vessels of New England," 58:120

"Tacks to Trunnels," 45:115

"Teak," 27:20

"The Wood/Paint Interface: Will It Stick?", 98:113

"The Yeoman Oak, Part I," 64:108

"The Yeoman Oak, Part II," 65:112

"Tree Immigration Quotas?", 86:105

"Tropical Forest Exploitation," 78:100

"Tropical Forests Revisited," 94:114

"Under-Utilized Boatbuilding Woods, Part I," 42:123

"Under-Utilized Boatbuilding Woods, Part II," 43:120

"Using the Rest of the Tree: Heating a Wooden Boat With Wood," 31:25

"Water-Curing of Timber," 69:119

"Wood: A Source of Food," 34:91

"Wood Preservation Update," 77:116

"Wood Technology," 49:124, 50:116, 52:118, 61:123, 62:113, 63:14, 66:109, 67:109, 72:105

"Woods of Australia," 95:102

"Woods of Australia and New Zealand, Part I," 46:131

"Woods of Australia and New Zealand, Part II," 47:123

"Woods of the West," 68:103

"Woodworkers Alliance for Rainforest Protection," 99:125

letter on iroko (wood), 47:9

letter on Osage orange (wood), 42:9

letter on trunnels, 46:5

letter on white cedar, 32:9

reviewer of *The Adirondack Guideboat* (book), 37:110

reviewer of *Understanding Wood: A Craftsman's Guide* (book), 39:104

Jagels, Richard, author and photographer:
"Bayou Lumberman," 26:83

James and Son, builder:
comments, 28:20

James, Joe, author:
"Built to Win: Thunderbird Class," 28:90

J & E RIGGIN (schooner):
comments, photo, 39:32

JANE (21' class):
history, 4:25

history, photo, plan, 8:62

JANET MAY (schooner):
design and construction commentary, launching, photos, 63:74

Janggolan (lateen rig):
design and construction commentary, photos, 77:52

Jannasch, Niels W.:
letter on wooden block maintenance, 53:6

JAN VAN GENT (Shpountz 44–40):
design and construction commentary, photos, plans, 71:74

Japan, builders: (*See* Sano, Ichiro; Sano Shipyard)

Japanese tools:
critique, 72:21

Jaquette, Leslee, author:
"Product Review: Flounder Bay Boat Lumber," 99:107

Jasperse, David E.:
letters on Project Lakewell, 51:7, 54:5

JAVA (Concordia yawl):
history, painting, photo, 80:72

Jay Brothers, builder:
comments, 14:26

J class:
design comments, 46:30

J class, RANGER:
comments, photo, 74:42

J class, SHAMROCK V:
cover photo/Onne Van Der Wal, 95:0

J class, WHIRLWIND:
comments, 46:30, 55:32

J class, YANKEE:
comments, photo, 85:74

JEANNE (sloop):
comments, photo, 78:30

JEFF BROWN (Key West smackee):
comments, photo, 69:48

Jelliffe, Bill, author:
"Bears on the Bay," 50:34

Jenkins, Nancy, author:
"Ancient Masterpiece: The Royal Ship of Cheops," 38:28

JENNY NORMAN (bugeye):
builder, construction commentary, photos, 65:32

JERILYN (Alaska limit seiner):
cover photo/Joe Upton, 37:0

Jespersen, Bent, author:
"Another REALITY," 34:20
reviewer of *Wooden Boat Restoration & Repair* (book), 100:120

Jespersen, Bent, builder (British Columbia):
cat-ketch MIST, 35:98
cold-molded hull-overlay techniques, 61:104
cold-molded hull repairs, 52:92
cold-molded repair of cutter FALCON, 60:76
comments, 27:89
Eight-Meter REALITY, 34:20
McCurdy and Rhodes cutter AERIEL, 100:108
sloop SAANICH BEAGLE, 12:70
wedge-seam construction technique, 98:82

JESSE JAMES (offshore raceboat):
cover photo/A.E. Reed, 73:0
design and construction, racing, photos, 73:86
editorial by Jon Wilson, 73:2

JESSICA (commuter):
comments, photo, 94:74

Jester, Herb, builder:
Chincoteague scows, 49:81

Jigs: (*See* Molds)

J.M. WHITE (steamboat):
comments, photo, 64:64

Joachim, Kurt:
letter on projection lofting, 52:10

JOANN (schooner):
drawing, 55:32

Jogglestick:
construction and use as scribing tool, 39:106

Johansson, Georg, builder (Sweden):
Swedish kåg, 58:48

Johansson, Lars, author and photographer:
"A New Kåg," 58:48

John dory:
comments, photo, 70:74

JOHN F. LEAVITT (schooner):
account of abandonment, photos, 33:20
comments, 14:7, 33:2
cover photo/Jon Wilson, 31:0
launching, photos, plan, 31:18
letters on, 34:5

Johnson, Bruce R., author:
"Ask the Pros: Wood Preservatives," 19:98

Johnson, C. Lowndes, designer:
Comet class, 31:90

Johnson, Clay, designer:
daysailer, 29:20

Johnson, Dick:
letter on Albert Strange, 50:5

Johnson, Forest E., builder:
profile, photo, 86:44

Johnson, Irving:
eulogy for, 99:2

Johnson, Julius, author:
"Money to Spare," 17:66

Johnson, Palmer, builder:
comments, 26:70

Johnson, Peter, author:
"PILGRIM's Progress," 64:76

Johnson, Robert K., author and photographer:
"LIGHTFOOT," 22:53

Johnston, W.J., Jr., builder (Ontario):
Dispros, 55:68

Joinerwork: (*See* Cabin sole, Cabin interior, Doors, louvered; Dovetail construction method; Hatches; Icebox; Interior arrangements; Lockers, cabin; Raised panels; Skylights, Teak gratings)

JOLIE BRISE (pilot cutter):
design and construction commentary, history, photos, 38:54
letter on, 48:12

Jolly, Jean, builder (France):
comments, 39:44

Jones, Al and Alma, authors:
"The Liveaboard Experience," 11:40

Jones, Ginny,
comments on Gannon and Benjamin (builder), 95:70

Jones, Gordon P., author:
"Forget the Alehouses," 10:70

Jones, Harold Patrick:
owner of fly-fisherman TROUT UNLIMITED, 64:70

Jones, Howland B., Jr., author:
"SILVER HEELS," 1:32

Jones, Howland B., III, photographer:
cover photo/schooner SILVER HEELS, 1:0

Jones, Martin, designer (England):
Merlin Rocket, 58:100

Jones, Robert, author:
"As She Was Meant to Be," 71:94

Jones, Ted, author and photographer:
"NIMBLE," 84:21
letter about NIMBLE's hull speed, 86:7

Jones, Tristan:
letter on OUTWARD LEG, 55:5

Jones Shipyard, builder (Scotland):
Scottish fishing boats, 62:68

JOSEF W (Delaware ducker):
comments, plans, 48:86
cover photo/Benjamin Mendlowitz, 35:0
performance commentary, 48:83

JOSEPHA (Tahiti ketch):
cover photo/George Day, 8:0
cruising on, photos, 8:36
design commentary, photo, 16:66

JOSEPH CONRAD, lifeboat for:
construction commentary, photo, plans, 43:72

JOY (ketch):
owner's comments, 17:69

JOYCE MARIE (sardine carrier):
comments, photo, 59:70
cover photo/Ed Elvidge, 59:0

J.P. Downes Memorial Bifurcating Dinghy:
designs/Kaufman Design, Inc., 99:116

JULIA DELACRUZ (Biloxi schooner):
comments, photo, 37:80

Julian, Jeff, photographer:
"A Classic in Plywood, Part I," 41:63
"A Classic in Plywood, Part II," 42:44
"A Classic in Plywood, Part III," 43:96
"Keeping a Cutting Edge: Handsaws," 47:91

Junge, Gustav, designer:
schooner WANDERBIRD, 55:56

JUNIPER (trimaran):
comments, photo, 42:66, 92:34
cover photo/Alden Charles, 54:0
design and construction commentary, performance, photos, 54:56

Junk: (*See* Chinese junk)

Junk rig:
commentary by Iain Oughtred, 78:66
commentary by Colin Palmer, 92:76
letter by Iain Oughtred, 65:4
letter by Colin Palmer, 94:6
See also Chinese junk

JUNO (cutter):
design and construction comments, photo, plans, 79:64

JUST HOOKED (power launch):
comments, detail photo, 69:104

JZERO (Pacific proa):
comments, photos, 83:58

Kaarhus, Tom, builder:
McKenzie River drift boats, 52:80
Kåg (Swedish ketch):
construction commentary, making and
installing trunnels, photos, 58:48
Kaiser, Bryan, author and photographer:
"The Janggolans of Madura," 77:52
KAIULANI (bark):
comments, 38:36
history, 61:88
Kalayjian, Rolly:
profile (modelmaker), photo, 88:70
KALMAR NYCKEL (Dutch merchant ship):
comments, 96:64
Kane, Herb Kawainui, illustrator:
"Polynesia's Honored Beings," 19:25
Kaplan, Marion, photographer:
"No Passage to Zanzibar," 46:88
Kapur (wood):
comments, 10:35
Karosis, Robert, photographer:
cover photo/pulling boat MOCKINGULL,
48:0
Kasanof, David, author, "Fo'c's'le":
"A Midwinter Morale Booster," 92:8
"A Softening of Nautical Sinew," 73:14
"Aground in a Trailer Park," 91:8
"As Time Goes By," 90:23
"Bowsprit Envy," 89:19
"Call of the Wild," 76:8
"Carrying the Principle of Fakery to Its
Logical Conclusion," 100:15
"Delicate Arts of the Sailor," 98:12
"Inventions of the Devil," 97:16
"Irregular Fellow," 77:8
"Just Measure and Cut," 93:10
"Letting the Electrons Do It All," 96:10
"Life With Your Top Off," 68:11
"Messing Around with Words," 85:15
"Messy...but CONTENT," 87:17
"Navel Preparedness," 72:12
"'Progress' Viewed with Grave Suspicion,"
82:13
"Sailors' Luck," 83:17
"Seamanship Fettucine Style," 78:10
"Supernatural Stresses," 88:18
"The Check Is in the Mail," 94:10
"The Imperfect Tool for Every Job," 74:8
"The Old Second Sea Dog Trick," 75:10
"The Real Truth About Navigation," 84:14
"The Umbilical Cord," 79:9
"Tumblehome Sweet Home," 81:15
"What Makes Boats Go," 95:10
on anchoring, 19:16, 36:18
on authentic saltiness, 26:18

on bowsprits, 49:15, 71:11
on caulking, 4:30
on deck repair/CONTENT, 66:13
on electronic communications, 44:13
on etiquette at marinas, 45:12, 50:16, 55:15
on etiquette at sea, 31:16, 50:16
on high-tech marine hardware, 14:15
on installing engines, 10:11, 22:18, 24:18,
28:16
on leaky boats, 3:7, 4:30
on living aboard, 11:14, 12:13, 16:14, 20:15,
40:13, 53:17, 56:15, 62:11, 63:13, 65:11,
70:9
on maintenance standards, 8:17, 25:16,
47:16, 58:13, 59:13
on materials, 18:18
on nautical jargon, 31:16, 54:13
on navigation, 18:18, 34:18, 42:12
on new design concepts, 69:12
on newfangled anchors, 5:23
on newfangled equipment, 5:23, 48:16,
54:13
on plywood deck, 67:11
on reefing for gaff rig, 30:16
on romance of wooden boats, 13:13
on running aground, 46:26, 57:15
on schooner CONTENT, 7:30, 27:16
on scrounging, 14:15, 43:13
on seamanship, 15:20, 34:18, 37:24
on teenagers, 64:11
on the bilge, 32:18
on the fo'c's'le, 2:69
on traditional materials, 61:11
on Turk's Head knot, 35:18
on VHF, 44:13
on whitewater canoeing, 6:43
on winter liveaboard, 21:14, 38:24, 39:13
on *WoodenBoat*, 59:13, 60:15
KATHERINE (catboat):
designs/Paul Kotzebue, 50:130
KATOURA (commuter launch):
comments, photo, plans, 52:40
KATOURA (cutter):
comments, photo, 74:42
KATOURA (schooner):
comments, photo, 84:34
KATY G (sloop):
cruise of, 11:62
Kaufman Design, Inc.: (*See* Designs,
Kaufman Design, Inc.)
KAURI (Pacific proa):
comments, photos, 83:58
cover photo/Jim Brown, 83:0
Kauri (wood):
for boatbuilding, 47:123
in modified Bounty ketch LA FILLE D'OR,
67:82
Kayak, DK 13:
construction methods, photos, plans, 70:56
materials and tool list, 71:8
Kayak, folding:
design and construction commentary,
photos, use, 53:75
owner's comments, 8:5, 53:2
Kayak, folding, Klepper:
design and construction commentary,
photos, use, 53:75, 53:80
Kayak, folding, Nautiraid:
comments, 53:80
Kayak, Hooper Bay:
construction commentary, photos, use,
58:74

Kayak, Kodiak:
construction commentary, photos, plans,
58:68
Kayak, lapstrake:
designs/L.F. Herreshoff, 19:82, 60:140
Kayak, Olympic contenders:
comments, photos, 13:34
Kayak, plywood:
comments, plans, 7:64
Kayak, QUEEN CHARLOTTE:
computer-generated lines, photo, plan,
79:84
Kayak, strip:
design and construction commentary,
photos, plans, 57:60
Kayak, Struer:
construction commentary, history, photos,
82:44
Kayak, touring:
designs/Mike Alford and Eric Wahlman,
97:108
Keel: (*See* Ballast keel, Scheel keel)
Keel batten:
defined, 18:79
letters on, 13:6, 19:13
Keelbolts:
boring for/Joel White, 50:59
letter by Joseph Arnell, 35:5
letter by Ken Wilson, 90:6
making, boring for/Fred Ajootian, 14:38
making, boring for/Bud McIntosh, 37:89
removing/Michael Dziubinski, 89:105
removing/Paul Stubing, 35:30
removing/Joel White, 16:70
removing/James Woodward, 17:20
Keel construction:
for Beetle Cat/Leo Telesmanick, 51:99
for Biscayne Bay 14 daysailer/Eric Dow,
96:24
for Whitehall/Bob Baker, 45:108
for small craft/Maynard Bray, 28:56
laminating techniques/Allan Vaitses, 15:33
technique/Bud McIntosh, 33:66
Keel rabbet:
technique/Sam F. Manning, 14:42
Keel repair:
for Herreshoff 12½/Steve Ballentine, 57:93
for cold-molded construction/Reuel
Parker, 89:92
for ketch TARNE/Joel White, 49:97, 50:59
for power cruiser ARLINE/Clifton
Andrews, 18:82
Keelson:
defined, 18:79
letters on, 13:6, 19:13
repair technique/cold-molded construction, 89:92
Keel straps:
comments on, 19:72
Keith, David, author:
"Boatbuilder's Forum: Strip Planking for
Chine Boats," 4:63
"Opinion: On Flatness," 9:12
"What Good Is Wood," 10:43
reviewer of *Boatowner's Sheet Anchor* (book),
5:74
reviewer of *Eric the Red* (book), 1:76
reviewer of *Gaff Rig* (book), 7:74
reviewer of *How-to-Build Tahiti* (book),
12:78
reviewer of *How-to-Build Gulfweed* (book),
12:78

Keith, David, author (*continued*)
reviewer of *Sensible Cruising Designs* (book), 1:76
reviewer of *Shipshape and Bristol Fashion* (book), 6:72
reviewer of *Small Boats* (book), 8:72
reviewer of *The Arts of the Sailor* (book), 14:38
reviewer of *The Care and Maintenance of Small Boats* (book), 7:74
reviewer of *The Common Sense of Yacht Design* (book), 2:65
reviewer of *The Good Little Ship* (book), 9:73
reviewer of *The Ocean Sailing Yacht* (book), 11:79

Kelley, Kevin, and Susan Kelman, authors:
"Something of a Legend," 20:80

Kelley, Kevin, photographer:
"How the Legend Began," 20:82

Kellum, Tony and Ray:
profile, photo, 69:54

Kelly, William, builder:
Barnegat Bay sneakbox, photo, 68:25

KELPIE (cutter):
designs/William Garden, 64:98

KELPIE (Fishers Island 31):
history, photo, plan, rig conversion, 34:42

KELPIE II (cutter):
designs/William Garden, 64:98

Kemp, Dixon, designer (England):
comments, 15:29

Kemp, Molly:
letter on Alaska yellow cedar, 78:6

Kendall, David, author:
"The Building of RANDOM SCOOT," 31:50
"The Theft of RANDOM SCOOT," 53:66

Kendall Whaling Museum (MA):
comments, 63:8

Ken Hankinson and Associates, designers:
review of plans catalog, 93:118

Kenly, Bob, author:
"Designs: Winthrop Warner's Catboat BOB CAT," 36:94

Kenney, Susan, author:
"Building the First Lightning," 53:68

Kentucky coffeetree (wood):
characteristics, 43:120

Kenyan dugout canoe:
design commentary, 40:78

Kenyon, Gordon, builder:
Alexandria Bay boats, 49:58

Kenyon, Lew, builder:
Alexandria Bay boats, 48:66

Kercher, Bob, author:
"Teak Care Among the Palm Beach Sportfishing Fleet," 77:66

KESTREL (troller):
comments, photo, 38:78

Ketch: (*See* ALACRAN [sharpie ketch]; ALPHARD; ANNE MARGRETHE [Danish ketch]; ARAMINTA; ARETE [Rozinante ketch]; ATHENA; ARIEL [Rozinante ketch]; AUGUST MOON; BLUE SEA III; BLUE STAR; BOUNTY; CALYPSO; CARRIE L; Cogge ketch; COLIN ARCHER; DEFENDER [trading ketch]; DIABLESSE; DOG STAR; DOVEKIE; EXCALIBUR; FARMILY; FELISI; FRI [Danish ketch]; GALATEA [Nereia ketch]; GIPSY JAC; H-28; HARBINGER; HORIZON; Indonesia, Makassar ketch; IONIA; ISABELLE; JOSEPHA [Tahiti ketch]; JOY; JUNIPER

[trimaran]; Kåg [Swedish ketch]; LA TROPICANA; LA FILLE D'OR [modified Bounty ketch]; LANDFALL; LENE MARIE [Baltic ketch]; LONE STAR; MAYA; Meadow Lark [sharpie ketch]; MELITA [Tahiti ketch]; MEROE OF KENT; MERMAID; NARAINA; NIRVANA; ONDINE; PATIENCE; PEGGY; PROSPECTOR; QUIET TUNE; Redningskoite; RESOLUTE; R S COLIN ARCHER; ST. MARY; SANDPIPER; SHADOWFAX; SPELLBOUND; STORMY PETREL; SUMURUN; SUNRISE [pinky ketch]; SVAAP; SYLTU; TARNE; Ti Shpountz; TICONDEROGA; WHITEHAWK)

Kevlar:
for BOC Challenger AIRFORCE, 68:72
for Geodesic Airolites, 76:72
for Snowshoe canoe, 76:77
for sportfishing boats, 76:44

Kevlar cord:
for Cutts method of double planking, 78:30

Keyhaven yawl:
designs/Laurent Giles, Ltd., 63:116

Key West smackee, JEFF BROWN:
comments, photos, 69:48

Kielb, Debbie:
letter on Harry Dring, 63:6

Kiln drying:
DH kiln system, 79:103
solar-heated kiln design, 79:103

Kimber, Harold, builder (England):
comments, 4:31

Kincheloe-Nickerson, builder:
sportfishing boats, 76:44

King, Bruce P., designer:
ketch WHITEHAWK, 25:56
letter on marine hardware for ketch WHITEHAWK, 29:8
sloop WHITEFIN, 57:80
yawl UNICORN, 20:27
See also Designs, King, Bruce P.

King, David C.:
letter on painting technique, 64:4

King, Edie and Bruce, authors and photographers:
"Liberating the Unicorn," 20:27

King, Graeme, author, designer, and builder:
"Building the KINGFISHER, Part I," 61:60
"Building the KINGFISHER, Part II," 62:103
"Building the KINGFISHER, Part III," 63:63

King, JoAnn, author:
"A Howard Chapelle Chronology," 84:76

King & Davis, designers: (*See* Designs, King & Davis)

KINGFISH (sharpie):
comments, 56:76

KINGFISHER (recreational shell):
construction methods, photos, plans, 61:60, 62:103
rigging instructions, safety tips for using, sculling technique, storage and maintenance, transporting, 63:63

KINGFISHER (sardine carrier):
comments, photo, 59:70

King's Cruiser:
removing keelbolts, 16:70

King's Landing Museum (New Brunswick):
building the St. John River boat BRUNSWICK LION, 15:34

Kingston lobsterboat:
history, photo, plans, 1:65

Kirby, Bruce, designer: (*See* Designs, Kirby, Bruce)

Kirby, George Jr., Paint Co.:
history, photo, 28:50

Kiremidjian, David, author:
"The New York Thirties: Then, But Mostly Now Also," 35:20

Kirk, Arlington W.:
letter on building cabintop, 22:6

Kirkpatrick, Carl, illustrator:
"DREOILIN," 96:36

Kirschenbaum, Jerry, author and illustrator:
"ENDEAVOUR: A Motorsailer Lifestyle," 28:29
"Electrolysis and Corrosion, Part I," 23:30
"Electrolysis and Corrosion, Part II," 24:78
"Electrolysis and Corrosion, Part III," 25:61
"Marine Batteries, Part I," 34:72
"Marine Batteries, Part II," 35:69
"Marine Electrical Systems," 32:79
"William Hand: The Evolution of an Architect, Part I," 28:20
letter on corrosion, 26:7
letter on grounding, 28:7

Kirschenbaum, Jerry, author and photographer:
"Giffy's Hammer: Surveying Wooden Boats," 26:57

Kirschenbaum, Jerry, Maynard Bray, and Jon Wilson, authors:
"William Hand: The Evolution of an Architect, Part II," 29:38

Kit boats:
Blue Jay class/Robert MacKean, 15:42
Blue Jay class/Roberts Industries, 15:42
Destiny ketch/Rosborough Boats, 39:69
DN iceboats/Norton Boat Works, 38:84
Great Lakes Sharpie/Healy Boatworks, 38:84
Mirror dinghy/Bell Woodworking, 39:69
Mirror dinghy/Holt-Allen, 39:69
NAJA 30 sloop/A & T Marine Services, 38:84
Nutshell pram/WoodenBoat, 60:100
Old Town Stripper/Old Town Canoe Company, 38:84
Olympic Tornado (catamaran)/Houlton Boat Works, 38:84
plywood canoe/Granta Boats Ltd., 31:50
power cruiser GO-SUM, 40:117
Quintet 6 (sloop)/Clark Craft, 39:69
sailing pram TULIP/Camber Craft, 39:69
SIB 32 (trimaran)/Constant Camber Boat Works, 39:69
Wayfarer dinghy/Wayland Marine, 38:84, 51:88

Kitimat Centennial Museum (British Columbia):
project/Haisla dugout canoe, 69:64

KITTIWAKE III (Cadet dinghy):
history, photo, 52:100

KITTY (spritsail barge):
comments, photo, 38:88

KIYI (power cruiser):
comments, detail photo, 69:104

Klepper, Johann, designer (Germany):
Klepper folding kayaks, 53:75, 53:80

Klepper folding kayak:
design and construction commentary, photos, use, 53:75, 53:80

Kludas, Monika, photographer:
"The Smaller Boats of Kaszuby," 89:80
KLYSMA (cutter):
comments, photo, 90:84
Knapp, Douglas, author:
"No Passage to Zanzibar," 46:88
Knees, bronze:
design and construction for cutter
TALEISIN, 51:72
design of George F. Lawley & Son, 26:80
Knees, natural crook:
bandsaw cutting/Bob Baker, 37:57
bandsaw cutting/Bud McIntosh, 44:86
chainsaw milling/Will Malloff, 50:38
design for schooner CORONET, 32:20
flat-bottomed skiff or sharpie, 66:48
harvesting/Carl Hathaway and Ralph
Morrow, 59:64
harvesting/Frank Morse, 30:66
selecting/Richard Jagels, 40:120
Knees, quarter:
design for small craft, 26:80
installation in Biscayne Bay 14 daysailer,
97:31
installation in Catspaw dinghy (Herreshoff
Columbia model), 28:64
installation in Martha's Tender skiff, 47:58
Knees, seat:
design for small craft, 26:80
installation in Catspaw dinghy (Herreshoff
Columbia model), 28:64
Knees, stern:
installation in Martha's Tender skiff, 47:58
KNICKERBOCKER (fishing schooner):
comments, photo, 61:32
Knife, rigger's:
how to make one of beryllium-copper,
39:84
Knife, sailor's:
product review by Daniel Porter, 88:109
Knight, Nicholas, author:
"Boatbuilding Report: Machin Knight &
Sons Ltd.," 15:29
Knipmeyer, William B.:
on origins of Acadian folk boats, 62:44
Knots: (See Cordage, techniques for)
Knowles, Bill, builder:
design comments about sportfishing boats,
photo, 76:44
Knowles, Marianna, author:
introduction to "A RIVERKEEPER for the
Hudson," 61:72
Knowles, Robert, photographer:
"A RIVERKEEPER for the Hudson," 61:72
cover photo/utility outboard launch
RIVERKEEPER, 61:0
KOALA (sloop):
comments, photo, 55:32
KOCHAB (Friendship sloop):
designs/John Atkin, 1:72
Kocot, Chester:
on finish work, 46:66
Kodiak kayak:
construction commentary, photos, plans,
58:68
KOLUTOO (scow sloop):
comments, 72:44
Kortum, John, photographer:
"Between a Rock and a Hard Place," 72:60
Kortum, Karl:
association with Harry Dring, 61:88
comments, 44:70
maritime preservation/philosophy of, 61:88

on maritime preservation, 38:36
profile, photo, 72:60
Kotalac, Rick, author:
"A Cold-Molded Rejuvenation," 52:92
Kotzebue, Paul R., author:
letter on John Hyslop and Albert Strange,
51:6
letter on wave-form theory, 51:7
on boat plans and public domain, 48:105
Kotzebue, Paul R., designer: (See Designs,
Kotzebue, Paul R.)
Kragejollers: (See Spidsgatters)
Krick, Ray:
letter on cordage, 32:5
Krogen, James S., designer: (See Designs,
Krogen, James S.)
Krotenko, Linda, author:
"RELIANCE—A Pinky Schooner," 18:46
Kubiak, David, builder:
Kodiak kayak, 58:68
Kuchenbecker, George, author:
"Spring Fitting Out," 33:81
"The Structure of a Winner," 90:108
Kuna dugout canoe:
construction, history, sailing techniques,
97:62
Kunhardt, C.P., designer:
comments, 43:64, 44:24
KYRENIA II (Greek trading ship):
comments, photo, 96:64

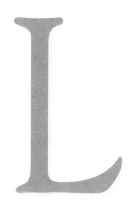

Labaree, Benjamin, W.:
letter about maritime history, 87:7
LA BERA (barque catalane):
comments, photo, 85:64
Ladder, boarding:
comments, detail photo, 70:82
how to build, illustrations, plans, 84:91
Ladder, companionway:
detail photo, comments, 66:90
L.A. DUNTON (schooner):
history, photos, plans, 6:44
photos, stem replacement, 39:97
LADY GENEVIEVE (power launch):
comments, photo, 57:72
LADY JEANNE (power cruiser):
design and construction commentary,
photos, plans, 37:72
letter on, 40:7
LADY MONA (power cruiser):
comments, photos, 22:57
LADY OF BERMUDA (sharpie schooner):
comments, plans, 71:74
LA FILLE D'OR (modified Bounty ketch):
design, construction, performance, photos,
plans, 67:82

Lafitte skiff:
comments, photos, 26:83
construction commentary, photos, 14:73
LaFlamme, Philip, builder:
comments about Lyle Hess cutter
THAENO, 76:60
**LA GANGALAISE (three-masted chasse-
marée):**
comments, photo, 85:64
Lagner, Richard, author and illustrator:
"Saving Time in the Mold Loft, Part II:
Pick 'Em Up with Precision," 31:66
LAGODA (whaleship replica):
comments, photo, 96:64
Lakeboat: (See Reelfoot Lake Stumpjumper)
Lake Tahoe, builder: (See Clarke, Dick)
Lake Tahoe, Concours d'Élégance (CA):
commentary, photos, 62:74
Lake Union Dreamboat:
comments, 94:62
comments, photos, 94:54
Lallow, Clare, Yard, builder (England):
apprenticing at, 6:20
Lamary, Ted:
letter on SEA BIRD yawl construction, 45:4
Laminated deckbeams:
technique/Bud McIntosh, 42:53
technique/Jon Wilson, 20:52
Laminated frames:
letters on reframing, 60:5
technique/Scott Cain, sloop WHITE
WINGS, 23:50
technique/Arch Davis, 97:44
technique/Harold Ford, Adirondack
guideboat, 18:55
technique/John Gardner, McInnis bateau,
51:66
technique/George I. (Sonny) Hodgdon, Jr.,
Swampscott dory, 51:50
technique/Daniel MacNaughton, 99:63
technique/Peterson Builders, MCM class,
58:90
technique/Robert Vespa, sloop RONDO,
51:59
technique/Joel White, Nutshell pram,
60:100
Laminated keel:
technique/Allan Vaitses, 15:33
Laminated plywood: (See Cold-molded hull
construction)
Laminated stem:
technique/Bob Baker, sailing canoe
PICCOLO, 36:44
Laminating: (See Cold-molded hull construc-
tion, Constant Camber, Vacuum bagging)
LA MOUETTE (canoe yawl):
construction commentary, photo, 75:62
sailing critique, 75:69
LAMPOONER (power cruiser):
comments, 56:38
Lamprell, William, photographer:
"Building a Dinghy for Oar and Sail,
Part I," 26:48
"Building a Dinghy for Oar and Sail,
Part II," 27:63
"Building a Dinghy for Oar and Sail,
Part III," 28:64
Landecker, Heidi, author:
"Clear Morning," 32:40
"ISH-TY-IQUE," 31:48
LANDFALL (ketch):
comments, photo, 56:38

LANDFALL (schooner):
photos, racing, 13:79
Landing School of Boatbuilding & Design, The (ME):
boatbuilding and design program, 42:100
letter by John T. Burgess, 76:7
Landis, Scott, author and photographer:
"Built to Portage," 21:54
Lange, Bob, builder:
profile, photo, 77:34
Langeland, Martin:
letter on clench nails, 28:7
Langevin, Sylvester, designer (France):
sloop NAJA 30, 38:84
Lappen, Alyssa A., author:
"VOLSUNGA II: Thimble Islands Ferryboat," 7:14
Lapstrake planking: (*See* Planking, lapstrake)
LAPWING (cutter):
comments, photo, 91:92
Larch (wood):
species for boatbuilding, 9:31
Western/comments, 68:103
See also Hackmatack
Larson, David, illustrator:
"Clamps and Cleverness," 12:62
"The Care and Feeding of Teak Decks," 11:70
Lashing:
technique/David Kubiak, Kodiak kayak, 58:68
technique/Brion Toss, cordage, 50:101
Laskornwy (Polish fishing craft):
comments, photos, plans, 89:80
Lateen rig:
commentary by Iain Oughtred, 78:66
comments by Colin Palmer, 92:76
See also Janggolan
Latimer, Tony, author:
"Endless Summer," 18:32
LA TROPICANA (ketch):
designs/Winthrop Warner, 4:66
LAUAN (Concordia 31 sloop):
comments, plan, 48:126
Lauan (wood):
comments, 10:35
decay resistance, 49:124
Launch:
at Lake Tahoe Concours d'Élégance, 62:74
Burgess design/comments, plan, 72:44
designs/Eldredge-McInnis, 12:68
designs/Nelson Zimmer, 43:124
photos, repair comments, 95:82
restorations by Peter Freebody & Co., 57:72
See also Alexandria Bay boats; ALOHA; BALOCCARF; Bassboat; Cabin launch; CASTALIA (steam launch); CHAR-LOTTE; CHEROKEE (cabin launch); CHIMO; COMET; Cowes steam launch; DISCOVERY's launch; DISPATCH; Dispro (Disappearing Propeller Boat); FALCON; Fantail launch; FAWN; FLOTSAM; FREE-LANCE; Hampton boat; JUST HOOKED; KATOURA (commuter launch); LADY GENEVIEVE; Lafitte skiff; MANATEE; MELISANDE; MERGANSER (lobster-boat); Motonautico launch (Italy); MRS. JONES; PANTHER; PETREL; POOR RICHARD; REDSKIN; RIVERKEEPER (utility outboard launch); ROSE PLUN-KETT (utility launch); SACHEM; SIM-PLEX; TERRIBLE; TINAVETTE; WREN; XANTHO (steam launch)

Laurel, California (wood):
characteristics, 35:45
for boatbuilding, 35:45, 43:120
letter on, 41:6
Laurent Giles, Ltd.: (*See* Designs, Giles, Laurent, Ltd.)
Lavin, Chris and Mark:
comments about, photos, 73:86
letters by Tim Cahill and Daniel J. Pusateri, 75:6
Lavin, Mark:
obituary, 74:4
LAWANA (power cruiser):
comments, photo, 65:76
Lawley, Fred, designer:
association with Walter McInnis, history, 52:40
Lawley, George F., designer:
association with W. Starling Burgess, 72:44
association with Walter McInnis, 52:40, 53:38, 54:34
comments, 46:30
21' knockabout ASPENET, 7:17
Lawley, George F., & Son Corp., builder:
association with Bror Tamm, 46:30
association with Walter McInnis, history, 52:40, 53:38
comments, 85:74
40' class, 48:58
Herreshoff dugout canoe, 14:54
power cruiser POT O' GOLD, 48:38
21' knockabout ASPENET, 7:17
Winter Harbor 21 class, 93:76
Lawley yacht tender:
design and construction commentary, photos, plans, 50:88
Lawrence, Anne, author:
"SHEARWATER," 59:48
Lawrence, Thomas, designer (England):
profile, 14:31
Lawson, Hank:
advice about engine layup, 72:25
Lawton, Bruce:
on finish work, 46:66
Lazarus, Paul, author:
"Boatbuilder, Beware," 93:86
"Building a Skylight: Fine Joinerwork with Duffy Dodge," 92:28
"William Crosby's Snipe," 89:36
LAZY JACK (sharpie sloop):
designs/Ed Frost, 54:130
owner's comments, 19:70
LAZY SUSAN (catamaran):
design and construction commentary, photo, plan, 42:66
Leach, Eric:
comments on Athenian trireme, 75:44
Lead keel: (*See* Ballast keel)
Leary, Joseph, author and photographer:
"Mock Turtle," 21:74
Leather, David, author:
"An Apprentice in England," 6:20
Leather, John F., author:
"The Return of the Steam Launch," 13:76
letter about minesweepers, 81:9
Leatherwork:
tools and technique with photos, 68:64
Leavitt, Dustin W., author:
"Clean Tools," 37:40
letter on Third World boatbuilding, 41:5
reviewer of *Archaeology of the Boat* (book), 36:110

reviewer of *The Sea-Craft of Prehistory* (book), 49:117
reviewer of *The Ship* (book), 59:120
reviewer of books by Basil Greenhill, 44:120
reviewer of books by Edgar J. March, 52:129
Leavitt, John F., author:
"Murray Peterson: A Brief Biography," 1:30
on 21' class EDNA, 1:58
Le Chasse-Marée **(French periodical):**
comments, 85:64
Lee, Douglas, author:
"Round-Up of Woodworking Videos" (video review), 76:119
reviewer of *How Wooden Ships Are Built* (book), 58:124
Lee, Douglas, designer and builder:
schooner HERITAGE, 53:52
Lee, Jan, photographer:
cover photo/Friendship sloop ESTELLA A, 19:0
Lee, Lance, author:
"A Celebration of the Traditional North Shore Dory," 36:82
"Less is More," 71:44
"Our Thanks to John Gardner," 90:36
"Shavings on the North Wall," 28:34
"The Apprenticeshop," 4:31
"The Case for the Restoration of Skillfulness," 38:48
"The Delaware Ducker: Why the Ducker Today," 48:86
"Viking Replica," 11:15
comments on, 95:90
comments on Howard I. Chapelle, 84:76
on sculling techniques, 100:60
reviewer of *Inshore Craft of Norway* (book), 35:89
Lee, Linda, builder:
schooner HERITAGE, 53:52
Lee, Madeline, author:
"Common Sense and the Energy 48," 47:40
Lee, Nicholas J., author and photographer:
"The Aegean Tradition," 21:42
Leeboard:
comments, plans, 22:71
design for Dutch boeier, 27:32
design for Polish craft, 89:114
design for sailing canoe, 22:33
designs for small craft, 38:98
Leek, Charles Platt, builder:
Pacemakers, 23:96
Lees, David, author:
"Vic Carpenter, A Superior Craftsman, Part I," 45:50
"Vic Carpenter, A Superior Craftsman, Part II," 46:50
LEGACY (Gemini class):
comments, photo, 12:24
cover photo/Michael Monahan, 12:0
LEILANI (Hawaiian koa dugout canoe):
comments, 59:80
Leland, Capt. Glen:
letter on carryaway boats, 62:9
Lemon, Rosine and Peter, photographers:
"The Adirondack Guideboat," 18:55
cover photo/Adirondack guideboat, 18:0
LENA (New York 30):
comments, 35:27
LENE MARIE (Baltic ketch):
photo, racing, 13:79

Loc

Lentini, Peter, author and builder:
  "TROUT UNLIMITED: The Compleat Fly
    Fisherman," 64:70
Lestabåt, VARIN:
  design, construction, photos, plans, rig,
    use, 95:90
LESTER ROWE (New Haven sharpie):
  comments, photos, 2:32
  construction commentary, photos, 1:8
  construction commentary, performance,
    photos, 3:24
Leth, Peter, photographer:
  "The Archer Poised," 20:38
Lettering:
  technique, photos/Dave Gross, 99:54
  technique/Karl MacKeeman, 21:50
Leve, Bob, author:
  "Why Aren't Heads Called Tails?", 46:49
Levin, Dan, author:
  "Chris White and His Multihulls," 54:56
LEWIS R. FRENCH (schooner):
  comments, photo, 39:32
Liability suits:
  boatbuilders' protection against, 57:39
LIBERTÉ (Bantry Bay gig):
  comments, photo, 71:44
LIBERTY (sardine carrier):
  comments, 59:70
LIBERTY (sloop):
  comments, photo, 95:70
LIBERTY (steamboat):
  comments, photo, 64:64
LIBRA (motorsailer):
  comments, photo, 29:38
Liener, Joe, builder:
  comments, 34:86
  Delaware ducker, 48:86
  small-craft outfitting, 38:98
Lie-Nielsen, O., builder:
  ketch WHITEHAWK, 25:56
Lifeboat, BANFIELD:
  comments, photo, 65:76
Lifeboat, converted Coast Guard:
  owner's comments, photos, 21:49
Lifeboat, Danish:
  construction commentary, photos, plans,
    43:72
LIGHTFOOT (cat-ketch):
  design and construction commentary,
    photos, plans, 22:53
LIGHTNING (New York 30):
  construction details, restoration comments,
    35:30
Lightning class:
  design and construction commentary,
    photos, plans, 34:97
  history, photos, 53:68
  owner's comments, 31:56
Lignum vitae (wood):
  comments, 10:35
LILLIAN (sardine carrier):
  comments, 59:70
LILY (pulling boat):
  comments, detail photo, 69:104
LILY (scow sloop):
  operation, 31:18
LILY (Whitehall):
  cover photo, 53:0
  design and construction commentary,
    photos, 53:86
Lincoln, Robin, author:
  "Surveying Your Sails," 93:60
  letter on battenless mainsail, 66:7

on patching techniques for cotton sails,
  81:75
Lincoln, Spencer, delineator:
  Adirondack guideboat, 18:55
  Asa Thomson skiff, 29:50
  Barnegat Bay sneakbox, 20:23
  Catspaw dinghy (Herreshoff Columbia
    model), 26:48, 27:63, 28:64
  Chris-Craft 23, 21:96
  Chumash tomol canoe, 35:82
  Dory No. 2, 36:83
  Fishers Island 31 class, 34:42
  halibut schooner, 16:63
  Herreshoff double-paddle canoe, 19:83,
    60:140
  Indian class (Cox & Stevens), 21:21
  New York 30 class, 35:20
  power cruiser LADY JEANNE, 37:72
  schooner JOHN F. LEAVITT, 31:18
  schooner ROB ROY, 32:66
  sloop TORETTA, 22:46
  Tumlaren class, 19:18
  Yankee Tender skiff, 30:74, 31:71
  yawl SCUD, 21:58
Lincoln, Spencer, illustrator:
  "Building the Banks Dory," 19:32
  "CORONET: Whither Away?", 32:20
  "Cradles for Storage and Shipping," 18:51
  "Leaking Decks: Watertight Solutions,"
    25:89
  "Leeboards," 22:71
  "Matter of Detail: Stems and Breasthooks,"
    25:52
  "SQUAW: A Sharpie Schooner," 33:36
Lincolnville wherry:
  construction commentary, history, photos,
    plans, 2:44
  photos, taking off lines, 19:42
Linder, George, designer:
  offshore raceboat JESSE JAMES, 73:86
Linderman, John:
  on rigging schooner WANDERBIRD, 55:56
LINDØ (schooner):
  chartering, 42:82
  cover photo/Robert Foley, 16:0
  maintenance schedule, photos, 42:92
Lindsay Disappearing Propeller Boat Co.,
  builder:
  history, 55:68
Lindsay, Ricki, author:
  "Craftsmanship in Sarasota," 66:56
Line, Lila, author:
  "JENNY NORMAN Comes Alive," 65:32
Linear polyurethane:
  application, maintenance, properties,
    repair, 78:21
  comments by Dick Clarke, 65:90
Linen, Gordon, author:
  "Opinion: How to Begin," 10:13
Lines:
  computer-generated/sea kayak QUEEN
    CHARLOTTE, 79:84
  reorienting lines plan/Steve Redmond,
    64:102
  taking/Lincolnville wherry/David
    Littleton-Taylor, 19:42
  understanding boat plans, 21:30
Linseed oil:
  as preservative, 76:36
  comments/Richard Jagels, 82:117
  comments/Walter J. Simmons, 81:75
  for wood-and-canvas canoe, 79:72

LION'S WHELP (power cruiser):
  comments, 53:38
  comments, photo, plans, 54:34
Lipke, Paul, author:
  "A Conversation with John Coates," 75:48
  "Legs for Boats," 70:52
  "On the Road to Quality," 34:32
  "The Self-Survey," 83:22
  letter on article "The Self Survey," 86:5
  on historic vessel reproduction, 96:64
LIRIS (40′ class):
  design commentary, photo, 49:66
Little, John D.:
  letter on caulking, 38:9
LITTLE BLACKFISH (dugout canoe):
  construction method, photos, 69:64
Littledyke, Ken, designer:
  plywood canoe RANDOM SCOOT, 31:50
LITTLE FLOWER (dragger):
  cover photo/Peter Prybot, 79:0
LITTLE HASTE (Massachusetts Bay 21):
  comments, photo, 72:44
LITTLE HOPE (cutter):
  comments, plans, 73:32
LITTLE JAMES (trawler-yacht):
  comments, plans, 54:34
LITTLE JOSIE (Acorn class):
  owner's comments, photo, plans, 30:46
LITTLE SEAL (motorsailer):
  design commentary, plans, 29:38
Littleton-Taylor, David, author:
  "Taking the Lines," 19:42
LITTLE VIGILANT (power cruiser):
  brief history, 54:34
LIVELY (extreme sharpie):
  comments, 84:64
LIVELY LADY (Vineyard Haven 15):
  comments, 47:68
Live oak (wood):
  for boatbuilding, 19:98
  logging technique/Sonny Lee, 46:80
  management, 46:76
Liverpool, England:
  comments by Peter H. Spectre, 66:35
LIVE YANKEE (R class):
  design commentary, photo, plan, 55:32
Livingston, Kimball, author:
  "West Coast Traditions," 13:79
LIZZIE ANNIE (Essex smack):
  comments, photo, 85:64
Ljungstrom rig:
  commentary by Iain Oughtred, 78:66
Lloyd's Register of American Yachting:
  comments, 100:70
Lloyd's Register of Shipping, author:
  "Electrical Installations in Wood Yachts,
    Part I," 2:24
  "Electrical Installations in Wood Yachts,
    Part II," 3:31
Lobsterboat:
  built by Arno Day, photos, 63:38
  built by Carroll Lowell, photos, 70:84
  designs/Philip C. Bolger, 77:101
  designs/Glen-L Marine, 38:120
  See also Bush Island boat, Cape Island boat,
    Grand Manan lobsterboat, Kingston lob-
    sterboat, Maine lobsterboat, Maine sloop-
    boat, MERGANSER, MRS. JONES
    (launch), Noank (Connecticut) lobster-
    boat, Novi boat, Plymouth lobsterboat
Lockers, cabin:
  construction methods, drawings/Aldren
    Watson, 76:89, 77:87

Lockwood, John, builder:
computer software/sea kayak QUEEN CHARLOTTE, 79:84

Locust (wood):
characteristics, 43:120
for boatbuilding, 9:31, 35:45

Lofting:
by projection/Paul Haist, 51:94
by projection, letters on, 52:10, 52:12
comments by Pete Culler, 4:4
comments by Arch Davis, 94:29
comments by Jack Ehrhorn, 12:43
comments by Sam Manning, 11:43
picking up for patterns/Richard Lagner, 31:66
picking up for patterns/Ed and Dave Minch, 35:95
picking up for patterns/Dave Porter, 31:64
reducing offsets for inside of plank/Ralph Morris, 52:69
technique for transom/Arno Day, 98:41
technique/Thomas MacNaughton, 23:53, 24:68
technique/Sam Manning, 12:44
technique/Bud McIntosh, 11:48
technique/James L. Meriam, 63:106
technique/Kenneth C. Mobert, 43:44
tools for, 11:48, 20:68, 31:66

Log canoe, Hawaiian koa:
construction commentary, history, photos, 59:80

Log canoe, Mexican dugout:
construction commentary, photos, 20:61

Logging operations:
sawmilling procedures, 51:106
technique/Doug Andersen, 51:106
technique/Jon Bielinski, 45:46
technique/Bob Darr, 37:98
technique/Bob Darr, letter on, 38:7
technique/Charles Page, equipment for, 9:36
technique/Charles Page, letter on, 11:4
See also Woodlot management

Loken, Marty, author:
"More Than Boats for Hire: An Interview with Dick Wagner," 24:36

Loken, Marty, author and photographer:
"MER-NA: Last of the Blanchard Dreamboats," 94:62

Loken, Marty, photographer:
"Getting the Feel of Caulking," 24:40
cover photo/outboard boat TROUT UNLIMITED, 64:0

Lone Gull (sloop):
comments, photo, plans, 91:78

LONE STAR (ketch):
designs/Jay E. Paris, Jr., 89:114

Long, Phil, builder:
sloop WHITEFIN, 57:80

Long, Roger, designer: (*See* Designs, Long, Roger)

Longboat, Pitcairn:
construction sequence, photos, plans, 13:22

Longleaf yellow pine:
using recycled timber, 93:134

Longsplice schooner (nesting dinghies):
designs/Charles Strayer, 99:116

Lord, Lindsay, designer:
comments, 48:38

LORRAINE (Folkboat):
comments, photo, 65:76

Loud, Francis, builder:
obituary, 87:27

LOUIS A. THEBAUD (fishing schooner):
comments, photo, 61:32

Lovric, Tony, builder:
comments, 43:104

Low, Andrew S.:
letter on marine insurance, 69:5

Lowe, Bill, builder:
sloop WHITEFIN, 57:80

Lowell, Carroll, builder:
profile, photo, 70:84

Lowell, Hiram, builder:
comments, 19:32, 36:83

Lowell, Pert:
construction method for mast hoops, 65:40

Lowell, Royal, author and illustrator:
"Planking the Maine Lobster Boat," 16:39

Lowell, Royal, builder:
Maine lobsterboat, 16:39

Lowell's Boatshop, builder:
comments, 19:32
dories, history, 18:71, 27:26
letter on, 19:11

Lowell, Simeon, builder:
comments, 36:78

Lowestoft College of Further Education (England):
letter by Rory Williams, 75:7

Lubec Boat (sloop):
lofting of, 12:44

Luberoff, Ben, author:
"How I Almost Used My Kayak as Firewood," 8:5

Lucander, Nils:
letter on design concepts, 43:4
letter on the Scheel keel, 67:6
letter on Third World boatbuilding, 43:4

Luders, A.E. (Bill), author:
"Laminating at Luders," 55:100

Luders, A.E. (Bill), designer:
comments, 55:68
letter on L.F. Herreshoff designs and MSO Class, 59:4

Luders Marine Construction Co., builder:
laminating techniques, 16:27, 55:100
sloop DYON, 64:40

Luders 16 class:
rebuilding, photos, plan, 55:102

Lug rig:
commentary by Iain Oughtred, 73:80
comments on, 71:44
See also Dipping lugsail, FANNY DUNKER (Class A Frostbite dinghy)

Lug rig, Chinese:
commentary by Iain Oughtred, 78:66

Luke, Paul, builder:
yawl TIGRIS, 53:109

Lumber: (*See* Wood, for boatbuilding)

Lumbert, Henry, builder:
Cape Cod catboats, 3:51

Lunenburg Foundry (NS):
profile, 94:64
technique for bronze propeller, 94:72

Lusa, Charles, builder (Tasmania):
Cadet dinghy, 52:100

Luxton, James, author:
"In a New Light: The Creation of LA FILLE D'OR," 67:82

Luzier, George, builder:
profile, photo, 66:56

Lydia Boat Yard, builder:
sportfishing boats, 76:44

Lyle, Rupert, author:
"Product Review: Plastic Fastenings," 99:110

Lyman, A.T., author:
"Inside the Insurance Business," 72:28
"The Huckins Yacht Corporation, Part II," 57:102

Lyman, Lois M.:
letter on Malcolm Brewer, 50:10

Lyman Boat Works, builder:
history, photos, 82:60
production methods, history, 82:68

LYRA (sloop):
designs/Tom Tucker, 10:65

LYRA II (sloop):
designs/Tom Tucker, 31:97

M

MAB (catboat):
comments, photo, 91:92

MacAdam, R. Bruce, author:
"ROYONO Gets Some New Planking," 1:4

Macalpine-Downie, J.R., designer (England):
Shark catamaran, 69:29

MacAodha, Risteard, author:
"The Galway Bay Púcan," 50:78

Macatawa Bay Boat Works, builder:
Grand Craft, 44:80

Macau-Coloane Shipbuilding and Ship Repair Co., builder (China):
comments, 44:104

MacDougall's Cape Cod Marine:
on boat covers, 54:92

MacDuff Boatbuilding & Engineering Co., builder (Scotland):
Scottish fishing boats, 62:68

MacGregor, Charles G., designer:
comments, 32:66, 84:106
See also Designs, MacGregor, Charles G.

MacGregor, John:
comments, 90:56
on canoe building, 60:140

MacGregor sailing canoe:
designs/Iain Oughtred, 84:106

Machin Knight & Sons Ltd., builder (England):
steam launches, 15:29

Mackaness, Tim:
on importing tropical woods, 69:35

MacKeeman, Karl, author:
"For Her Name's Sake," 21:50

MacKenzie, Tom, builder:
birchbark canoes, 36:36

Mackinac Island State Park Commission, photographer:
cover photo/armed sloop replica WELCOME, 10:0

Mackinaw boat:
designs/Nelson Zimmer, 23:90
history, photos, plans, 45:100

Mackinaw boat, EDITH JANE:
history, photos, plans, 45:100

Mackinaw boat, WABESI:
history, plans, 45:100

MacMillan, Donald B.:
owner of schooner BOWDOIN, 47:30

MacMillan, Donald B., author:
"Notes for Arctic Cruiser," 47:34

MacNaughton, Daniel, author:
"A Dynamic Tradition," 23:77
"Ask the Pros: Plywood," 24:100
"Ask the Pros: Questions and Answers," 18:94
"Battle Below the Waterline," 22:64
"Before You Set Sail," 27:74
"Built to Win: International 14 Class Boats," 20:84
"Cradles for Storage and Shipping," 18:51
"Healing the Break," 99:63
"Missing Links," 26:79
"Rolling and Tipping," 81:78
"Side by Side: The Lure of the Multihull," 23:63
"The Fine Art of Stripping Paint," 15:55
"The Light-Displacement Controversy," 61:42
"The Sharpie: Flat is Back," 25:36
"Tool Critic: Tools for Cruising," 17:78
"Topsides Never Lie," 21:79
"Where Do I Start?," 21:69
"Zahniser's: The Quality Comes with Experience," 42:75
letter on disc sanding, 95:4
letter on keelson and keel battens, 18:79
reviewer of *An L. Francis Herreshoff Reader* (book), 25:104
reviewer of Gordon Bok records, 19:90
reviewer of *The Cruising Cook* (book), 18:100
reviewer of *The Folding Schooner and Other Adventures in Boat Design* (book), 17:76

MacNaughton, Thomas, author:
"Designs: VOYAGER 30," 5:64
"Estimating Construction Costs," 7:36

MacNaughton, Thomas, author and illustrator:
"SIMPLICITY for the Amateur Builder, Part I," 23:53
"SIMPLICITY for the Amateur Builder, Part II," 24:68

MacNaughton, Thomas, designer:
sharpie, 25:36
See also Designs, MacNaughton, Tom

MacNeill, Robert F., designer: (*See* Designs, MacNeill, Robert F.)

Macramé:
comments, 18:19

MADCAP (Bristol Channel pilot cutter):
comments, photo, 85:64

MADGE (cutter):
comments, 43:64
comments, photos, 91:92
comments, plan, 41:26
racing against SHADOW, 44:24
racing history, 37:42

Madura: (*See* Indonesian janggolans)

Magerl, Caroline, illustrator:
"Quick and Dirty Repairs," 93:29
"Railboat," 95:34

Maggio, Joe, author:
"The Americanization of a Fuukien Junk," 16:35

MAGIC CARPET (sloop):
design and construction, photos, plans, 90:108

Mahogany:
comments, 10:35
decay resistance, types discussed, 49:124
identification of types, 55:120

Maiden, Meg Davis, author:
"Up to the Mark," 65:76

Maiden, Meg Davis, Paul Stubing, and Maynard Bray, authors:
"From Sail to Power: The Evolution of the Noank Lobsterboat," 69:42

MAID OF ENDOR (cutter):
designs/John Atkin, 22:89, 59:116

Maier, Spence F., author:
"A Non-Professional's Working Perspective," 7:52

MAINE (pinky schooner):
comments, photo, 32:66

Maine Cruise Schooner Fleet:
cruising on ADVENTURE, history, illustrated list, photos, 39:32

Maine cruise schooner, HERITAGE:
construction commentary, launching, photos, plans, 53:52

Maine cruise schooner, JANET MAY:
design and construction commentary, launching, photos, 63:74

Maine lobsterboat:
planking technique/Royal Lowell, 16:39

Maine Marine Vocational Center (ME):
boatbuilding program, 42:100
on maintenance, 46:66

Maine Maritime Museum (ME):
apprenticeshop program, 4:31, 42:100
boat types at, 29:102
comments, 31:18, 36:82, 44:117

Maine sardine carrier: (*See* Sardine carrier)

Maine sloop-boat:
design commentary, history, photos, plans, 2:15

Mainsails:
battened vs. battenless, 64:34
comments by Tom Clark 64:34
comments by Fritz Seyfarth, 64:34
letters on battenless mainsail, 66:7

Maintenance:
advice for fitting out, 93:36
advice for underwater seams, 74:17
advice from professionals, 46:66, 81:75
advice on painting for decoration, 93:42
advice on safety gear and procedures, 79:41
antifouling bottom paints, 67:30
boatyard hazards commentary, 79:34
caulking compounds/types and application techniques, 92:23
copper sheathing of ISKRA, 67:35
copper sheathing of GAZELA PHILADELPHIA, 74:19
editorial by Jon Wilson, 65:2
fiberglass vs. wood/survey of yard managers, 100:38
for iron fastenings/Robert Gardner, 29:77
for recreational shell, 63:63
for tropical conditions, 83:48
layup procedures/Maynard Bray, 54:88
layup procedures/Daniel MacNaughton, 18:94
layup procedures/Hilda Marvin, 13:30

layup procedures/Riverside Boatyard, 48:91
layup procedures/Jon Wilson, 12:59
layup procedures afloat/Maynard Bray, 30:54
letters on wood blocks, 53:7
of batteries/Nigel Calder, 99:41
of batteries/Jerry Kirschenbaum, 34:72, 35:69
of batteries/Lloyd's Register of Shipping, 3:31
of decks, 77:60
of decks/Giffy Full, 27:40
of decks/Donald Street, 25:89
of diesel engines/George Cadwalader, 54:106
of gasoline engines/Fritz Seyfarth, 54:101
of mast from bosun's chair, 42:27
of seams/Maynard Bray, 57:112
of teak decks/Jim Emmett, 11:70
of tools/Dustin Leavitt, 37:40
of wooden blocks/Phil and Gerry Troy, 50:67
of wooden blocks/letter on, 53:6
paint adhesion on wood, 98:113
prevention of decay/letter on, 43:9
prevention of drying out/Maynard Bray, 54:88
prevention of drying out/Daniel MacNaughton, 18:94
prevention of drying out/Ed McClave/letter on, 55:6
prevention of leaks/Maynard Bray, 57:112
prevention of leaks/letter on, 58:7
prevention of mildew from boat interiors, 100:128
prevention of surface checking/Richard Jagels, 50:116
procedures for early launching/Anne and Maynard Bray, 63:87, 64:58
procedures for maritime museums/Maynard Bray, 38:40
procedures for protecting paint and varnish, 99:66
procedures/Francis Birra/Baltic trader LINDØ, 42:92
procedures/Paul Bryant, 40:56, 48:91
procedures/Giffy Full, 27:40
procedures/Wayne Mocksfield/speedboats, 41:72
procedures/Lin and Larry Pardey/cutter SERAFFYN, 11:36, 18:65
safety checks/Daniel MacNaughton, 27:74
schedule for wooden boats, 75:30
swelling up dried-out hulls/Maynard Bray, 57:112
swelling up dried-out hulls/letter on, 58:7
using judgment/Daniel MacNaughton, 21:69
See also Arabol (adhesive), Engines, Paintbrush, Paintbrush spinner, Painting techniques, Sanding, Scraper, Scribing (marking) waterlines, Seacocks, Seam compounds, Stripping paint, Stripping varnish, Varnishing

Main-trysail ketch: (*See* DIABLESSE)

Mair, Robin, designer:
comments, 59:40

Mair 30 (sloop):
designs/Rafel Marine, 63:116

Mait, Edey, author:
"Designs: DAKINI, One Man's 'Shorey,'" 92:96

Makassar ketch:
construction comments, photo, 14:66
MAKO (motorsailer):
design commentary, plan, 29:38
Malabar Jr. (sloop and yawl):
comments by Waldo Howland, plan, 32:66
designs/John G. Alden, 41:128
Malabar Jr., IMAGINE:
repair commentary, photos, 65:56
Malabar schooners:
Bermuda race history, comments by Waldo
Howland, 32:66
MALABAR I (schooner):
comments, plans, 32:66
MALABAR II (schooner):
comments, photo, 38:71, 65:76
comments, plans, 32:66
designs/John G. Alden, 41:127
MALABAR III (schooner):
comments, plans, 32:66
MALABAR VI (schooner):
comments, plans, 32:66
MALABAR VII (schooner):
comments, plans, 32:66
MALABAR X (schooner):
comments, plan, 32:66
MALIBU (motoryacht);
comments, photo, 94:54
Malibu Outrigger class:
design commentary, photos, plan, 33:86
Malloff, Will, author:
"Chainsaw Lumbermaking: Natural
Knees," 50:38
Mallon, Tom, builder (Ireland):
púcan, 50:78
Mallory, Clifford D.:
comments, 100:70
Malmquist, Lea, author:
"Calling a Cruiser Home," 25:24
Malone, Mark, author:
"VORTEX," 100:84
MANATEE (power launch):
comments, photo, 55:32
Mancebo, Dave, designer:
comments, 44:90
MANDALAY (sloop):
comments, plans, 75:34
Mangrove (wood):
characteristics, 51:121
Manning, Sam F., author:
"Lofting the Lubec Boat," 12:44
"The ALVIN CLARK Revisited," 52:66
"The Rabbet," 14:42
cover photo/Tom Stewart, 99:0
letter on bevels, 15:12
letter on caulking, 17:6
letter on lead pouring, 80:6
Manning, Sam F., author and illustrator:
"Bevels," 13:50
"Building a Classic Yacht Boarding
Ladder," 84:91
"Building the Cardboard Dory," 90:63
"Caulking," 16:47
"How to Scull a Boat," 100:60
"Scrapers," 90:113
"Singlehanded Boatbuilding," 99:94
"Some Thoughts on Lofting," 11:43
"Sticks and String," 22:33
Manning, Sam F., illustrator:
"A Close Look at Wood Screws,
Part I," 54:47
"A Close Look at Wood Screws,
Part II," 55:43

"A New Cabin Top," 20:52
"A Simple Wooden Plane," 69:70
"A Smooth and Fair Hull," 55:107
"ALVIN CLARK: An Unfinished Voyage,"
52:52
"ALVIN CLARK: The Challenge of the
Challenge," 52:59
"An Introduction to Refastening," 12:30
"Bending SPARTAN's Frames," 58:107
"Building a Skylight: Fine Joinerwork with
Duffy Dodge," 92:28
"Building the House," 42:53
"Casting Lead Keels," 89:52
"Ceilings," 47:69
"Centerboards and Trunks," 78:41
"Fairing," 94:29
"Final Fairing," 94:35
"Fitting the Deck Framing," 41:91
"Floor Timbers," 44:43
"Hatches and Other Deck Joinery," 67:91
"How Firm a Foundation?", 36:53
"Making Your Boat Tight Again," 57:112
"Ordering Lumber," 87:46
"PASSIONELLA: A Ten-Dollar Skiff,"
20:44
"Patternmaking for Custom Hardware,"
39:58
"Plywood Lapstrake Construction," 43:44
"Skill of Hand: The Planking Process,
Part I," 18:38
"Skill of Hand: The Planking Process,
Part II," 19:50
"Spars," 60:125
"Stopwaters," 56:116
"The Anatomy of a Wooden Boat," 60:115
"The Backbone, Part I," 33:66
"The Backbone, Part II," 34:66
"The Backbone, Part III," 35:56
"The Backbone, Part IV," 37:89
"The Backbone, Part V," 38:95
"The Case for Simple Edge-Gluing," 59:93
"The Making of Molds," 13:53
"The New York Thirties: The Restoration
of Number 14," 35:30
"To Fit a Bulkhead," 43:61
"To Lay a Deck," 46:103
"VARIN the Lestabåt," 95:90
Manning, Sam F. and Susan, authors:
reviewers of *Knots* (book), 97:98
reviewers of *Knowing the Ropes* (book),
97:98
reviewers of *Seagoing Knots* (book), 97:98
Man-overboard drill:
aboard Tancook whaler VERNON
LANGILLE, 58:82
maneuvers of Roger Taylor, 45:62
Manson, Arthur, builder:
construction methods, power cruisers, 9:56
Manson Boat Works, builder:
construction methods, power cruisers, 9:56
MANXMAN (yawl):
comments, photo, 74:42
Maple:
for constructing a canoe paddle, 67:44
March, John P., author:
reviewer of *The Hidden Canyon: A River
Journey* (book), 23:101
Marchaj, C.J. (Tony):
comments, 92:76
Marconi rig:
commentary by Iain Oughtred, 77:44
comments by Colin Palmer, 92:76

Marco Polo (schooner):
design commentary, photo, 56:38
Marcus, Daniel, designer: (*See* Designs,
Marcus, Daniel)
MARIKA (power skiff):
comments, photo, plans, 88:76
MARILEE (New York 40):
comments, photo, 33:50
Marine archaeology: (*See* Archaeology,
nautical)
Marine Design, Inc., designer:
designs/36′ sloop, 65:104
Marine insurance: (*See* Insurance, marine)
Marine photography:
interview with Stanley Rosenfeld, 90:46
Mariners' Museum (VA):
boat types at, 29:102
comments, 63:8
Crabtree model collection, 63:80
Rosenfeld photo collection, 90:46
Marinette Marine Corporation, builder:
MCM-class ships, 58:90
MARIQUITA (40′ class):
history, photo, 49:66
Marisol (sailing dinghy):
design and construction commentary,
photos, plans, 12:54
Maritime art:
commentary by Llewellyn Howland III,
86:21
profile on William Gilkerson, 89:64
Maritime history:
editorial by Peter H. Spectre, 84:2
letter by Benjamin W. Labaree, 87:7
See also Yachting history
Maritime preservation:
commentary by Peter H. Spectre, 38:36,
41:36, 44:62, 72:60, 77:21, 96:64, 96:72
editorial by Jon Wilson, 86:2
historic ships, 72:60, 61:88
letter by Peter J. Brennan, 97:6
letter by Capt. A.F. Reynaud, 91:4
letter by Peter Stanford, 97:4
letters on, 44:7, 47:9, 48:5, 53:9
letters on Project Lakewell (MI), 51:7, 54:5
maintenance for museum ships, projects
discussed, 38:36, 61:88
museum objectives/small craft, 6:34, 8:30
See also ALVIN CLARK (schooner), BOW-
DOIN (schooner), CHARLES W. MOR-
GAN (whaleship), GAZELA PRIMEIRO
(barkentine), Historic vessel reproduc-
tion, L.A. DUNTON (schooner)
Maritime preservation, philosophy of:
Badham, Michael, 41:36
Berryman, Eric, 41:36
Bray, Maynard, 38:40
Carr, J. Revell, 41:36
Dring, Harry, 61:88
Durham, Bill, 41:36
Exeter Maritime Museum (England), 46:54
Gardner, John, 6:34
Goddard, David, 46:54
Greenhill, Basil, 46:54
Hull, David, 44:70
Kortum, Karl, 61:88
Lee, Lance, 34:48, 38:48
Manning, Sam, 52:66
National Maritime Museum at San
Francisco (CA), 61:88
National Maritime Museum (England),
46:54
National Park Service, 61:88

National Trust for Historic Preservation, 62:13
Neill, Peter, 62:13
Penn's Landing Corp., 44:62
Philadelphia Maritime Museum (PA), 44:62
Sail Gazela, Inc., 44:62
Sands, John O., 8:30
Spectre, Peter H., 38:36, 41:36, 44:62, 72:60, 96:64, 96:72
Stanford, Norma, 41:36
Stanford, Peter, 38:45
Throckmorton, Peter, 41:36
Walker, Matthew, 41:36
Wilson, Jon, 38:2

Marking gauge:
for making eight-sided oars, plan, 71:28
Mark II sharpening system:
critique, 21:94
MARLIN (commuter):
comments, photo, 94:74
MARLIN (power cruiser):
comments, photo, 52:40
Marlinespike seamanship: (*See* Cordage, techniques for)
MARNA (Wianno Senior class):
comments, photo, 91:58
Marples, John, author:
"Backyard Vacuum Bagging," 44:99
"Designs: A Folding Multihull Mini-Cruiser," 49:112
Marples, John, designer:
comments, 92:34
kit boats SIB 32 (trimaran) and TULIP (sailing pram), 39:69
skiff GULL, 64:83, 65:97
See also Designs, Marples, John R.
Marples, John, photographer:
"Bagging the GULL, Part I," 64:83
"Bagging the GULL, Part II," 65:97
Marples, John, Jim Brown, and Dick Newick, authors:
"Bagging the GULL, Part I," 64:83
"Bagging the GULL, Part II," 65:97
Marsh, Nim, photographer:
"The Lincolnville Wherry," 2:44
Marshall, Aubrey, builder:
dories, 18:71
Marshall, Roger, author:
"Ask the Pros: Buoyancy," 14:81
"The Most Notable of All Distinctions," 22:42
Marshall, Roger, designer: (*See* Designs, Marshall, Roger)
Marsland, John E., author:
"ACTIVE to England," 7:20
"Mast Making: The Hollow Spar," 15:60
"The Ship's Wheel: A New Turn," 14:70
Marstal Trækskibsværftet Anchor Seiner:
comments, plans, 88:40
MARTHA (sloop):
compiling lumber list, photo, plans, 87:46
designs/Samuel S. Crocker, 62:100
MARTHA JANE (sharpie):
designs/Philip C. Bolger, 80:102
Martha's Tender (skiff):
how to build, photos, plans, 45:92, 46:94, 47:58
Martha's Vineyard:
profile on builders Gannon and Benjamin, 95:70
Martin, Arthur, designer:
profile, 47:40

Martin, David P., designer:
power cruiser BLACK MAGIC, 30:96
See also Designs, Martin, David P.
Martin, Douglas, author:
"MOCKINGULL: A Wing in the Water, A Wing in the Wind," 48:50
Martin, Douglas, designer:
on sculling techniques, 100:60
pulling boat MOCKINGULL, 48:50
Martin, J. Rodger, author:
"In My View: Sharpie Points and Counterpoints," 59:36
Martini, Jerry, photographer:
"The Kodiak Kayak," 58:68
Martino, Horace, builder (Grenada):
comments, 50:106
Martin, Paul Ray, builder:
Caddo Lake bateau, 62:44
Martin, Tyrone G., author:
"Aboard 'Old Ironsides,'" 83:32
Martsolf, John:
letter about sailing canoe YAKABOO, 82:5
Marvin, Hilda, author:
"Winter Layup: Doing It Now," 13:30
letter on varnishing techniques, 18:7
MARY (dragger):
comments, 79:48
MARY ALICE (motorsailer):
comments, plan, 28:20
MARY AND ELLEN (pungy schooner):
comments, plans, 45:56
MARY ANN (Barnegat Bay A-cat):
history, photo, 62:60
MARY ANNE (sardine carrier):
comments, 59:70
MARY B (iceboat):
comments, photo, 39:88
MARY CELESTE (brigantine):
history, painting, 6:60
MARY DAY (schooner):
comments, photo, 39:32, 88:60
cover photo/Bill Fisher, 39:0
cover photo/Sherry Streeter, 60:0
MARY DE COSTA (fishing schooner):
comments, photos, 87:56
MARY FOSTER (Biloxi schooner):
comments, photo, 37:80
Maryland crabbing skiff:
comments, plan, 69:100
MARY LORING (sloop):
comments, photo, plan, 75:34
MARY MARGARET (Biloxi schooner):
history, 37:80
MARY ROSE (schooner):
comments, photo, 84:34
MASHNEE (Buzzards Bay 30):
comments, photo, 43:91, 65:76
Mason, Al, designer:
comments, 97:76
Mason, Mark:
profile, 60:84
Masone, Steve, author:
"Coppering GAZELA," 74:19
Massachusetts Bay 21 class, CHEWINK III:
comments, photo, 72:44
Massachusetts Bay 21 class, EAGLET:
comments, photo, plan, 72:44
Massachusetts Bay 21 class, GREAT HASTE:
comments, photo, 72:44
Massachusetts Bay 21 class, LITTLE HASTE:
comments, photo, 72:44
Mast: (*See* Spars)

Mast collar:
comments, detail photo, 70:82
comments, photo, 47:74
Masterman, Nick:
comments, 90:102
Master Mariner's Regatta, 1976:
comments, photos, 13:79
Masthead knot:
how to tie, 21:16
Masthead rig:
commentary by Iain Oughtred, 77:44
Mast hoops:
construction method/Pert Lowell, scantlings, photos, 65:40
Maststep:
framing technique/Aldren Watson, 82:75
in Biscayne Bay 14 daysailer, 97:31
Mathewson, Duncan, nautical archaeologist:
ATOCHA project, 68:56
MATILDA D (felucca replica):
builder, photo, 42:30
construction commentary, drawings, history, 13:43
drawings, performance, plans, 14:45
MATTHEW J. BOYLE (fireboat):
comments, photo, 53:38
Mathew Walker Knot:
how to tie, 52:112
Matthews, Scott J., builder:
power cruisers, 31:92
profile, 38:114
Matthews Boat Owners Association:
comments, 31:92
Matthews 38 (power cruiser):
history, photos, plan, 38:114
Matthews 42 DCFB (power cruiser):
history, photos, plans, 31:92
MATTIE (schooner):
comments, photo, 39:32
Mauric, André, designer (France):
comments, 39:44
Maxi racer, CHRISTINE:
construction commentary, history, photos, 56:86
Maxwell Cutter:
designs/Kaufman and Ladd, 21:84
May, Curtis, author:
"The Decay of Wood in Boats," 2:36
MAYA (ketch):
cruising aboard, 9:16
design commentary, photo, 16:66
MAYFLOWER (fishing schooner):
comments, plan, 74:42
MAYFLOWER II (colonial ship replica):
comments, 67:38
comments, photo, 96:64
Mayher, Bill, author:
"The Lobsterboats of Grand Manan," 45:82
Maynard, Mary R., author:
"Sailing Together Around the World," 21:58
See also Drake, Mary Maynard, author
McAlear, Robin, author:
"Grand Craft," 44:80
McAllister, Iain, author:
"The Fifes of Fairlie," 90:84
McCaffery, Lloyd, modelmaker:
letter on ship models, 100:6
profile, photo, 73:52
McCaffery, Lloyd, photographer:
"Modelmaker Lloyd McCaffery," 73:52

McCaffrey, Frank, builder:
　sailing dinghy Tender Ten, 22:77
McCarthy, Henry ("Mac"), author:
　"Strip-Building a Double-Paddle Canoe,"
　　100:92
McCarthy, Leo:
　letter on Excalibur Leisure Skills Center,
　　62:7
McCarthy, Lucy, builder:
　profile, photo, 79:22
McClain, John:
　letter on nautical archaeology, 72:5
McClave, Ed, author/builder:
　"A Close Look at Wood Screws, Part I,"
　　54:47
　"A Close Look at Wood Screws, Part II,"
　　55:43
　"An Unpressured Approach to Steaming,"
　　88:50
　"Bending Rangeley Stems at Mystic
　　Seaport," 33:74
　"Bending SPARTAN's Frames," 58:107
　"Bent Frames: Why They Break, and How
　　to Fix Them," 68:87
　"Butt... The Butt-Block Chronicle
　　Continues," 67:23
　"Corrosion-Related Problems," 93:94
　"In My View: To Bond or Not to Bond,"
　　65:114
　"Painting for Longevity," 93:70
　"Plank Curvature," 100:31
　"Stopwaters," 56:116
　"Ways That Work: Canvasing Decks," 75:89
　"Ways That Work: Proper Poppets," 78:93
　"Ways That Work: Shellac, The Neglected
　　Helper," 76:18
　"Ways That Work: That's Right, Roofing
　　Tar," 74:17
　comments on, 71:44
　letter on galvanized fastenings, 56:8
　letter on laminated frames for repair, 60:5
　letter on prevention of drying out of
　　wooden hull, 55:6
McClave, Ed, delineator:
　Rangeley Lake boat, 39:26
McClennen, Douglas, author:
　"The Art of Finding Your Way," 59:102
McClure, Darrell, illustrator:
　"A Different Kind of Love," 19:48
　"Marine Insurance: Objectivity vs.
　　Subjectivity," 36:29
　"Other Ways: Delivering Small Boats,"
　　44:117
　"Why Aren't Heads Called Tails?", 46:49
　obituary by Jon Wilson, 76:2
McCutcheon, C.T. (Ted), Jr., author:
　"ALVIN CLARK: An Unfinished Voyage,"
　　52:52
McCutcheon, C.T. (Ted), Jr., delineator:
　schooner ALVIN CLARK, 52:52
McCutcheon, C.T. (Ted), Sr., builder:
　armed sloop replica WELCOME, 10:60
McEvoy, Michael:
　comments, 90:56
McGann, Peter D.:
　letter on Australian Cadet dinghy, 55:9
McGowan, Gordon, photographer:
　"Producing a Bronze Propeller at the
　　Lunenburg Foundry," 94:72
　"The Marine Industries of Lunenburg,
　　Nova Scotia," 94:64
McGrail, Sean:
　on historic vessel reproduction, 96:64

McGuane, Thomas, author:
　"A Bird for Thin Water," 38:58
McGuire, Paul, author:
　"The Rangeley Tradition," 39:26
McInnis, Alan, author:
　"The Bassboat," 12:68
McInnis, Walter J., designer:
　bateau, 51:66
　New England draggers, 79:48
　profile, 52:40, 53:38, 54:34
　Richardson Cruisabouts, 28:92, 29:101
　schooner PILGRIM, 8:12
　See also Eldredge-McInnis, Inc., designer
McInnis bateau (rowing craft):
　how to build, photos, 51:66
McIntosh, David C. (Bud), author/builder:
　"A Simple Wooden Plane," 69:70
　"A Smooth and Fair Hull," 55:107
　"Building the House," 42:53
　"Ceilings," 47:69
　"Centerboards and Trunks," 78:41
　"Fitting the Deck Framing," 41:91
　"Floor Timbers," 44:43
　"Hatches and Other Deck Joinery," 67:91
　"How Firm a Foundation," 36:53
　"On Laying Down and Taking Off," 11:48
　"Ribbands and Timbering Out," 15:74
　"Set Work: A Show of Force," 85:99
　"Skill of Hand: The Planking Process,
　　Part I," 18:38
　"Skill of Hand: The Planking Process,
　　Part II," 19:50
　"Spars," 60:125
　"The Backbone, Part I," 33:66
　"The Backbone, Part II," 34:66
　"The Backbone, Part III," 35:56
　"The Backbone, Part IV," 37:89
　"The Backbone, Part V," 38:95
　"The Making of Molds," 13:53
　"To Fit a Bulkhead," 43:61
　"To Lay a Deck," 46:103
　"To Stop a Leak," 84:44
　advice to boatbuilders, on boatbuilding
　　books, on design, profile, 51:40
　comments, 43:61, 48:126
　letters on, 52:7, 52:8
　reviewer of *Building the Blackfish* (book),
　　89:110
　technique for cutting a knee, 44:86
McIntosh, David C. (Bud), designer:
　APPLEDORE I, II, and III, 76:36
　ketch DOVEKIE, 5:55, 7:31
McIntosh, Ned, builder:
　comments, 48:126
McIntosh's Stone Crusher:
　for bending frames, 15:74
McKee, Eric:
　comments, 57:2
　on origins of strip planking, 57:55
McKee, Jack, author:
　"Oarlocks on Your Own," 73:21
McKenzie River drift boat:
　construction commentary, history, photos,
　　52:80
　letter on, 53:8
McKie, Robin A.:
　letter on surveying, 61:8
M class, ISTALENA:
　comments, photo, 55:32
M class, PRESTIGE:
　comments, photo, 74:42
McLaughlin, Mike, author:
　"Reviving MAKE WAY," 89:43

McManus, Thomas F., designer:
　fishing schooners, 56:102
　New England draggers, 79:48
　schooner L.A. DUNTON, 6:44
MCM class (mine countermeasure ships):
　construction commentary, painting,
　　photos, plan, 58:90
　letter by Robert C. Baldwin, 83:8
　letter by R.H. Fred, 61:9
　letter by John Leather, 81:9
McMenemy, Michael, and Debbie Pointer,
　authors:
　"R.O. Davis," 97:76
　"The Three Davis-Nevins Motorsailers,"
　　97:86
McMillan, Bruce, author and photographer:
　"EMME," 35:41
McNaughton, Samuel, builder:
　sardine carriers, 58:52
McNeil, Charles R., author:
　"Unemployed—But Happy," 6:6
McNeil, Charles R., and Michael Alford,
　authors:
　"Sailing the Carolina Sharpie IDIE," 13:68
McQueen, George, builder (British
　Columbia):
　Monk-designed power cruiser, 12:66
McVey, A.G., designer:
　40' class, 49:66
McVicker, Lynn, illustrator:
　"Murray G. Peterson," 1:29
Mead, Ted, builder:
　Mead Skeeter iceboat, 39:88
MEADOWLARK (power cruiser):
　living aboard/owner's comments, 25:24
Meadow Lark (sharpie ketch):
　cruise in Florida, design commentary,
　　drawing, 38:58
　design commentary, photo, 56:38
Mecray, John:
　letter on Tom Benson, 79:8
Mecray, John, illustrator:
　"Lest We Forget," 39:76
Mediterranean molding:
　commentary, history, photos, 66:84
MEDRIC (sardine carrier):
　comments, 59:70
Mefferd, Boyd:
　letter on *BUC Used Boat Price Guide*, 79:7
Melaleuca (wood):
　comments by Richard Jagels, 91:118
　decay resistance, 54:120
　letter by Tim and Pauline Carr, 88:10
Mele, Andre, author/designer/builder:
　"A RIVERKEEPER for the Hudson," 61:72
MELE KAI (sloop):
　construction commentary, photos, plans,
　　63:106, 64:92
MELISANDE (steam launch):
　comments, photo, 98:66
MELITA (Tahiti ketch):
　comments, photo, 99:48
Mellemværftet Shipyard:
　history, photos, 84:58
Mellor, John, author:
　"They Never Stopped Working: British
　　Sail," 17:63
Melrose, Robert G.:
　letter on Antique and Classic Boat Society,
　　63:4
Mench, Ahoi, builder:
　letter on scrapers, 18:6
　profile, 55:88

Mendlowitz, Benjamin:
letter on Roger Taylor, 42:7
Mendlowitz, Benjamin, author and photographer:
"Confidence," 22:74
Mendlowitz, Benjamin, photographer:
"A Conversation with Dick Clarke," 65:90
"A Lineage of Craftsmanship," 78:30
"A Matter of Family Tradition," 57:72
"ACE Speedboat," 45:77
"ANNIE," 41:78
"Alfred Bain and the UNITY B," 81:34
"Bienvenue à Douarnenez 88," 85:64
"Building Martha's Tender, Part I," 45:92
"Building Martha's Tender, Part II," 46:94
"Building Martha's Tender, Part III," 47:58
"Building the Beetle Cats, Part I," 51:99
"Building the Beetle Cats, Part II," 52:107
"Building the Beetle Cats, Part III," 53:101
"Class Without Flash," 95:60
"Concours D'Élégance...and Hang the Expense," 62:74
"Cutting an Apple Knee," 44:86
"Damaged Planks: Their Repair and Replacement," 53:109
"Eddie Crosby's Last Boat," 34:82
"Fitting Out: A Guide to Getting Her Ready Again," 93:36
"Gathering the Finest," 43:91
"Harvesting Hackmatack Knees: A Conversation with Frank Morse," 30:66
"Interior Arrangements," 93:52
"Keeping Up With LINDØ," 42:92
"Looking Good Again: A Refinishing Story," 40:56
"Maintenance With Meaning: An Interview with Giffy Full," 27:40
"Onboard a Davis-Designed Motorsailer," 97:80
"Other Ways: Liberated Caulking," 37:86
"PAULINE: A Working Sardine Carrier," 59:74
"Pete Culler's Workshop, Part I," 27:81
"Pete Culler's Workshop, Part II," 28:83
"Planking the MORGAN," 36:98
"Quick and...er...Dirty Boatbuilding," 49:89
"Restoration of 12½-Footers, Part I," 56:93
"Restoration of 12½-Footers, Part II," 57:93
"The Finishing Touch," 46:66
"The Foundry in Use," 73:24
"The Great Ones Gather," 38:71
"The Reliable One-Lunger," 30:59
"The Whitehall Backbone," 45:108
"The Wizard of Speed," 58:100
"Vic Carpenter, Part II," 46:82
"Ways and Means at Riverside Boatyard," 48:91
"Whitehall to Windward," 24:58
"Wooden Yachts Earning Their Keep," 42:82
cover photo/Bahamian smack UNITY B, 81:0
cover photo/Bar Harbor 31´-class DESPERATE LARK, 84:0
cover photo/Beetle Cats, 30:0
cover photo/caulking the deck, CHARLES W. MORGAN, 36:0
cover photo/classic speedboats, 65:0
cover photo/Delaware ducker JOSEF W, 35:0
cover photo/express cruiser THUNDERBIRD, 62:0
cover photo/Fries jacht HILTJE, 85:0

cover photo/ketch HORIZON, 66:0
cover photo/maintaining the Baltic Trader LINDØ, 42:0
cover photo/motorsailer BURMA, 97:0
cover photo/Nereia ketch GALATEA, 56:0
cover photo/rowing wherry Bangor Packet, 52:0
cover photo/schooner EAGLE, 40:0
cover photo/Shew & Burnham Whitehall, 45:0
cover photo/sloop MICKY FINN, 51:0
cover photo/sportfishing boat TINTINA-JO, 76:0
cover photo/Stulen faering, 43:0
cover photo/Wianno Senior One-Design, 91:0
cover photo/schooner EAGLE, 40:0
cover photo/yawl ANNIE, 41:0
MERCANTILE (schooner):
comments, photo, 39:32
MERCEDES U.S.A. (autoboat):
comments, plan, 73:32
Mercury class:
comments, photo, 50:31
MERGANSER (duckboat):
designs/Daniel Marcus, 65:108
MERGANSER (lobsterboat):
comments, plan, 70:84
Meriam, James L., author and builder:
"The Careful Creation of MELE KAI, Part I," 63:106
"The Careful Creation of MELE KAI, Part II," 64:92
'MERICAN MOR (Galway hooker):
construction commentary, history, photos, 50:74
MERIDIAN (yawl):
comments, plans, 75:34
Merkel, Jeanne St. Andre, author:
"LADY JEANNE," 37:72
letter on power cruiser LADY JEANNE, 40:5
MERLIN (power cruiser):
comments, photo, 60:96
MERLIN (schooner):
comments, photo, 71:52
Merlin Rocket class:
comments, photo, 74:64
construction commentary, photos, 58:100
MERMAID (ketch):
comments, photo, 95:55
MER-NA (Blanchard 36 Standardized Cruiser):
comments, detail photo, 69:104
comments, photos, 94:62
comments, plans, 94:54
MEROE OF KENT (ketch):
comments, photo, 91:50
Merrill, Keith:
profile, photo, 94:64
MERRY MONARCH (cruise ship):
comments, 12:9
Merseyside Maritime Museum (England):
comments, 46:54, 63:8, 66:35
Mesdag, Rob Von, author:
"Voga Is Again in Vogue," 40:54
Mesquite (wood):
characteristics, 43:120
Mexico, watercraft: (See Dugout canoe, Mexican)
Meyer, Douglas:
letter on Caribbean boatbuilding, 52:6

Michaud, Jacqueline, author:
reviewer of *Junks and Sampans of the Yangtze* (book), 16:69
reviewer of *My Waterfront*, and *The Oxford Companion to Ships and the Sea*, 22:100
Mickleburgh, Timothy, author:
"Jack Holt, A Brilliant Career in Dinghies," 74:64
"VARUA: Soul of the Southern Sea," 65:44
MICKY FINN (sloop):
comments, photo, 51:40
cover photo/Benjamin Mendlowitz, 51:0
MICRO (cat-yawl):
comments, illustration, 86:76
Micron 22 (bottom paint):
critique, 46:66
Micronesia, watercraft: (See Paopao canoe)
Mildew:
commentary by Richard Jagels, 100:128
Miles, Jan:
profile, photo, 96:58
Millar, Gordon H., author:
"Unleaded Gas: For Antique and Classic Marine Engines," 91:70
Miller, Jas., & Sons, builder (Scotland):
Scottish fishing boats, 62:68
Miller, Malcolm, builder (New Zealand):
cutter PASTIME, 40:68
Miller, Richard T.:
letter on rig design, 94:4
Millie Hill (houseboat):
comments, plans, 85:52
Mills, Clark, designer/builder:
profile, 36:73
Windmill class, 26:88
Milne, Peter, designer (England):
Fireball class, 22:83
Milwaukee power screwdriver:
critique, 22:96
MINAS PRINCE (fishing schooner):
comments, photos, 87:56
letter by Stanley T. Spicer, 88:11
Minch, Ed and Dave, authors:
"Other Ways: Picking Up Through Plastic," 35:95
Mine countermeasure ship, MCM class:
construction commentary, photos, plan, 58:90
letter by Robert C. Baldwin, 83:8
letter by R.H. Fred, 61:9
letter by John Leather, 81:9
letter on construction, 59:4
MINERVA (40´ class):
comments, 41:26
comments, photo, 90:84
history, photo, 49:66
Minett, Albert, builder (Ontario):
comments, 45:50
Minett, H.C., builder (Ontario):
comments, 50:52
MING HAI (Chinese junk):
owner's comments, photo, 16:35
Mirror class:
comments, photo, plans, 74:64
history, photos, 3:49, 23:88
Mishler, Neal, photographer:
cover photo/DN-class iceboat, 86:0
MISS ABU (power cruiser):
comments, photo, plan, 5:67
MISS ALEXIE (speedboat):
comments, photo, 62:74
MISS COLUMBIA (speedboat):
brief history, 60:84

MISS LINDWOOD (Chesapeake Bay log canoe):
construction commentary, photos, 6:26
MISS RUTH (runabout):
comments, photo, 80:24
Miss Simplette (sharpie):
designs/Daniel J. Bombigher, 74:96
letter by Daniel J. Bombigher, 76:6
MISS STROHS (hydroplane):
comments, drawing, photo, 80:24
MIST (cat-ketch):
comments, photo, 60:96
designs/William Garden, 35:98
MISTRESS (schooner):
comments, photo, 39:32
MITENA (power cruiser):
comments, plan, 75:34
MITENA (12-Meter):
comments, photo, 68:40
design commentary, 56:38
design commentary, photo, 55:32
MIZPAH (cutter):
drawings, salvaging of, 60:120
Mobert, Kenneth C.:
letter on, 45:11
Mobert, Kenneth C., author:
"In My View: The Dream Business," 74:25
"Plywood Lapstrake Construction," 43:44
Mobjack-type design: (*See* GIPSY JAC [ketch])
MOCCASIN (yawl):
design commentary, photos, plans, rig, 18:20
MOCKINGULL (lapstrake pulling boat):
cover photo, 48:0
design and construction commentary, photos, 48:50
Mocksfield, Wayne, builder:
runabout restoration, 41:72
Model building:
advice from Jay Hanna, 66:29
Bolger Cartopper/construction model, how to build, 85:36, 86:29
cardboard dory/Sam Manning, 90:63
critique of model kits/Jay Hanna, 85:109
critique of sandbagger model/Steve Redmond, 63:112
half model by the lift method/George I. (Sonny) Hodgdon, Jr., 33:41
how to build AMERICA's half model/Eric Dow, 54:67
letter by Lloyd McCaffery, 100:6
letter on small-scale models by Bill Durham, 99:4
models in National Watercraft Collection, 77:21
profile of August Crabtree, 63:80
profile of Robert H. Eddy, Jr., and Jay S. Hanna, 97:52
profile of Rolly Kalayjian/photos, ketch WHITE WINGS II, 88:70
profile of Lloyd McCaffery, 73:52
Ratty's Boat (Thames skiff)/Lois Darling, 94:44
Modrell, Bill, author and builder:
"Ask the Pros: Butt Blocks," 15:7
"Ask the Pros: Deck Finish," 21:90
"Ask the Pros: Exhaust Systems and Cockpit Scuppers," 14:81
"Ask the Pros: Mooring Boats," 13:85
"Ask the Pros: Planking and Floor Timber Repair," 16:70
"Ask the Pros: Scarfing Planks," 15:7

"Ask the Pros: Transom Repair," 20:100
Moen's Boatshop, builder (Norway):
comments, 28:36
Moffat, Tom, author:
"Friendship Charter," 11:65
MOHAWK (schooner):
comments, 37:42, 43:64
Mohr, Merilyn, author:
"The Bear Mountain Canoes," 31:58
Molds:
comments on Herreshoff construction method, 100:70
compiling lumber list/20' sloop/Joel White, 87:46
for Biscayne Bay 14 daysailer/plywood construction, 96:24, 98:28
for casting lead keels, 89:52
for double-sawn frames/schooner SPIRIT OF MASSACHUSETTS, 82:48
for laminating frames, 97:44
for Mediterranean molding, 66:84
for sailing canoe PICCOLO/Bob Baker, 36:44
for strip-planked Constant Camber/skiff GULL, 64:83
for Wee Lassie double-paddle canoe, 100:92
from lofting, 24:68, 31:64, 31:66
shown in illustrated glossary, 60:115
technique/Bud McIntosh, 13:53
See also Frame templates, Shadow molds
Molds, setting up:
Acorn skiff/Iain Oughtred, 56:60
Catspaw dinghy/Joel White, 26:48
Gloucester Light Dory/Harold Payson, 41:63
Nutshell pram/Joel White, 60:100
sailing canoe PICCOLO/Bob Baker, 36:44
technique/Bud McIntosh, 15:74, 35:56
Yankee Tender skiff/Joel White, 30:74
Moliceiros (Portuguese workboats):
construction, history, photos, plans, 95:48
MOLLYHAWK (schooner):
comments, 91:50
Molly's Cove Boatworks, builder:
cold-molded hull repair, 60:76
Monahan, Michael, photographer:
cover photo/Gemini-class sloops, 12:0
Monfort, Platt, designer/builder:
comments, 90:56
profile, photo, 76:72
Monk, Edwin, Sr., designer:
association with George McQueen, 12:66
comments, photo, 94:54
obituary, 10:71
profile, 10:70
Monkey Fist knot:
how to tie, 26:20
Monomoy surfboat:
construction commentary/carvel planked vs. cold-molded, photos, 44:90
Monomoy surfboat, CARL M. LARKIN:
comments, drawing, 77:34
Mons, Jackie, builder (Ireland):
lapstrake dinghy, 50:88
Monson, Alex, author:
"The Perfect Material," 12:24
MONTAUK II (Indian class, Atwater):
construction commentary, photos, plans, 21:21
Monterey clipper (power fishing boat):
history, photos, 18:28

Monterey Marine, builder:
sportfishing boats, 76:44
Montgomery, David, builder:
yawl PETREL, 75:70
Montgomery, Larry, author:
"An Open and Shut Case for Seacocks," 71:69
"Dubbin' the Latigo," 68:64
"Engine Systems Checkup," 69:22
"Heavy Metal," 82:27
"Lessons from Prince William Sound," 90:145
"The Shipwright's Toolbox," 79:29
letter on transmission coupling, 71:5
Moodie, David, author:
"FRI: Taking Care of a Ship—and the World," 87:36
"Fire Bending," 44:104
Moody, Glenn, photographer:
"Just the Right Medium," 54:82
"Three Friends," 54:74
Moody & Son, builder: (*See* A.H. Moody & Son)
MOONBEAM (motorsailer):
comments, plan, 28:20
MOONGLOW II (yawl):
comments, photo, 50:31
Moore, C. Philip, author:
"Forest E. Johnson," 86:44
"The Commuters," 94:74
Moore, Denton R.:
on ketch PROSPECTOR, 45:9
Moore, Wyatt A., builder:
methods for Caddo Lake bateau, 62:44
Moores, Ted, builder (Ontario):
profile, 31:58
Moran, E.D., designer:
comments, 4:25
MORAY ENDEAVOUR (Scottish fishing vessel):
comments, photos, 62:68
Morch, Erik, author:
"Building the BRUCE," 20:87
Morgan, Bill, builder:
profile, photo, 71:82
Morgan, E.D.:
comments, 100:70
MORNING CLOUD (sloop):
comments, photo, 6:20
MORNING STAR (Galway hooker):
comments, photo, 50:74, 85:64
Morocco:
boatbuilding in, 43:76
Morris, Ev:
comments on New York 32 class, 73:42
Morris, Ralph, author and illustrator:
"Lofting by Numbers," 52:69
Morrison, John:
comments on trireme, photo, 75:44
Morrison, Len, designer (Australia):
International Moth class, 37:104
Morrison, Philip, designer (England):
Merlin Rocket class, 58:100
Morrow, Ralph, builder:
Adirondack guideboat, 59:64
Morse, Charles A., builder:
Malabar schooners, 32:66
schooner MALABAR II, 41:127
Morse, Frank:
on harvesting knees, 30:66
Morse, Wilbur A., builder:
Maine sloop-boats, 2:15
sloop PRINCESS, 4:14

Mosquitia Indians (Honduras):
WoodenBoat School project, 88:76
WoodenBoat School project, boat designs, 88:82

Moss, Michael, author:
"L.A. DUNTON: A Brief Encounter," 6:44

Moss, Robert, author:
"Spidsgatters," 78:50

Moth class:
history, photos, plan, 37:104

Motonautico launch (Italy):
construction commentary, photos, 52:86

Motorsailer: (*See* ANTARES, ANZAC, AT LAST, BEN ALLEN, BLUEBILL, BLUE-FISH, BLUE JACKET, BUCKAROO, BURMA, ENDEAVOUR, FLYING CLOUD, FLYING FIFTY, GOOSANDER, GOS-SOON, HALAIA, HOCI, IMELDA, LIBRA, LITTLE SEAL, MAKO, MARY ALICE, MOONBEAM, NOR'EASTER, ONZA, PASSAGEMAKER, PETER DUCK, SEAL, SEA TAR, SEER, Stonington motorsailer, TAMARACK, VIAJERO, VIGILANT, VOYAGEUR, WATER WITCH)

Motorsailer, William Hand designs:
design commentary, photos, plans, 28:20, 29:38

Motorwell, outboard:
construction/outboard runabout DOWN-EASTER 18, 75:53

MOUETTE (12-Meter):
comments, photo, 68:40

Mount Desert Yacht Yard, builder:
Controversy series, 61:42

Moving boats:
advice from lift operators, 80:85
cartop/recreational shell KINGFISHER, 63:63
comments/Jon Wilson, 12:59
cradle design for storing and shipping boats, 18:51
cradle technique/Paul Bryant, 48:91
cradle technique/Bill Modrell, 13:85
jacking up the hull/Bud McIntosh, 37:89
plank and roller, cradle and trailer techniques, 69:86
techniques for small craft, 34:86
transporting for delivery, 44:117
See also Turning over boats

Mower, Charles D., author:
"How to Build SEA BIRD," 43:38

Mower, Charles D., designer:
Barnegat Bay A-cats, 62:60
sloop WHITE WINGS, 23:50
yawl SEA BIRD, 43:26

MOXIE (trimaran):
comments, photo, 91:38

MP7 (metal conditioner):
use of on fastenings, 29:77

MRS. JONES (launch):
owner's comments, repair comments, photos, 68:80

MSO class (minesweeper):
letter on construction, 59:4

Mt. Gay Cup Race:
comments, 2:8

Mudgett, Bernie:
on finish work, 46:66

Mudie, Colin, designer (England): (*See* Designs, Mudie, Colin)

Muirhead, Ross, author:
reviewer of *The Stripper's Guide to Canoe-Building* (book), 42:114

Mulberry (wood):
characteristics, 43:120

Multihulls:
commentary by James W. Brown, photos, 69:76, 91:38, 92:34
designs by Chris White, 54:56
letter on French-designed multihulls, 92:4
See also Catamaran, Pacific proa, Trimaran

Mulville, Frank, author:
"ISKRA Sails Down East," 53:90
"Resheathing a Copper Bottom," 67:35

Mulville, Frank, author and photographer:
"Singlehanding an Old Gaffer," 40:72

Munder, Emil, builder:
scow schooners, 3:8

Munroe, Commodore Ralph M., designer:
sharpie EGRET, 56:2, 56:76, 71:94
sharpies, 25:36

Munson, Perry:
letter on portable venting system, 81:5

MURIEL (cutter):
comments, plan, 41:26

Murphy, Billy:
profile, photo, 94:64

Murphy, David, author:
"The Restoration of the Trading Ketch DEFENDER," 92:62

Murray, Darien, author:
"A Taste of the Twenties," 22:57

Murray, Timothy F., author:
"CORONET: Whither Away?", 32:20

Murray G. Peterson & Assoc., designer: (*See* Peterson, Murray G.)

Museum of Yachting (RI):
Classic Yacht Regatta/comments, photos, 65:76
comments, 39:76

Museums, maritime:
guide to England, 46:54
guide to United States, 29:102
maritime highlights, 1984, 59:32
news from International Congress of Maritime Museums, 63:8
See also Center for Wooden Boats (WA), Kendall Whaling Museum (MA), Kitimat Centennial Museum (British Columbia), Mariners' Museum (VA), Merseyside Maritime Museum (England), Mystic Seaport Museum (CT), National Maritime Museum at San Francisco (CA), National Maritime Museum (England), Norsk Sjofartsmuseum (Norway), Smithsonian Institution (DC), South Street Seaport Museum (NY), Viking Ship Museum (Denmark), Windermere Steamboat Museum (England)

MUSTANG (New York 32):
comments, photo, 73:42

Muttersbach, Les, builder:
sloop SKIDOO, 51:80, 51:83, 51:85

MVI (lobsterboat, sloop):
comments, photo, 69:42

MYA (schooner):
comments, photo, 38:71

Mygaard, Gerry:
letter on Dudley Davidson, 40:5

Mylar, use:
patterns for canoe yawl LA MOUETTE, 75:62
stem pattern for outboard runabout Downeaster 18, 73:67

MYRA (sailing punt):
designs/Johan Selmer-Larsen, 71:105

MYRTLE LEAF (schooner):
comments, photo, 6:60

Mystic Seaport Museum (CT):
association with John Gardner, 40:30, 90:36
boat types at, 29:102
boatbuilding program, 42:100
BOWDOIN project, 47:30
comments, 10:9, 29:50, 33:74, 39:26, 43:72, 46:66, 47:30, 48:78, 48:86, 63:8
comments, preservation project, 38:36
restoration of schooner L.A. DUNTON, 6:44
restoring (planking) the CHARLES W. MORGAN, 36:96
Rosenfeld photo collection, 90:46
Small Craft Workshop, 1975, 5:24

MYTH OF MALHAM (sloop):
comments, photo, plan, 24:24

Nabb, Michael:
on historic vessel reproduction, 96:64

Naddy, Bill, photographer:
cover photo/schooner ACTIVE, 7:0

NAHEMA (schooner):
comments, photo, 66:84

NAJA 30 (sloop):
kitboat, photo, 38:84

NANCY (21' class):
history, photo, plans, 8:62

Nancy's China (sloop):
comments, plans, 85:52

Nansen, Fridtjof:
comments, 85:44

NARAINA (ketch):
charter, 42:82

Narrowboat (English canal boat):
design and construction commentary, drawings, history, plans, 41:98

NATHANIEL BOWDITCH (schooner):
comments, 39:32
comments, photos, 9:10

National Maritime Museum (England):
comments, 63:8
comments, interview with director Basil Greenhill, 46:54

National Maritime Museum at San Francisco (CA):
association with Harry Dring, 61:88
boat types at, 29:102
comments, 3:8, 13:43, 72:60
letter by Glennie Wall, 73:6
maritime preservation philosophy, 61:88
preservation project, 38:36

National Park Service:
association with Harry Dring, 61:88
comments, 72:60

National Park Service (*continued*)
  letter by Peter H. Spectre, 90:4
  letter by Glennie Wall, 73:6
  maritime preservation policy, 61:88
National Trust for Historic Preservation:
  BOWDOIN grant, 47:30
  history, 38:36
  maritime projects, 62:13
  on ALVIN CLARK, 52:59
National 12 class:
  history, 58:100
National Watercraft Collection (DC):
  commentary by Peter H. Spectre, 77:21
  letter by Robert C. Post, 79:5
  letters on, 78:5
Nation, John, author:
  "The Building of a Tancook Whaler,
    Part I," 5:44
  "The Building of a Tancook Whaler,
    Part II," 7:56
Nation, John, builder:
  Tancook whaler ELLEN IVY, 5:44, 7:56
NATIVE GIRL (schooner):
  comments, photo, 20:82
Nautical archaeology: (*See* Archaeology,
  nautical)
NAUTI MIRAGE (converted lifeboat):
  owner's comments, photos, 21:49
Nautiraid (folding kayak):
  comments, 53:80
NAVAHOE (cutter):
  comments, photo, 91:92
Naval craft: (*See* MCM class [mine countermeasure ships], USS CONSTITUTION
  [frigate])
NAVETTE (commuter):
  comments, photo, 94:74
Navigation:
  by sounding pole, 15:40
  comments/David Kasanof, 18:18, 34:18,
    42:12
  comments/Douglas McClennen, 59:102
  comments/Roger Taylor, 41:42
  letter on electronic aids, 60:10
  loss of schooner TYEHEE, 83:74, 83:86,
    83:88
  loss of schooner TYEHEE, letters on, 84:5
Navigational tools: (*See* Dividers, Parallel
  rules)
NAWALILKHIL (African dhow):
  a passage on, 46:88
N class, PONTIAC:
  comments, photo, 73:32
NEFERTITI (12-Meter):
  comments, photo, 65:76
Neill, Peter, author:
  "In My View: A Past in Search of a Future,"
    62:13
  letter on South Street Seaport Museum,
    90:4
NEITH (sloop):
  comments, 63:116
  comments, photo, 43:94
  interior arrangement, photos, plan, 93:52
NELLIE (Itchen cutter):
  comments, photo, 14:22
NELLIE (sailing dinghy):
  construction commentary, photos, plans,
    1:20
NELLYROSE (Bequia sloop):
  owner's comments, photo, 68:29
Nelson, Barry C., author:
  "The Self-Apprenticing Alternative," 43:56

NEPSI (New York 30):
  comments, photo, 35:27
Neptune 47 (power cruiser):
  comments, photo, 57:102
Nereia ketch, GALATEA:
  cover photo/Benjamin Mendlowitz, 56:0
Nerney, Dan, photographer:
  "Interior Arrangements," 93:52
Nesting dinghies: (*See* Chameleon dinghy,
  Longsplice schooner, J.P. Downes
  Memorial Bifurcating Dinghy)
Netherlands, watercraft: (*See* Dutch boeier,
  PHOENIX; Vlet [Dutch pram])
Netting, fish:
  how to make, 27:18
Nettlewood:
  for boatbuilding, 47:123
Nevins, Henry B., Inc., builder: (*See* Henry
  B. Nevins, Inc.)
Newbert and Wallace, builder:
  New England draggers, 79:48
  sardine carrier PAULINE, 59:74
  schooner JOHN F. LEAVITT, 31:18
New England draggers:
  origins and development, photos, 79:48
New England smack:
  comments, plan, 58:116
Newfoundland trap skiff:
  design commentary, origins of, photos,
    plans, 26:76
  origins of, 26:79
New Haven sharpie:
  design commentary, 25:36, 56:76
New Haven sharpie, LESTER ROWE:
  comments, photos, 2:32
  construction and performance commen-
    tary, photos, 3:24
  construction commentary, photos,
    plans, 1:8
Newick, Dick, author:
  "Designs: STRIDER: A 24′ Catamaran,"
    73:106
Newick, Dick, designer:
  comments, 83:58, 91:38
  comments, photo, 92:34
  kit boat SIB 32, 39:69
  multihulls, 54:56
  trimaran ROGUE WAVE, 23:68
**Newick, Dick, Jim Brown, and John Marples,
  authors:**
  "Bagging the GULL, Part I," 64:83
  "Bagging the GULL, Part II", 65:97
Newport boats:
  design commentary, 43:64
Newport 29, DOLPHIN:
  comments, photo, 43:92
Newport (RI) Wooden Boat Show, 1981:
  commentary, photos, 43:84
NEWQUAY (pilot gig):
  comments, photo, 25:28
New York 30 class:
  history, 35:25
  history, list of boats, 35:32
  history, photos, plans, 35:20
New York 30 class, ADELAIDE II:
  history, 35:20
New York 30 class, AMORITA:
  history, 35:20
New York 30 class, AQUILA:
  comments, photo, 43:91
New York 30 class, BANZAI:
  comments, photo, 35:20

New York 30 class, CARA MIA:
  construction details, photo, rebuilding
    comments and illustrations, 35:30
  history, 35:20
New York 30 class, COCKATOO II:
  comments, 35:20
  letter on, 37:7
  performance, 35:27
New York 30 class, HUNTRESS:
  history, 35:20
  letter on, 38:10
New York 30 class, IBIS:
  history, 35:20
New York 30 class, LIGHTNING:
  history, 35:20
  photos, rebuilding commentary/illus-
    trations, 35:30
New York 30 class, NEPSI:
  photo, 35:27
New York 30 class, OLD TIMER:
  history, 35:20
New York 30 class, PHRYNE:
  history, photo, 35:25
New York 32 class:
  design and construction comments, his-
    tory, photo, plans, 73:42
New York 32 class, APACHE:
  history, 73:42
New York 32 class, FALCON:
  letter by Mike Sloan, 74:7
New York 32 class, MUSTANG:
  comments, photo, 73:42
New York 32 class, SAPPHIRE:
  history, 73:42
New York 40 class:
  comments, photos, 33:50
New York 50 class, SPARTAN:
  comments, photos, 38:71
  photos, reframing, 58:107
New Zealand, builder: (*See* Orams Marine
  Ltd.)
New Zealand, designer: (*See* Jackson,
  Gifford)
New Zealand, watercraft: (*See* PASTIME
  [cutter])
New Zealand, wood:
  comments by Richard Jagels, 97:104
Neyman, R. Mark, author:
  "Three Men and a Boat," 66:23
NIAGARA (brig):
  comments, painting, 78:76
  letter by Eric Blumensaadt, 98:4
Ni-Cad batteries:
  comments, 82:100, 99:41
Nicholson, Charles, designer (England):
  12-Meter-class boats, 68:40
Nicholson, L.E., author:
  "An Introduction to Refastening," 12:30
  "Gathering the Finest: The Classic Yacht
    Regatta," 43:91
  letter on refastening, 14:9
Nicholson, L.E., author and photographer:
  "Lest We Forget," 39:76
  "TLC at East Bay Boat Works," 22:77
  "The Tradition of Burnside St.," 23:25
Nicholson, Nick, author:
  "Shpountz: A French Designer's Vision,"
    71:74
Nicholson, Peggy C., author:
  "Gathering the Finest: The Herreshoff
    Rendezvous," 43:94
Nickerson, John, builder:
  sportfishing boats, 76:44

Nicolson, Ian, author:
"Nicolson's Notes," 3:49, 5:67, 6:66, 7:35,
8:57
"Scottish Fishing Boat Conversions," 4:50
Niederer, Cliff, builder:
Friendship sloop, 8:53
Nielsen, K. Aage, designer:
schooner TYEHEE, 83:74
yawl TIGRIS, 53:109
NIGHTFALL (cutter):
cruising account, photo, 91:89
NIGHT RUNNER (cutter):
comments, photo, 77:34
cover photo/Neil Rabinowitz, 77:0
design and construction commentary,
drawing, photos, plan, 77:40
NIGHTWIND (12-Meter):
cover photo, 68:0
Nilson, Russell:
owner of brigantine VARUA, 65:44
NIMBLE (Nimble 30):
design and construction, photos, plans,
84:21
letter by Ted Jones, 86:7
Nimphius, Ferdinand (Red), builder:
comments, 19:18
letter on use of epoxy, 27:6
profile, 25:42
NIÑA (schooner):
comments, photo, plan, 74:42
Nine-Meter, TANGO II:
cold-molded hull repair, photo, 60:76
19-Meter class:
letter by David Ryder-Turner, 83:5
NINGUI (cutter):
comments, photo, 4:66
NIRVANA (cutter):
comments, photo, 65:76
NIRVANA (yawl):
comments, photo, 38:71, 43:92, 65:76
NISMIME (research vessel):
design commentary, plans, 30:20
Nite iceboat:
comments, 39:88
Nixon, W.M., author:
"Meetings with Mature Ladies," 70:17
Nixon, W.M., author and photographer:
"The Time Warp of a Gaff Cutter," 61:80
Noank (Connecticut)-built boats:
letter by William N. Peterson, 71:7
of builder Jack Wilbur, history, photos,
69:48
Noank (Connecticut) lobsterboats:
evolution, photos, 69:42
wet-well construction commentary with
drawings, 69:42
Noank sloop, SIM SEK:
comments, photos, 69:48
Noank sloop, STAR III:
comments, photo, 69:48
Noble, Alex, & Sons, builder (Scotland):
Scottish fishing boats, 62:68
Noble, Earl, builder:
comments, 5:33
NOBLE 41 (sloop):
designs/Robert Perry, 5:33
Nock, F.S., builder:
association with Walter McInnis, 52:40
NO GO 8 (sloop):
comments, photo, 63:56
design and construction commentary,
photos, 17:48

NOKOMIS (sardine carrier):
comments, photo, 58:52
No Man's Land boat, ORCA:
comments, photo, 5:24
Nordfjord faering:
comments, photo, plans, 28:36
Nordland boat:
history, plan, 28:39
NORDSØ (trawler-yacht):
construction commentary, photo, plans,
74:74
NOR'EASTER (motorsailer):
comments, photo, plans, 28:20
comments, plan, 97:76
Norfolk School of Boatbuilding (VA):
boatbuilding program, 42:100
Norgrove, Ross, author:
"Shovels & Pails: An Antipodal
Instructional Recalled," 60:120
Normand, Robert R., photographer:
"Paddling Like an Ancient," 55:79
NORNOUR (pilot gig):
comments, photo, 25:28
Norsk Sjofartsmuseum (Norway):
comments, 84:58
North Carolina Maritime Museum (NC):
boat types at, 29:102
boatbuilding program, 42:100
comments, 6:6, 13:68
comments, plans source, 13:5
**North Country Community College (NY),
builder:**
Adirondack guideboat, 59:64
North End Shipyard, builder:
comments, 39:32
schooner HERITAGE, 53:52
NORTHERN LIGHT (fishing schooner):
comments, photo, 87:56
Northern white pine: (See Pine, Northern
white)
North Haven dinghy:
history, photos, plans, 38:111
Northius, Steve, builder:
Grand Craft, 44:80
Northrup, Bruce, author:
"In My View: I'm an Artist, Dammit!," 63:11
Northrup, Bruce, designer: (See Designs,
Northrup, Bruce)
North Shore dory:
builder, photo, plans, 36:82
NORTH STAR (schooner):
comments, photo, 49:53
NORTH STAR (sloop):
drawings, repair commentary, 26:24
NORTHWEST (iceboat):
comments, photo, 38:64
**Northwest School of Wooden Boatbuilding
(WA):**
boatbuilding program, 42:100
boatbuilding program/critique by Ray
Speck, teaching methods of Bob
Prothero, 62:82
Norton, Joe, builder:
builder profile, 86:52
Norton, Tom, designer:
comments, 84:21
Norton Boat Works, builder:
DN iceboat kit boat, 38:84
profile, photos, 86:52

Norwalk Island sharpie:
designs/Bruce Kirby, 74:96
Norway, builders: (See Bjørkedal, Sigur;
Brenne, Harald P.; Drange, Ole;
Gregersen's Boatshop; Hansen, Verner;
Mellemværftet Shipyard; Moen's Boatshop;
Oma, Sigurd; Sovik, Alfred)
Norway, designer: (See Archer, Colin)
Norway, boatbuilding school: (See Saltdal
Videregående Skole)
Norway, maritime museum: (See Norsk
Sjofartsmuseum)
Norway, watercraft: (See Bjørkedal boats;
Faering; FRAM [Norwegian polar explo-
ration ship]; Norwegian sailing freighters;
PAULINA [jekt]; Pram, Norwegian;
RAKEL [skøyte]; RANA [Nordlands boat];
SAGA SIGLAR [Viking Age merchant ship
replica]; Seksaering; VARIN [Norwegian
Lestabåt])
Norwegian sailing freighters:
restoration comments, photos, 73:96
NOSTALGIA (speedboat):
comments, photo, 62:74
Nova Scotia, Lunenburg:
marine industries of, 94:64
Novi boat:
design and construction commentary,
photos, 45:88
letter on, 47:5
NOW VOYAGER (power cruiser):
charter, 42:82
Nugent, John, builder:
repair to schooner BOWDOIN, 47:30
Nunes, Antonio, builder:
profile, 50:31
Nunes, Ernie, designer:
profile, 50:31
Nunes, Manuel, designer:
profile, 50:31
**Nunes Brothers Boat and Ways Company,
builder:**
Bear class, 50:34
history, 50:31
Nunes Jet (runabout):
comments, 50:31
Nutshell pram:
how to build, photos, plans, 60:100
offset corrections, 64:26
NYALA (12-Meter):
comments, photo, 68:40
Nyce, Tom, builder (British Columbia):
construction method for dugout canoes,
69:64
Nylon sailcloth:
commentary by Robin Lincoln, 93:60
NYMPH (40' class):
history, photos, plans, 48:58
NYSSA (cutter):
comments, plans, 37:42

Oak:
decay resistance, 2:36
species for boatbuilding, 9:31
Oak, live:
for boatbuilding, 19:98
logging technique/Sonny Lee, 46:80
management, 46:76
review of *Live Oaking: Southern Timber for Tall Ships* (book), 48:117
Oak, red:
decay resistance and identification, 1:48
decay resistance, strength properties, 65:112
for mast hoops, 65:40
identification of, 64:108
Oak, white:
characteristics, 35:45
decay resistance and identification, 1:48
decay resistance, strength properties, 65:112
identification of, 64:108
Oarlock for sculling:
comments, detail photo, 76:70
Oars:
building technique/E.A. Ayling & Sons Ltd., 23:47
built by Water Power Products, 94:64
design commentary/Douglas Martin, 48:50
design commentary/Roger Taylor, 42:38
for Norwegian lestabåt, 95:90
for recreational shell KINGFISHER, 63:63
for sculling/commentary by Sam Manning, 100:60
how to build, photo, plans/Pete Culler design, 71:28
Obituaries:
Baker, Robert H. (Bob), 55:2
Baker, William Avery, 44:78
Bemis, Alan, 99:2
Chapelle, Howard I., 5:1
Crosby, Eddie, 34:82
Culler, R.D. (Pete), 23:2
Gamage, Harvey, 13:38
Johnson, Capt. Irving, 99:2
Lavin, Mark, 74:4
Loud, Francis, 87:27
McClure, Darrell, 76:2
Monk, Edwin, 10:70
Rosencrantz, Donald C., 44:78
Sloan, Bob, 70:2
Stone, Lester, 9:10
O-Boat class:
advice on painting for decoration, 93:42
designs/John G. Alden, 32:102, 42:126
O'Brien, Frank, illustrator:
"A Classic in Plywood, Part I," 41:63

O'Brien, Mike, author:
"Boat Plans Catalogs, Part I," 89:112
"Boat Plans Catalogs, Part II," 93:118
"Boat Plans Catalogs, Part III," 96:98
"Designs: CALICO JACK," 79:106
"Designs: Iota and Gray Seal," 94:110
"Designs: Nesting Dinghies," 99:116
"Designs: Outboard Cruisers," 82:108
"Designs: Schooner and Flashboat," 86:94
"Designs: Simple Daysailers, Chesapeake Fashion," 88:114
"Designs: Touring Kayaks," 97:108
"Designs: Two Outboard-Powered Garveys," 91:96
"Designs: Wee Rob and MacGregor," 84:106
"Designs: WENDA and MARTHA JANE," 80:102
"Double-Paddle Canoes," 90:56
"Flat-Bottomed Skiffs," 87:90
"Phil Bolger Cartopper," 85:38
"Product Review: DuraKore," 79:93
"Russell Brown and His Proven Proas," 83:58
comments on centerboard trunks, 80:85
reviewer of *Small Craft Plans* (book), 98:97
OCEAN BIRD (cutter):
comments, photo, 20:82
OCEAN SURFER (trimaran):
comments, photo, 92:34
OCEANUS (sloop):
designs/William Garden, 81:106
O'Ciobhain, Tomas, builder (Ireland):
curraghs, 50:80
Odell, Jim, builder:
comments, 44:117
profile, 27:26
Odell, Malcolm, builder:
letter on Lowell's Boat Shop, 19:11
OF COURSE (speedboat):
comments, photo, 62:74
Offshore raceboat: (*See* JESSE JAMES)
Oil-type finish:
removal technique/Rebecca Wittman, 81:88
Oker, Jay, author:
"Pocket Cruisers From the Past: East Coast," 75:70
Oker, Jim, photographer:
cover photo/yawl PETREL, 75:0
Okie, William T., Jr., author:
"The New York Thirties: Restoration of Number 14," 35:30
Okoume (wood):
comments, 10:35
Old Boathouse, The: (*See* Center for Wooden Boats [WA])
Old Time Barnegat Bay Decoy & Gunning Show (NJ):
comments, 68:25
OLD TIMER (New York 30):
history, 35:20
Old Town Canoe Company, builder:
comments, 38:84
Old Town Stripper:
kit boat, 38:84
Oliver, Bet, author:
"LILY—A Boat Lover's Dream," 53:86
OLLIE (Friendship sloop):
comments, photo, 29:61
Olmsted, Nick:
letter on Alaska yellow cedar, 78:6

Olofsson, Richard, author:
"Opinions: Is Symmetry a Lost Word?", 6:71
Olsen, David and Ray:
profile, photo, 69:54
Olsen, Stephen, author:
"A Shortcut to Castings," 46:52
Olsen, Terje, photographer:
"Building a Norwegian Pram," 49:28
Olson, Stephen:
letter on electrical systems, 95:7
Olympic contender:
ANGELITA, Eight-Meter sloop, 59:40
Olympic games:
boats for, 13:34
kayaks and canoes, 82:44
Oma, Sigurd, builder (Norway):
comments, 28:43
ONAWA (12-Meter):
comments, photo, 68:40
ONDINE (ketch):
comments, 20:58
O'Neil, Timothy F., author:
"The Return of an Olympic Eight-Meter," 59:40
O'Neill, Brian:
comments on, 72:60
Onion River Boatworks, builder:
recreational pulling boats, 54:82
See also Bassett, Ken, builder
Ontario, builders: (*See* Bear Mountain Canoe Co.; Botting, Sam; Carpenter, Vic and Hazel; Disappearing Propeller Boat Co.; Greavette Boat Co.; Greavette, Tom; Johnston, W.J., Jr.; Minett, Albert; Minett, H.C.; Moores, Ted; Port Carling Boat Works Ltd.; Superior Boats)
ONZA (motorsailer):
comments, plans, 54:34
Opera House Cup Race, 1980:
comments, 38:75
photos and results, 38:71
Opheim, Ed, builder:
dories and skiffs, 43:40
Opheim dories and skiffs:
design and construction commentary, photos, 43:40
Optimist pram:
comments, 26:88
design comments, 36:73
Orams Marine Ltd., builder (New Zealand):
Bounty ketch LA FILLE D'OR, 67:82
ORCA (No Man's Land boat):
comments, photo, 5:24
ORESTES (Q class):
comments, 73:32
ORIANDA (schooner):
comments, photo, 65:76
ORIOLE (30-Square-Meter):
comments, photo, 55:32
ORIVA (cutter):
comments, photo, plan, 41:26
ORLO III (Sea Sled):
comments, photo, 100:46
Orr, George D., Jr., author:
"Other Ways: Stretching Canoe Canvas," 35:94
Osage orange (wood):
characteristics, 43:120
letter on, 42:9
Osea Brig (sloop):
comments, photo, 70:74

Oselver boats:
construction commentary, 28:42
history, plans, 28:39
OSHA (Occupational Safety and Health Administration):
boatyard hazards, regulations, 93:86
Osmun, Mark, author:
"The Koa Canoe," 59:80
OSTAR: (*See* C-STAR [Singlehanded Transatlantic Race])
Ostkust cruising sloop:
detail photo, comments, 76:60
OTTER (bateau):
comments, photo, 55:88
Oughtred, Iain, author and illustrator:
"Exotic Rigs, " 78:66
"Sprit Rigs," 76:80
"The Bermudian Rig," 77:44
"The Gaff Rig," 75:80
"The Gunter Rig," 74:100
"Variations on the Lugsail," 73:80
letter on junk rig, 65:4
Oughtred, Iain, designer (England):
Acorn skiff, 56:60
letter on Cadet dinghy, 57:7
profile, photo, 70:74
See also Designs, Oughtred, Iain
Oughtred, Iain, photographer:
"A Plywood Lapstrake Classic," 56:60
OUR TERN (power cruiser):
owner's comments, photo, plan, 11:40
Outboard boat:
design commentary/David P. Martin, 30:96
designs/David D. Beach, 23:93
designs/Eric Dow, 21:86
Outboard boat, Cackler:
comments, photos, plans, 85:52
designs/Sam Devlin, 91:96
Outboard boat, Camp skiff:
designs/Howard I. Chapelle, 82:108
Outboard boat, Downeaster 18:
construction methods, photos, plans, 73:67, 74:87, 75:53
design commentary/Charles Wittholz, 73:77
Outboard boat, lapstrake skiff:
construction comments, photos, 91:34
Outboard boat, Lyman Boat Works:
history, photos, 82:60
production methods, 82:68
Outboard boat, MRS. JONES:
owner's comments, repair comments, photos, 68:80
Outboard boat, RIVERKEEPER:
cover photo/Robert Knowles, 61:0
design and construction comments, operation, photos, plans, 61:72
Outboard boat, Stauter Boat Works:
cover photo/Morry Edwards, 72:0
design and construction commentary, photos, 72:90
Outboard boat, TROUT UNLIMITED:
cover photo/Marty Loken, 64:0
design and construction commentary, photos, 64:70
Outboard boat, TRUMPET:
designs/Weston Farmer, 82:108
Outboard boat, WATERMAN:
designs/Howard I. Chapelle, 82:108
Outboard motorwell:
construction method/outboard runabout Downeaster 18, 75:53

Outboard racing speedboats:
commentary by Peter H. Spectre, 80:32
OUTLOOK (scow sloop):
comments, photo, 72:44
comments, plan, 37:42
Outrigger canoe:
construction commentary, history, photos, 59:80
Outrigger canoe, Micronesian:
design and construction commentary, performance, photos, 31:42
Outriggers:
installation in recreational shell KINGFISHER, 63:63
Outward Bound (school):
history, comments, 71:44
OUTWARD LEG (multihull):
letter on, 55:5
Owen, George, designer:
comments, 10:30
cutter FALCON, 60:76, 61:104
Owen, Greg, author:
"Timber, Sail and Oar," 28:36
Owen, James G.:
letter on Chart Kit, 86:5
Owens cutter, FALCON:
cold-molded hull overlay/Bent Jespersen, 61:104
cold-molded hull repair, photos, 60:76
OWL (Wianno Senior class):
comments, photos, 91:58
cover photo/Benjamin Mendlowitz, 91:0
OX (steam tug):
comments, plans, 73:32
Oyster dredger, BOADICEA (England):
history, performance, photos, plan, 36:20
Oyster dredger, SIGSBEE:
photos, racing, 3:34
Oyster dredger, STANLEY NORMAN:
photos, rebuilding commentary, 35:62
Oysterman 22 (cutter):
designs/Paul Gartside, 36:92
Oyster tonger, New Haven sharpie:
comments, plans, 25:36

Pacemaker, TOMKAT III (power cruiser):
transom repair, 16:20
Pacemaker Day Boat (power cruiser):
history, photo, plan, 23:96
PACIFICA (yawl):
comments, photo, 65:76
Pacific Coast class, ROBIN:
comments, photo, 65:76
Pacific proa:
comments, photos, plans, sailing technique, 83:58
Pacific proa, CIMBA:

comments, photos, plans, 83:58
Pacific proa, JZERO:
comments, photos, 83:58
Pacific proa, KAURI:
comments, photos, 83:58
PACIFIC TRADER (cutter):
leatherwork on, 68:64
Packard, Alpheus, designer:
Winter Harbor 21 class, 93:76
comments about, 72:44
Packer: (*See* Alaska packer)
Paddle, canoe:
building instructions for double paddle, 37:67, 57:60
construction method of Alexandra Conover, plans, 67:44
Paddlewheel tug, EPPLETON HALL:
comments, photo, 72:60
Paddling techniques:
attempted by an old salt, 6:43
for double paddle/Mike O'Brien, 90:56
letter on, 56:6
of Alexandra Conover, 55:79
Padebco Custom Boats, builder:
comments, 20:58
Page, Charles, author:
"Seasoning Science," 10:39
"Wood Harvest," 9:36
Page, William:
comments as a yacht broker, 60:62
letter on brokerage business, 61:6
Page, William, builder:
sailing dinghy NELLIE, 1:20
Pagels, Steven F.:
comments on Maine cruise schooner JANET MAY, 63:74
Pagels, Steven F., and Philip Shelton, authors:
"SQUAW: A Sharpie Schooner," 33:36
Paine, Art, author:
"Designs: Shoalwater Mini-Yachts," 74:96
"Racing Gently," 95:55
"Redesigning the Swede 55," 100:88
Paine, Art, author and photographer:
"The Artist's Eye," 99:48
Paine, Art, designer:
BOC Challenger AIRFORCE, 68:72
comments about, 75:22
Paine, Belknap & Skene, designer:
power cruiser POT O'GOLD, 48:38
Paine, C.W., designer: (*See* Designs, Paine, C.W.)
Paine, Frank, designer:
association with W. Starling Burgess, 74:42
comments, 46:30
fishing schooners, 56:102
Paint:
bottom prep all temp (undercoater)/ product review, 99:112
Imron, use of, 47:80
letter on, 47:7
matching bottom paints, 81:75
critique of MICRON 22 and Sharkskin, 46:66
safety precautions when using, 79:34, 79:41
selecting and mixing, 63:87
selection for longevity, 93:70
wood/paint adhesion, 30:94, 98:113
See also Linear polyurethane, Red lead
Paintbrush:
critique, 18:98
for applying varnish, 83:66
for lettering, 21:50, 99:54

Paintbrush (*continued*)
  letters on solvent for cleaning, 65:6
  maintenance, 10:56, 16:56, 21:79, 27:40,
    46:66, 48:91, 63:87, 99:104
Paintbrush spinner:
  letter by David Biggs, 92:4
Paint company, George Kirby Jr.:
  history, photos, 28:50
Painting techniques:
  advice for fitting out/Paul Bryant, 93:36
  advice on painting for decoration/
    Maynard Bray, 93:42
  bottom painting/Paul Bryant, 40:56
  bottom painting/Daniel MacNaughton,
    22:64
  during construction process, 93:70
  for early launching/Anne and Maynard
    Bray, 63:87, 64:58
  for galvanized steel, 82:27
  for linear polyurethanes, 78:21
  for plywood/Harold Payson, 43:96
  for scribe lines, 63:87
  for tropical conditions, 83:48
  general/Paul Bryant, 40:56
  general/Giffy Full, 27:40
  general/Daniel MacNaughton, 21:79,
    22:64
  general/Jim Walker, 10:56
  general/letter by D.C. King, 64:4
  general/survey of professional painters,
    46:66
  gold leafing/Dave Gross, 99:54
  layup procedures/Maynard Bray, 54:88
  lettering/Dave Gross, 99:54
  lettering/Karl MacKeeman, 21:50
  priming/Jim Walker, 10:56
  priming/survey of professional painters,
    46:66
  procedures for low maintenance/David L.
    Jackson, 99:66
  rolling and tipping/Daniel MacNaughton,
    81:78
  topsides/Paul Bryant, 40:56
  topsides/Jim Walker, 10:56
  topsides/Daniel MacNaughton, 21:79
  topsides/survey of professional painters,
    46:66
**Palmer, Colin, author, illustrator, and
  photographer:**
  "Sail and Hull Performance," 92:76
  letter on rig and hull performance, 94:6
Palmer Boat Company, builder:
  Skeeter iceboat, 39:88
Palmer Johnson, builder:
  on boat covers, 54:92
Palmer Scott, builder:
  comments, 44:108
Panama, watercraft: (*See* Kuna dugout canoe,
  Piragua [Panamanian dugout canoe])
PANDA (schooner):
  comments, photo, 6:66
PANDORA (catboat):
  cold-molded hull repair, photos, 60:76
Panels for Constant Camber construction:
  skiff GULL, how-to-build series, 65:97
Panels for stitch-and-glue construction:
  Bolger Cartopper dinghy, how-to-build
    series, 87:29
PANTHER (power launch):
  comments, photo, 57:72
Paopao canoe:
  design and construction commentary,
    performance, photo, 31:42

PAPOOSE (40' class):
  comments, 85:74
  history, photos, plans, 41:26, 48:58
  racing history, photos, 44:24
Parallel rules:
  product review/Jon Wilson, 100:124
PARAMOUR (Concordia yawl):
  comments, photo, 43:92
Pardey, Lin and Larry, authors:
  "Mast Making: Build a Practical Wooden
    Spar," 15:64
  "The Once in 3-Year Refit," 18:65
  "Understanding, Appreciating, Preventing
    Rot," 11:36
  letter on *Practical Yacht Joinery: Tools,
    Techniques, and Tips* (book), 55:5
**Pardey, Lin and Larry, authors and photog-
  raphers:**
  "Bronze: The Non-Timber," 51:72
Pardey, Lin and Larry, builders:
  cutter TALEISIN, 51:72
Paris, Jay E., Jr., designer:
  comments on Olin F. Stephens II, 98:50
  designs/54' ketch LONE STAR, 89:114
Parker, Reuel, author and builder:
  "A Story of Priorities," 65:56
  "Repair Strategies for Cold-Molded
    Construction," 89:92
  "Two Contemporary Centerboard
    Schooners," 80:44
Parks, Robert, illustrator:
  cover illustration/Tancook schooner, 5:0
Parry, Muriel H.:
  letter on schooner ISAAC H. EVANS, 40:9
Particle board:
  for boatbuilding, 60:145
PASSAGEMAKER (power cruiser):
  designs/Robert P. Beebe, 93:128
PASSIONELLA (skiff):
  owner's comments, rig commentary, 20:44
PASTIME (cutter):
  history, photos, 40:68
PAT & ROBBIE (Grand Manan lobsterboat):
  comments, photo, 45:82
PATIENCE (ketch):
  designs/Ed Frost, 95:110
PATRICE (sloop):
  designs/Paul Kotzebue, 43:128
PATRICIA (tugboat):
  photos, rebuilding commentary, 21:54
PATRICIA A (schooner):
  comments, 31:18
PATRIOT (sardine carrier):
  comments, photo, 59:70
Patris, Gordon, builder (Grenada):
  comments, 50:106
Patrol Boat (military craft):
  design and construction commentary,
    photo, 39:44
PAT'S (multihull):
  comments, photos, 92:34
Pattern for stem:
  repair/wood-and-canvas canoe/Rollin
    Thurlow, 79:72
Patternmaking:
  Biscayne Bay 14 daysailer/plywood con-
    struction/Eric Dow, 96:24
  for ballast keel/technique of Thomas
    MacNaughton, 24:68
  for ballast keel/technique of Bud
    McIntosh, 36:53
  for castings/technique of Michael
    Podmaniczky, 39:58

  for castings/technique of Richard
    Remsen, 46:52
  from lofting, jogglestick method/tech-
    nique of Roger Simpson, 39:106
  from lofting/technique of Thomas
    MacNaughton, 24:68
  tic spiling method/technique of Gary
    Weisenburger, 63:48
Pattinson, George:
  profile, photos, 98:66
PAULINA (jekt):
  comments, 84:58
PAULINE (sardine carrier):
  comments, photos, 59:70
  operation of, photos, 59:74
Paxton, Roland, author and illustrator:
  "Mr. Souter's New Boat," 24:47
Paxton, Roland, designer (England):
  comments, 24:47
Payne, Jim, author:
  reviewer of *The Gougeon Brothers on Boat
    Construction* (book), 70:120
Payne, Jim, builder:
  sloop WHITEFIN, 57:80
Payne, William, author:
  "California Friendships," 8:53
  "RESTLESS," 3:41
  "The Weather Side of Gaff Rig," 53:48
  "When the Keel Drops Off," 2:28
Payson, Harold H. ("Dynamite"), author:
  "A Boatbuilding Shop," 85:27
  "Build a Construction Model,
    Build a Boat, Part I," 85:36
  "Buying Used Tools," 70:31
  "Scarfs and Butts," 86:109
  "The Japanese Edge," 72:21
  reviewer of *Ultralight Boatbuilding* (book),
    81:97
**Payson, Harold H. ("Dynamite"), author
  and builder:**
  "A Classic in Plywood, Part I," 41:63
  "A Classic in Plywood, Part II," 42:44
  "A Classic in Plywood, Part III," 43:96
  "Instant Boats," 7:64
  "Keeping a Cutting Edge: Handsaws," 47:91
  "Keeping a Cutting Edge: Power Saws,"
    48:44
  "Plywood Scarphing," 18:77
**Payson, Harold H. ("Dynamite"), author and
  photographer:**
  "Build a Construction Model,
    Build a Boat, Part II," 86:29
  "Build a Construction Model,
    Build a Boat, Part III," 87:29
  "Build a Construction Model,
    Build a Boat, Part IV," 88:31
Pazereskis, John, author:
  "Icky, Sticky, Goo," 19:46
Pazereskis, John, author and photographer:
  "The Timeless Tumlarens," 19:18
P class, CHIPS:
  comments, photo, 74:42
PCP: (*See* Pentachlorophenol [wood preser-
  vative])
Peabody Museum of Salem (MA):
  comments, 13:40
Peapod:
  construction methods of Jimmy Steele,
    photos, 77:74
  cruising Maine and Nova Scotia coasts,
    70:68
  outfitting for cruising, 70:68

Peapod, sailing:
designs/Howard I. Chapelle, 33:104
Peapod, sailing, built by Tom Rubino:
builder's comments, photos, 13:61
Peapod, sailing, built by Jim Steele:
construction commentary, performance, photos, rig, 27:52
Peapod, sailing, built by Jon Wilson:
construction commentary, photos, plan, 1:42
Pease, Greg, photographer:
"A New PRIDE for Baltimore," 96:50
Pedersen, Ivan, builder:
lapstrake plank repair methods, 71:38
Peffer, Randall, author:
"A Boatbuilder's Trade School," 14:34
"Cut and Look: Building a Chesapeake Bay Sailing Log Canoe," 6:26
"Gentleman Jim," 24:52
"PILGRIM's People Get Ready," 8:12
"The Oysterman's Race," 3:34
PEG (wood preservative):
comments by Richard Jagels, 63:14, 73:108, 82:117
PEGGOTTY (catboat):
building, photos, plans, 23:39
PEGGY (ketch):
comments, plan, 72:44
PEGGY (schooner):
history, photo, plan, 70:17
PEKING (bark):
comments, photo, 38:45
Pelican class, San Francisco:
design and construction commentary, photos, plans, 30:29
Pelican Harbour (CA):
photo essay on, 25:80
Penbo cruiser:
design commentary, photos, 37:112
Pendleton, F.F., builder:
comments, 32:66
Penetrol:
use as varnish additive, 76:22
Penguin class:
history, photos, plans, 27:94
Penn's Landing Corporation:
comments, 44:62
Penobscot Boat Works, builder:
Lubec Boat, 12:44
Penbo cruiser, 37:112
Penobscot Marine Museum (ME):
boat types at, 29:102
Pentachlorophenol (wood preservative):
comments by Richard Jagels, 61:123
toxic effects of, 59:111, 79:34
use of, 52:118
Perkins, Bert, builder:
Lightning No. 1, 53:68
Peroba de Cambo (wood):
comments, 10:35
Perrine, J. Howard, builder:
sneakboxes, 20:23, 47:102
Perry, Robert, author:
"NOBLE 41," 5:33
Perry, Robert, designer:
comments about cutter NIGHT RUNNER, 77:40
See also Designs, Perry, Robert
Persson, Jon, author:
"Obituary: Donald C. Rosencrantz," 44:78
Persson, Seth, builder:
comments, 37:2
letter on, 36:9

PETALUMA (recreational shell):
comments, photo, 73:60
PETER DUCK (motorsailer):
comments, plans, 24:24
Peters, Frank, builder (England):
pilot gigs, 25:28
Peters, Harry:
on cold-molded hull repair, 60:76
Peterson, Charles L., illustrator:
"ALVIN CLARK: An Unfinished Voyage," 52:52
"JAVA, Father, and Capt. Hardy," 80:72
"Just an Overnighter," 57:66
"RUBY's Bloom," 25:48
cover illustration/sloop VALKYRIE, 27:0
Peterson, Douglas B., designer:
sloop BROWN SUGAR, 30:50
See also Designs, Peterson, Douglas B.
Peterson, Murray G., designer:
association with Malcolm Brewer, 49:44, 49:51
comments, 32:66, 33:41
designs compared to William Garden's, 60:134
obituary, 1:29, 1:30
schooner ACTIVE, 7:20
schooner SILVERHEELS, 1:32
Peterson, Murray G., & Assoc., designer: (*See* Designs, Peterson, Murray G., & Assoc.)
Peterson, Susan J., author:
"Built to Win: Lightning Class," 34:97
Peterson, William E. (Pete), author:
"Always a Gentleman," 49:51
on boat plans and the public domain, 48:105
Peterson, William M. (Bill), author:
"A Tribute to Murray Peterson," 1:29
"Always Right," 49:53
"Friendship Sloop Days," 2:22
on cargo schooners, 31:18
Peterson, William N.:
letter on Noank fishing vessels, 71:7
Peterson Builders, Inc., builder:
MCM class, 58:90
Peterson 33:
designs/Douglas B. Peterson, 11:76
PETREL (cutter):
comments, plan, 41:26
PETREL (launch):
designs/William Garden, 66:120
PETREL (yawl):
construction comments, photos, plans, 75:70, 75:72
cover photo/Jim Oker, 75:0
sailing critique, 75:73
PETRIFIED (sloop):
comments, photos, 26:70
Petty, George, author:
"Barnegat Bay's A-Cats," 62:60
Phair, W. A., author:
"20-Minute Job," 9:50
Phalen, Dan, author:
"Asa Thomson's Elegant Skiffs," 29:50
"Notes on the Opera House Cup," 38:75
PHANTOM II (commuter):
comments, photo, 94:74
Phelps, Ivan:
advice on planking repair, 81:75
Philadelphia Maritime Museum (PA):
GAZELA PRIMEIRO program, 11:24
Philadelphia Ship Preservation Guild:
comments on, 74:19

Philbrick, Ben, builder:
reframing New York 50 SPARTAN, 58:107
Philbrick, Don, builder:
construction methods/runabouts, 29:33
Phillipps, Jeanette, photographer:
"A Boat Worth Keeping," 33:90
Phillipps, Peter, author:
"A Boat Worth Keeping," 33:90
"Two Weeks on the Ways," 69:94
Phillips-Birt, Douglas:
comments, 57:55
Phillips, Myfanwy, author:
"In My View: Larry Dahlmer Speaks His Mind," 58:34
Phillips, W. Lyman, author:
"Manson Boat Works," 9:56
"The Same After 75 Years," 9:24
"Tool Critic: Powered Screwdriver," 22:96
editorial on pleasure-boat documentation, 9:2
editorial on wooden boatbuilding as small business, 10:3
reviewer of *Building the Herreshoff Dinghy* (book), 21:92
reviewer of *Marine Metals Manual* (book), 9:73
Phillips, W. Lyman, author and illustrator:
"Butt Blocks As They Should Be," 21:66
Phillips, W. Lyman, photographer:
cover photo/Idem-class sloop, 9:0
Phillips, W. Lyman, and Jim Walker, authors:
"A Pro Speaks On Painting," 10:56
PHOENIX (Dutch boeier):
design and construction commentary, performance, photos, plans, 27:32
Phoenix Boatshop Cooperative (MA):
boatbuilding program, 42:100
PHRYNE (New York 30):
comments, 35:25
PHYLLIS (sloop):
owner's comments, photos, 16:17
PICCOLO (sailing canoe):
how to build, photos, plans, 36:44, 37:57
Pike, Dag, author and photographer:
"Oars By Aylings," 23:47
PILGRIM (AMERICA's Cup boat):
comments, photo, 85:71
PILGRIM (schooner):
design and construction commentary, photos, 64:76
history, photos, 8:12
Pilot-boat, SANDY HOOK:
comments, plan, 53:38
Pilot-boat, Swedish:
comments, plan, 46:30
Pilot cutter, HIRTA:
sailing techniques, photos, 71:60
Pilot cutter, JOLIE BRISE:
design and construction commentary, history, photos, 38:54
Pilot cutter, OLGA:
comments, photo, 17:63
Pilot gig:
history, photos, plans, 25:28
Pilot gig, ACTIVE:
comments, photo, 25:28
Pilot gig, CAMPERNELL:
comments, photo, 25:28
Pilot gig, CZAR:
comments, photo, 25:28
Pilot gig, NEWQUAY:
comments, photo, 25:28

Pilot gig, NORNOUR:
comments, photo, 25:28

Pilot gig, TREFFRY:
plans, history, 25:28

Pilothouse:
comments, detail photo, 69:104

Pilot schooner:
comments, photos, 62:88

Pilot schooner, CAPRICE:
account of voyage, 62:88

Pilot schooner, WANDER BIRD:
design commentary, history, photos, plans, 55:56

Pina, John, builder:
comments, 60:76

Pine:
comments, 28:94, 29:14, 31:88, 33:72
species for boatbuilding, 9:31

Pine, Canadian:
comments, 70:101

Pine, Northern white:
comments by Richard Jagels, 88:100

Pine, Southern:
comments by Richard Jagels, 66:109

Pines, Southern yellow:
comments by Richard Jagels, 76:115
using recycled timber, 93:134

Pine, Western white:
comments, 68:103

PINE LAND (passenger vessel):
comments, photo, 73:32

Pine tar:
use, 19:98

Pinky, BLOODSTONE:
racing of, 58:52

Pinky, Crotch Island:
comments, photo, plan, 4:31

Pinky, DOVE:
designs/Edward S. Brewer, 3:65

Pinky, Eastport:
designs/Brewer, Wallstrom and Associates, Inc., 18:89
lofting, 12:44

Pinky, GLAD TIDINGS:
comments, photo, plans, 84:76

Pinky, RELIANCE:
design and performance commentary, photos, plans, 18:46

Pinky, SUNRISE:
designs/Jay Benford, 3:61

Pinnace, DOVE:
comments, 24:52
construction commentary, photos, 26:30, 26:36

PINTAIL (New York 30):
comments, 35:27

Pioneer Marine School (NY):
boatbuilding program, 42:100

Pipante: (*See* The Pipante)

Pipe fittings:
defined and illustrated, 81:82

PIQUANT (power launch):
comments, 47:40
design commentary, photo, 56:38

Piragua (Panamanian dugout canoe):
construction commentary, photos, 74:27

Pirogue:
origins of, 62:44

Pitcairn Island longboat:
construction commentary, photos, plans, 13:22

Pitch pine:
comments by Richard Jagels, 66:120

Pittaway, Robert, author:
"The Antique Boat Show," 2:66

Pittaway, Robert, designer: (*See* Designs, Pittaway, Robert)

Pittaway, Robert, photographer:
cover photo/power launch FAWN, 2:0

PIUTE III (runabout):
comments, plans, 28:20

Piver, Arthur, designer:
association with Jim Brown, 69:76
comments, 91:38

Plane, smoothing:
how to build, 11:52

Plane, spar:
how to build, 11:52

Plane, Ulmia:
critique, 4:72

Plane, wooden:
advice on buying used, 70:31
construction methods, with plans, 69:70

Planer blade:
sharpening method/Harold Payson, 48:44

Plane tree (wood):
comments, 70:101

Planking:
estimating for planking stock/Joel White, 22:94, 87:46
guide for self-survey/Paul Lipke, 83:22
plank curvature/commentary by Ed McClave, 100:31
tools for/commentary by Jim Emmett, 17:40
See also Edge-setting; Fairing, hull; Spiling; Stitch-and-glue construction

Planking, Ashcroft system:
comments, 4:17
letters on, 11:4
scantling table, described, 27:78
used in Rangeley Lake boat/R.R. Richardson, 8:50

Planking, batten-seam:
comments by George Luzier, 66:56

Planking, bottom:
Caddo Lake bateau, 62:44
flat-bottomed skiff or sharpie/Bob Baker, 66:48
plywood panel/Percy Blandford, 28:80
plywood panels/outboard runabout Downeaster 18, 74:87
plywood, Gloucester Light Dory/Harold Payson, 42:44
plywood, Martha's Tender skiff/Belford Gray, 46:94
plywood/recreational shell KINGFISHER, 61:60
Yankee Tender skiff/Joel White, 30:74

Planking, bottom, repair:
runabout/advice from Ivan Phelps, 81:75

Planking, carvel:
Catspaw dinghy/Joel White, 27:63
commentary on plank curvature/Ed McClave, 100:31
comments on butt seam construction/ Editors of *WoodenBoat*, 1:75
comments on butt seam construction/ William Garden, 3:71
compiling lumber list/20′ sloop MARTHA/ Joel White, 87:46
from a float/Jim Emmett, 17:41
Maine lobsterboat/Royal Lowell, 16:39
perahu lambot, SIOLA TAU, 10:16
Portuguese moliceiros, 95:48

schooner HERITAGE/North End Shipyard, 53:52
sloop MELE KAI, 64:92
sloop SIMPLICITY/Thomas MacNaughton, 24:68
technique/Bud McIntosh, 18:38, 19:50
wedge-seam construction techniques, 98:82
whaleship CHARLES W. MORGAN/ Mystic Seaport Museum, 36:98

Planking, carvel, firebending:
Baltic Trader FRI/China, 44:104

Planking, carvel, repair:
ketch TARNE/Belford Gray, 50:59
sloop RONDO/Robert Vespa, 51:59
sloop WHITE WINGS/Scott Cain, 24:72
spiling template technique/Allen Taube, 80:56
yawl TIGRIS/Steve Ballentine, 53:109

Planking, cold-molded: (*See* Cold-molded hull construction)

Planking, deck:
(*See* Deck construction, Deck repairs)

Planking, double:
Cutts Patent method, 78:30
Herreshoff method, 45:68

Planking, lapstrake:
Adirondack guideboat/Howard Ford, 18:55
canoe yawl LA MOUETTE, 75:62
Grand Banks dory/Jan Zimmermann, 19:32
letter by John Breiby, 77:4
letter by Ray Speck, 77:4
Norwegian faering/Chip Stulen, 95:38
Norwegian pram/Arne Emil Christensen, 49:28
Norwegian pram/Mark Swanson, 49:36
pulling boats/Shew & Burnham, 77:76
sailing canoe PICCOLO/Bob Baker, 36:44
shadow mold, 75:68
techniques/Simon Watts, 73:60
Whitehall/William B. Southworth, 5:12
Yankee Tender skiff/Joel White, 30:74

Planking, lapstrake, repair:
powerboat/Ivan Pedersen, 71:38
St. Lawrence skiff/Keith Quarrier, 32:57
small craft/Walter J. Simmons, 92:90

Planking, plywood:
Biscayne Bay 14 daysailer, 96:24
Bolger Cartopper dinghy, 87:29
DK 13 kayak, 70:56
Gloucester Light Dory/Harold Payson, 42:44
Lyman Boat Works, 82:68
Martha's Tender skiff/Belford Gray, 46:94
outboard runabout Downeaster 18, 74:87
recreational shell KINGFISHER, 61:60
skiff GULL, 64:83

Planking, plywood lapstrake:
Acorn skiff/Iain Oughtred, 56:60
canoes/Tom Hill, 54:74
Nutshell pram/Joel White, 60:100
panels/outboard runabout Downeaster 18, 74:87
technique/Kenneth C. Mobert, 43:44

Planking, repair:
Chris-Craft Riviera/Ken Bassett 96:87
cold-molded construction, 89:92
wood-and-canvas canoe/Rollin Thurlow, 79:72
See also Planking, carvel, repair; Planking, lapstrake, repair

Planking, skiff construction:
 Caddo Lake bateau, 62:44
 flat-bottomed skiff or sharpie, 66:48
Planking, skin boat construction:
 catamaran TAULUA, 72:70
Planking, strip:
 Bear Mountain canoe/Ted Moores, 31:58
 comments by Cyrus Hamlin, 22:94
 comments by David Keith, 4:63
 comments by Joe Trumbly, 89:44
 Hampton boat/Dick Pulsifer, 57:50
 kayak/Curtis Rindlaub, 57:60
 origins of, 57:55
 techniques/Formula 40 ADRENALIN,
  87:66
 techniques/Mt. Desert Yacht Yard, 61:42
 techniques/Wee Lassie double-paddle
  canoe/Henry McCarthy, 100:92
Planking, transom: (*See* Transom construction, Transom repair)
Plank patterns:
 peapod/Jimmy Steele, 77:74
Plank scarfer:
 comments, plans, 67:30
Plank scriber:
 design of Ed McClave, 67:30
Plans for boatbuilding:
 commentary by Joel White, 75:111
 copyright, letter on, 49:5
 copyright comments/forum, 48:105
 copyright comments/John Gardner, 47:46
 copyright comments/Jon Wilson, 32:2, 47:2
 illustrated glossary of boat parts, 60:115,
  77:79, 87:46
 review of plans catalogs/Mike O'Brien,
  89:112, 93:118, 96:98
 review of *Small Craft Plans* (book)/Mike
  O'Brien, 98:97
 understanding, 21:30
Playmate 34 (power cruiser):
 construction commentary, photo, plan,
  25:102
PLEASURE (yawl):
 comments, photo, 100:70
Pletten, Otto:
 comments on, 71:44
Plymouth (MA) lobsterboats:
 history, photos, plans, 1:65
Plywood, Bruynzeel:
 comments by Kenneth C. Mobert, 43:44
Plywood, grading:
 comments by Richard Jagels, 72:105
Plywood, marine:
 applications to boatbuilding, 18:94, 57:122
 characteristics, manufacturing problems,
  56:125
 letter on, 57:8
Plywood, use:
 comments by Joel White, 70:110
 for Biscayne Bay 14 daysailer, 96:24, 98:28
 for Bolger Cartopper (construction
  model), 86:29
 for Bolger Cartopper dinghy, 87:29, 88:31
 for DK 13 kayak, 70:56
 for Dynel-and-epoxy deck overlay, 66:64
 for Dynel-and-epoxy deck repair, 66:64
 for Dynel-and-epoxy deck/outboard runabout Downeaster 18, 75:53
 for offshore raceboat JESSE JAMES, 73:86
 for outboard runabout Downeaster 18,
  73:67, 74:87, 75:53
 for outboard utility launch RIVERKEEPER,
  61:72

 for recreational shell KINGFISHER, 61:60
 for sharpies TERESA and SARAH, 80:44
 for three-fathom sharpie, 67:60
 ordering information/Joel White, 87:46
 recommendations for finishing fir ply-
  wood/Glen L. Witt, 81:75
 recommendations for painting plywood/
  Harold Payson, 43:96
 stitch-and-glue construction, 85:52
Plywood boatbuilding:
 comments by Daniel MacNaughton, 24:100
 comments by Jon Wilson, 41:2
 See also Planking, plywood; Planking, plywood lapstrake; Scarfing, plywood
Plywood decks:
 repair of Malabar Jr. IMAGINE, 65:56
 techniques of Bud McIntosh, 46:103
POCAHONTAS (scallop dragger):
 model, photo, 97:52
Pocock, George, designer:
 profile, 21:36
Pocock, Stan, builder:
 profile, 21:36
Podmaniczky, Michael, author:
 "Patternmaking for Custom Hardware,"
  39:58
 "The Butt Block in Its Place," 66:45
 "The Case for Simple Edge-Gluing," 59:93
 letter on butt blocks, 69:11
 letter on Seth Persson, 36:9
Poillon Brothers, builder:
 schooner CORONET, 32:20
**Pointer, Debbie, and Michael McMenemy,
 authors:**
 "R. O. Davis," 97:76
 "The Three Davis-Nevins Motorsailers,"
  97:86
Poland, watercraft (fishing craft): (*See* Bot
  cezowy, Bot kôn, Bot żakowy, Laskornwy,
  Pomeranka)
Polar exploration:
 history of Norwegian ship FRAM, 85:44
 history of schooner BOWDOIN, 47:30
Pole for canoe:
 building instructions, 49:40
Poling a canoe:
 history, techniques, 49:40
Polk, Milbry, photographer:
 "The Vanishing Craft of the Nile," 33:61
Polyester: (*See* Fiberglass)
Polynesia, sailing canoe:
 design and construction commentary,
  history, plans, 19:25
Polysulfide:
 comments and application tech-
  niques/Aimé Ontario Fraser, 92:23
 comments by Fred Barter, 17:32
 comments by Jon Wilson, 28:76
 See also Detco (seam filler)
Polysulfide, Thiokol:
 comments by Barry Thomas and Jon
  Wilson, 2:64
 use of, 1:8
Polyurethane: (*See* Linear polyurethane)
Polyurethane caulking:
 advice on cleanup, 80:85
 types and application techniques/Aimé
  Ontario Fraser, 92:23
POMELION (sloop):
 comments, photo, 74:42
Pomeranka (Polish fishing craft):
 history, photos, plans, 89:74

PONTIAC (N class):
 comments, photo, 73:32
Pool, Andrew, author:
 "Extending the Limits: The Gift of Laurent
  Giles," 24:24
 "Masterpiece: The VERTUE and Her
  Achievement," 24:32
Poole, Ann McCormish, illustrator:
 "In My View: A Rowboat for Our Times,"
  85:95
Poole Maritime Museum (England):
 comments, 46:54
Pool, Kathy, photographer:
 cover photo/wherries, 21:0
POOR RICHARD (power launch):
 design and construction commentary,
  plans, 20:76
Poplar, yellow:
 use of, 43:120
Poppets:
 commentary by Ed McClave, 78:93
PORPOISE (sportfisherman):
 comments, photo, 49:44
 designs/Geerd Hendel, 61:127
**Port Carling Boat Works Ltd., builder
 (Ontario):**
 history, 55:68
Porter, Daniel, author:
 "Product Review: Keeping the Edge,"
  91:103
 "Product Review: Searching for the Perfect
  Knife," 88:109
 "Product Review: The Chain Mate Anchor
  Chain Scrubber," 93:116
 "Product Review: Vise-Grip Pliers and
  Clamps," 93:120
 reviewer of *Once is Enough* (book), 84:97
 reviewer of *TREKKA Round the World*
  (book), 84:97
Porter, Dave, author and illustrator:
 "Saving Time in the Mold Loft," 31:64
Porter-Cable:
 product review of Random Orbit Sander,
  96:97
Portland cement:
 use as seam compound, 81:75
Port Orford cedar:
 for planking/canoe yawl LA MOUETTE,
  75:62
 for planking/sloop MELE KAI, 64:92
 for planking/trawler-yacht NORDSØ,
  74:74
**Port Townsend's (WA) Wooden Boat
 Festival, 1977:**
 commentary and photos, 19:56
Portugal, fishing craft:
 cover photo/Rebecca Hirte, 33:0
Portugal, watercraft:
 photo essay/fishing ports of, 72:80
 See also GAZELA PHILADELPHIA
  (barkentine), Moliceiros
Portuguese Grand Banks fleet:
 exploits of dorymen, 44:62
Portuguese Grand Banks schooner: (*See*
  GAZELA PRIMEIRO [barkentine])
Post, Franklin G., builder:
 comments, 100:58
Post, Robert C.:
 letter on National Watercraft Collection,
  79:5
Poston, Clark, author:
 "A Cutter's Story," 85:21

POT O'GOLD (power cruiser):
design commentary, history, photos, plan, 48:38

Pott, Kenneth R.:
letter on nautical archaeology, 69:5

Potter, Lincoln, photographer:
"Fire Bending," 44:104

Potter, Nicholas, designer:
Eight-Meter sloop ANGELITA, 59:40
profile, photo, 83:38

Potts, Louise, photographer:
"The Schooner AMERICA: How to Build Her Half Model," 52:40

Power craft: (*See* A.C.F. 41; ALBACORE III; Alexandria Bay boats; ALICE; ALOHA; AMIGO MIO; APHRODITE; ARLINE; ARROW; Atlantic 53; BANFIELD; BARNACLE IV; Bartender; Bassboat; BIG KEX; BLACK KNIGHT; BLUE HERON; BLUE STAR; CALISTO V.; CANDID GYPSY; CANELLI; CANIM; CARIBE MONIQUE; CARIBOU; CERO; Chris-Craft; CHRISTABEL; CIGARETTE; Constellation; Corinthian; COUNTESS; CUTTERHEAD; CZARINNA; Elco; EXPRESS; Express cruisers; FAIRFA; Fairform Flyer; FANTASY; FAVONIA; GENNY W; GO-SUM; Grand Manan 45; HERCULES; Huckins Offshore 64; Hydroplanes; IMOVA; ISLAND RAVEN; JESSE JAMES; JESSICA; KATOURA; KIYI; LADY JEANNE; LADY MONA; LAMPOONER; Launch, power; LAWANA; LION'S WHELP; LITTLE JAMES; LITTLE VIGILANT; Lobsterboat; MALIBU; MARLIN; Matthews; MEADOW-LARK; MERLIN; MER-NA; MISS ABU; MITENA; Narrowboat; NAVETTE; Nep-tune 47; NOW VOYAGER; OUR TERN; Outboard boat; Pacemaker; PASSAGEMAKER; Penbo cruiser; PHANTOM II; Playmate 34; PORPOISE; POT O'GOLD; Power dory; Power skiff; Prowler power craft; RAGTIME; RASCAL; RESOLUTE; Richardson Cruisabout; ROSE PLUNKETT; Runabout; SAGA; SAMONA; SCELP; SEA SCRIBE; SIVA; SLY MONGOOSE; SNIPE; SOLARIA TOO; SOONER; Speedboat; Sportfishing boat; Sportsman; STING RAY V; Surf Scoter; TARANTULA; THE JUDGE; TIGER; TLINGIT; TOMKAT III; TRADITION; TWISTER; USS SUISUN; VINTAGE ROSE; Vlet; WALRUS; WANDA; Wheeler 34; WHISPER; WHITECAP; WHITE RABBIT; WILLOW; WINCHESTER IV; WOODPECKER; YAZOO)

Power craft designs: (*See* Designs appearing in *WoodenBoat* design section)

Power dory:
WoodenBoat School project, comments, plans, 88:82

Power skiff:
comments, plans, 87:90
lapstrake, outboard-powered/construction, photos, 91:34
WoodenBoat School project, comments, plans, 88:82

PQ-8 (wood preservative):
comments by Richard Jagels, 61:123

Pram:
design comments by Steve Redmond, 71:105

See also Designs, Gougeon Brothers; Designs, Peterson, Murray G. & Assoc.; Designs, Strayer, Charles M.

Pram, Herreshoff design:
comments, photo, 73:60

Pram, Norwegian:
construction commentary, plans/Arne Emil Christensen, 49:28
construction commentary, photos/Mark Swanson, 49:36

Pram, Nutshell:
how to build, photos, plans, 60:100
offset corrections, 64:26

Pram, plywood:
plans, 7:64

Pram, Dutch vlet:
history, photos, plans, 52:75

Preiss, Fred, builder:
sloop CHRISTINE, 56:86

PRELUDE (sloop):
comments, photo, 43:92

Preservation: (*See* Maritime preservation)

Preservatives, wood:
comments by Richard Jagels, 52:118, 59:111, 76:115, 77:116
comments by Frank Prothero, 48:30
for canvas, 22:94
health hazards of, 59:111
paraquat injections, 31:88
salt, 19:98
types discussed, 2:36
See also CCA, Cuprinol, Git-Rot, IPBC, Linseed oil, PFG, Pentachlorophenol, PQ-8

Pressure-treated wood:
comments by Richard Jagels, 28:94, 76:115, 77:116, 85:121, 89:106

PRESTIGE (M class):
comments, photo, 74:42

PRIDE OF BALTIMORE (schooner):
comments, 96:50, 96:56
comments, photos, 55:56, 78:76
design and construction commentary, photos, plans, 14:16
loss of, editorial by Jon Wilson, 71:2
operation of, photos, voyage, 44:72

PRIDE OF BALTIMORE II (schooner):
comments, 96:56, 96:64
design and construction commentary, photos, 96:50
editorial by Jon Wilson, 96:2

Prime, Stephen R.:
letter on Newport (RI) Wooden Boat Show, 76:4

PRINCE DE NEUFCHATEL (Baltimore clipper):
model, photos, 97:52

PRINCESS (Friendship sloop):
history, 4:14

PRISCILLA (sloop):
comments, 41:26, 71:52

PRISM (cutter):
comments, photo, 79:64

Proa: (*See* FISH TRUCK, Pacific proa)

Proctor, Ian, designer (England):
Merlin Rockets, 58:100
Wayfarer dinghy, 51:88

Product reviews: (*See* Reviews [product], appearing in *WoodenBoat*)

Professional Yacht Racing Association:
comments, 39:123

Profiles: (*See* Builder profiles, Designer profiles)

Projection lofting:
letters on, 52:10, 52:12
techniques/Paul Haist, 51:94

Project Lakewell (MI):
letters on, 51:7, 54:5

Project Seal (MA):
boatbuilding program, 11:7

Propeller:
bronze/casting technique at Lunenburg Foundry, photos, 94:72

Propeller drag:
defined, 54:101

PROSPECTOR (ketch):
letter on, 45:9
owner's comments, photos, plans, 44:108

Prothero, Bob, builder:
profile, 62:82

Prothero, Frank, builder:
profile, 48:30

Prothero Boat Company, builder:
history, 48:30

Prowler power craft:
history, photos, 86:44

PRUDENCE (catboat):
comments, photo, 32:36

Prybot, Peter, photographer:
cover photo, dragger LITTLE FLOWER, 79:0

Pryor, Walter, builder:
comments, 36:73

PT boats by Huckins:
design commentary, history, 56:48
letter on, 57:7

Púcan (Irish fishing craft):
builder of, photos, 50:78
design and construction commentary, photos, 10:25

PUFFIN (yawl):
comments, 51:72

Pulsifer, Dick, builder:
profile, 57:50

Pump, bilge:
design, 23:44
selection/Roger Taylor, 40:38

Pungy schooner:
designs/R.D. (Pete) Culler, 55:122
drawing, history, photos, plan, 45:56

Pungy schooner, AMANDA F. LEWIS:
drawing, photo, 45:56

Pungy schooner, MARY AND ELLEN:
comments, plan, 45:56

Pungy schooner, RUBEN DE CLOUX:
designs/Bruce Northrup, 68:110

Punt, MYRA:
designs/Johan Selmer-Larsen, 71:105

Punt, plywood:
comments, plans, 7:64

Punty (waterfowl boat):
comments, photo, 92:52

Purdon, John R., designer:
comments, 37:42, 73:32, 85:74

Pure Sound Society (WA):
comments, 89:86, 89:89

PURITAN (cutter):
comments, 41:26
comments, photo, 71:52

PURITAN (schooner):
racing, 56:102

Purpleheart (wood):
comments, 10:35

Pusateri, Daniel:
letter on Mark and Chris Lavin, 75:4

Push-pole:
design, 34:86
PUSS (lobsterboat, sloop):
comments, photo, 69:42
Putty:
application technique, 63:87
comments by Ed McClave, 74:17
Putz, George, author:
"A Boatbuilder's Garden, Part I," 44:50
"A Boatbuilder's Garden, Part II," 45:36
"Buying a Wooden Boat," 60:62
"The Outlook for World Timber," 59:56
reviewer of *A Life in Boats* (book), 61:117
reviewer of *From Tree to Sea: The Building of a Wooden Steam Drifter* (book), 71:121
reviewer of *Go Build Your Own Boat* (book), 57:124
reviewer of *The American Challenge* (video), 64:38
reviewer of *The Boatbuilding Video Series: The Lines* (video), 66:104

Q-boat, BAT:
comments, photos, 85:74
Q-boat, ORESTES:
comments, 73:32
Quarrier, Keith, author:
"Extending the Life of a Skiff," 32:57
QUEEN CHARLOTTE (sea kayak):
computer-generated lines, photos, plans, 79:84
Quick-and-dirty boats:
boatbuilding contest, photos, plans, 49:89
repairs for/commentary by Peter Spectre, 93:29
QUIET TUNE (ketch):
comments, 84:21
comments, photo, 56:38
QUINTET 6 (sloop):
kit boat/Clark-Craft, 39:69

Rabbet:
backbone/Bud McIntosh, 33:66, 34:66, 35:56
backbone/Whitehall pulling boat/Bob Baker, 45:108
planking/Hampton boat/Dick Pulsifer, 57:50
stem/from lofting/Fred Ajootian, 14:38
stem/from lofting/Sam Manning, 14:42
stem/peapod/Jimmy Steele, 77:74
stem and stem knee/Fred Ajootian, 14:38
Rabinowitz, Neil, author:
"The Blanchard Boat Company," 94:54
Rabinowitz, Neil, photographer:
"The ADVENTURESS and Mrs. B," 90:94
cover photo/Blanchard 36 Standardized Cruiser CUTTERHEAD, 94:0
cover photo/CHALLENGER (Peterson 41), 100:0
cover photo/schooner ALCYONE, 82:0
Racing:
AMERICA's Cup, 18:32, 37:42, 41:26, 68:40, 71:52
Ancient Mariner's Regatta, 65:76
Barnegat Bay A-cats, 62:60
BOC Challenge, 68:72, 75:22
BOC Challenge, letter by Dick Cross, 69:5
Classic Yacht Regatta, 38:71, 43:91
classic yacht regattas/preparing for, 95:55
comments by Jon Wilson, 59:2
comments, history, 73:86
correspondence/N.G. Herreshoff and W.P. Stephens, 100:70
C-STAR (singlehanded transatlantic race), 91:38
Delaware duckers, 48:82
DN-class iceboats, 86:52
evolution of Universal and International Rules, 68:40
Foxy's Wooden Boat Regatta, 65:76
Friendship Sloop Race, 2:22, 29:64
Gold Cup, 48:66, 60:84
Gold Cup Challenge, 71:82
Great Schooner Race, 13:82
Great South Bay Scooters, 92:52
Ice Yacht Challenge Pennant of America, 14:26
International Fishermen's Race, 13:82, 56:102
International Schooner Race, 13:82
IOR Transpac Race, 30:50
letter on French-designed multihulls, 92:4
Master Mariners' Regatta, 1976, 13:79
Mt. Gay Cup Race, 2:8
Museum of Yachting's Classic Yacht Regatta, 65:76

Mystic Seaport Schooner Race, 13:5
offshore power craft/Prowler cruisers, 86:44
offshore raceboats, 73:86
Olympic Games, 13:34
Olympic Games/Struer kayaks, 82:44
Opera House Cup Race, 38:75
outboard speedboats/commentary by Peter H. Spectre, 80:32
Oysterman's Race, Chesapeake Bay Appreciation Day, 3:34
profile of Charles Francis Adams III, 85:74
Staudacher-built hydroplanes and run-abouts, 80:24
Swiftsure, 34:21
Victoria Classic Boat Festival, 65:76
Wianno Senior class, 91:58
Racing canoes, Hawaiian koa canoe:
construction commentary, history, photos, 59:80
Racing canoes, Olympic contenders:
comments by John Hanson, 13:34
Racing history:
Cruising-class canoe, 24:90
cutter MADGE, 37:42, 44:24
40' class, 48:58, 49:66
iceboats, 1600–1930, 38:64
iceboats, 1930–1980, 38:88
New York 30 class, 35:20, 35:25, 35:27
sloop SHADOW, 37:42, 43:64, 44:24
yachts, 1850–1900, 37:42, 41:26
RACING SPLASHER (sloop):
comments, plan, 37:42
Racing tactics:
Wianno Senior class/Jack Fallon, 91:67
Rader, Amy, photographer:
"A Proper Lady," 68:80
cover photo/yawl SAGA, 49:0
Rafel Marine:
designs/sloop MAIR 30, 63:116
RAGTIME (commuter):
comments, photo, 94:74
RAIN BIRD (schooner):
designs/William Garden, 68:114
RAINBOW IV (speedboat):
comments, 60:84
Raised panels:
how to build, photos, plans, 99:86
RAKEL (skøyte):
comments, photo, 84:58
Ramin (wood):
comments, 59:56
RANA (Nordlands boat):
comments, photo, 85:64
RANDANDY (bateau-type rowing skiff):
history, racing, photo, 66:23
Rander, Steve, builder:
comments, photo, 90:108
RANDOM SCOOT (canoe):
construction commentary, photos, 31:50
essay on theft, 53:66
Rangeley Lake boat:
design and construction commentary, photos, plans, 39:26
photos, planking of, 8:50
steam-bending stems for, 33:74
RANGER (J class):
comments by Olin J. Stephens II, 98:50
comments, photo, 74:42
Ranger 23 (power cruiser):
design commentary, photo, 27:96
Ransom, Edward A., builder:
Plymouth lobsterboats, 1:65

RAPIER (10-Meter):
construction commentary, photo, 3:71

Rapoza, Frank, builder:
restoration of schooner L.A. DUNTON, 6:44

RASCAL (commuter):
comments, photo, 94:74

Rasmussen 20-Tonner (Danish seiner):
comments, plans, 88:40

Rating rules:
evolution of Universal and International Rules, 68:40

Ratty's Boat (Thames skiff model):
design and construction comments, history, photos, 94:44

RAY OF HOPE (Friendship sloop):
performance commentary, 53:48

R class, DANDELION:
comments, photo, 85:74

R class, FRIENDSHIP:
comments, photo, 83:38

R class, GOSSOON:
comments, photo, 85:74

R class, LIVE YANKEE:
design commentary, photo, plan, 55:32

R class, SIR TOM:
comments, photo, 94:54

R class, YANKEE:
comments, 55:32

REALITY (Eight-Meter):
cold-molded hull construction, photos, 34:20

REBELLION (sloop):
comments, photo, 78:30

Recreational shells: (*See* Bangor Packet [rowing wherry], KINGFISHER, PETALUMA)

Red bay (wood):
characteristics, 43:120

RED JACKET (Friendship sloop):
performance and charter, photos, 11:65

RED JACKET (schooner):
comments, photo, 94:54

Red lead:
for priming underwater seams, 74:17
in preventing wood from checking, 63:14
in repairing a fantail launch, 63:48
letter on using, 55:6

Red maple:
for boatbuilding, 60:145

Redmond, Steve, author:
"Designs: A Logical Sheer," 65:108
"Designs: A Representative National Type," 58:116
"Designs: An Antique-Shop Sandbagger, Part I," 63:112
"Designs: An Antique-Shop Sandbagger, Part II," 64:102
"Designs: Chesapeake Crabbing Skiffs," 69:100
"Designs: Herreshoff's Double-Paddle Canoe," 60:140
"Designs: Keel Shapes: The AMERICA's Cup and a New Daysailer," 66:124
"Designs: Open-Boat Cruisers Compared," 70:104
"Designs: Open-Boats, Part II, and MYRA, a Punt," 71:105
"Designs: Pretty Enough to Save," 62:96
"Designs: Quick and Simple Boats," 67:117
"Designs: The Versatile Sneakbox," 61:124
"Designs: Three Skiffs—Variations on a Traditional Theme," 57:118
"Designs: Two Little Keel Yachts," 59:116

"Designs: Two Multi-Purpose Skiffs," 72:98

Redmond, Steve, designer:
comments, 54:74, 57:2
See also Designs, Redmond, Steve

Redningskoite (ketch):
design commentary, plan, 47:46
history, plan, 20:35
letter on, 50:5

Red oak:
decay resistance, identification of, 1:48
decay resistance, strength properties, 65:112
for mast hoops, 65:40
identification of, 64:108

REDSKIN (launch):
comments, photo, 62:74, 65:90

REDWING (sloop):
comments, photo, 92:42

Redwood:
comments, 9:31, 18:94

Reed, A.E., photographer:
cover photo/offshore raceboat JESSE JAMES, 73:0

Reefing a sail:
aboard Bristol Channel pilot cutter, 71:60
comments by Rod Stephens, 73:42
for sharpie ALACRAN, 5:36
gunter rig/comments by Iain Oughtred, 74:100
lateen rig/comments by Iain Oughtred, 78:66
lug rig/comments by Iain Oughtred, 73:80
small spritsail/Ernie Cassidy, 89:30
small spritsail, letter by David Scarborough, 78:8

Reefing deck seams:
tools and techniques, 77:60

Reefing hook (for seams):
how to make and use, 12:30, 16:47, 57:112

Reef knot:
how to tie, 18:19

Reef nettles:
sewing of, 38:100

Reeks, Walter, designer:
comments on steam yacht ENA, 90:102

Reelfoot Lake Stumpjumper:
construction commentary, history, photos, 82:19

Refastening:
advice from Paul Coble, 80:85

Refastening with wood screws:
technique/Ed McClave, 55:43
technique/L.E. Nicholson, 12:30, 14:9, 16:9

Refinishing:
E.H. Gerrish wood-and-canvas canoe/ Rollin Thurlow, 78:56
brightwork/Rebecca Wittman, 81:88

Reframing: (*See* Frame repair)

REGINA MARIS (barkentine):
cover photo/John Barnes, 11:0

Rehor, Milanne, author:
"A New Life for HIPPOCAMPUS JR," 6:54
"HIPPOCAMPUS JR: Adventure Challenges the Will," 8:46
"HIPPOCAMPUS JR: Back to Virginia," 9:66

Reimers, Knud, designer (Sweden):
Swede 55 VORTEX, 100:84, 100:88
Tumlaren class, 19:18

Reinell powerboat:
repair technique/Wallace Whitford, 80:14

Reisland, David L.:
letter on McKenzie River drift boat, 53:8

Reithel, Kitty, author:
"Not Just Boats but Craftsmen, Too," 62:82

RELIANCE (schooner):
design and construction commentary, photos, plans, 18:46
photos, racing, 13:79

RELIANCE (schooner, sardine carrier):
comments, photo, 58:52

Remsen, Richard, author:
"Casting Lead Keels," 89:52
on casting technique for small-boat hardware, 73:24

Renaissance Yachts, builder:
cutter SASKIANNA, 83:112

RENEGADE (cutter):
comments, photo, 76:60
comments, photos, 55:88
construction commentary, photos, 35:45

Renegades (iceboats):
design and construction commentary, photos, 39:88

Repair:
Baltic trader FRI, 87:36
Baltic trader FRI/Macau-Coloane Shipbuilding and Ship Repair Co., 44:104
barkentine GAZELA PRIMEIRO, 11:24, 44:62, 46:5
Barnegat Bay sneakbox/Eric Stark, 47:102
brigantine VARUA, 65:44
cabintop, 20:52
Celebrity class SEOLADAIR/George Hill, 22:60
Chris-Craft Riviera/Ken Bassett, 96:87
Concordia 33 FREE SPIRIT, 66:64, 99:28
copper sheathing of barkentine GAZELA PHILADELPHIA, 74:19
copper sheathing of cutter ISKRA, 67:35
cutter ELLY/Dean Stephens, 58:40
cutter VAGRANT, 61:80
Falmouth Quay punt CURLEW, 86:36
fantail launch, 63:48
Fishers Island 31, CIRRUS, 66:64
Herreshoff 12½ class/Steve Ballentine, 56:93, 57:93
Idem class/W. Lyman Phillips, 9:24
ketch TARNE/Brooklin Boat Yard, 49:97, 50:59
lapstrake powerboat/Ivan Pedersen, 71:38
launch CHEROKEE, 61:100
Luders 16 SILHOUETTE/Steve White, 55:102
Malabar Jr. IMAGINE, 65:56
methods of Peter Freebody & Company, 57:72
methods of Wayne Mocksfield, 41:72
museum guidelines for, 8:30
New York 30 CARA MIA/Paul Stubing, 35:30
New York 50 SPARTAN/Ed McClave, 58:107
Norwegian sailing freighters, 73:96
outboard launch MRS. JONES, 68:80
Owens cutter FALCON, 61:104
Pacemaker/George Clapp, 16:20
patching technique for cotton sails/Robin Lincoln, 81:75
power cruiser ARLINE/Clifton Andrews, 18:82
power cruiser USS SUISUN, 81:21
power launch/Ulf Henrikson, 47:109

quick-and-dirty rowboat/Peter H. Spectre, 93:29

Reinell powerboat/Wallace Whitford, 80:14

removal of keelbolts, 89:105

Royal Ship of Cheops (Egypt), 38:28

runabouts/Wayne Mocksfield, 41:72

schooner ALVIN CLARK, 52:59

schooner L.A. DUNTON, 6:44

schooner VOYAGER, 69:94

scow sloop ALMA, 3:8

skipjack FLORA/W.A. Phair, 9:50

skipjack STANLEY NORMAN/Ed Farley, 35:62

sloop GAUNTLET/critique of repairs, 70:23

sloop HIPPOCAMPUS JR/Gus Eckhoff, 6:54

sloop IOLAIRE/Donald Street, 3:59, 13:65, 25:89

sloop RONDO/Robert Vespa, 51:59

sloop WHITE WINGS/Scott Cain, 23:50, 24:72

Snipe class, 89:43

speedboat BABY BOOTLEGGER/Bruce Barnard, 60:84

St. Lawrence skiff/Keith Quarrier, 32:57

Thistle class/Mike Baird, 47:80

torpedo-sterned launch ALOHA, 95:82

Trading ketch DEFENDER, 92:62

whaleship CHARLES W. MORGAN/Mystic Seaport, 36:98

Winter Harbor 21 class WHIPPET, 93:76

wood-and-canvas canoe/Jerry Stelmok, 29:68

wood-and-canvas canoe/Rollin Thurlow, 78:56, 79:72

yawl ISLA TROTHE/Rick Kotalac, 52:92

yawl ROYONO/Elmer Dion, 1:4

yawl TIGRIS/Steve Ballentine, 53:109

See also Canvas-covered decks; Canvas-covered hulls; Canoe repair; Caulking; Centerboard; Coaming; Cold-molded hull repair; Deck repair; Floor timbers; Frame repair; Keel repair; Keelson; Planking, bottom, repair; Planking, carvel, repair; Planking, lapstrake, repair; Refastening; Seam compounds; Shaftlog, repair; Stem repair; Stopwaters; Transom repair

Replicas: (*See* Athenian trireme, BRUNSWICK LION [St. John River boat], DOVE [pinnace], Historic vessel reproduction, HMS ROSE, KALMAR NYCKEL [Dutch merchant ship], KYRENIA II [Greek trading ship], MATILDA D [felucca replica], MAYFLOWER II [colonial ship replica], PRIDE OF BALTIMORE [schooner], PRIDE OF BALTIMORE II [schooner], SAGA SIGLAR [Viking Age merchant ship replica], SEBBE ALS [Viking ship replica], SPIRIT OF MASSACHUSETTS [schooner], SUSAN CONSTANT, WELCOME [armed-sloop replica])

Rescribing waterlines:
technique, 63:87

Research vessel, NISMIME:
design commentary, plans, 30:20

Research vessel, VARUA:
design and repair commentary, history, photos, plans, 65:44

Resheathing, copper:
barkentine GAZELA PHILADELPHIA/ Steve Masone, 74:19

cutter ISKRA/Frank Mulville, 67:35

RESOLUTE (AMERICA's Cup defender):
comments, photo, 84:34, 85:74

RESOLUTE (Blanchard 36):
comments, photo, 94:54

RESOLUTE (dragger):
comments, 79:48

RESOLUTE (ketch):
owner's comments, 8:7

RESOLUTION (cat-yawl):
comments, photos, 61:38, 92:42

Resorcinol glue:
commentary by Aimé Ontario Fraser, 84:48

commentary by John Pazereskis, 19:46

commentary by Gerald Schindler, 4:47

comments, 15:64

comments by John Guzzwell, 84:64

use by George I. (Sonny) Hodgdon, Jr., 59:88

use by Lin and Larry Pardey, 11:36

use in Controversy class/Mt. Desert Yacht Yard, 61:42

use in MCM class, 58:90

Respirators:
advice for selecting and using, 79:41

RESTLESS (steam tug):
history, photo, 3:40

Restoration, philosophy:
Dick Clarke/classic speedboats, 65:90

Bill Morgan/classic speedboats, 71:82

Reuel Parker/Malabar Jr. sloop, 65:56

Rollin Thurlow/wood-and-canvas canoe, 78:56

Hans and Hetti van de Vooren/Norwegian sailing freighter, 73:96

Restorations: (*See* Preservation, Repair)

Restorationshop of Maine Maritime Museum, builder:
restoration of schooner BOWDOIN, 47:30

Reviews (book) appearing in *WoodenBoat,* **listed by author and title:**
Abbey, Edward, *The Hidden Canyon: A River Journey,* 23:101

Adams, Bill, *Ships and Memories,* 37:50

Allen, Joseph Chase, *The Wheelhouse Loafer,* 37:50

American Bureau of Shipping, *Guide for Building and Classing Offshore Racing Yachts,* 87:108

Ayer Company, *The Historic American Merchant Marine Survey,* 62:115

Barlow, Peter, *The Marine Photography of Peter Barlow,* 6:72

Barrett, Wayne, and David A. Walker, *Small Wooden Boats of the Atlantic,* 97:97

Beekman, W. Boerhare, *Elsevier's Wood Dictionary, Vol. I,* 75:99

Benford Design Group, *Small Craft Plans,* 98:97

Bingham, Fred P., *Practical Yacht Joinery,* 54:132

Blunt, Edmund M., *The American Coast Pilot,* 5:73

Bolger, Philip C., *Small Boats,* 8:72, 37:50

Bolger, Philip C., *The Folding Schooner and Other Adventures in Boat Design,* 17:76

Borland, Loren, *Shipshape and Bristol Fashion,* 6:72

Brann, Christian, *The Little Ships of Dunkirk,* 94:99

Braund, Stephen R., *The Skin Boats of Saint Lawrence Island, Alaska,* 90:140

Bray, Maynard, *Mystic Seaport Museum Watercraft,* 31:94

Bray, Maynard, and Carlton Pinheiro, *Herreshoff of Bristol,* 92:108

Bunting, William H., *Portrait of a Port: Boston,* 37:50

Bureau of Ships, U.S. Navy, *Wood: A Manual for Its Use as a Shipbuilding Material,* 75:99

Calder, Nigel, *Boatowner's Mechanical and Electrical Manual,* 95:115

Cantin, Donald, *The Care and Maintenance of Small Boats,* 7:74

Carrick, Robert, and Richard Henderson, *John G. Alden and His Yacht Designs,* 56:128

Carter, Glen, *My Waterfront,* 22:100

Case, Betsy, and Ben Dennis, *Houseboat,* 22:100

Chapelle, Howard, *American Small Sailing Craft,* 37:50

Chevalier, François and Jacques Taglang, *AMERICA's Cup Yacht Designs,* 82:97

Chudnoff, Martin, *Tropical Timbers of the World,* 75:99

Cole, Guy, *Best of Uffa,* 29:108

Creagh-Osborne, Richard, *Dinghy Building,* 17:76

Crocker, Sturgis S., *Sam Crocker's Boats: A Design Catalog,* 68:105

Cruising Club of America, Technical Committee, *Desirable and Undesirable Characteristics of Offshore Yachts,* 79:95

Culler, R.D., *Building the SPRAY,* 26:98

Day, Cyrus L., *The Art of Knotting and Splicing,* 28:95

Deal, Shirley Herd, *The Cruising Cook,* 18:100

de Hartog, Jan, *The Distant Shore,* 37:50

de Kerchove, René, *International Maritime Dictionary,* 37:50

Dennis, Ben, and Betsy Case, *Houseboat,* 22:100

Dixon, June, *Uffa Fox: A Personal Biography,* 29:108

Dunbaugh, Edwin L., and William duBarry Thomas, *William H. Webb: Shipbuilder,* 100:119

Durant, Kenneth, and Helen, *The Adirondack Guideboat,* 37:110

Durham, Bill, and Lowell North, *Steamboats and Modern Steam Launches,* 37:50

Dye, Frank and Margaret, *To Iceland and Norway in an Open Boat,* 24:102

Eastland, Jonathan, *Great Yachts and Their Designers,* 81:98

Estep, H. Cole, *How Wooden Ships Are Built,* 58:124

Faerøyvik, Bernhard and Øystein, *Inshore Craft of Norway,* 35:89

Forest Products Laboratory, *Some Books About Wood,* 2:65

Forest Products Laboratory, *Wood Handbook: Wood as an Engineering Material,* 3:72, 75:99

Forester, C.S., *Hornblower Saga,* 37:50

Fostle, D.W., *Speedboat,* 87:105

Frost, Ted, *From Tree to Sea: The Building of a Wooden Steam Drifter,* 71:121

Gardner, John, *Building Classic Small Craft, Vol. II,* 63:120

Reviews, book (*continued*)

Garland, Joseph, *ADVENTURE: Queen of the Windjammers*, 66:101

Gerr, Dave, *Propeller Handbook*, 92:107

Gilpin, Vincent, *The Good Little Ship*, 9:73

Giono, Jean, *The Man Who Planted Trees*, 68:13

Glasspool, John, *Open Boat Cruising*, 24:102

Gougeon Brothers, Inc., *The Gougeon Brothers on Boat Construction*, 31:94, 70:120

Gougeon Brothers, Inc., *Wooden Boat Restoration & Repair*, 100:120

Grayson, Stan, *The Dinghy Book*, 46:118

Greenhill, Basil, *Archaeology of the Boat*, 36:110

Greenhill, Basil, *Literature of the Boat*, 44:120

Greenhill, Basil, *The Evolution of the Wooden Ship*, 90:136

Greenhill, Basil, *The Ship*, 59:120

Griffiths, Maurice, *Dream Ships*, 12:78

Griffiths, Maurice, *The Magic of the Swatchways*, 37:50

Guthorn, Peter J., *The Sea Bright Skiff and Other Jersey Shore Boats*, 18:100

Guzzwell, John, *TREKKA Round the World*, 84:97

Hamlin, Cyrus, *Preliminary Design of Boats and Ships*, 94:102

Hanna, John, *How-to-Build Gulfweed*, 12:78

Hanna, John, *How-to-Build Tahiti*, 12:78

Hayward, Charles H., *Woodwork Joints*, 14:76

Hazen, David, *The Stripper's Guide to Canoebuilding*, 42:114

Henderson, Richard, and Robert Carrick, *John G. Alden and His Yacht Designs*, 56:128

Herreshoff, L. Francis, *An L. Francis Herreshoff Reader*, 25:104

Herreshoff, L. Francis, *Sensible Cruising Designs*, 1:76

Herreshoff, L. Francis, *The Common Sense of Yacht Design*, 2:65

Hill, Thomas, *Ultralight Boatbuilding*, 81:97

Hill, Utegaard, and Riordan, *Dutton's Navigation and Piloting*, 37:50

Hoadley, R. Bruce, *Understanding Wood: A Craftsman's Guide to Wood Technology*, 39:104, 75:99

Howland, Llewellyn, *Sou'West and By West of Cape Cod*, 80:89

Howland, Waldo, *A Life in Boats*, 61:117

International Wood Trade Publications, Inc., publisher, *Imported Wood Purchasing Guide*, 75:99

Johnstone, Paul, *The Sea-Craft of Prehistory*, 49:117

Kemp, Peter, editor, *The Oxford Companion to Ships and the Sea*, 22:100

Lane, Carl D., *Boatowner's Sheet Anchor*, 5:74, 21:92

Lang, Steven, and Peter Spectre, *On the Hawser: A Tugboat Album*, 42:114

Lansing, Alfred, *Endurance*, 69:107

Leather, John, *Colin Archer and the Seaworthy Double-Ender*, 32:86

Leather, John, *Gaff Rig*, 7:74

Leavens, John M., *The Catboat Book*, 3:72

Lewis, Charles Lee, *Books of the Sea*, 37:50

Lewis, John, *Restoring Vintage Boats*, 10:72

Lindquist, William C., *The Richardson Story*, 100:123

Lipke, Paul, *Plank on Frame: The Who, What, and Where of 150 Boatbuilders*, 41:117

Little, Elbert L., Jr., *Checklist of United States Trees (Native and Naturalized)*, 75:99

Livingston Marine Services, *The North American Yacht Register*, 26:98

Manley, Atwood, *Rushton and His Times In American Canoeing*, 37:50

Manry, Robert, *TINKERBELLE*, 37:50

March, Edgar J., *Inshore Craft of Britain in the Days of Sail and Oar*, 52:129

March, Edgar J., *Literature of the Boat*, 52:129

March, Edgar J., *Sailing Drifters*, 52:129

March, Edgar J., *Sailing Trawlers*, 52:129

March, Edgar J., *Spritsail Barges of the Thames and Medway*, 52:129

Marshall, Michael W., *Fishing—The Coastal Tradition*, 92:104

Matthiessen, Peter, *Men's Lives: The Surfmen and Baymen of the South Fork*, 73:112

McKee, Eric, *Working Boats of Britain: Their Shape and Purpose*, 55:118

Mendlowitz, Benjamin, and Joel White, *Wood, Water & Light*, 87:107

Mudie, Rosemary and Colin, *Power Yachts*, 20:96

Mulville, Frank, *Schooner INTEGRITY*, 40:114

Neill, Peter, editor, *Maritime America*, 90:135

Nielsen, Christian, *Wooden Boat Designs*, 38:102

Nordhoff, Charles, and James N. Hall, *BOUNTY Trilogy*, 37:50

North, Lowell, and Bill Durham, *Steamboats and Modern Steam Launches*, 37:50

Oughtred, Iain, *Wooden Boatbuilding in Britain: A Guide to Designers, Builders, and Suppliers*, 70:74

Pardey, Lin and Larry, *Cruising in SER-AFFYN*, 14:76

Parker, Reuel, *The New Cold-Molded Boatbuilding*, 95:118

Payson, Harold H., *Boat Modeling with Dynamite Payson*, 95:116

Payson, Harold H., *Go Build Your Own Boat*, 57:124

Peterson, William N., *Mystic Built: Ships and Shipyards of the Mystic River, Connecticut, 1784–1919*, 92:106

Pinheiro, Carlton, and Maynard Bray, *Herreshoff of Bristol*, 92:108

Pretzer, Robert, *Marine Metals Manual*, 9:73

Prout, Geoffrey, *Simple Boat-Building*, 67:117

Pyle, Douglas C., *Clean Sweet Wind: Sailing Craft of the Lesser Antilles*, 47:118

Rabl, Sam, *Boatbuilding in Your Own Backyard*, 37:50

Remote Area Conflict Information Center, *Blue Book of Coastal Vessels—South Vietnam*, 86:89

Richards, Joe, *PRINCESS*, 4:63

Richards, Joe, *PRINCESS—New York*, 37:50

Ridler, Donald, *Eric the Red*, 1:76

Rodengen, Jeffrey L., *The Legend of Chris-Craft*, 87:110, 88:6, 89:4

Ronnberg, Erik A.R., *To Build a Whaleboat: Historical Notes and a Modelmaker's Guide*, 67:103

Rosenow, Frank, *Seagoing Knots*, 97:98

Rousmaniere, John, *The Golden Pastime: A New History of Yachting*, 75:101

Rousmaniere, John, *The Annapolis Book of Seamanship*, 90:138

Rousmaniere, John, editor, *Desirable and Undesirable Characteristics of Offshore Yachts*, 79:95

Salaman, R. A., *Dictionary of Tools Used in Woodworking*, 13:18

Simmons, Walter, *Finishing*, 64:106

Slocum, Joshua, *Sailing Alone Around the World*, 37:50

Smeeton, Miles, *Once is Enough*, 84:97

Smith, Hervey Garrett, *The Arts of the Sailor*, 8:72

Spectre, Peter, and Steven Lang, *On the Hawser: A Tugboat Album*, 42:114

Speltz, Robert, *The Real Runabouts*, 25:104

Speltz, Robert, *The Real Runabouts IV: Outboard Edition*, 53:122

Spurr, Daniel, *Yacht Style*, 99:108

Steele, Virginia, *Live Oaking: Southern Timber for Tall Ships*, 48:117

Stelmok, Jerry, and Rollin Thurlow, *The Wood & Canvas Canoe*, 85:112

Stephens, W.P., *Traditions and Memories of American Yachting*, 43:117, 91:92

Steward, Robert M., *Boatbuilding Manual*, 78:90

Story, Dana, *Frame Up!*, 72:113

Story, Dana, narrator, *Building the Blackfish*, 89:110

Street, Donald M., Jr., *The Ocean Sailing Yacht*, 11:79

Taube, Allen, *The Boatwright's Companion*, 74:109

Taylor, Roger C., *Knowing the Ropes*, 97:98

Thomas, Barry, *Building the Herreshoff Dinghy*, 21:92

Toss, Brion, *Knots*, 97:98

Upton, Joe, *Alaska Blues*, 37:50

Watson, Aldren, *Hand Tools: Their Ways and Workings*, 51:118

Weiner, Michael A., *Plant a Tree*, 27:108

White, Chris, *The Cruising Multihull*, 98:98

White, Joel, and Benjamin Mendlowitz, *Wood, Water & Light*, 87:107

Worcester, G.R.G., *The Junks and Sampans of the Yangtze River*, 16:69

Zimmerly, David, *Hooper Bay Kayak Construction*, 45:115

Reviews (film) appearing in *WoodenBoat*:

Ghosts of Cape Horn, 45:29

letter on review of *Ghosts of Cape Horn*, 46:9

Reviews (product) appearing in *WoodenBoat*:

Arabol (latex-type adhesive), 91:110

battery-powered tools, 82:100

blocks, wooden and metal, 83:93

boat plans catalogs, 89:112, 93:118, 96:98

Bottom Prep All Temp (undercoater), 99:112

Chain Mate anchor chain scrubber, 93:116

computer software for ABS standards applications, 87:108

DuraKore (balsa/hardwood composite), 79:93

Flounder Bay Boat Lumber, 99:107

hardware chandlers and manufacturers, 86:91

knives, 88:109

model kits, 85:109

plastic fastenings, 99:110

Porter-Cable Random Orbit Sander, 96:97

solar panels, 78:87

T & L Screw Extractors, 93:117

tool catalogs, 85:107
Vise-Grip pliers and clamps, 93:120
Womanswork gloves, 80:93
waterstones, sharpening systems, 91:103
Weems and Plath parallel rules and
  dividers, 100:214
Wooden Boat Shop, Seattle, Washington,
  93:115
Reviews (video) appearing in *WoodenBoat*,
  listed by title:
  Bahamas Video Cruise Guide, 84:101
  Basic Celestial Concepts, 77:109
  Bowl Turning, 68:107
  Carve a Ball-and-Claw Foot, 68:107
  Carving Techniques and Projects, 83:97
  Cats Conquer Offshore Racing: Big Seas '85,
    73:110
  Celestial Navigation, 77:109
  Celestial Navigation Simplified, 77:109
  Classic Speedboats of Tahoe, 69:116
  Concordia—A Classic Wooden Yacht, 94:101
  Dovetail a Drawer, 68:107
  Radial-Arm-Saw Joinery, 68:107
  Runabout Renaissance, 98:102
  The American Challenge, 64:38
  The Boatbuilding Video Series: The Lines,
    66:104
  The Gloucester ADVENTURE, 89:109
  The Great Lakes, Volume I: Lake Michigan,
    84:101
  The Keys Video Cruising Guide, 84:101
  The Riddle of the Sands, 67:101
  The Shape of Speed, 80:93
  Virgin Islands Video Cruise Guide, 84:101
  Voyage to Understanding, 78:90
  Wood Finishing, 68:107
  Wooden Planes and Cabinet Scrapers, 72:103
Reviews (video), navigation:
  comments by Steve Woycke, 81:100
Reviews (video), woodworking:
  comments by Douglas Lee, 76:119
Reynaud, Capt. A.F.:
  letter on maritime preservation, 91:4
RHIANNON (sloop):
  owner's comments, photos, plans, 8:18
Rhodes, Philip L., designer:
  comments, 47:46, 97:76
  Penguin class, 27:94
  See also Designs, Rhodes, Philip L.
Rhuland, Fred, builder (Nova Scotia):
  schooner VOYAGER, 33:90
Ribbands:
  illustrated glossary, 60:115
  installation method/Bud McIntosh, 15:74
Ribs:
  repair technique/wood-and-canvas canoe/
    Rollin Thurlow, 78:56
  technique/birchbark canoe/Henri
    Vaillancourt, 87:80
  See also Frames
Rice, Larry, author:
  "The Folding Kayak," 53:75
Rice, Randall H., author:
  "Built to Win: Windmill Class," 26:88
Richards, Joe, author:
  "Old John's Kicker," 9:22
  "The Fish and the Bird," 4:14
Richards, Myron N.:
  letter on deck canvasing, 25:8
Richards, Peter B.:
  letter on Bud McIntosh, 53:8
Richardson, George, builder:
  sardine carriers, 58:52

Richardson, James B. (Jim), builder:
  interview by Randall Peffer, methods, 24:52
  pinnace DOVE, 26:30, 26:36
  profile, photos, 65:32
Richardson, R.R., author:
  "Ashcroft Construction," 8:50
Richardson Boat Co., builder:
  Cruisabouts, 28:92, 29:101
  31' Cruisabout, 22:92
  31' Sedan, 22:92
Richardson Boat Owners Association:
  history, 35:37
Richardson Cruisabout:
  design commentary, photos, plans, 28:92,
    29:101
Rieff, Brion, author:
  "Product Review: The Porter-Cable
    Random Orbit Sander," 96:97
Rieff, Brion, builder:
  transom replacement/Concordia 33 FREE
    SPIRIT, 99:28
Riess, Warren:
  comments on Ronson ship, 63:96
Rig design:
  Bermudian rig/Iain Oughtred, 77:44
  commentary by Colin Palmer, 92:76
  comments by Rod Stephens, 73:42
  comments by Joel White, 75:111
  exotic rigs/Iain Oughtred, 78:66
  for boeier PHOENIX, 27:32
  for canoe, 22:33
  for canoe yawl SHEILA, 64:49
  for Chesapeake crabbing skiff, 69:100
  for converting knockabout to yawl, 6:14
  for Maine sloop-boat, 2:15
  for main-trysail ketch DIABLESSE, 81:52
  for Micronesian canoe, 31:42
  for pulling boat MOCKINGULL, 48:50
  for schooner APPLEDORE III, 76:36
  for sharpie, 25:36
  for skiff SAM WISE, 29:56
  for yawl MOCCASIN, 18:20
  gaff rig/Iain Oughtred, 75:80
  gaff rig/William Payne, 53:48
  gunter rig/Iain Oughtred, 74:100
  junk rig/Iain Oughtred, 65:4
  letter by Lloyd Bergeson, 98:6
  letter by Rick Day, 94:4
  letter by Richard T. Miller, 94:4
  letter by Russ Vinden, 94:4
  lug rig/Iain Oughtred, 73:80
  sprit rig/Ernie Cassidy, 89:30
  sprit rig/Iain Oughtred, 76:80
  See also Boom jaws
Riggers (outriggers):
  installation in recreational shell KING-
    FISHER, 63:63
Rigger's knife:
  beryllium-copper, making of, 39:84
Rigging:
  on Bahamian smack UNITY B, 81:34
  on Norwegian lestabåt VARIN, 95:90
  procedures aloft, 70:92
  swaged terminals inspection, 81:75
  technique for 1x19 wire splice, 81:45
  See also Blocks, wooden and metal;
    Cordage, techniques for
Riggs, Malcolm McB.:
  letter on wooden block maintenance, 53:7
Rig tuning:
  commentary by Art Paine, 95:55
Rindlaub, Curtis, author and designer:
  "The Tale of a Strip-Planked Kayak," 57:60

Rindlaub, Curtis, author and photographer:
  "Pert Lowell and the Art of the Mast
    Hoop," 65:40
Riordon, Frank:
  founder of Chesapeake Academy of
    Traditional Boatbuilding, 14:34
Ripsaw:
  method of sharpening/Harold Payson,
    47:91, 48:44
Rist, Walter R., photographer:
  cover photo/Colorado River dory, 15:0
Riva, Carlo, builder (Italy):
  Riva speedboats, 17:70
Riva speedboat:
  builder, photos, 17:70
  cover photo/John Watney, 17:0
Riverboat: (*See* Au Sable River boats,
  Colorado River dory, McKenzie River drift
  boat, RIVERKEEPER [utility outboard
  launch]; Steamboat, river)
River Boyne coracle:
  construction commentary, history, photos,
    79:17
RIVERKEEPER (utility outboard launch):
  cover photo/Robert Knowles, 61:0
  design and construction comments, opera-
    tion, photos, plans, 61:72
Riverside Boat Yard, builder:
  comments on boat covers, 54:92
  method for storing boats, 48:91
  refinishing techniques, 40:56
River skiff, English:
  design and construction commentary,
    history, photos, 30:36
Rivets:
  compared to screws, 51:72, 55:43
  removal from lapstrake planking, 71:38,
    92:90
  removal from planking, letter by John S.
    Bennett, 73:8
  technique for Catspaw dinghy (Herreshoff
    Columbia model), 27:63
  technique for Herreshoff 12½/Steve
    Ballentine, 56:93
  technique for lapstrake canoe PICCOLO/
    Bob Baker, 37:57
  technique for Lawley dinghy/Jackie Mons,
    50:88
  technique for Norwegian pram/Arne Emil
    Christensen, 49:28
  technique of Bud McIntosh, 19:50
Roach, Patrick, photographer:
  cover photo/Fife schooner ALTAIR, 90:0
ROAMER (steam yacht):
  comments, photo, 84:34
ROBERT E. LEE (steamer):
  comments, photo, 64:64
ROBERT SCOTT (iceboat):
  history, 38:64
Roberts, David, author:
  "Product Review: Bottom Prep All Temp,"
    99:112
Roberts, Richard R.:
  letter on U.S. Coast Guard boardings, 91:6
Robertson, Malcolm, builder:
  Sea Sled, 100:58
ROBERTSON II (schooner):
  comments, photo, 65:76
Robichaux, Francis:
  comments, 26:83
ROBIN (cat-ketch):
  designs/Rob Pittaway, 51:131

ROBIN (Pacific Coast class):
comments, photo, 65:76
Robinhood Marina, builder:
schooner ACTIVE, 7:20
Robinson, Barbara, author:
"Polynesia's Honored Beings," 19:25
Robinson, Robby, author:
"Designer Olin J. Stephens II," 98:50
Robinson, W.A., Inc., builder:
brigantine VARUA, 65:44
Robinson, William Albert:
profile, photos, 65:44
ROB ROY (schooner):
comments, plans, 32:66
ROB ROY (yawl):
comments, photo, 65:76
Rob Roy canoe:
comments, photo, 55:88
comments, plan, 70:104
Rockport Apprenticeshop:
builder of Norwegian lestabåt VARIN,
95:90
comments on, 71:44
Rodengen, Jeffrey L.:
letter on review of *The Legend of Chris-Craft*,
88:6
Rogers, John, author:
"A Shark with Teeth," 69:29
Rogers, Nick, photographer:
"A Week Along the Thames," 74:54
cover photo/Thames skiff, 74:0
ROGUE'S ROOST (sloop):
comments, 23:25
ROGUE WAVE (trimaran):
cover photo/Polly Brown, 23:0
design and construction commentary,
photos, plans, 23:68
Rolling and tipping: (*See* Painting techniques)
Rollins, Paul, builder:
repair of brigantine VARUA, 65:44
RONDINA (cutter):
comments, photo, 91:92
RONDO (sloop):
repair, 51:59
Ronson Ship:
archaeological dig, construction commentary, photos, 63:96
history, 63:101
Roofing tar, use:
application for underwater seams, 74:17,
81:75
bedding butt blocks, 67:23
Rooney, Jim, author:
"The Makassar Ketch," 14:66
Rope grommet:
making, 32:49, 55:114
Roper, David, author:
"When Boats Are Proud," 16:17
Ropework: (*See* Cordage, techniques for)
Roping technique:
for ditty bag and sails, 32:49
ROSA LEE (skipjack):
comments, plan, 79:106
Rosborough Boats, builder (Nova Scotia):
kit boats, 39:69
Rose, Donald, author:
"Two Elcos: Vintage Rose," 13:27
Rose, Peter, photographer:
"Sam Devlin," 85:52
Rose Brothers Boat Works, builder:
Harkers Island power skiff, 17:23

Rosencrantz, Donald C., designer:
association with Ken Bassett, 54:82
obituary, 44:78
Rosenfeld, Howard, author:
"No Wrinkles: Canvasing the Deck," 14:64
Rosenfeld, Morris and Sons, photographer:
"A Decade of Legendary 12s," 68:40
"New York 30s, Then, But Mostly Now
Also," 35:20
cover photo/12-Meters ZIO and
NIGHTWIND, 68:0
Rosenfeld, Stanley, photographer:
interview, 90:46
Rosenfeld photo collection:
comments by Revell J. Carr, 90:46
ROSE NOELLE (trimaran):
comments, photos, 92:34
ROSE PLUNKETT (utility launch):
builder (Lucy McCarthy), photos, 79:22
ROSEWAY (schooner):
comments, photo, 39:32
cover photo/Sherry Streeter, 60:0
Rosewood:
comments, 36:89
ROSIE B (runabout):
comments, photo, 50:31
Ross, Mitchell K., M.D., author:
"First Aid: A Primer for the Boatshop,"
96:74
Ross Bandmill Portable Sawmill:
operation of, photos, 62:110
Rössel, Greg:
WoodenBoat School/Miskito (Honduras)
Indian project, photo, 88:76
Rot: (*See* Decay in wooden boats)
Rotating rigs:
commentary by Iain Oughtred, 78:66
Roth, McKie W., builder:
Friendship sloop kit boat, 39:69
letter on projection lofting, 52:10
Rousmaniere, John, author:
"Looking for the One Shot," 90:46
reviewer of *Herreshoff of Bristol* (book),
92:108
Router:
advice on buying used, 70:31
for building louvered doors, 94:84
for cutting rabbets/peapods, 77:74
for dovetail construction, 98:89
for plank repair/Chris-Craft Riviera, 96:87
for scarfing planks, 67:30
Rover class:
designs/Philip L. Rhodes, 28:97
ROWDY II (sloop):
comments, photo, 75:34
Rowe, Lester, designer:
sharpie, 25:36
Rowe, Spencer, author:
"The Chincoteague Scow: Form Follows
Function," 49:81
ROWENA: (*See* RESOLUTE [Blanchard 36])
Rowing:
comments on technique, 42:38
sculling technique for recreational shell,
63:63
technique for Norwegian lestabåt, 95:90
Rowing events:
Muskingum regatta, 66:23
Rowsell, Spud, builder (England):
profile, 58:100
Royal Naval Museum (England):
comments, 46:54

Royal Ship of Cheops:
history, photos, plans, restoration commentary, 38:28
ROYONO (yawl):
photos, repair, 1:4
Rozinante (ketch):
design commentary, 56:38
design commentary, performance, photos,
plans, rig, 26:40
R S COLIN ARCHER (ketch):
comments, photo, 20:35
RUBEN DE CLOUX (pungy schooner):
designs/Bruce Northrup, 68:110
Rubicam, Stephen, photographer:
"The Swampscott Dory—Hodgdon Style,"
51:50
cover photo/ketch WHITEHAWK, 25:0
Rubino, Tom, author:
"A Peapod for Passage," 13:61
RUBY (sloop):
owner's comments, 25:48
Rudder:
design for Cape Cod catboat, 31:84
design for Herreshoff 12½, 32:76
for Biscayne Bay 14 daysailer, 98:28
materials and building technique/Philip
Teuscher, 20:70
Rudderport:
repair technique/Bud McIntosh, 84:44
Ruge, Raymond A., author:
"The History and Development of the
Iceboat, Part I," 38:64
"The History and Development of the
Iceboat, Part II," 39:88
RUGOSA II (New York 40):
comments, photo, 33:50
Runabout:
at Lake Tahoe Concours d'Élégance, 62:74
comments by Robert Speltz, 10:53
designs/W.S. Baber, 22:88
Florida antique-boat cruise, 90:78
letter by Don Benjamin, 79:8
letter on BUC Boat Price Guide, 79:7
restoration philosophy of Dick Clarke,
65:90
restoration philosophy of Bill Morgan,
71:82
restorations by Wayne Mocksfield, 41:72
surveying guide with drawings, 77:79
See also ACE, Alexandria Bay boats, BABY
BOOTLEGGER, Chris-Craft Riviera,
Downeaster 18, Grand Craft, Hacker
Boat Company, MISS RUTH, Nunes Jet,
PIUTE III, RAINBOW IV, ROSIE B,
Speedboat
Rushton, J. Henry, designer/builder:
comments, 31:58, 90:56
comments about, 61:124, 65:66
on canoe paddles, 37:67
Wee Lassie canoe, 100:92
Rushton canoe:
comments by R.D. Culler, 11:2
Rushton Princess (canoe):
comments, 31:58
Russell, Marylyn, author:
reviewer of *Houseboat* (book), 22:100
Russia, watercraft: (*See* SEDOV [four-masted
bark])
RUTH-MARY (sardine carrier):
comments, 59:70
Ryder-Turner, David, author:
letter about 19-Meters, 83:5

SAANICH BEAGLE (sloop):
design and construction commentary, plans, 12:70

SABINO (steamboat):
comments, 9:10
comments, photo, 38:36

SACHEM (launch):
comments, photo, 84:34

SAFARI (Concordia yawl):
comments, photo, 80:64

Safety precautions:
accident-prevention comments, 79:45
advice on safety gear, 79:41
advice on steam-generating rigs, 88:50
advice when sanding and grinding epoxy coatings, 94:35
commentary on boatyard hazards/Paul Lazarus, 93:86
commentary on boatyard hazards/Peter H. Spectre, 79:34
comments by Larry Montgomery, 90:145
editorial by Jon Wilson, 79:1
editorial on noise pollution, 81:2
first-aid procedures, 96:74
first-aid procedures, letter on, 98:4
for using recreational shell KINGFISHER, 63:63
letter by Wallace D. Whitford, 84:8
letter on hearing protection, 81:7
letter on portable venting system, 81:5

SAGA (commuter):
comments, photo, 94:74

SAGA (yawl):
cover photo, 49:0
history, photos, 49:74

SAGA SIGLAR (Viking Age merchant ship replica):
construction commentary, launching, voyage, photos, 68:19

Sail area-to-displacement ratio:
explained, 59:116

Sail-assisted workboats:
comments/Jim Brown, 42:66

Sail design:
battened vs. battenless mainsail, 64:34
commentary by Colin Palmer, 92:76
commentary by Iain Oughtred, 73:80, 74:100, 75:80, 76:80, 77:44, 78:66
editorial on sail plan efficiency, 92:2
for Cape Cod catboat, 3:51
for Catspaw dinghy, 28:64
for flatiron skiff, 29:56
for iceboats, 38:64
for peapods, 27:52
for pulling boat MOCKINGULL, 48:50
for sailing canoe, 22:33

for schooner WANDER BIRD, 55:56
letter on angelwing rig by Tom Godfrey, 63:7
letters on battenless mainsail, 66:7
See also Rig design

Sail Gazela, Inc.:
comments, 44:62

Sailing canoe: (*See* Canoe, sailing)

Sailing critique:
canoe yawl LA MOUETTE, 75:69

Sailing dinghies:
designs by Jack Holt, 74:64
designs/Robert P. Beebe, 45:110
designs/R.D. Culler, 24:96, 57:118
designs/Joseph Dobler, 57:118
designs/Frederick Goeller, 25:95
designs/Rob Pittaway, 51:131
designs/S.S. Rabl, 57:118
See also Acorn skiff (sailing skiff), Catspaw dinghy (Herreshoff Columbia model), DINGUS, Fatty Knees sailing dinghy, H-14, Marisol, Mirror class dinghy, NELLIE, Nutshell pram, Sid Skiff, TELKKÄ (Swedish ship's boat), Tender Ten

Sailing skiff, Chapelle sharpie:
designs/Howard I. Chapelle, 88:114

Sailing skiff, WHISP:
designs/Steve Redmond, 72:98

Sailing skiff, Windward 15:
designs/Karl A. Stambaugh, 88:114

Sailing techniques:
Bahamian smack UNITY B, 81:34
Bristol Channel pilot cutter, 71:60
Concordia yawl/Waldo Howland, 80:72
English cobles, 86:58
Great South Bay Scooter, 92:52
Indonesian janggolan, 77:52
lobstering under sail, 1:65
Norwegian lestabåt, 95:90
Pacific proas/Russell Brown, 83:58
professional skippers on traditional vessels, 96:58
rudderless peapod sailing, 27:52
square-rigged ships, 50:96
yawl rig, 64:49
See also Reefing a sail, Seamanship

Sailmaker's eyesplice:
how to make, 32:49

Sailmaking:
herringbone stitch, 37:95
letter on, 54:11
roping technique, 32:49
sewing a patch, 36:86
sewing details, 32:49
sewing reef nettles, 38:100
tools for, 31:30

Sail preservatives:
comments, 22:94
letter on, 23:8

Sails:
cut and trim of, 53:48
maintenance and repair, 93:60
patching technique for cotton sails, 81:75

SAILSKI (catamaran):
comments, photo, 55:32

Sail training:
commentary by Lance Lee, 71:44
history of schooner ADVENTURESS, 90:94

Sail training vessels: (*See* FOUDROYANT [frigate], GAZELA PRIMEIRO [barkentine])

St. John River boat, BRUNSWICK LION:
construction commentary, history, photo,

plans, 15:34

St. Katherine's Dock (England):
comments, 46:54

St. Lawrence River skiff:
design and construction commentary, history, plans, 20:48
design and construction commentary, photos, plan, 21:26
drawings, frame and plank repairs, photos, 32:57
history, photos, plans, 11:58

St. Lawrence yawl:
history, photos, 8:58

St. Lawrence yawl replica:
designs/Tim Evans, 85:117

ST. MARGARET II (schooner):
docking under sail, 17:26

ST. MARY (dragger):
comments, photo, 79:48

ST. MARY (ketch):
design commentary, photo, 6:66

St. Mary's City Commission:
comments, 26:30

ST. PETER (dragger):
operation of, photos, 69:54

St. Pierre dory, EMME:
owner's comments, photos, 35:41

Salentine Boat Works, builder:
Penguin class, 27:94

Salisbu, Kirby G.:
letter on tropical deforestation, 93:4

Sallee Rover (sloop):
compiling lumber list, photo, plans, 87:46
illustrated glossary of wooden boat terms, 60:115

SALLY MAY (Canvasback):
comments, photo, 95:70

SALLY II (sloop):
comments, plan, 72:44

SALLY VII (knockabout sloop):
comments, photo, plans, 52:40

Salt Boatbuilding School (ME):
boatbuilding program, 42:100

Saltdal Videregående Skole (Norway):
program, 23:80

Salting of hulls:
as a preservative, 2:36

Salvage:
of cutter MIZPAH, 60:120
of schooner ALVIN CLARK, 52:59

SAMONA (motoryacht):
comments, 94:54

SAM WISE (skiff):
design and performance commentary, photos, 29:56

Sandbagger:
critique of model, 63:112, 64:102

Sandbagger, CRUISER:
comments, plan, 63:112

Sander, Porter-Cable Random Orbit:
product review by Brion Rieff, 96:97

Sanders, K.E., author:
"A Little Irish Fleet," 10:25

Sanderson, Jill, author:
"Eye-Sweet & Spacious," 22:46

Sanding:
advice from professionals, 40:56
letter by Daniel MacNaughton, 95:4
technique for brightwork, 16:56, 27:40, 40:56, 82:88, 83:66
technique for early launching, 63:87, 64:58
technique for epoxy fairing, 94:35
technique for fitting out, 93:36

Sanding (*continued*)
technique for topsides, 21:79
with spar-finishing machine, 60:125
See also Disc sanding
Sanding blocks:
for sanding belts, 67:30
Sanding machine, Flintstone:
comments, photo, 66:56
Sandpaper:
commentary by Rebecca Wittman, 82:88
grades and storage, 15:82
SANDPIPER (ketch):
comments, detail photos, plan, 74:80
Sands, John O., author:
"Small Craft Restoration," 8:30
SANDY HOOK (pilot-boat):
comments, plan, 53:38
Sanford, Alfred F., builder:
on cold-molded hull repairs, 52:92
Sanford, John J., author:
reviewer of *Bowl Turning* (video), 68:107
reviewer of *Carve a Ball-and-Claw Foot* (video), 68:107
reviewer of *Dovetail a Drawer* (video), 68:107
reviewer of *Radial-Arm-Saw Joinery* (video), 68:107
reviewer of *Wood Finishing* (video), 68:107
San Francisco Bay felucca, MATILDA D:
comments, photo, 42:30
construction commentary, drawings, history, 13:45
drawings, performance, plans, 14:45
San Francisco Bear class:
cover photo/Jay Daniel, 50:0
history, photos, 50:34
San Francisco Pelican class:
design and construction commentary, photos, plans, 30:29
Sano, Ichiro, builder (Japan):
profile, 80:50
profile, photo, 80:54
Sano Shipyard, builder (Japan):
profile, 80:50, 80:54
SANTA LUCIA (dragger):
comments, 79:48
SANTA MARIA (Eight-Meter sloop):
comments, 59:40
SANTANA (yawl):
racing, 13:79
SAPPHIRE (New York 32):
history, 73:42
Sapwood:
comments, 1:48, 2:36
discussed/Richard Jagels, 20:20
SARAH (sharpie):
design and construction commentary, photos, plans, 80:44
SARAH MEAD (Friendship sloop):
racing, 29:64
Sardine carrier (power and sail):
history, photos, 58:52
history, photos, plans, 59:70
Sardine carriers: (*See* AMARETTO, BLACK DIAMOND, CHESTER L. PIKE, DOUBLE EAGLE, EDWARD M, EL PLACIDA, EVA H, HAZEL LEAH, HELEN McCOLL, HENRY O. UNDERWOOD, IDA MAE, JACOB PIKE, JOYCE MARIE, KINGFISHER, LIBERTY, LILLIAN, MARY ANNE, MEDRIC, NOKOMIS, PATRIOT, PAULINE, RELIANCE, RUTH-MARY, SEWANHAKA, SYLVINA W. BEAL)

Sarsfield, John, author:
"From the Brink of Extinction: Mediterranean Molding," 66:84
SASKIANNA (cutter):
designs/Bruce King, 83:112
Sassafras (wood):
commentary by D.W. Blake, 80:82
comments, 43:121
SASSOON (knockabout yawl):
photos, plans, rig modification, 6:14
SAUK (cutter):
designs/Norman Boettcher, 27:91
Saw, Disston:
history, 47:91
Saw, hand:
sharpening and rebuilding technique/ Harold Payson, 47:91
Saw, hand crosscut:
tooth design, 14:52
Saw, hand rip-:
tooth design, 14:52
Saw, power:
sharpening technique/Harold Payson, 48:44
Sawdust:
use in leaking hulls, 71:38
See also Wood dust
Sawmill operation:
comments/Richard Jagels, 38:108
methods explained, 51:106
Ross Bandmill Portable Sawmill, 62:110
Saws:
advice on buying used, 70:31
Scaling of timber:
procedure for, 51:106
Scantling rules:
for cold-molded construction/Thomas MacNaughton, 4:17
Herreshoff and Nevins, 68:87
Scantlings:
for mast hoops, 65:40
Scottish fishing vessels, 62:68
Scarborough, David:
letter on reefing small spritsails, 78:8
Scarfing, planks:
plank scarfer, 67:30
technique/Bill Modrell, 15:7
technique/W. Lyman Phillips, 9:24
Scarfing, plywood:
for fiberglass butts/Harold Payson, 87:29
technique/Dennis Davis/DK 13 kayak, 70:56
technique/John Gardner, 51:66
technique/Tom Hill, 54:74
technique/Graeme King/recreational shell Kingfisher, 61:60
technique/Lyman Boat Works, 82:68
technique/Iain Oughtred, 56:60
technique/Harold Payson, 18:77, 86:109
Scarfing, spars:
technique for Biscayne Bay 14 daysailer/ Eric Dow, 98:28
technique for hollow spars/Arch Davis, 91:25
jig design for/Bud McIntosh, 60:125
jig design for/Lin and Larry Pardey, 15:64
SCAT (catboat):
cruising in Maine, 24:64
SCELP (power cruiser):
comments, photo, plans, 54:34
Scheel, Henry A., author:
"Designs: Scheel 36, A Simple Cruiser," 49:114

Scheel, Henry A., designer:
profile, photo, 62:36
See also Designs, Scheel, Henry A.
Scheel keel:
comments, plan, 62:36
design comments, 66:124
letter by Nils Lucander, 67:6
Scheel 30 (sloop):
comments, plans, 62:36
Scheel 36 (sloop):
designs/Henry Scheel, 49:114
Scheffer, T.C., Catherine Duncan, and George Englerth, authors:
"A Technical Comparison of Red and White Oaks," 1:48
SCHEMER (cutter):
history, photo, plans, 37:42
Scherpel, Cornelus, builder (Netherlands):
construction methods, Vlets, 52:75
Schindler, Gerald, author:
"Adhesives and the Boatbuilder," 4:47
"Boatbuilders' Forum: Sheathing," 19:94
"Sheathing: What We Know," 17:54
Schmid, Peter, illustrator:
"Lapstrake Plank Repair," 71:38
"Legs for Boats," 70:52
Schmidt-Fonseca, Susan, author:
"A Core Sound Sharpie," 35:76
Schnaufer, Joe:
on boat covers, 54:92
Schneider, K.M.:
letter on Ashcroft construction, 11:4
Schools: (*See* Boatbuilding schools)
Schooner Bowdoin Inter-Island Expeditions:
comments, 47:30
Schooner design commentary:
by William Garden, 68:114
Schooners: (*See* ACTIV [Danish topsail schooner], ACTIVE, ADVENTURE, ADVENTURESS, ADVENT, ALCYONE, ALMA, ALTA C, ALTAIR, ALVIN CLARK, AMANDA F. LEWIS [pungy schooner], AMBASSADRESS, AMBERJACK, AMERICA, ANNA KRISTINA [Norwegian sailing freighter], ANNA ROSA [Norwegian sailing freighter], ANNIE CHRISTENSON [steam schooner], APPLEDORE I, APPLEDORE II, APPLEDORE III, ATTU [halibut schooner], Banks fisherman, BILL OF RIGHTS, Biloxi schooner, BLACKFISH, BLACK HAWK, BLUENOSE, BLUENOSE II, BOUNDING HOME, BOWDOIN, BRIGADOON, BRILLIANT, BUT & BEN, CALIFORNIAN, CAPRICE [pilot schooner], CAPT. R.D. CULLER [scow schooner], Cargo schooner, C.A. THAYER, CECELIA J, CHALLENGE, Chesapeake Bay pungy schooner, COASTER, COASTER I, COASTER III, COLUMBIA, COMET II, CORONET, CURTIS FOUNTAIN [Biloxi schooner], DAGNY IV [Norwegian sailing freighter], DAUNTLESS, DENYCE, Designs appearing in *WoodenBoat* design section, DON QUIXOTE, DOROTHY B, DOROTHY G, DOUBLE EAGLE, DOVE [pinky schooner], DYRAFJELD [Norwegian sailing freighter], EAGLE, EASTWARD, ELIZABETH SILSBEE, ELLEN IVY [Tancook schooner], ELSIE, ENDYMION, FEARLESS, FIDDLERS' GREEN, FORTUNE, FREDONIA, GERTRUDE L. THEBAUD, GLAD TIDINGS [pinky schooner], GLEAM,

Gloucester fishing schooner, Grand Banks fishing schooner, HALF MOON [Alden schooner], Halibut schooner, HARVEY GAMAGE, HENRY FORD, HERITAGE, ISAAC H. EVANS, J & E RIGGIN, JANET MAY, JAN VAN GENT [Shpountz 44-40], JENNY NORMAN [bugeye], JOANN, JOHN F. LEAVITT, JULIA DELACRUZ [Biloxi schooner], KATOURA, KNICKER-BOCKER, L.A. DUNTON, LADY OF BERMUDA [sharpie schooner], LAND-FALL, LEWIS R. FRENCH, LINDØ, Longsplice schooner [nesting dinghies], LOUIS A. THEBAUD, MAINE [pinky schooner], Maine Cruise Schooner Fleet, Malabar schooners, Marco Polo, MARY AND ELLEN [pungy schooner], MARY DAY, MARY DE COSTA, MARY FOSTER [Biloxi schooner], MARY MARGARET [Biloxi schooner], MARY ROSE, MATTIE, MAYFLOWER, MERCANTILE, MERLIN, MINAS PRINCE, MISTRESS, MOHAWK, MOLLYHAWK, MYA, MYRTLE LEAF, NAHEMA, NATHANIEL BOWDITCH, NATIVE GIRL, NIÑA, NORTHERN LIGHT, NORTH STAR, ORIANDA, PANDA, PATRICIA A, PEGGY, PILGRIM, Pilot schooner, PRIDE OF BALTIMORE, PRIDE OF BALTIMORE II, Pungy schooner, PURITAN, RAIN BIRD, RED JACKET, RELIANCE, ROBERTSON II, ROB ROY, ROSEWAY, RUBEN DE CLOUX [pungy schooner], ST. MARGARET II, Scow schooner, SEA CALL, SERENA, SERENITY, Sharpie [schooner-rigged], SHERMAN ZWICKER [Banks fishing schooner], SHNA TAK [steam schooner], SILVER HEELS, SOPHIA CHRISTINA, SPIKE AFRICA, SPIRIT OF MAS-SACHUSETTS, SQUAW [sharpie schooner], STAR II, Steam schooner, STEPHEN TABER, SUCCESSOR, SWIFT, SYLVINA W. BEAL, Tancook whaler, TAP-PAN ZEE, THEO G, TIGRESS, TIMBER-WIND, TOADSTOOL, TOLE MOUR [three-masted schooner], TYEHEE, UNION JACK, VAHINE, VERNON LANGILLE, VICTORY CHIMES, VOY-AGER, WANDER BIRD, WAPAMA [steam schooner], WESTWARD, ZACA)

Schroeder, Ernest, designer:
daysailer, 29:20

Schroeger, J.F., author:
"WELCOME Once Again," 10:60

Schuyler, Roosevelt, designer:
comments, 41:26

Schweiss, Paul, author/builder:
"Norwegian Finger Clamps," 24:77
comments, 17:14
reviewer of *Wooden Boat Designs* (book), 38:102

Schwicker, Bill, author/builder:
"A Three-Fathom Sharpie," 67:60
"In My View: Sharpie Points and Counterpoints," 59:36
"Pieces of Eight," 68:56
"What More Could the Commodore Ask?", 56:76
sharpie EGRET, 56:76, 59:36
three-fathom sharpie, 67:60

Sciuto, Dick, author:
"Buying and Selling Wooden Boats," 2:71, 3:69, 4:70

comments on surveyors, 4:70

Scooter: (*See* Great South Bay Scooter)

Scotland, builders: (*See* Culzean Ship & Boatbuilding Company Limited; Eyemouth Boatbuilding Co.; Forbes, J. & G., Co.; Gerrard Bros.; Henderson, John and Son; Herd & MacKenzie; Jones Shipyard; MacDuff Boatbuilding & Engineering Co.; Miller, Jas., & Sons; Noble, Alex, & Sons; Thomson's Shipyard)

Scotland, designers: (*See* Douglass, Gordon [Sandy]; Fife, William, I, II, and III [design-ers and builders]; Skidmore, A.G.; Watson, G.L.)

Scotland, watercraft:
fishing vessels, 4:50, 62:68

Scott, Alan, author:
"The Shipsmith's Art," 50:46

Scott, Katherine, author:
"Gannon & Benjamin," 95:70

SCOTTY TOO (speedboat):
comments, photo, 65:66

Scow, A-class:
history, photo, plan, 39:123

Scow, Chincoteague:
construction commentary, photos, 49:81

Scow, power:
designs/Roger Haddock, 30:98

Scow schooner, ALMA:
comments, photo, 61:88, 72:60
history, photos, plans, 3:8

Scow schooner, CAPT. R.D. CULLER:
design and construction commentary, plans, 30:42

Scow sloop, CORINTHIAN:
comments, 73:32

Scow sloop, KOLUTOO:
comments, 72:44

Scow sloop, LILY:
as cargo vessel, 31:18

Scow sloop, OUTLOOK:
comments, photo, 72:44

Scraper:
technique for sharpening, 64:58
technique for sharpening/Giffy Full, 27:40
technique for sharpening and using/Sam Manning, 90:113
technique for using/Paul Bryant, 48:91
technique for using/Rebecca Wittman, 81:88

Scraper (serrated):
for hull bottom paint removal, 63:87
sharpening and using/Sam Manning, 90:113

Screen:
comments, detail photo, 74:80

Screwdrivers, electric:
critique, 22:96

Screw extractor:
product review by Maynard Bray, 93:117

Screws, wood: (*See* Wood screws)

Scribing:
for cabin lockers/technique of Aldren Watson, 76:89
for ceiling planks/technique of Bud McIntosh, 47:69
frames/Yankee Tender skiff/Joel White, 31:71
jogglestick method/Roger Simpson, 39:106
See also Plank scriber

Scribing, waterlines:
Catspaw dinghy (Herreshoff Columbia model)/Joel White, 28:64

rescribing technique/Maynard Bray, 63:87
scribing boot-top from scum line, 81:75
technique/Biscayne Bay 14 daysailer/Eric Dow, 98:28
technique/Paul Bryant, 40:56
technique/Bud McIntosh, 55:107

SCRIMSHAW (trimaran):
comments, photo, 69:76

SCUD (yawl):
construction commentary, performance, photos, plans, voyage, 21:58

Scull: (*See* Basque racing scull, Shell)

Sculling:
rowing technique for recreational shell, 63:63
technique of Sam Manning, 100:60
technique of Douglas Martin, 48:50
technique (yuloh)/Roger C. Taylor, 42:38

Scully, J.M.:
letter on Cantiere-Motonautico Works, 54:9

Sea Bird yawl:
construction and performance commen-tary, plans, 43:35
construction commentary, photo, plans, 43:38
design and performance commentary, photos, 43:26
designs/Charles MacGregor (plywood), 50:132
letter on construction, 45:4
painting, transatlantic voyage, 44:32
performance commentary, plans, sea trials, 43:30

Seaborn, Ben, designer:
Thunderbird class, 28:90

Sea Bright skiff:
photos, surfing techniques, 17:29

SEA CALL (schooner):
design commentary, 52:40

Seacocks:
design, installation, maintenance, 71:69

SEAGULL (Scottish fishing vessel):
comments, photo, 62:68

SEA HAWK (Concordia yawl):
comments, photo, 80:64

Sea kayak: (*See* Kayak)

Sea kayaking:
history, voyaging, 53:80

SEAL (motorsailer):
comments, photo, plan, 28:20

Sealers:
for wood preservatives, 61:123

Seaman, Hazelton, builder:
sneakboxes, 20:23

Seaman, Warren, designer:
Malibu Outrigger class, 33:86

Seamanship:
comments by Michael Badham, 34:51
comments by Roger Taylor, 40:38, 41:42, 42:38, 43:50, 45:62, 47:13, 58:82
competitive racing and good judgment/ comments by Jon Wilson, 59:2
docking under sail, 17:26
letter on, 47:13
loss of schooner TYEHEE/account, 83:74
loss of schooner TYEHEE/letters on, 84:5
man-overboard maneuvers, 34:51, 58:82
navigation comments/loss of schooner TYEHEE, 83:86, 83:88
ocean voyaging, anchoring procedures, 34:51

Sea

Seamanship (*continued*)
pumping, avoiding knockdowns, avoiding shipping seas, 40:38
rowing and sailing English cobles, 86:58
safety checks, 27:74
sailing a Tancook whaler, 58:82
singlehanded sailing, 40:72
speed under sail, speed under oars, 42:38
surfing with Sea Bright skiff, 17:29
See also Navigation, Reefing a sail, Sailing technique, Sail training, Sculling

Seam compounds:
application technique, 63:87
letter on application of, 55:6
recommendations by Allen Taube, 81:75
recommendations by Ed McClave, 74:17
traditional vs. modern, 2:64
use/professional advice, 17:32, 46:66
See also Caulking compounds, Portland cement, Putty, Roofing tar, Splash Zone)

Seams:
repair methods/Maynard Bray, 57:112
tools for/Jim Emmett, 17:40
use of cedar "feathers"/William Garden, 17:86

Seams, garboard:
repair technique/Bud McIntosh, 84:44

Seams, reefing out:
tools and methods/Benjamin River Marine, 93:76
tools and methods/Maynard Bray, 57:112
tools and methods/Sam Manning, 16:47
tools and methods/L.E. Nicholson, 12:30

Searunner Trimaran (sloop):
comments, photo, 69:76, 91:38, 92:34

SEA SCRIBE (power cruiser):
comments, photo, 70:84

Sea Sleds:
design and construction commentary, photos, plans, 100:46
design and construction comments, photos, 100:58

Seasoning of wood:
drying properties and techniques, 10:39, 23:32

SEA TAR (motorsailer):
comments, plan, 29:38

Seat assembly:
DK 13 kayak, 70:56
outboard runabout Downeaster 18, 75:53
recreational shell KINGFISHER, 62:103

Seat knees:
design and construction, 26:80, 27:86

Seats:
design for small craft, 34:86

Seattle Community College (WA):
boatbuilding program, 42:100
comments, 20:33

SEA URCHIN (sailing skiff):
comments, photo, 73:60

SEA WITCH (clipper ship):
comments, painting, 78:76

Seaworthiness:
comments by Jim Brown/multihulls, 92:34
comments by Joel White, 75:111

SEBBE ALS (Viking ship replica):
construction commentary, history, photos, plans, 11:15

SEDOV (four-masted bark):
comments, photo, 85:64

SEER (motorsailer):
comments, photo, 97:76, 97:86
design commentary, photo, 29:38

Segal, Dan, author:
"Philip C. Bolger, Boat Designer," 92:42

SEGUIN (tugboat):
comments, 10:9

Seidman, David, author:
"A New Sea Sled from Mystic," 100:58
"Damned by Faint Praise," 100:46
"The Great South Bay Scooters," 92:52

Seiner, Alaska limit:
history, photos, plans, 37:31

Seiner, Alaska limit, TINY ROY II:
comments, plans, 37:31

Seiner, Danish:
fishing techniques, history, photos, plans, 88:40

Seizing:
technique, 35:80, 48:100

Seksaering (Norwegian rowing craft):
comments, photo, 28:36
history, photo, plans, 28:39

Selmer-Larsen, Johan: (*See* Designs, Selmer-Larsen, Johan)

Senior, Eric, builder:
sailing dinghy Tender Ten, 22:77

SEOLADAIR (sloop):
rebuilding commentary, 22:61

SERAFFYN (cutter):
fitting-out procedures, 18:65

SERENA (schooner):
comments, 47:11

SERENADE (sloop):
comments, photos, 83:38

SERENITY (schooner):
comments, photos, 49:44

Servais, Bob, author:
"CAPT. R.D. CULLER: A Scow Schooner Dream," 30:42

Service (serving):
technique, 48:100
wire techniques for splices and shrouds, 59:106

Sesse, African sailing canoe:
design and construction commentary, history, photos, 40:78

Setting up:
Acorn skiff/Iain Oughtred, 56:60
Biscayne Bay 14 daysailer, 96:24
Caddo Lake bateau, 62:44
Catspaw dinghy (Herreshoff Columbia model)/Joel White, 26:48
flat-bottomed skiff or sharpie, 66:48
Gloucester Light Dory/Harold Payson, 41:63
Martha's Tender skiff/Belford Gray, 45:92
McInnis bateau/John Gardner, 51:66
outboard runabout Downeaster 18, 73:67
recreational shell Kingfisher, 61:60
sailing canoe PICCOLO/Bob Baker, 36:44
schooner SPIRIT OF MASSACHUSETTS, 82:48
technique/Fred Ajootian, 14:38
technique/Bud McIntosh, 15:74
Yankee Tender skiff/Joel White, 30:74

SEVEN SEAS (12-Meter):
comments, photo, 68:40

Sewall, J.R., photographer:
"PILGRIM's Progress," 64:76

SEWANHAKA (sardine carrier):
comments, 59:70

Seyfarth, Fritz, author:
"Auxiliary Power—Views from Experience: A Preference for Gas," 54:101
"Bequia Beauty," 68:29

"In My View: The Battenless Mainsail," 64:34
"In My View: To Err Is Human, To Admit Divine," 60:41
letter on battenless mainsail, 66:7

Seyfarth, Fritz, builder:
on cold-molded hull repair, 52:92

Seymour, John, author:
"DREOILIN," 96:36

SHADOW (Falmouth oyster boat):
design and construction commentary, photo, plan, 31:36

SHADOW (sloop):
drawings, history, photos, plan, 43:64
history, 37:42
history, photos, 44:24

SHADOWFAX (ketch):
maintenance of, photos, 16:56

SHADOWFAX (trimaran):
comments, 54:56

Shadow molds:
lapstrake planking, 75:62
letter by John Breiby, 77:4
letter by Ray Speck, 77:4

Shaftlog, boring:
technique/Bud McIntosh, 33:66
technique/James L. Meriam, 63:106

Shaftlog, repair:
comments, 40:102

SHAMROCK (23-Meter):
comments, photo, 90:84

SHAMROCK (Tamar sailing barge):
comments, 60:68

SHAMROCK I (AMERICA's Cup boat):
comments, photo, 90:84

SHAMROCK III (AMERICA's Cup boat):
comments, photo, 90:84

SHAMROCK IV (AMERICA's Cup boat):
comments, photo, 85:74

SHAMROCK V (AMERICA's Cup boat):
cover photo/Onne Van Der Wal, 95:0

Shapiro, Scotty, author and photographer:
"Basque Racing Sculls," 40:52

Shark catamaran:
design and construction commentary, history, photos, 69:29

Sharkskin (bottom paint):
critique, 46:66

Sharp, Jim:
captain of schooner ADVENTURE, 39:32
captain of schooner BOWDOIN, 47:30
letter on schooner BLUENOSE II, 58:9

Sharpening systems:
critique of Sharpenset Whetstone grinder, 20:98
critique of Woodcraft Mark II grinder, 21:94
product review by Daniel Porter, 91:103

Sharpening techniques:
cabinet scrapers/Giffy Full, 27:40
handsaws/Harold Payson, 47:91
Japanese chisels/Harold Payson, 72:21
power saws/Harold Payson, 48:44
scrapers/Maynard Bray, 64:58
scrapers/Sam Manning, 90:113

Sharpie:
design commentary, history, plans by various designers, 25:36
method for turning over, 22:30
See also Advanced Sharpie (yawl); ALACRAN (sharpie ketch); Carolina sharpie, IDIE; Core Sound sharpie, TORTUGA; Egret sharpie, EGRET; Egret

sharpie, GRIMALKIN; Great Lakes sharpie (sloop); Hooper Island sharpie; KINGFISH; LADY OF BERMUDA (sharpie schooner); LAZY JACK (sharpie sloop); LIVELY (extreme sharpie); MARTHA JANE; Meadow Lark (sharpie ketch); Miss Simplette; New Haven sharpie; Norwalk Island sharpie; SARAH; SHARPIE (three-fathom sharpie); SQUAW (sharpie schooner); TASHTEGO (Black Skimmer sharpie)

Sharpie, Chapelle design:
comments, plans, 84:76

Sharpie, Chesapeake Bay:
comments, plan, 69:100

Sharpie (bugeye-rigged):
design commentary, plan, 36:62

Sharpie (schooner-rigged):
construction commentary, 33:33

SHARPIE (three-fathom sharpie):
design, construction, and performance commentary, photos, plans, 67:60

Sharptown barge:
designs by Pete Culler and Robert Steward/ comments, plans, 87:90

SHAWNEE II (Concordia 28):
comments, plan, 48:126

Sheahy, Danny, builder (Ireland):
curraghs, 50:80

SHEARWATER (cat-ketch):
design and construction commentary, photos, plans, 59:48

SHEARWATER (sloop):
designs/Henry A. Scheel, 66:124

Sheathing for wooden hulls:
comments, 19:94
fiberglass/Gloucester Light Dory, 43:96
fiberglass/Martha's Tender skiff, 47:58
types discussed, 17:54
See also Copper sheathing

Sheehan, Kevin, author:
"Hankins Heritage: Boatbuilding Report," 18:26

Sheer clamp:
Biscayne Bay 14 daysailer, 97:31
construction technique/Bud McIntosh, 41:91
repair technique for sloop RONDO/ Robert Vespa, 51:59

Sheerline:
comments, detail photo, 76:70
comments by Joel White, 75:111
fairing technique/Arch Davis, 94:29

Sheerstrakes:
outboard runabout Downeaster 18, 74:87
spiling/peapods/Jimmy Steele, 77:74

Sheet bends:
cordage technique, 53:96

SHEEVRA (National 30' Restricted class):
comments, photo, 90:84

SHEILA (canoe yawl):
comments, photo, 85:64
construction and rig commentary, history, photos, plans, 64:49

SHEILA II (yawl):
letter by Paul Titchener, 67:5

Sheldon, Irving C., author:
"Don't Give Up the Ship," 26:24
"Other Ways: Fixing a Leaky Shaftlog," 40:102

Shell, racing, built by J. Garofolo:
design and construction commentary, photos, 21:40

Shell, racing, built by George Pocock:
construction commentary, performance, photos, 21:36

Shell, racing, Olympic contenders:
comments, 13:34

Shell, recreational, Bangor Packet:
cover photo/Benjamin Mendlowitz, 52:0
designs/Joel White, 52:122

Shell, recreational, Best Boat:
designs/Uffa Fox, 54:130

Shell, recreational, built by Ken Bassett:
construction commentary, photos, 54:82

Shell, recreational, Cosine Wherry:
design and construction commentary, photo, plans, 100:100

Shell, recreational, KINGFISHER:
how to build, photos, plans, 61:60, 62:103
maintenance and storage, transporting, 63:63
rigging instructions, safety tips for using, sculling technique, 63:63

Shell, recreational, MOCKINGULL:
cover photo, 48:0
design and construction commentary, photos, 48:50

Shell, recreational, PETALUMA:
comments, photo, 73:60

Shellac, use:
comments by Ed McClave, 76:18

Shelton, Gail, author and photographer:
"Return of a Classic," 21:21

Shelton, Philip, builder:
Atwater Indian class, MONTAUK II, 21:21
methods for Maine cruise schooner JANET MAY, 63:74
sharpie schooner SQUAW, 33:36

Shelves: (See Cabin lockers)

Shepard, Ernest H., illustrator:
"Ratty's Boat," 94:44

Shepard, Warren, illustrator:
"Across the Atlantic in SEA BIRD, Part II," 44:32

Sheppard, Fred, designer (England):
ketch MAYA, 9:16, 16:66

SHERMAN ZWICKER (Banks fishing schooner):
model, photo, 97:52

Shetterly, Robert, illustrator:
"A Boatbuilder's Garden," 45:36
"Binds that Tie," 72:40
"Grommeting," 55:114
"Lashmanship," 50:101
"Living Aloft," 70:92
"Product Review: A Guide to Block Selection," 83:93
"Seven Bends," 53:96
"Spike Knots," 48:100
"The 1x19 Splice Made Possible," 81:45
"The Comforts of Service," 59:106
"The End of Your Rope," 52:112

Shew, Dick, builder:
comments, 44:117
profile, photo, 77:70

Shew & Burnham, builder:
Whitehall pulling boat, 24:58

SHIMAERA (Concordia yawl):
comments, photo, 80:64

Shipbuilding, colonial:
wood for, 58:120

Shipbuilding, Emergency Fleet, 1917–1920:
history, photos, plan, 40:94

Shipbuilding, MCM class:
construction commentary, painting,

photos, plan, 58:90

Ship model building: (See Model building)

Ships Preservation Trust of Hartlepool (England):
comments, 56:68

Ship's wheel:
how to build, photos, plans, 14:70

Shipwrights' Co-op, Sausalito:
guidelines, history, 34:38
methods, 34:36

SHIRIS (cutter):
comments, photo, 65:76

SHNA TAK (steam schooner):
comments, photos, 61:100

SHONA (cutter):
comments, photo, 41:26
racing history, 44:24

Short, Derrell, author:
"The Kodiak Kayak," 58:68

Short, William H., designer:
San Francisco Pelican class/design and flotation commentary, 30:29

Shortall, John W., III, author:
"Cold-Molded Construction: A Critique," 7:45
reviewer of Wood Handbook: Wood as an Engineering Material (book), 3:72

Shpountz 44-40, JAN VAN GENT:
design and construction commentary, photos, plans, 71:74

Shrouds:
serving technique/Brion Toss, 59:106

SIB 32 (trimaran):
comments, photo, 41:50, 69:76
design and construction commentary, 54:56
kit boat, 39:69

Sid Skiff (sailing dinghy):
design and construction commentary, photo, plan, 40:88

Siemer, Fred, builder:
scow schooner ALMA, 3:8

Sierra Boat Company, builder:
restoration of classic speedboats, 65:90

SIGMA-T (Wayfarer dinghy):
construction commentary, photos, 51:88

SIGSBEE (skipjack): photos, racing, 9:34

Sika Challenge Cup:
comments, 67:117

Sikaflex, use:
outboard boat TROUT UNLIMITED, 64:70
Quick and Dirty Boatbuilding Contest, 49:89
repair of lapstrake planking, 71:38
teak deck overlay repair, 72:53

SILHOUETTE (Luders 16 class):
photos, plan, rebuilding, 55:102

SILHOUETTE (New York 30):
history, 35:20

Silk, George, photographer:
cover photo/Thistle-class sloops, 47:0

Silveira, Mark, photographer:
cover photo/Bahama sloops AVENGER and UNITY B, 26:0

Silverballi (wood):
comments by Richard Jagels, 73:108
for repair of schooner VOYAGER, 69:94

SILVER HEELS (schooner):
comments, photos, plans, 1:32
cover photo, 1:0

SILVERHEELS (Vineyard Haven 15):
comments, 47:86

Silviculture:
comments/George Putz, 44:50, 45:36
See also Wood harvesting, Woodlot management

Simmons, Walter J., author:
"Clamps and Cleverness," 12:62
"The Lincolnville Wherry," 2:44
on finishes, 81:75
reviewer of *Building Classic Small Craft, Volume II* (book), 63:120

Simmons, Walter J., author and illustrator:
"The Trap Skiff's Delicate Daughter," 26:76

Simmons, Walter J., author and photographer:
"Repairing Lapstrake Planking," 92:90

Simmons, Walter J., builder:
comments, 19:42
Newfoundland Trap skiffs, 26:76

Simonson, Chris, author:
"Other Ways: How Archimedes Hauled Our Boat," 36:96

SIMPLEX (launch):
comments, plan, 78:30

SIMPLICITY (sloop):
design commentary, lofting, plans, 23:53
lofting, plans, 24:68

Simpson, Dwight, designer:
New England draggers, 79:48

Simpson, Roger C.E., author and photographer:
"Other Ways: The Incredible Jogglestick," 39:106

Sims, Billy Ray, author:
"Open-Boat Cruising," 70:68

SIM SEK (Noank sloop):
comments, photo, 69:48

Singh, Umbi, photographer:
"India's Teak Harvest," 32:42

SIOLA TAU (perahu lambot sloop):
design and construction commentary, photos, 10:16

SIR TOM (R class):
comments, photo, 94:54

Sisk, Hal:
comments about, photo, 61:80

Sister frames:
frame repair techniques/Ed McClave, 68:87
installation in schooner VOYAGER/Nat Benjamin, 69:94
installation in sloop RONDO/Robert Vespa, 51:59
installation in yawl TIGRIS/Steve Ballentine, 53:109

Sitka spruce:
for Biscayne Bay 14 daysailer spars, 98:28
for E.M. White guide canoe, 67:54
for sloop MELE KAI, 64:92

Sitton, Thad, and James H. Conrad, authors:
"The Caddo Lake Bateau," 62:44

SIVA (power cruiser):
comments, photo, 56:38

Sixern:
comments, photo, 71:44

Six-Meter, CAPRICE:
comments, photo, 83:38

Six-Meter, WASP:
comments, photo, 55:32

6.63-Meter sloop, AN TRI VREUR:
comments, photo, 85:64

Skahill, Thomas G., author:
"California Designer: Nick Potter," 83:38

Skaneateles Boat Company, builder:
Lightning class, 34:97, 53:68

Skauge, Bjørn, author:
"The Brenne Clamp: Norwegian Finger Clamps II," 29:67

Skauge, Bjørn, and Gunnar Eldjarn, authors:
"A Norwegian Boatbuilding School," 23:80

Skean, Cheryl, delineator:
Kodiak kayak, 58:68

Skeates, Nick, author:
"Just an Overnighter," 57:66

Skeeter iceboat:
history, photo, 39:88

Skerry Cruiser:
comments, 100:88

Skidmore, A.G., designer (Scotland): (*See* Designs, Skidmore, A.G.)

SKIDOO (Burns 30):
design and construction commentary, photos, 51:85
design commentary, performance, photos, plans, 51:83
design commentary, photos, plans, 51:80

Skiff, dory: (*See* Dory skiff, Chamberlain)

Skiffs: (*See* Acorn skiff [sailing skiff]; Amesbury skiff; Asa Thomson skiff; BLUEGILL [sailing skiff]; Bolger Cartopper dinghy; Camp Skiff [outboard cruiser]; Carolina skiff; Chamberlain dory skiff; Chesapeake Bay crabbing skiff; Chesapeake Bay outboard skiff; Cotuit skiff [daysailer]; Designs appearing in *WoodenBoat* design section; Dory skiff; GULL; Harkers Island skiff [power]; Lafitte skiff; MARIKA [power skiff]; Martha's Tender; Newfoundland trap skiff; Opheim dories and skiffs; PASSIONELLA; Power skiff; RANDANDY [bateau-type rowing skiff]; River skiff, English; Sailing skiff, WHISP; Sailing skiff, Windward 15; St. Lawrence River skiff; SAM WISE; Sea Bright skiff; SEA URCHIN [sailing skiff]; Sharptown barge; Sid Skiff [sailing dinghy]; Smith Island crabbing skiff; Southard skiff; Susan [flat-bottomed skiff]; Thames River skiff; The Pipante [power skiff]; Westport skiff; Yankee Tender skiff)

SKIMMER (Friendship sloop):
construction commentary, photos, 8:53

Skimming-dish:
history, photos, plans, 37:42

Skipjack:
designs/Charles Coad, 19:82

Skipjack, CALICO JACK:
designs/Joseph Gregory, 79:106

Skipjack, FLORA:
centerboard maintenance, 9:50

Skipjack, ROSA LEE:
comments, plan, 79:106

Skipjack, SIGSBEE:
photos, racing, 3:34

Skipjack, STANLEY NORMAN:
photos, restoration commentary, 35:62

SKOAL (spidsgatter):
design and construction, history, photos, plans, 78:50

Skookum Fastenings:
comments, 10:9, 43:104

SKYHOOK (sloop):
comments, 23:25

Skylight:
construction method of Bud McIntosh, 67:91

construction method, photos, plans/Duffy Dodge, 92:28

Slaymaker, Sam, author:
reviewer of *Boatowner's Mechanical and Electrical Manual* (book), 95:115

Sliding gunter rig: (*See* Gunter rig)

Slings:
tying technique, 20:18, 25:18, 28:18, 29:18

Sloan, Bob:
eulogy by Jon Wilson, 70:2
letter by Alice Jackson, 71:5
profile, photo, 70:42

Sloan, Mike:
letter on New York 32 FALCON, 74:7

Sloops: (*See* Acorn class, LITTLE JOSIE; ALERION III; ALERT; ALICE; AMARYLLIS [catamaran]; Amphibi-Con class; Amphibi-ette class; ANDURIL; ANGELITA [Eight-Meter]; ANNA KAY [catamaran]; AN TRI VREUR [6.63-Meter sloop]; AQUILA; Arctic Tern sloop; AREOI [catamaran]; A-scow class; ASHUMET; AVENGER [Bahamian sloop]; Balboa 26; BAMBINO; Bar Harbor 31′ class; Bear class, San Francisco; Bermuda fitted dinghy; Blanchard Knockabout; Blue Jay class; BOSWELL; BRAINSTORM [sloop-rigged lobsterboat]; Brewer 39; BROWN SUGAR; BRUCE [International 14 class]; Buzzards Bay 25′ class; Buzzards Bay 30′ class; Cadet class; Cadet dinghy; CALICO JACK [skipjack]; Cal 32 class, Camden class; CARDHU; CAROL; Celebrity class, SEOLADAIR; CHEERIO [Eight-Meter]; CHIPS [P class]; CHRISTINE; CHRISTOPHER COLUMBUS; COFFEE GRINDER; Comet class; Concordia sloop-boat; Concordia 28; Concordia 31; Concordia 33; CONDOR; Controversy class; Core Sound sharpie, TORTUGA; CRUISER [sandbagger]; CRUISING CLUB; CURLEW; CYGNET; Dark Harbor 12½′ class; Dark Harbor 17½′ class; Designs appearing in *WoodenBoat* design section; Development class; Diamond class; DILEMMA; DINGUS [sailing dinghy]; DOLPHIN [Newport 29]; Dutch boeier, PHOENIX; DYON; EAGLE [lobsterboat, sloop]; EARTHLIGHT [catamaran]; Eastport pinky; Eastward Ho! class; Eight-Meter class; EILEEN; ELECTRA; ELEUTHERA; ELMAC; Ensenada 25; Enterprise class; Eventide; FILSADAR [Concordia sloop-boat]; Fireball class; Fishers Island 23′ class; Fishers Island 31′ class; 510 class; FLIRT; Flying Dutchman class; Folkboat class; 40′ class; 46′ class; FRANCES; FREE SPIRIT [Concordia 33]; FRIENDSHIP [R-class sloop]; Friendship sloop; FROG PRINCESS; GAUNTLET; GeLu class; GENESTA; GIPSY MOTH III; GOLDEN DAZY; GOLDEN GOOSE; GOOD HOPE; GP 14 class; Great Lakes sharpie; GREAT REPUBLIC; GREAT WESTERN; GYPSY [knockabout]; HALCYON; Halfhander; HATTIE [Maine sloop-boat]; Herreshoff 12½′ class; HIPPOCAMPUS JR; Hornet class; Idem class; IDIE [Carolina sharpie]; IMAGINE [Malabar Jr.]; Indian class; International 14 class; International One-Design class; International 210 class; IOLAIRE; ISTALENA [M class]; J class; JEANNE; JEFF BROWN [Key West smackee]; KATY G;

KELPIE [Fishers Island 31]; King's Cruiser; KOALA; LAUAN [Concordia 31 sloop]; LAZY JACK [sharpie sloop]; LAZY SUSAN [catamaran]; LEGACY [Gemini class]; LIBERTY; Lightning class; LIVE YANKEE [R-class]; Lone Gull; Lubec Boat; Luders 16 class; LYRA; LYRA II; M class; MAGIC CARPET; Mair 30; Maine sloop-boat; Malabar Jr. [sloop and yawl]; MANDALAY; MARTHA; MARY LORING; Massachusetts Bay 21 class; MELE KAI; Mercury class; Merlin Rocket class; MICKY FINN; Mirror class; Miss Simplette [sharpie]; MORNING CLOUD; MVI [lobsterboat, sloop]; MYRA [sailing punt]; MYTH OF MALHAM; NAJA 30; Nancy's China; National 12 class; NEITH; NELLIE [sailing dinghy]; NELLY-ROSE [Bequia sloop]; Newport boats; New York 30 class; New York 32 class; NISMIME [research vessel]; NOBLE 41; NO GO 8; NORTH STAR; O-Boat class; OCEANUS; ORESTES [Q class]; ORIOLE [30-Square-Meter]; Osea Brig; Ostkust cruising sloop; PATRICE; Pelican class, San Francisco; Penguin class; Peterson 33; PHYLLIS; POMELION; PONTIAC [N class]; PRELUDE; PRESTIGE [M class]; PRISCILLA; PURITAN; PUSS [lobsterboat, sloop]; QUINTET 6; RACING SPLASHER; RAPIER [10-Meter]; R class; REBELLION; REDWING; RHIANNON; ROBIN [Pacific Coast class]; ROGUE'S ROOST; ROGUE WAVE [trimaran]; RONDO; ROSA LEE [skipjack]; Rover class; ROWDY II; RUBY; SAANICH BEAGLE; Sallee Rover; SALLY II; SALLY VII [knockabout sloop]; SANTA MARIA [Eight-Meter sloop]; Scheel 30; Scow sloop; Searunner Trimaran; SEO-LADAIR; SERENADE; SHADOW; SHADOWFAX [trimaran]; SHAWNEE II [Concordia 28]; SHEARWATER; SIMPLICITY; SIM SEK [Noank sloop]; SIOLA TAU [perahu lambot sloop]; Six-Meter class, CAPRICE; SKYHOOK; SNAPPER BLUE II; Sonderklasse sloops [Sonder boats]; SOPRANINO; Spidsgatter; STAR DUST [Concordia 31]; STAR III [Noank sloop]; STRATUS; STRIDER [catamaran]; TANGO II [Nine-Meter]; TARANTELLA [catamaran]; TAULUA [catamaran]; Thames sailing barge; THAT [trimaran]; Thistle class; Thunderbird class; TIFFANY JANE; TOM COD; TORETTA; Tornado class; TROPIC BIRD [trimaran]; Trumbly 38; TUESDAY; Tumlaren class; 12-Meter class; 21' class; 210 class; Typhoon class, RONDO; UNITY B [Bahama sloop]; Vagabond class; VALKYRIE; Vertue class; Vineyard Haven 15; VITI-VITI [trimaran]; VOYAGER 30; WANDERER III; Waterwag class; Wayfarer dinghy; WELCOME [armed-sloop replica]; WENDIGO; WHITEFIN; WHITE WINGS; WINDANCE; Windmill class; Winter Harbor 21 class; Winter Wren; YANKEE GIRL III; YANKEE [R-class sloop])

SLY MONGOOSE (express cruiser):
brief history, 54:34

Smack, BOADICEA:
history, performance, photos, plans, 36:20

Smack, Itchen ferry:
design and construction commentary, photos, plans, 14:22

Smack, New England:
comments, plan, 58:116

Smackee, Key West: (*See* Key West smackee, JEFF BROWN)

Small, Ron, author:
"Built to Win: The Thistle Class," 29:106

Smith, A. Cary, designer:
comments, 41:26
40′ class, 48:58, 49:66

Smith, Bert, author:
"An Exceptional Man," 14:31

Smith, Buckley, illustrator:
"A Bird for Thin Water," 38:58
"Milling Your Own," 37:98
"North Atlantic Shakedown: The Abandonment of the JOHN F. LEAVITT," 33:20
"The Biloxi Schooners," 37:80
cover illustration/waterborne home, 24:0

Smith, Buckley, photographer:
cover photo/Portuguese fishing craft, 33:0

Smith, Bulkeley, Jr., author:
"PASSIONELLA: A Ten-Dollar Skiff," 20:44

Smith, Charles:
letter on solvent for cleaning brushes, 65:6

Smith, Charles W.:
letter on historic vessel reproduction, 99:4

Smith, Chris, builder:
Grand Craft, 44:80

Smith, Don and Fred, builders:
Pelican class, 30:29

Smith, Everett, builder:
profile, 65:66
restorer of speedboat BABY BOOTLEG-GER, 60:84

Smith, E.W. (Ernie), Jr.:
on boat covers, 54:92

Smith, Herb, builder:
profile, photo, 76:36

Smith, James, author:
"The Greatest Little Motorboat Afloat," 55:68

Smith, Jim, builder:
sportfishing boats, photo, 76:44

Smith, Kevin:
letter on Kenneth Mobert, 45:11

Smith, Linda, builder:
comments about Lyle Hess cutter, 76:60

Smith, Mason, author:
"Arno Day: From Master Builder to Master Teacher," 63:38
"BABY BOOTLEGGER," 60:84
"My Brother Everett," 65:66

Smith, Melbourne, builder:
letter on maritime preservation, 44:7
letter on projection lofting, 52:12
schooner PRIDE OF BALTIMORE, 14:16, 44:72

Smith, Melbourne, designer and builder:
comments on Howard I. Chapelle, 84:76
letter by Craig Chipman, 79:5
profile, photo, 78:76

Smith, Melbourne, illustrator:
"Pungy Boats of the Chesapeake," 45:56
"The Remarkable Sloop SHADOW," 43:64

Smith, Nathan, designer: (*See* Designs, Smith, Nathan)

Smith, Phillip L.:
profile, 64:40

Smith, Robert, designer:
comments, 90:108

Smith, Sheli, illustrator:
"Manhattan's Mystery Merchant Ship: Her Probable Past," 63:96

Smith, William, builder:
comments, 37:42

Smith Island crabbing skiff:
comments, plan, 69:100

Smithsonian Institution (DC):
National Watercraft Collection, 77:21
National Watercraft Collection, letters on, 78:5, 79:5

Smokestacks:
design for, 49:86

Smutz, Tim, photographer:
"A New ERA," 50:52
cover photo/Disappearing Propeller Boats, 55:0

Smyth, Pete, and Maynard Bray, authors:
"On the Hunt," 76:44

SNAPPER BLUE II (sloop):
comments, photo, 75:34

Sneakbox:
designs/Glen-L Marine, 61:124
designs/John Gardner, 61:124
letter on Glen-L Marine design by Glen L. Witt, 62:7
See also Barnegat Bay sneakbox

Snider, Tim, author:
"Northwest Passage," 17:14
"The Great Wooden Boat Festival," 19:56
reviewer of *Restoring Vintage Boats* (book), 10:72

SNIKERSNEE (canoe yawl):
comments, photo, 100:70

SNIPE (commuter):
brief history, 54:34

Snipe class:
history, photos, plans, 89:36

Snipe class, MAKE WAY:
repair comments, photo, 89:43

Snipe Class International Racing Association:
comments, 89:36

Snow, Ralph, author:
"Manhattan's Mystery Merchant Ship: Her Probable Past," 63:101

Snowshoe canoe kit:
construction commentary, photos, 76:77

Snyder, David, author:
"Boatbuilding Report: The Lafitte Skiff," 14:73

Society for Spritsail Barge Research (England):
comments, 38:88

Solar-heated kiln:
comments by Richard Jagels, plan, 79:103

SOLARIA TOO (power cruiser):
comments, photo, 39:44

Solar panels:
product review by Steve Henkel, 78:87

Sole, cabin: (*See* Cabin sole)

SOLITAIRE (Plymouth lobsterboat):
comments, 1:65

Solvents:
safety precautions when using, 79:34

SOLWAY MAID (cutter):
comments, photo, 90:84

Sommer, Harold and Annaliese:
owners of schooner WANDER BIRD, 55:56

Sonderklasse sloops (Sonder boats):
comments, 73:32
comments, photo, 85:74

SOONER (power cruiser):
comments, photo, 49:44

SOPHIA CHRISTINA (schooner):
maintenance, photos, 99:66

SOPRANINO (sloop):
comments, plans, 24:24

Sounding pole:
use of, 15:40

Souter, Wilfred, builder (England):
comments, 24:47

Southampton Boatbuilding School (England):
program, 5:67

Southard sharpie:
comments, plans, 66:48

Southard skiff:
comments, plans, 66:48

Southern yellow pines:
comments by Richard Jagels, 76:115

South Shore Outboard Association (SSOA):
commentary by Peter H. Spectre, 80:32

South Street Seaport Museum (NY):
comments, 10:9
letter by Peter Neil, 90:4

Southworth, Anchea King, photographer:
"An Amateur-Built Boat," 5:12

Southworth, William B., author:
"An Amateur-Built Boat," 5:12

Southworth, William B., builder:
Whitehall pulling boat, 5:12

Søvik, Alfred, builder (Norway):
Norwegian oselvers, 28:34

Spain, Basque racing scull:
history, photos, 40:52

Spanish cedar:
comments, 10:35

Sparbuilding:
comments, vacuum bag system, 54:56
compiling lumber list/20' sloop
Martha/Joel White, 87:46
See also Spar maintenance, Spar repair

Sparbuilding, hollow:
technique/Arch Davis, 91:25
technique/Biscayne Bay 14 daysailer/Eric
Dow, 98:28
technique/John Marsland, 15:60
technique/Bud McIntosh, 60:125
technique/Lin and Larry Pardey, 15:64

Sparbuilding, solid:
construction commentary/Jim Emmett,
15:58
for Catspaw dinghy (Herreshoff Columbia
model), 28:64
for sailing canoe PICCOLO/comments by
Bob Baker, 37:57
technique/Bud McIntosh, 60:125

Sparbuilding, tools:
bench design/Bud McIntosh, 60:125
clamp design/John Marsland, 15:60
clamp design/Bud McIntosh, 60:125
clamp design/Lin and Larry Pardey, 15:64
scarfing jig/Bud McIntosh, 60:125
spar gauge and sanding machine/Bud
McIntosh, 60:125
spar plane/James Curry, 11:52

SPARKLE (cutter):
comments, drawing, 77:34

Sparkman, Drake, designer:
comments, 47:86

Sparkman & Stephens, designer:
Richardson Cruisabout 31, 22:92
12-Meter-class boats, 68:40

Sparks, E.L.:
letter on use of epoxy, 21:12

Spar maintenance:
in tropical conditions, 83:48
methods from bosun's chair, 42:27

Spar repair:
lengthening and patching/Bud McIntosh,
60:125

SPARTAN (New York 50):
comments, photos, 38:71
photos, reframing, 58:107

Spaulding, Matthew, author:
"The Search for Insurance," 72:35

Spaulding, Myron, builder:
sloop RONDO, 51:59

Speck, Ray, author:
"Lapstrake Planking, English Style," 75:68
"Pocket Cruisers From the Past: West
Coast," 75:62
letter on lapstrake planking, 77:4

Speck, Ray, builder:
construction methods/canoe yawl LA
MOUETTE, 75:62
critique of Northwest School of Wooden
Boatbuilding, 62:82
Sid Skiff, 40:88

Spectre, Peter H., author:
"A Cloud of Sawdust and Simon Watts,"
73:60
"A Conversation with Dick Clarke," 65:90
"A Conversation with C.A. Goodall,
Coblebuilder," 86:70
"A Matter of Family Tradition," 57:72
"A New Coaster: The Schooner HER-
ITAGE," 53:52
"A New Era," 50:52
"A Week Along the Thames," 74:54
"ACE Speedboat," 45:77
"Between a Rock and a Hard Place," 72:60
"Boatyard Hazards," 79:34
"Concours d'Élégance...and Hang the
Expense!", 62:74
"Conversations with Bud McIntosh," 51:40
" 'Do You Have a Moment?' He Asked,"
66:35
"Float Like a Butterfly, Sting Like a Bee,"
80:32
"Give 'Em Hell, Harry," 61:88
"How to Build a Double Paddle," 37:67
"In Search of the British Wooden Boat
Revival," 70:74
"John Gardner: In His Own Words," 40:30
"Just the Right Medium," 54:82
"Knocking on Boat Heaven's Door: A
Survey of English Maritime Museums,"
46:54
"Marine Insurance: Objectivity vs.
Subjectivity," 36:29
"Maurice Griffiths," 91:78
"Melbourne Smith and the Art of the
Possible," 78:76
"Newport's Wooden Boat Show," 43:84
"North Atlantic Shakedown: The Aban-
donment of JOHN F. LEAVITT," 33:20
"Olde-Tyme Shyppes," 96:64
"Producing a Bronze Propeller at the
Lunenburg Foundry," 94:72
"Product Review: Seattle's Wooden Boat
Shop," 93:115
"Professional Sailors, Traditional Vessels,"
96:58
"Quick and Dirty Repairs," 93:29
"Quick and...er...Dirty Boatbuilding," 49:89
"Speedboats from the Golden Era," 71:82
"Ten Years After," 60:44
"The Boats of Autumn," 68:25
"The BOWDOIN Project," 47:30
"The Challenge of the Challenge," 52:59

"The Gilkersonian Imperative," 89:64
"The Greatest Little Motorboat Afloat,"
55:68
"The Hands of August Crabtree," 63:80
"The Heaving Deck of History," 96:72
"The Issues of Maritime Preservation,"
38:36
"The Legacy of Howard Chapelle," 84:76
"The Lyman Legend," 82:60
"The Maine Schooners," 39:32
"The Marine Industries of Lunenburg,
Nova Scotia," 94:64
"The National Watercraft Collection,
Whither Away?," 77:21
"The Politics of Maritime Preservation,"
44:62
"The Reliable One-Lunger," 30:59
"The Shipwrights' Co-op," 34:36
"The Unretired Frank Prothero," 48:30
"The Windermere Steamboat Museum,"
98:66
"The Wizard of Speed," 58:100
"Three Friends," 54:74
"Three of What? The Reconstruction of an
Ancient Athenian Trireme," 75:44
"Trimaran Jim," 69:76
"Two Modelmakers," 97:52
"WARRIOR's Figurehead," 56:68
"Welcome to Hard Times: A Conversation
with Dean Stephens," 42:30
"Winter Reading: An Editor's Choice,"
37:50
critique of The Taunton Press (publisher),
50:121
editorial on maritime history, 84:2
letter on book review, *The Legend of Chris-
Craft*, 89:4
letter on steam schooner WAPAMA, 90:4
on maritime preservation, 41:36
on schooner PRIDE OF BALTIMORE,
44:72
reviewer of *ADVENTURE: Queen of the
Windjammers* (book), 66:101
reviewer of *Boatbuilding Manual* (book),
78:90
reviewer of *Boat Modeling with Dynamite
Payson* (book), 95:116
reviewer of *Clean Sweet Wind: Sailing Craft
of the Lesser Antilles* (book), 47:118
reviewer of *Endurance* (book), 69:107
reviewer of *Frame-Up!* (book), 72:113
reviewer of *Live Oaking: Southern Timber for
Tall Ships* (book), 48:117
reviewer of *Maritime America* (book),
90:135
reviewer of *Mystic Built: Ships and Shipyards
of the Mystic River, Connecticut, 1784–1919*
(book), 92:106
reviewer of *Plank on Frame: Who, What,
Where of 150 Boatbuilders* (book), 41:117
reviewer of *Sam Crocker's Boats: A Design
Catalog* (book), 68:105
reviewer of *The Dinghy Book* (book), 46:118
reviewer of *The Gloucester ADVENTURE*
(video), 89:109
reviewer of *The Little Ships of Dunkirk*
(book), 94:99
reviewer of *The Real Runabouts IV: Outboard
Edition* (book), 53:122
reviewer of *The Richardson Story* (book),
100:123
reviewer of *The Riddle of the Sands* (video),
67:101

reviewer of *Traditions and Memories of American Yachting* (book), 43:117

reviewer of *Wooden Boatbuilding in Britain: A Guide to Designers, Builders, and Suppliers* (book), 70:74

Speedboat, ACE:
design and construction commentary, photos, 45:77

Speedboat, Alexandria Bay boats:
comments, photos, 49:58

Speedboat, BABY BOOTLEGGER:
history, photos, plans, restoration commentary, 60:84

Speedboat, ERA:
construction commentary, photos, 50:52

Speedboat, FINAL FLING:
comments, photos, 71:82

Speedboat, HAPPY TIMES:
comments, photos, 71:82

Speedboat, MISS COLUMBIA:
brief history, 60:84

Speedboat, RAINBOW IV:
comments, 60:84

Speedboat, Riva:
builder, photos, 17:70

Speedboat, SCOTTY TOO:
comments, photo, 65:66

Speedboat, TEASER:
comments, 60:84

Speedboats:
at Lake Tahoe Concours d'Elegance, 62:74

photos of classics, 23:48

See also Hydroplanes, JESSE JAMES (offshore raceboat), Outboard racing speedboats, Runabouts

SPELLBOUND (ketch):
comments, photo, 78:30

Speltz, Robert G., author:
"The Real Runabouts," 10:52

reviewer of *Classic Speedboats of Tahoe* (video), 69:116

reviewer of *Runabout Renaissance* (video), 98:102

Spicer, Stanley, T., author:
"MARY CELESTE: The Story of a Mystery Ship," 6:60

letter on fishing schooners, 88:11

Spidsgatter:
design and construction commentary, history, photos, plans, 78:50

Spidsgatter, AIDA:
comments, photos, 78:50

Spidsgatter, DOXY:
comments, photos, 78:50

Spidsgatter, SKOAL:
design and construction commentary, history, photos, plans, 78:50

Spiegel, Ted, photographer:
cover photo/Norwegian craft, 28:0

SPIKE AFRICA (schooner):
cover photograph/Matthew Walker, 70:0

history, photos, plan, 70:42

Spiling:
cabin sole risers/Aldren Watson, 81:65

carvel planking repair/Allen Taube, 80:56

transom replacement/Brion Rieff, 99:28

using the tic method/stem pattern/fantail launch, 63:48

Spiling cabinsides:
technique/Bud McIntosh, 42:53

Spiling planks, new construction:
Catspaw dinghy (Herreshoff Columbia model)/Joel White, 27:63

Grand Banks dory/Jan Zimmermann, 19:32

Maine lobsterboat/Royal Lowell, 16:39

peapod/Pemberton Drinker, 13:56

peapod/Pemberton Drinker (letter on), 16:13

technique/Bud McIntosh, 18:38, 19:50

Spiling planks, repair:
ketch TARNE/Belford Gray, 50:59

sloop RONDO/Robert Vespa, 51:59

sloop WHITE WINGS/Scott Cain, 24:72

whaleship, CHARLES W. MORGAN, 36:98

yawl TIGRIS/Steve Ballentine, 53:109

SPIRIT OF BERMUDA (Bermuda fitted dinghy):
design commentary, photo, 57:42

SPIRIT OF MASSACHUSETTS (schooner):
comments, 78:76

comments, photo, 96:73

framing technique, photos, 82:48

Splash Zone (seam compound):
comments, 81:75

Splice:
service technique/Brion Toss, 59:106

Splice, back-:
how to make, 52:112

Splice, Cleopatra's Eye:
how to make, 24:20

Splice, wire:
technique/1x19 splice/Brion Toss, 81:45

Spline-joint gluing:
compared to simple butt-joint gluing, 59:93

Splines:
use for glue joints, 59:93

Sponberg, Eric W., author:
reviewer of *Propeller Handbook* (book), 92:107

Sportfisherman:
designs/David P. Martin, 24:95

Sportfisherman, CERO:
comments, plan, 54:34

Sportfisherman, PORPOISE:
comments, photo, 49:44

designs/Geerd Hendel, 61:127

Sportfisherman, THAT'S MY HON:
comments, photo, 76:41

Sportfisherman, TINTINAJO:
cover photo/Benjamin Mendlowitz, 76:0

Sportfishing boats of Florida:
builders, design and construction commentary, photos, 76:44

Sportsman 36 (power cruiser):
comments, photos, 57:102

comments, photos, plan, 56:48

design commentary, photos, plan, 35:92

Sportsman 40 (power cruiser):
comments, photo, 57:102

Sportsman 42 (power cruiser):
comments, plan, 56:48

Sportsman 80 (power cruiser):
comments, photo, 57:102

Sprague, Eli, builder:
sloop HIPPOCAMPUS JR, 6:54

Sprague, Scott, designer: (*See* Designs, Sprague, Scott)

SPRAGUE (steamboat):
comments, photo, 64:64

SPRAY (yawl):
comments, plans, 21:58

Sprit boom:
commentary by Iain Oughtred, 77:44

Sprit rig:
commentary by Ernie Cassidy, 89:30

commentary by Iain Oughtred, 76:80

comments by Colin Palmer, 92:76

Spritsail:
reefing technique, letter by David Scarborough, 78:8

Spritsail barge (England):
construction commentary, history, photos, plan, research society, 38:88

Spruce:
species for boatbuilding, 9:31

SPY (Barnegat Bay A-cat):
history, photo, 62:60

SQUAW (sharpie schooner):
design and construction commentary, photos, 33:36

SS GREAT BRITAIN (England):
comments, 46:54

Stability:
comments by Jim Brown/multihulls, 92:34

comments by Joel White, 75:111

Stack, Charley Noble:
design for, 49:86

Stackpole, Charles:
letter on sardine carrier EDWARD M, 62:8

Stadel, George, designer:
sloop NORTH STAR, 26:24

See also Designs, Stadel, George

Stainton, David M., designer:
letter on cold-molded construction, 10:5

Stambaugh, Karl A., designer: (*See* Designs, Stambaugh, Karl A.)

Stammers, Michael:
comments about, 66:35

Stanchion supports:
detail photo, comments, 66:90

Standing lugsail:
commentary by Iain Oughtred, 73:80

Stanford, Norma:
on maritime preservation, 41:36

Stanford, Peter, author:
"The Testimony of the Thing Itself," 38:45

letter on historic vessel reproduction, 97:4

on maritime preservation, 38:36

on Wianno Senior class, 91:58

STANLEY NORMAN (skipjack):
photos, restoration commentary, 35:62

Staples:
cold-molded hull overlay/Owens cutter FALCON, 61:104

use in plywood lapstrake planking, 56:60

STAR (cutter):
design, construction, and rig commentary, photos, plans, 54:114

STAR (dragger):
comments, photo, 69:48

STAR (lobsterboat, power):
comments, photo, 69:42

STAR DUST (Concordia 31):
comments, photo, 51:40

comments, plan, 48:126

letter on, 50:8

STAR II (schooner):
comments, photo, 69:48

STAR III (Noank sloop):
comments, photo, 69:48

Stark, Eric L., author and photographer:
"The Barnegat Bay Sneakbox," 47:102

Starkweather, Frank, author:
"A Modern Composite," 16:27

"Au Sable River Boats," 5:6

Staudacher, Jon, builder:
profile, photo, 80:24

Stauter, Lawrence, builder:
profile, photo, 72:90

Stauter Boat Works, builder:
construction methods, 72:90

Staysail:
commentary by Iain Oughtred, 78:66

Steam-bending:
commentary by Ed McClave, 88:50
commentary by Simon Watts, 88:58
for building a Haisla dugout canoe, 69:64
wood characteristics for, 29:14
See also Chines, steam-bent; Frames, steam–
bent; Steambox

Steam-bending, canoe ribs:
technique/Jerry Stelmok, 29:68

Steam-bending, coamings:
Herreshoff 12½/Steve Ballentine, 57:93
technique/Joel White, 44:86

Steam-bending, planks:
schooner HERITAGE/North End
Shipyard, 53:52

Steam-bending, stems:
Rangeley Lake boat/Ed McClave, 33:74

Steamboat, ECHO:
design and construction commentary,
photos, 67:70

Steamboat, river:
builder (Howard Ship Yard and Dock Co.),
64:64
history (Mississippi & Ohio), photos, 64:64

Steamboat, river, CITY OF HELENA:
comments, photo, 64:64

Steamboat, river, INDIANA:
comments, photo, 64:64

Steamboat, river, J.M. WHITE:
comments, photo, 64:64

Steamboat, river, LIBERTY:
comments, photo, 64:64

Steamboat, river, ROBERT E. LEE:
comments, photo, 64:64

Steamboat, river, SPRAGUE:
comments, photo, 64:64

Steambox:
comments on use by Ed McClave, 88:50
comments on use by Simon Watts, 88:58
examples from readers/photos, plans,
88:50

Steamer, CAPE COD:
comments, photo, 61:32

Steamer, COMET:
design commentary, photos, 3:49

Steam launch:
restorations by Peter Freebody & Co.,
57:72

Steam launch, CASTALIA:
design and construction commentary,
photos, 15:29

Steam launch, Cowes:
design and construction commentary,
plans, 13:76

Steam launch, MELISANDE:
comments, photo, 98:66

Steam launch, SULTAN:
comments, photo, 57:72

Steam launch, XANTHO:
comments, photo, 84:34

Steam schooner: (*See* ANNIE CHRISTEN-
SON, SHNA TAK, WAPAMA)

Steam tug, OX:
comments, plans, 73:32

Steam tug, RESTLESS:
history, photo, 3:40

Steam yacht: (*See* BRANKSOME, DOLLY,
HANNIEL)

Steele, Jim, builder:
building methods, 77:74
peapods, 27:52, 28:56
profile, photo, 77:70

Steele, Keith, builder:
McKenzie River drift boats, 52:80

Steering systems:
comments, detail photo, 69:104

Steever, Andrew, author:
"Native to the Thousand Islands, Part I,"
20:48
"Native to the Thousand Islands, Part II,"
21:26

Steiner, Peter, designer:
comments, 87:66

Steinlein, Eric J., author:
"Pungy Boats of the Chesapeake," 45:56

Steinmetz, Ken, author/builder:
"Our Thanks to John Gardner," 90:36
comments, 54:82

STELLA (Folkboat):
comments, photo, 5:67

Stelmok, Jerry, author/builder:
"A Mentor Would Appear: Mick Fahey and
the North Woods Way," 67:38
"Canvasing a Canoe," 79:77
"Henri Vaillancourt and the Bark Canoe,"
87:80
cover photo, 96:0
profile, photo, 67:54

Stelmok, Jerry, author and illustrator:
"Rebuilding the Wood & Canvas Canoe,"
29:68

Stem construction:
Beetle Cat/Leo Telesmanick, 52:107
Bolger Cartopper dinghy, 87:29
cutting the rabbet/Fred Ajootian, 14:38
Gloucester Light Dory/Harold Payson,
41:63
marking the rabbet/Sam Manning, 14:42
outboard runabout Downeaster 18/
Graham Ero, 73:67
shaping and finishing/Maynard Bray, 25:52
steam bending for Rangeley Lake boat/Ed
McClave, 33:74
technique/Bud McIntosh, 34:66

Stem pattern:
repair/wood-and-canvas canoe/Rollin
Thurlow, 79:72
tic spiling method/fantail launch, 63:48

Stem rabbet:
peapods/Jimmy Steele, 77:74

Stem repair:
cold-molded construction/Reuel Parker,
89:92
Herreshoff 12½/Steve Ballentine, 56:93
replacement methods/Willits Ansel, 39:97
Winter Harbor 21 class/Benjamin River
Marine, 93:76

Stephan, Herb and Jay, builder:
Au Sable River boats, 5:6

Stephens, Dean, author/builder:
"Product Review: Arabol," 91:110
felucca replica MATILDA D, 13:45, 14:45
pinky schooner RELIANCE, 18:46
profile, 42:30
repairs to cutter ELLY, 58:40

Stephens, Jim, builder:
bateau-type rowing skiff RANDANDY, 66:23

Stephens, Olin, designer:
Blue Jay class, 15:42

comments, 47:86
Lightning class, 34:97, 53:68
New York 32 class, 73:42
profile, photos, 98:50

Stephens, Robert W., designer: (*See* Designs,
Stephens, Robert W.)

Stephens, Rod, designer:
comments, 45:50, 98:50
comments about New York 32 class, photo,
73:42

Stephens, William P., designer:
comments, 37:42, 41:26, 44:24, 48:58
comments about, 75:70, 75:72
comments on 21' class, 8:62
comments on 40' class, 49:66
correspondence with N.G. Herreshoff,
photo, 100:70

STEPHEN TABER (schooner):
comments, photos, 39:32

Sternpost:
construction technique of Bud McIntosh,
33:66, 34:66

Stern sheets:
design and construction commentary,
27:86

Stevens, David, builder (Nova Scotia):
profile, 34:26

Stevens, Harold, sailmaker (Nova Scotia):
methods, 34:26

Stevens, Jim, builder:
on Malcolm Brewer, 49:44
repair of schooner BOWDOIN, 47:30

Stevens, Murray, builder (Nova Scotia):
construction methods, 34:26

Stevens, Skip:
letter on marine insurance, 70:8

Stevenson, J. Paul:
comments on USS SUISUN, 81:21

**Stevenson, Kevin M., author and photog-
rapher:**
"The Bermuda Fitted Dinghy," 57:42

Steward, Robert M., designer:
comments on Huckins Yacht Corporation,
57:102
letter on fastenings, 47:11
Sharptown barge and skiff SUSAN, 87:90

Stewart, Thomas R., photographer:
"Boatyard Hazards," 79:34
"Float Like a Butterfly, Sting Like a Bee,"
80:32
cover photo/Sam Manning, 99:0
cover photo/Willow canoe/Jerry Stelmok,
96:0

Stewart & Binney, designer and builder:
21' class, 4:25, 8:62

STING RAY V (power cruiser):
designs/C. Raymond Hunt Associates,
98:104

Stitch-and-glue construction:
DK 13 kayak, 70:56
commentary by Tom Brown, 85:52
See also Designs, Devlin, Sam; Tack-and-
tape construction

**Stitching Stamboek Ronde-en-
Platbodemjachten (Netherlands):**
comments, 27:32

Stoller, Lincoln, author and photographer:
"The Indian's Apprentice," 74:27

Stone, Dick, builder:
on finish work, 46:66

Stone, Doug, builder:
North Haven dinghy, 38:111

Stone, Lester, builder:
obituary, 9:10
Stonington motorsailer:
comments, plan, 62:36
Stopper knot:
tying technique, 52:112
Stopwaters:
commentary by Ed McClave, 56:116
comments, 50:59
installation technique/Bud McIntosh,
19:50
letter on, 57:12
repair technique/Bud McIntosh, 84:44
Storage:
cradle and trailer design, 69:86
grounding-out techniques, 70:52
poppeting techniques, 78:93
See also Boathouse, Moving boats, Winter
layup
STORMY PETREL (ketch):
comments, plan, 55:32
STORMY WEATHER (yawl):
charter, 42:82
comments, photo, plan, 98:50
Story, A.D., Shipyard, builder:
history, photo, 61:32
Story, Arthur, builder:
schooner L.A. DUNTON, 6:44
Story, Arthur Dana (A.D.), builder:
comments, photo, 61:38
profile, photo, 61:32
Story, Brad, builder:
profile, photo, 61:38
Story, Dana, builder:
comments, photo, 61:38
profile, photo, 61:32
Story, Elizabeth, author:
"The Storys of Essex," 61:32
Story 20 (Bolger yawl):
comments, plan, 92:42
Stoves (heating) for marine use:
comments, 25:27, 31:25
Stowe, Nick, author:
"The Huckins Yacht Corporation, Part I,"
56:48
Stowell, Robert, author:
"PASTIME," 40:68
Strange, Albert, designer (England):
canoe yawl ISOBEL, 97:70
comments, 47:46
letters on, 50:5, 51:6, 51:7
profile, 64:49
See also Designs, Strange, Albert
Stratton, Gil:
design for wooden cleat, 14:14
STRATUS (sloop):
designs/Warwick & Associates, 22:86
**Straumbaten seksaering (Norwegian rowing
craft):**
comments, photo, plans, 28:36
Strawbery Banke (NH):
comments, 19:32
Strayer, Charles, designer: (*See* Designs,
Strayer, Charles M.)
Streamline Cruiser by Chris-Craft:
construction commentary, history, photo,
39:119
Street, Donald M., Jr., author:
"Check the Bilge," 3:59
"Improving the Classic Dinghy," 50:88
"IOLAIRE: 1905 to ?", 2:48
"Keeping the Structure Together," 13:65

"Leaking Decks: Watertight Solutions,"
25:89
letter on deck repair, 30:6
letter on IOLAIRE, 70:4
letter on laminated frames, 60:5
Street, Donald M., Jr., author and illustrator:
"The Herreshoff Connection," 19:72
Streeter, John, editor:
"Letters from the Masters," 100:70
Streeter, Sherry, illustrator:
"The Art of Finding Your Way," 59:102
Streeter, Sherry, photographer:
"A Boatbuilding Shop," 85:27
"Surveying Your Sails," 93:60
"Transom Replacement," 99:28
cover photo/wooden boats on Egge-
moggin Reach, 60:0
STRIDER (catamaran):
designs/Richard and Lilian Woods, 73:106
letter by Richard and Lilian Woods, 74:7
Strip planking: (*See* Planking, strip)
Struer kayaks and canoes:
construction, history, photos, use in
Olympics, 82:44
Stubbs, Laurie, author:
"The Steam Yacht ENA," 90:102
Stubing, Paul, builder:
restoration of New York 30, 35:30
**Stubing, Paul, Maynard Bray, and Meg
Maiden, authors:**
"From Sail to Power: The Evolution of the
Noank Lobsterboat," 69:42
Stuch, Lafayette, author:
"A Tempered Boat," 17:42
Stuffing box:
advice for fitting out/Paul Bryant, 93:36
Stulcken yard, builder (Germany):
schooner WANDER BIRD, 55:56
Stulen, Chip, builder:
profile, photos, 95:38
Sturgeon Bay Yacht Harbor:
on boat covers, 54:92
Sturges, Ed, builder:
profile, 54:74
Sturhahn, Larry, author and photographer:
"Ray Speck and the Sid Skiffs," 40:88
Styrene:
hazards of use, 93:86
Submarine, 6' TURTLE:
design and construction commentary,
photos, plans, 21:74
SUCCESSOR (schooner):
photo, 80:50
Sucher, Harry V., designer:
letter on Howard I. Chapelle, 85:7
sharpie ALACRAN, 59:36
sharpies, 25:36
Suffolk Marine Museum (NY):
boat types at, 29:102
SUISUN, USS (power cruiser): (*See* USS
SUISUN)
SULTAN (steam launch):
comments, photo, 57:72
Summer, Jackson P.:
letter on Concordia 31 STARDUST, 50:8
Summers, Greg, illustrator:
"Corrosion-Related Problems," 93:94
"Painting for Longevity," 93:70
Summers, John:
letter on Allen Farrell, 68:5
SUMURUN (ketch):
comments, photos, 91:50

SUNBEAM (English smack):
comments, photo, 85:64
Sun Cat (catboat):
design commentary, 36:73
SUN DANCE (outboard cruiser):
designs/Weston Farmer, 82:108
Sunden, Tore, designer (Sweden):
Folkboat, 10:30
Sunnfjord boat:
history, plans, 28:39
SUNRISE (pinky ketch):
design commentary, photos, plans, 3:61
Superior Boats, builder (Ontario):
cold-molded boats, construction methods,
45:50
comments, 45:2
construction methods, 46:82
speedboat ERA, 50:52
Surface checking of wood:
treatment for, 50:116
Surfboat, Monomoy: (*See* Monomoy surfboat)
Surf Scoter (power cruiser):
comments, photo, plans, 85:52
Surveying:
comments/Giffy Full and Jack Jacques,
60:62
comments/Richard Jagels, 41:123
comments/F.M. Kaufman, 13:12
comments/Ian Nicholson, 8:57
comments/Randy Peffer, 11:9
comments/Dick Sciuto, 2:71, 3:69
comments/W.J. Thomte, 13:12
comments/James Woodward, 17:20
E.H. Gerrish wood-and-canvas canoe/
Rollin Thurlow, 78:56
guide for antique/classic runabouts, with
drawings, 77:79
guide for self-survey/Paul Lipke, 83:22
letter by Ernest F. Braatz, 74:6
letter by Paul Lipke, 86:5
letter by Robin A. McKie, 61:8
techniques/Giffy Full, 14:8, 26:57
techniques/Dick Sciuto, 4:70
See also Buying a wooden boat
Susan (flat-bottomed skiff):
comments, plans, photo, 87:90
SUSAN CONSTANT:
comments, photo, 96:64
Sutcliffe, Rae, author:
"With Feeling: Varnishing, Music and
Love," 16:56
Sutter, Annie, author:
"CHEROKEE: The Several Lives of a
Launch," 61:100
"Rags to Riches," 81:21
"The Nunes Brothers Boat and Ways
Company," 50:31
"The Rebirth of WANDER BIRD," 55:56
Sutter, Peter:
on sails for schooner WANDER BIRD,
55:56
SUVERA (coble):
photo, 86:70
SVAAP (ketch):
comments, 65:44
Sverdrup, Otto:
comments, 85:44
Swampscott dory:
construction commentary/George I.
(Sonny) Hodgdon, Jr., 51:50
Swampscott dory, AMERICA:
comments, photo, 61:52

Swampscott-type dory, Alpha-Beachcomber:
history, photos, 36:78
owner's comments, photos, 36:83
Swampscott-type dory, North Shore:
comments, photo, plans, 36:82
Swan, Ken, designer:
review of plans catalog, 96:98
Swanson, Mark, builder:
Norwegian prams, 49:36
Swanson, Roger C., author:
"EDITH JANE: A Search for the Real
Mackinaw Boat," 45:100
Swanson, Roger C., delineator:
of Mackinaw boat, 45:100
Swasey, A. Loring, designer:
association with Walter McInnis, 53:38
Swede 55, VORTEX:
design and construction commentary,
racing, photos, 100:84
design and construction commentary,
photos, plans, 100:88
Sweden, builders: (*See* Ericson, Henry;
Johansson, Georg)
Sweden, designers: (*See* Chapman, Fredrik
Henrik; Eliasson, Rolf; Iversen, Jac N.;
Reimers, Knud; Sunden, Tore)
Sweden, watercraft: (*See* ELLY [cutter]; Kåg
[Swedish ketch]; Pilot-boat, swedish;
TELKKÄ [Swedish ship's boat])
Swedish furling:
technique, 50:101
Swift, Gordon, builder:
association with Bud McIntosh, 51:40
SWIFT (schooner):
comments, 65:44
Sydney Maritime Museum (Australia):
comments, 63:8
SYLTU (ketch):
design and construction commentary,
photos, plans, 12:14
Sylvester, Charlie, builder:
comments, 33:50, 37:2
SYLVINA W. BEAL:
as sardine carrier, 59:70
plan (as schooner), 39:32
SYRINX (cutter):
builders of, comments, photo, 63:38
cover photo/Vernon Cheek, 63:0
designs/Lyle Hess, 63:116
Szymkowiak, Ken, author:
"Sano Magic," 80:50

Taberly, Eric:
comments, photo, 91:38
Tack-and-tape construction:
Bolger Cartopper dinghy/how-to-build
series, 87:29, 88:31

See also Stitch-and-glue construction
Tacks:
removal/wood-and-canvas canoe/Rollin
Thurlow, 78:56
Tacoma Vocational School: (*See* Bates
Vocational-Technical Institute [WA])
Taft, Henry W., author:
"Rowing the Maine Coast," 47:52
Tahiti ketch, JOSEPHA:
cover photo/George Day, 8:0
cruising, photos, 8:36
design commentary, photos, 16:66
Taking off lines: (*See* Lines)
Talbot, Richard P., author:
"Snowshoe for Two," 76:77
TALEISIN (cutter):
bronze floor timbers and knees, photos,
51:72
comments, photo, 76:60
designs/Lyle Hess, 63:116
Tamagni, Henry, builder:
comments on, 76:44
TAMARACK (motorsailer):
comments, plan, 28:20
Tamar sailing barge, SHAMROCK:
comments, 60:68
Tamm, Bror, builder:
association with Walter McInnis, 52:40
Herreshoff dugout, 14:54
profile, 46:30
Tancook whaler:
comments, photo, 71:44
cover illustration, 5:0
Tancook whaler, ELLEN IVY:
construction commentary, photos, plans,
5:44
construction commentary, photos, 7:56
Tancook whaler, VERNON LANGILLE:
design and rig commentary, performance,
photos, plan, 58:82
operation of, photos, 31:18
Tanganyika liftnet canoe:
comments, plans, 41:50, 42:66
TANGO II (Nine-Meter):
cold-molded hull repair, photo, 60:76
TANNIS (Friendship sloop):
comments, photo, 29:61
Tanoak (wood):
characteristics, 43:120
Tanton, Yves-Marie, designer: (*See* Designs,
Tanton, Yves-Marie)
TAPPAN ZEE (schooner):
comments, 95:70
Tar:
use in catamaran TAULUA, 72:70
See also Roofing tar
TARANTELLA (catamaran):
performance, 23:64
TARANTULA (commuter):
comments, photo, 94:74
Tarbox, Fred, builder:
at Lowell's Boatshop, 27:26
Tarn, W.W.:
comments on trireme, 75:44
TARNE (ketch):
replacing keel, photos, 49:97, 50:59
TASHTEGO (Black Skimmer sharpie):
comments, photo, 92:42
Tasmania:
Cadet dinghy racing, 52:100
Taube, Allen, author:
"In My View: Surviving the Tropics," 83:48
"Replacing Planks," 80:56

recommendations for seam compounds,
81:75
TAULUA (catamaran):
design and construction commentary,
photos, voyage, 72:70
Taylor, Roger C., author:
"A Crewman's View of a Sloop Race," 29:64
"BOADICEA," 36:20
"Mr. Herreshoff's Wonderful Rozinante,"
26:40
"Sailing PETREL," 75:73
"Sailing a Tancook Whaler," 58:82
"The DISCOVERY's Launch," 89:86
"The Elements of Seamanship, Part I:
Keeping the Water Out," 40:38
"The Elements of Seamanship, Part II:
Keeping From Hitting Anything," 41:42
"The Elements of Seamanship, Part III:
Keeping Her Going," 42:38
"The Elements of Seamanship, Part IV:
Keeping Her Where You Want Her,"
43:50
"The Elements of Seamanship, Part V:
Keeping Your Reputation," 45:62
"The New York Thirties: Recollections
Under Sail," 35:27
"VARIN the Lestabåt," 95:90
comments on designer Henry A. Scheel,
62:36
letter about, 42:7
letter on seamanship, 47:13
reviewer of *Sou'West and By West of Cape Cod*
(book), 80:89
reviewer of *Yacht Style* (book), 99:108
Taylor, William H., author:
"The New York Thirties: A Salute to the
First One-Design Yachts to Reach the
Half-Century Mark," 35:25
"The New York Thirties: At 25, One of the
Best Classes Ever Built," 35:25
Teak:
comments by Richard Jagels, 67:109
finishes for interiors, 21:90
for boatbuilding, 10:35
harvesting and management (India), 32:42
refinishing/comments by Rebecca
Wittman, 81:88
substitutes for, 27:20
Teak decks:
comments by Bill Modrell, 21:90
construction technique/Seth Emmer,
15:26
construction technique/George I. (Sonny)
Hodgdon, Jr. 59:88
maintenance and repair comments, 64:58,
77:60
maintenance comments by Jim Emmett,
11:70
maintenance for tropical conditions, 83:48
repair technique/Donald Street, 25:89
repair/plywood-and-Dynel overlay/Fishers
Island 31, 66:64
repair/teak-and-fiberglass overlay/ketch
ISABELLE, 72:53
Teak gratings:
methods of Henry R. Hinckley Co., photos,
62:53
Teak-over-plywood decks:
maintenance and repair comments, 77:60
TEASER (speedboat):
comments, 60:84
Tea tree (wood):
for boatbuilding, 47:123

Ted Brewer Yacht Designs: (*See* Brewer, Edward S. [Ted], designer)

TE-KA Teak Wood Cleaner:
comments on using/Rebecca Wittman, 81:88

TELEGRAMME (trimaran):
comments, photos, 91:38

Telesmanick, Leo, builder:
Beetle Cats, 51:99, 52:107, 53:101
profile, 21:72

TELKKÄ (Swedish ship's boat):
design commentary, photos, plans, use, 60:68

TEMPEST (Cal 32 class):
comments, photo, plans, 83:38

Template:
for spiling carvel planking repair, 80:56
See also Patternmaking

Templin, Doug, author:
"Linear Polyurethanes," 78:21

TEMPO ALCOA (hydroplane):
comments, photo, 80:24

Tender Ten (sailing dinghy):
planking technique, photos, plans, 22:77

10-Meter, GRACIL:
comments, photo, 91:56

10-Meter, RAPIER:
construction commentary, photo, 3:71

TERESA (sharpie):
design and construction commentary, photos, plans, 80:44

TERRIBLE (power launch):
comments, 48:66

TESS (Cornish gig):
comments, drawing, 77:34

Teuscher, Philip, author:
"Building a Rudder," 20:70
"Runabout Renaissance," 41:72

TEVA (yawl):
comments, plan, 72:44

THAENO (cutter):
comments, photo, 76:60

Thames Barge Sailing Club (England):
comments, 38:88

Thames River skiff:
construction commentary, photos, 74:54
cover photo/Nick Rogers, 74:0
river cruise in, photos, 74:54

Thames sailing barge:
comments, photos, 17:63
construction commentary, history, photos, plans, 38:88

Thames skiff model, Ratty's Boat:
design and construction comments, history, photos, 94:44

THAT (trimaran):
comments, photo, 69:76

THAT'S MY HON (sportfisherman):
comments, photo, 76:44

Thayer, Bud, builder:
North Haven dinghy, 38:111

THE JUDGE (power cruiser):
designs/Tom Beard, 25:97

THELMA IV (cutter):
comments, photo, 90:84

THEO G (schooner):
designs/William Garden, 68:114

The Pipante (power skiff):
WoodenBoat School project, comments, plans, 88:82

The Tuk-Tuk (power dory):
WoodenBoat School project, comments, plans, 88:82

Thiokol:
comments by Barry Thomas and Jon Wilson, 2:64
for deck seams, 77:60
in repair of fantail launch, 63:48
in Sharpie construction, 1:8

Third World boatbuilding:
comments by Jim Brown, 40:78, 41:51, 42:66, 88:76
comments by James Wharram, 30:20
letters on, 41:5, 43:4

Third World projects:
Constant Camber projects/Jim Brown, 69:76
Danish ketch FRI, 87:36
WoodenBoat School/Miskito (Honduras) Indians project, 88:76
hospital ship TOLE MOUR/Marimed Foundation, 84:64

Third World sailing rigs:
commentary by Colin Palmer, 92:76
letter by Colin Palmer, 94:6

Third World timber supplies:
comments by Douglas M. Dayton, 59:56

30-Square-Meter, ORIOLE:
comments, photo, 55:32

THISTLE (cutter):
comments, 100:70

THISTLE (yawl):
comments, photo, 84:34

Thistle class:
cover photo, 47:0
design commentary, history, photos, plans, 29:106
letters on, 49:9, 50:4
photos, rebuilding commentary, 47:80

THISTLEDOWN (Concordia yawl):
comments, detail photos, 67:100, 68:70
comments, photo, 80:64

Thomas, Barry, author:
"Our Thanks to John Gardner," 90:36
letter on clench nails, 28:7
on Thiokol compounds, 2:64

Thomas, Barry, author and illustrator:
"Clench Nailing for Planks and Frames," 26:68

Thomas, Randy, author and photographer:
"Dragon Quest: In Search of the Chinese Junk," 66:76

THOMAS McDONOUGH (power fishing craft):
comments, photo, 50:70

Thomas Walters & Son, Ltd.:
profile, 94:64

Thomas Wylie Design Group, builder: (*See* Wylie, Thomas, Design Group)

Thomsen, Bob, builder:
cold-molded boats, 26:70
Eight-Meter sloop ANGELITA, 59:40

Thomson, Asa, builder:
profile, 29:50

Thomson's Shipyard, builder (Scotland):
Scottish fishing boats, 62:68

Thomte, W.J., and F.M. Kaufman, authors:
"Opinion: Surveyors," 13:12

Thonging chisel:
use in leatherworking, 68:64

Thorset, Ragnar:
Operation Viking project, photo, 68:19

Thousand Islands Shipyard Museum (NY):
comments, 2:66

Three-fathom sharpie, SHARPIE:
cover photo/Bob Beech, 76:0

Thuja (Shark catamaran):
construction commentary, 69:29

THUNDERBIRD (express cruiser):
at Lake Tahoe Concours d'Élégance, photos, 62:74
cover photo/Benjamin Mendlowitz, 62:0

Thunderbird class:
history, photos, plan, 28:90

Thunderboats:
Staudacher built/comments, 80:24

Thurlow, Rollin, author and builder:
E.M. White guide canoe, 67:54
"Wood-and-Canvas Canoe Restoration, Part I," 78:56
"Wood-and-Canvas Canoe Restoration, Part II," 79:72

Thwart:
comments, detail photos, 66:90, 69:104

Thwarts and benches:
design and construction for small craft, 27:86

Thygesen, Bent:
letter about edge-setting, 87:7
letter on Danish skiff, 50:8

TICONDEROGA (ketch):
comments, 25:56, 55:32, 56:38

Tic spiling:
stem pattern, fantail launch, 63:48

TIFFANY JANE (sloop):
designs/Paul R. Kotzebue, 34:102
racing against sloop SKIDOO, 51:83

TIGER (motoryacht):
comments, photo, 91:50

TIGRESS (schooner):
comments, photo, 28:20

TIGRIS (yawl):
repair, photos, plan, 53:109

Tiller:
for Biscayne Bay 14 daysailer, 98:28
for Cape Cod catboat, 31:84
for Herreshoff 12½, 32:76

Timber: (*See* Wood, for boatbuilding)

Timber Framers' Guild of North America:
letter about old-growth timber management, 85:5

Timbering out: (*See* Frames)

TIMBERWIND (schooner):
comments, photo, 39:32

TINAVETTE (power launch):
comments, 75:9
comments, photo, 74:42

TINTINAJO (sportfisherman):
cover photo/Benjamin Mendlowitz, 76:0

TINY BOY II (Alaska limit seiner):
comments, plans, 37:31

Tirrul-Jones, James, author and photographer:
"With Adze and Steam," 69:64

Ti Shpountz (ketch):
painting, 71:74
Titchener, Paul:
letter on Albert Strange design SHEILA II,
67:5
TLINGIT (power yacht):
designs/William Garden, 96:112
TOADSTOOL (schooner):
comments, photos, 60:96
designs/William Garden, 68:114
Toerail:
construction method/Bud McIntosh, 67:91
design and construction commentary,
29:94
TOLE MOUR (three-masted schooner):
comments, plan, 84:64
TOMAHAWK (40' class):
history, 49:66
TOM COD (sloop):
designs/George Stadel, Jr., 47:128
TOMKAT III (power cruiser):
transom repair, 16:20
Tomol canoe, Chumash:
design and construction commentary,
history, photos, plans, 35:82
Tompkins, Warwick:
on schooner WANDER BIRD, 55:56
Tonner, Nick:
on finish work, 46:66
Tools, battery-powered:
product review by Aimé Ontario Fraser,
82:100
Tools for boatbuilding:
accldent-prevention comments, 79:45
acquisition, maintenance, storage, transport, 79:29
advice on buying used tools, 70:31
availability of, 20:65
comments by Bob Baker, 32:32
comments by Larry Montgomery, photos,
79:29
critique of Japanese chisels, 72:21
critique of professional power tools, 68:35
critique of tool catalogs/Gary
Weisenburger, 85:107
for building Cartopper construction
model, 85:36
for building Norwegian pram, 49:28
for building raised panels, 99:86
for building recreational shell KINGFISH-
ER, 61:60
for leatherwork, 68:64
for making trunnels, 49:28
for reefing deck seams, 77:60
for rigging aloft, 70:92
for singlehanded boatbuilding, 99:94
letter by David W. Carnell, 69:7
maintenance procedures for, 37:40
of R.D. Culler, 27:81, 28:83
product review of Porter-Cable Random
Orbit sander, 96:97
product review of Vise-Grip pliers and
clamps, 93:120
sharpening device/Sharpenset Whetstone,
20:98
sharpening handsaws, 47:91
sharpening power saws, 48:44
sharpening systems, 21:94
toolbox for cruising, 17:78
traditional, 1:14
See also Adze; Axe; Bandsaws; Batlodd;
Bevel rule; Caulking; Chainsaw; Chisel;
Clamps, Vise-Grip; Drills, power;

Japanese tools; Knife, sailor's; Lofting;
Plane, wooden; Plank scarfer; Plank
scriber; Router; Scraper; Screwdrivers,
electric; Screw extractor; Sparbuilding,
tools
Toops, Connie, author:
"The Biloxi Schooners," 37:80
"The Mighty Maritime Oaks," 46:76
TOPAZ (cutter):
comments, photos, plans, 26:70
Topsail:
for Norwegian lestabåt, 95:90
Topsides:
guide for self-survey/Paul Lipke, 83:22
TORETTA (sloop):
design and construction commentary,
photos, plans, 22:46
Tornado class:
history, photo, 25:98
kit boat, 38:84
Olympic contender, plan, 13:34
Torpedo-sterned launch, ALOHA:
photos, repair comments, 95:82
TORTUGA (Core Sound sharpie):
design and construction commentary,
photos, plan, 35:76
Toss, Brion, author:
"Binds that Tie," 72:40
"Grommeting," 55:114
"Hitches: Improving on a Cylinder," 39:102
"Lashmanship," 50:101
"Living Aloft," 70:92
"Northwest Crannies," 43:104
"Product Review: A Guide to Block
Selection," 83:93
"Seven Bends," 53:96
"Spike Knots," 48:100
"The ADVENTURESS and Mrs. B.," 90:94
"The Comforts of Service," 59:106
"The End of Your Rope," 52:112
"The Handy Billy," 41:58
"The 1x19 Splice Made Possible," 81:45
letter on battenless mainsail, 66:7
letter on bosun's chair, 72:9
letter on making a handy-billy tackle, 42:10
Toss, Brion, and Malcolm Wehncke, authors:
"Sons of Hitches," 40:92
Totara (wood):
for boatbuilding, 47:123
Totman, Clayton O.:
on woodlot management, 35:50
Touring Quad (recreational pulling boat):
construction commentary, 54:82
Towboat, SPRAGUE:
comments, photo, 64:64
Townes, Brooks, author:
"A Smoky Mountains (?) Dory," 2:52
"Pelican Harbour," 25:80
on boat plans and public domain, 48:105
Townes, Brooks, builder:
plywood dory, 2:52
Town Marine Museum (NY):
boatbuilding program, 42:100
Trading ketch, DEFENDER:
history, repair commentary, photos, 92:62
TRADITION (commuter):
comments, photo, 94:74
Traditional Boat Association (Sweden):
comments, 58:48
Trailboards:
comments, detail photo, 65:52
Trailer:
design comments, photos, 69:86

See also Brownell hydraulic trailer
Tramontin, Nedis, builder (Italy):
gondolas, 15:21
Transom construction:
Bolger Cartopper dinghy, 87:29
Catspaw dinghy (Herreshoff Columbia
model)/Joel White, 26:48
Gloucester Light Dory/Harold Payson,
41:63
lofting technique/Arno Day, 98:41
outboard runabout Downeaster 18, 73:67
power cruiser YOREL, 95:67
technique/Bud McIntosh, 35:56, 55:107
Transom knot:
tying technique, 72:40
Transom repair:
Concordia 33 FREE SPIRIT/Brion Rieff,
99:28
Herreshoff 12½/Steve Ballentine, 56:93
Pacemaker/George Clapp, 16:20
letter by E. Barton Chapin III, 100:4
Transporting boats: (*See* Moving boats)
Travaco (seam filler), use:
teak deck overlay repair, 72:53
Trawler-yacht:
designs/Charles Wittholz, 15:72
Trawler-yacht, BLUE STAR:
comments, plans, 75:34
Trawler-yacht, NORDSØ:
construction commentary, photo, plans,
74:74
Trawler-yacht, OUR TERN:
owner's comments, photo, plan, 11:40
Traxler, Scott, author:
"Will It Last? A Lumber Forecast," 28:46
TREASURE (cutter):
comments, photo, 84:64
Tree identification books:
list, 44:50
TREFFRY (pilot gig):
comments, plans, 25:28
TREKKA (yawl):
comments, photo, plans, 84:64
comments, plan, 24:24
Trenholme, Bill, builder (British Columbia):
comments, 14:59
Trimaran:
commentary by Jim Brown, 69:76, 91:38,
92:34
See also ADRENALIN (Formula 40 class);
Designs appearing in *WoodenBoat* design
section; DRAGONFLY 15; GULF
STREAMER; IDENEK; JUNIPER;
MOXIE; NISMIME (research vessel);
OCEAN SURFER; ROGUE WAVE; ROSE
NOELLE; Searunner Trimaran (sloop);
SHADOWFAX; SIB; TELEGRAMME;
THAT; TROPIC BIRD; VITI-VITI
TRINCOMALEE (frigate):
history, photos, plans, 22:42
Tripp, Fred, builder:
flat-bottomed skiffs, 66:48
Tripple & Everett Marine Ways Inc., builder:
pinky ketch SUNRISE, 3:61
Trireme, Athenian:
reconstruction comments, photo, plans,
75:44
Troller (power fishing craft):
design commentary, operation of, photos,
38:78
designs/William Garden, 39:128
TRONDA (Fishers Island 23):
construction commentary, photos, 33:50

Tropical Timber, Inc.:
procedures for importing tropical woods, 69:35
TROPIC BIRD (trimaran):
design and construction commentary, photo, 42:66
TROUT UNLIMITED (outboard boat):
cover photo/Marty Loken, 64:0
design and construction commentary, photos, 64:70
Trowbridge, Clinton W., author:
"Consider the Peapod," 17:61
"Roque Island," 24:64
Trowbridge, Paul, illustrator:
"Pete Culler's Workshop, Part II," 28:83
"The Mighty Maritime Oaks," 46:76
Troy, Phil and Gerry, authors:
"Inside the Wood Block: A Maintenance Guide," 50:67
TRUCE (cutter):
interior mock-up, 84:29
Trull, Alden:
on boat covers, 54:92
Trumbly, Joe, designer and builder:
profile, photos, 89:44
Trumbly 38 (sloop):
comments, plan, 89:44
TRUMPET (outboard cruiser):
designs/Weston Farmer, 82:108
Trunnels (treenails):
comments by Richard Jagels, 45:115
installation/whaleship CHARLES W. MORGAN, 36:98
letters on, 46:5
making and installing/schooner DENYCE, 3:44
making and installing/Swedish kåg, 58:48
tools for making/Norwegian pram, 49:28
Tuberville, Jack, author:
"A Well-Used Boat," 82:19
Tucker, Tom, designer: (*See* Designs, Tucker, Tom)
TUESDAY (sloop):
comments, photo, 51:40
Tugboat: (*See* Designs, Sprague, Scott; ECHO [steamboat]; EPPLETON HALL [paddle-wheel tug]; GILLCREST; OX [steam tug]; PATRICIA; RESTLESS [steam tug])
Tuk-Tuk, The (power dory): (*See* The Tuk-Tuk)
Tulip (sailing pram):
kit boat, 39:69
Tumlaren class:
design and construction commentary, photos, plans, 19:18
Tung oil:
comments/Walter J. Simmons, 81:75
Tuplin, Basil, builder:
planking of whaleship CHARLES W. MORGAN, 36:98
restoration of schooner L.A. DUNTON, 6:44
Turk's Head knot:
tying technique, 19:17, 32:49, 40:92, 72:40
Turnabout class:
history, photos, plan, 36:105
Turner, Harold, designer and builder:
Turnabout class, 36:105
Turner, Rich, author:
"Colorado Dories," 15:47
Turning over boats:
at Herreshoff Manufacturing Company, 33:50
sharpie, 22:30, 33:36

Turpentine (wood):
for boatbuilding, 47:123
Turquoise Turtle knot:
tying technique, 72:40
Tursiops touring kayak:
designs/Mike Alford, 97:108
TURTLE (6′ submarine):
design and construction commentary, photos, plan, 21:74
Tuxworth, Greg:
comments on maintenance, 100:38
12-Meter class:
history, photos, 68:40
list of fleet before World War II, 68:50
12-Meter class, AUSTRALIA II:
comments on keel design, 62:36, 66:124
12-Meter class, COLUMBIA:
comments, photo, 68:40
12-Meter class, ENDLESS SUMMER:
design and construction commentary, photos, plan, 18:32
12-Meter class, GLEAM:
comments, 68:40
comments, photos, 38:75, 43:92
12-Meter class, INTREPID:
comments, 1:80
comments, photo, plan, 98:50
12-Meter class, MITENA:
comments, photo, 55:32, 68:40
history, 56:38
12-Meter class, MOUETTE:
comments, photo, 68:40
12-Meter class, NEFERTITI:
comments, photo, 65:76
12-Meter class, NIGHTWIND:
cover photo, 68:0
12-Meter class, NYALA:
comments, photo, 68:40
12-Meter class, ONAWA:
comments, photo, 68:40
12-Meter class, SEVEN SEAS:
comments, photo, 68:40
12-Meter class, VIM:
comments, 68:40
12-Meter class, WAIANDANCE:
account of passage from Halifax to New York, 68:50
12-Meter class, ZIO:
cover photo, 68:0
20-Square-Meter, Tumlaren class:
design and construction commentary, photos, plan, 19:18
21′ class:
comments, photo, 85:74
21′ class, ASPENET:
history, photos, plans, 7:17
letter on, 10:5
21′ class, BETSY:
history, photos, 1:58, 4:25
21′ class, EDNA:
history, photos, 1:58, 4:25
21′ class, JANE:
history, photo, plan, 8:62
21′ class, NANCY:
history, photo, plan, 8:62
T Wharf (Boston, Massachusetts):
photo essay, 87:56
TWILITE (sailing canoe):
builder of, comments, photos, 65:66
TWISTER (power cruiser):
comments, photo, 56:38
210 class:
history, photo, 40:105

TYEHEE (schooner):
account/loss of schooner, 83:74
letters on by various readers, 84:5
navigation comments/loss of schooner, 83:86, 83:88
thoughts on loss of schooner, 83:90
Typhoon class, RONDO:
photo, repair, 51:59
Tyrell, Jack, designer/builder (Ireland):
profile, 50:70
repair of cutter VAGRANT, photo, 61:80

ULLA (Danish seiner):
comments, photo, 88:40
Ulmia wooden planes:
critique, 4:72
Ultralight boats:
construction commentary by Tom Wylie, photos, 63:56
Controversy class, 61:42
designs/Scott Sprague, Nathan Smith, 70:110
Geodesic Airolites/Platt Monfort, 76:72
Robert Smith-designed sloop MAGIC CARPET, 90:108
Undergrove, A.N.S.:
letter about fuels for engines, 83:6
Unibond:
for deck repair, 25:89
UNICORN (yawl):
design and construction commentary, plans, 20:27
UNION JACK (schooner):
designs/William Garden, 68:114
United States Coast Guard:
letter on boardings, 91:6
small craft regulations, 3:1, 6:65, 50:16
vessel design by Walter McInnis, 53:38, 54:34
United States Forest Products Laboratory:
wood analysis report, 1:4
United States Forest Service: (*See* Forest Service, U.S.)
UNITY B (Bahamian smack):
construction comments, history, sailing techniques, photos, 81:34
cover photo/Benjamin Mendlowitz, 81:0
cover photo/Mark Silveira, 26:0
Universal Rule:
comments, 68:40, 73:32
discussed, 55:32
Unlimited-class hydroplanes:
Staudacher hydroplanes/comments, photos, 80:24
Upton, Joe, author:
reviewer of *Fishing—The Coastal Tradition* (book), 92:104

Upton, Joe, author and photographer:
"AMARETTO," 58:60
"Alaska Limit Seiners," 37:31
"Alaska Packers," 36:66
"Northwest Trollers and Gillnetters," 38:78
Upton, Joe, photographer:
cover photo/Alaska limit seiner, 37:0
USAID:
comments, 88:76
USS CONSTITUTION (frigate):
history, illustrations, photos, turnaround cruise, 83:32
USS SUISUN (power cruiser):
history, photos, restoration commentary, 81:21
Utzon, Aage, designer (Denmark):
spidsgatter designs, 78:50

Vacuum bagging:
Constant Camber construction/skiff GULL, 64:83, 65:97
letter on, 45:11
of sportfishing boat hulls, 76:44
pumps for, 64:83
technique for hull construction/Jim Brown, 41:50
technique for hull construction/John Marples, 44:99
technique for mast building, 54:56
Vacuum pump:
for vacuum bagging, 64:83
Vagabond class:
comments, photo, 74:64
VAGRANT (cutter):
comments, photo, 90:84
construction, history, photos, plan, rebuilding, 61:80
VAHINE (schooner):
designs/Herve Gloux, 22:90
Vaillancourt, Henri, builder:
profile, photos, 87:80
Vaitses, Allan, author and builder:
"Boatbuilders' Forum: Sheathing," 19:94
"Cold-Molded Opinion," 15:33
"Teak on Teak," 72:53
on cold-molded hull repair, 52:92, 60:76
VAKA BUSI (catamaran):
comments, photo, 69:76
cover photo/James W. Brown, 69:0
VALHALLA (pulling boat):
design and construction commentary, plan, 40:46
VALKYRIE (sloop):
cover illustration, 27:0
Valves: (See Seacocks)

Vancouver Maritime Museum (British Columbia):
comments, 63:8
Van Dam, Steve, builder:
sloop STAR, 54:114
Van Der Wal, Onne, photographer:
cover photo/SHAMROCK V, 95:0
Van Deusen, J.B., builder:
comments, 41:26
VanDevelder, Paul, photographer:
"GIPSY JAC," 98:74
Van de Vooren, Hans and Hetti:
profile, 73:96
Vanner, Samuel, builder:
sardine carriers, 58:52
Van Sant, Joel, designer:
International Moth class, 37:104
Van Voast, James T.:
on boat plans and public domain, 48:105
VARIN (Norwegian lestabåt):
design, construction, rig, use, photos, plans, 95:90
Varnishing:
advice for fitting out/Paul Bryant, 93:36
advice from professionals, 46:66
characteristics of varnish, 26:22
in tropical conditions/Allen Taube, 83:48
removal technique/Rebecca Wittman, 81:88
technique for early launching, 64:58
technique for hot-weather varnishing/Ian Bruce, 76:22
technique for varnish-and-epoxy combination/David Jackson, 99:66
technique/Paul Bryant, 40:56
technique/Giffy Full, 27:40
technique/Rebecca Wittman, 82:88, 83:66
technique/Rae Sutcliffe, 16:56
techniques, letter on, 18:7
See also Interior brightwork, Refinishing
VARUA (brigantine):
design and repair commentary, history, photos, plans, 65:44
Vassilopoulos, Peter, author:
"Boatbuilding Report: McQueen's Boat Yard," 12:66
Vaughan, W. Tay (Taylor), III, author:
"A Tale of Two Sisters: Carvel vs. Cold Molding," 44:90
on sail-powered commercial vessels, 31:18
Vaughn, Bill, author:
"Railboat," 95:34
Veneer:
use in BOC Challenger AIRFORCE, 68:72
use in cold-molded hull overlay/Owens cutter FALCON, 61:104
use in Constant Camber construction/skiff GULL, 64:83, 65:97
Venetian gondola:
design and construction commentary, photos, plan, 15:21
Venice, rowing craft:
photos, rowing event, 40:54
VENITA (power dory):
comments, photo, plans, 88:76
Ventilator, Dorade:
detail photo, comments, 66:90
VERENA (40' class):
history, photo, 49:66
Verhaegen, Quentin, builder and delineator (Morocco):
ketch BLUE STAR, 43:76

Verlicco, Paula Darois, author:
"The Passing of a New England Boatbuilder," 87:2
Vermandois, Karl, author:
"The Building of Lightning No. 13219," 31:56
Vermilya, Peter T., author:
"Building the Beetle Cats, Part I: Keel and Transom," 51:99
"Building the Beetle Cats, Part II: Stem and Centerboard Trunk," 52:107
"Building the Beetle Cats, Part III: Fitting and Bending Frames," 53:101
VERNON LANGILLE (schooner):
design commentary, performance, photos, plan, rig commentary, 58:82
operation of, photos, 31:18
Versatex:
for wooden hull sheathing, 17:54
Vertue class:
history, photos, plans, 24:32
VERTUE XXXV (cutter):
photo, plan, 24:32
Vespa, Robert, author and photographer:
"RONDO's Recovery," 51:59
Vesper-type canoe, TWILITE:
builder of/comments, photos, 65:66
VIAJERO (motorsailer):
design commentary, plan, 29:38
VICAR OF BRAY (ship):
comments, photo, 38:45
Victoria Classic Boat Festival (British Columbia):
comments, photos, 65:76
VICTORY CHIMES (schooner):
comments, photo, 39:32
VICTORY III (Bermuda fitted dinghy):
comments, 57:42
VICTURA (Wianno Senior class):
comments, photo, 91:58
Video reviews: (See Reviews [video] appearing in WoodenBoat)
VIGILANT (motorsailer):
construction commentary, history, photo, plans, 54:34
VIKING (pulling boat):
design and construction commentary, plan, 40:46
Viking Age merchant ship replica, SAGA SIGLAR:
construction commentary, 68:19
launching and voyage, photos, 68:19
Viking ship, SEBBE ALS:
construction commentary, history, photos, plans, 11:15
Viking Ship Museum (Denmark):
comments, 63:8
Viking ship replica, IMME GRAM:
comments, photo, 11:15
VIM (12-Meter):
comments on, 68:40
Vinal, Charles, designer:
research vessel NISMIME, 30:20
Vincent, J.G.:
comments, 60:84
Vinden, Russ:
letter on rig design, 94:4
VINDEX (cutter):
comments, 41:26
Vineyard Haven 15:
history, photos, plans, 47:86
VINTAGE ROSE (power cruiser):
comments, 14:2
owner's comments, photo, 13:26

VIPER II (Sea Sled):
comments, plans, 100:46
VIRGINIA (power cruiser): (*See* USS
SUISUN)
VIRGINIA REEL (motorsailer):
comments, plan, 97:76
Vise:
use for singlehanded boatbuilding, illustrations, 99:94
Vise-Grip tools:
product review of pliers and clamps/
Daniel Porter, 93:120
VITI-VITI (trimaran):
designs/John R. Marples, 23:92
VIXEN (Plymouth lobsterboat):
comments, photos, plans, 1:65
Vlet (Dutch pram):
construction, history, photos, plans, 52:75
VOLSUNGA II (ferryboat):
history, photos, 7:14
Voltage regulator:
comments, photo, 99:41
VORTEX (Swede 55):
design and construction commentary,
racing, photos, 100:84
design and construction commentary,
photos, plans, 100:88
VOYAGER (schooner):
comments, photos, 38:71
design and construction commentary,
photos, 33:90
sister-framing procedure, photos, 69:94
VOYAGER 30 (sloop):
designs/Thomas MacNaughton, 5:64
VOYAGEUR (freight canoe):
comments, photo, 67:38
VOYAGEUR (motorsailer):
design commentary, plan, 29:38

WABESI (Mackinaw boat):
design commentary, history, plans, 45:100
Wade, John C.:
letter on cold-molded hull repair, 53:6
Wagner, Dick:
interview with, 24:36
profile, photo, 90:72
Wagner, Dick, author:
"Our Thanks to John Gardner," 90:36
Wagner-Martin, Carol, author:
"Motonautico," 52:86
WAIANDANCE (12-Meter):
account of passage from Halifax to New
York, 68:50
Walker, B.W., designer (Bermuda):
Bermuda fitted dinghy, 57:42

Walker, Jim, and W. Lyman Phillips,
authors:
"A Pro Speaks On Painting," 10:56
Walker, Matthew:
fable of, 17:38
Walker, Matthew, author:
"Black Magic: Carbon Fiber Comes to
Wooden Boat Building," 25:76
"The Uncompromised Craftsmanship of
L'Estérel," 39:44
letter on Chinese maritime tradition, 67:5
letter on keel-vs.-keelson debate, 19:13
on maritime preservation, 41:36
reviewer of *Power Yachts* (book), 20:96
Walker, Matthew, author and photographer:
"From Rags to Riches," 17:48
"On Deck," 47:74
Walker, Matthew, photographer:
cover photo/schooner SPIKE AFRICA,
70:0
Walker, Ralph E.:
letter on refastening, 16:9
Wall, Glennie:
comments about, 72:60
letter on National Maritime Museum, 73:6
Wallace, Leroy (Roy), builder:
New England draggers, 79:48
sardine carrier PAULINE, 59:74
sardine carriers, 59:70
schooner JOHN F. LEAVITT, 31:18
Wallstrom, Bob, designer: (*See* Designs,
Brewer, Wallstrom and Assoc., Inc.)
Walnut, black:
comments by Richard Jagels, 72:105
WALRUS (power cruiser):
comments, photo, 75:34
Walters, Craig, author:
"GIPSY JAC," 98:74
Walters, Thomas, & Son, Ltd.: (*See* Thomas
Walters & Son, Ltd.)
Walters, Vernon:
profile, photo, 94:64
WANDA (motoryacht):
comments, photo, 94:54
WANDER BIRD (schooner):
design commentary, history, photos, 55:56
WANDERER III (sloop):
comments, plan, 24:24
Wanderer yawl:
designs/Cyrus Hamlin, 67:112
Wang, Finn:
letter on Deks Olje, 48:12
WAPAMA (steam schooner):
comments, photos, 72:60
history, photos, 61:88
letter by Capt. A.F. Reynaud, 91:4
letter by Peter H. Spectre, 90:4
Ward, Herschel B., builder:
for Huckins Yacht Corp., 56:48
Ward, Lynd, illustrator:
"A Boatbuilder's Garden," 45:36
Warner, Winthrop, designer:
comments, 97:76
profile, drawing, 75:34
See also Designs, Warner, Winthrop
WARRIOR II (iceboat):
comments, photo, 39:88
Warship, Athenian trireme:
reconstruction comments, photo, plans,
75:44
Warwick & Associates, designer: (*See* Designs,
Warwick & Associates)

Washbasin:
comments, detail photo, 74:80
WASP (Barnegat Bay A-cat):
history, photo, 62:6
WASP (40′ class):
comments, 41:26
WASP (Six-Meter):
comments, photo, 55:32
Water knot:
comments, 23:20
Waterlines: (*See* Scribing, waterlines)
WATERMAN (outboard cruiser):
designs/Howard I. Chapelle, 82:108
Water Power Products, oarmaker (Nova
Scotia):
profile, 94:64
WATER RAT (cutter):
comments, photo, 65:76
Waters, Rick, author:
"The North Woods Paddle," 67:44
Waterstones:
product review by Daniel Porter, 91:103
Waterwag Association (Ireland):
comments, 19:67
Waterwag class:
comments, 38:111
history, photo, plans, 19:67
letter on, 44:5
WATER WITCH (motorsailer):
comments, photo, plans, 28:20
Watkinson, John, designer (England):
Drascombe boats, 26:73
Watney, John, author:
"Riva," 17:70
Watney, John, photographer:
cover photo/Riva speedboat, 17:0
Watson, Aldren, author and illustrator:
"A Locker for the Main Cabin,
Part I," 76:89
"A Locker for the Main Cabin,
Part II," 77:87
"Building the Cabin Sole, Part I," 81:65
"Building the Cabin Sole, Part II," 82:75
Watson, Don, builder:
cold-molded hull repair, 60:76
Watson, Gavin:
letter on bungs, 84:5
Watson, George L., designer (Scotland):
comments, 41:26, 100:70
Watson, James and Nate, builders:
Plymouth lobsterboats, 1:65
Watson, Jim, author:
"Cold-Molded Repairs for Laminated
Boats," 55:96
Watts, Simon, author:
"A Steambox Primer," 88:58
"An Evolution from Sail to Power:
Boats of Eastern Nova Scotia," 46:42
"Pilot Gigs of Cornwall and the Scilly
Islands," 25:28
"The JOLIE BRISE," 38:54
"The Stevens Family: A Nova Scotia
Tradition," 34:26
"Wedge-Seam Construction," 98:82
letter on Bush Island boat, 47:7
Watts, Simon, builder:
profile, 73:60
Wave Form Theory:
letter on, 51:6
of Colin Archer, 20:35
WAVERTREE (ship):
comments, 38:36, 38:45

Wayfarer dinghy:
kit boat/comments, photos, 38:84
kit boat/construction commentary, photos, 51:88
Wayland Marine, builder (British Columbia):
Wayfarer dinghy kit boat, 38:84
Weatherford, Robbie:
sculling technique, 100:60
Weatherston, David:
letter on solvent for cleaning brushes, 65:6
Webster, Richard, author:
"A Byte at Tradition," 79:84
Webster, Sam, builder:
Chesapeake Bay log canoe, 6:26
Wedge-seam construction:
commentary by Simon Watts, 98:82
Wee Lassie (double-paddle canoe):
how to build, photos, plans, 100:92
Weems & Plath plotting tools:
product review of parallel rules and dividers/Jon Wilson, 100:124
Wee Rob (double-paddle sailing canoe):
designs/Iain Oughtred, 84:106
Wehncke, Malcolm, author and illustrator:
"A Ditty Bag Apprenticeship, Part I," 31:30
"A Ditty Bag Apprenticeship, Part II," 32:49
"Herringboning," 37:95
"Hitches: Improving on a Cylinder," 39:102
"Seizing Hanks," 35:80
"Sewing a Patch," 36:86
"Sewing Reef Nettles," 38:100
Wehncke, Malcolm, and Brion Toss, authors and illustrators:
"Sons of Hitches," 40:92
Weingand, Jack, author:
"Sailing LA MOUETTE," 75:69
Weisenburger, Gary, author:
"Product Review: Some Traditional Hardware Chandlers and Manufacturers," 86:91
"Product Review: Tools of the Trade," 85:107
Weisenburger, Gary, author and photographer:
"Lyman: A Sleeping Assembly Line," 82:68
"New Life at Ninety," 63:48
Weitz, Allan, photographer:
"Interior Arrangements," 93:52
WELCOME (armed-sloop replica):
cover photo, 10:0
design and construction commentary, history, photos, plan, 10:60
Weld, Phil:
association with Jim Brown, 69:76
comments, photo, 91:38
owner of trimaran ROGUE WAVE, 23:68
Weldwood glue:
comments, 15:64, 18:65
comments/Lin and Larry Pardey, 18:65
use by George I. (Sonny) Hodgdon, Jr., 59:88
WELLIFONT (power fishing craft):
comments, photo, 50:70
WENDA (canoe yawl):
designs/Albert Strange, 80:102
WENDIGO (sloop):
design and construction commentary, photo, plans, 19:18
Wenger, Greg, photographer:
"A Taste of the Twenties," 22:57
"RELIANCE—A Pinky Schooner," 18:46

Wertenbaker, William, author:
"Parting Thoughts," 83:90
Wescott, Earle, author:
"Cousin Sam's Friendship Sloop," 7:8
Western larch:
comments, 68:103
Western white pine:
comments, 68:103
Western yew:
comments, 68:103, 82:72
Westphal, David, photographer:
"Friendship Sloop Days," 29:61
Westport sharpie:
comments, plans, 66:48
Westport skiff:
comments, plans, 66:48
design commentary, photos, plans, 32:29
letter on towing of, 33:5
WESTWARD (schooner):
comments, photo, 54:34
Wetmore, Brad, author:
"The Pure Sound Society," 89:89
Wetstone, Richard J., author:
"Keeping Warm," 25:27
Wet-well:
construction comments/Bahamian sloop, 81:34
design and construction commentary with drawings, 69:42
Wetzler Clamp Co.:
critique of C-clamp, 1:77, 2:70
Whaleship, CHARLES W. MORGAN:
comments, 38:36, 41:36, 46:80
cover photo/Benjamin Mendlowitz, 36:0
planking technique, 36:98
Wharram, James, designer (England):
comments on Third World boatbuilding, 30:20
profile, 23:77
review of plans catalog, 89:112
Wheel, ship's:
how to build, photos, plans, 14:70
Wheeler, Chauncy, builder:
Alexandria Bay boats, 48:66
Wheeler, J.R., author and photographer:
"Whitehall Pulling Boats," 16:15
Wheeler Shipyard, builder:
Wheeler 34, 25:102
William Hand designs, 29:38
Wheeler 34 (power cruiser):
construction commentary, photo, plan, 25:102
Wherry: (See Bangor Packet, Lincolnville wherry)
WHIFF (iceboat):
comments, plan, 38:64
WHIPPET (Winter Harbor 21 class):
repair, illustrations, photos, 93:76
Whipping (cordage technique):
British Admiralty and palm-and-needle methods, 52:112
comments, 25:18, 52:112
WHIRLWIND (J class):
comments, 55:32
comments, photo, 46:30
WHISP (sailing skiff):
comments, photo, 54:74
designs/Steve Redmond, 72:98
WHISPER (commuter):
comments, photo, 94:74
WHISPER (Wianno Senior class):
comments, 91:58
Whisstock's Boatyard, builder (England):
Deben Four-Tonner, 8:67
kit boat NAJA 30, 38:84

White, Chris, author:
"Product Review: AMBUSH and YACHT," 87:108
reviewer of *Guide for Building and Classing Offshore Racing Yachts* (book), 87:108
White, Chris, designer and builder:
comments, 92:34
profile, 54:56
White, E.M., canoe: (See E.M. White canoe [wood-and-canvas])
White, Joel, author:
"A Design for the Indians," 88:82
"Ask the Pros: Planking Stock," 22:94
"Ask the Pros: Removing Keel Bolts," 16:70
"Designs: A Contemporary Cutter," 78:106
"Designs: A Design for a Designer," 65:104
"Designs: A Heavy Cruiser," 87:119
"Designs: A Lobsterboat with Traditional Flavor," 77:101
"Designs: A Modern Quay Punt," 63:116
"Designs: AERIEL, Excellence and Moderation," 100:108
"Designs: An Ultralight Double-Ender," 70:110
"Designs: BOUNTY and LONE STAR," 89:114
"Designs: Eye-Pleasing Pungy," 68:110
"Designs: Grace and Speed at Sea," 61:127
"Designs: Light for Its Length," 59:114
"Designs: Looking at Boat Plans," 75:111
"Designs: OCEANUS—Old and New," 81:106
"Designs: PASSAGEMAKER and ALBACORE III, Seagoing Powerboats," 93:128
"Designs: St. Lawrence Yawl," 85:117
"Designs: SASKIANNA," 83:112
"Designs: STING RAY," 98:104
"Designs: Simplicity, Not Extravagance," 62:100
"Designs: Strong Roots in the Region," 60:134
"Designs: TLINGIT and CZARINNA, Plain and Fancy Powerboats," 96:112
"Designs: 20' Sliding-Seat Rowing Wherry," 52:122
"Designs: 26' Canoe-Sterned Sloop," 56:130
"Designs: Unproved Potential, Cyrus Hamlin's Wanderer," 67:112
"Ordering Lumber," 87:46
"Other Ways: Liberated Caulking," 37:86
"Peapods Are For Sailing," 27:52
"The Feel of a Deepwater Vessel," 58:114
letter on stopwaters, 57:12
on maintenance of Fishers Island 31 CIRRUS, 34:42
on paint primers, 46:66
on sharpie-ketch EGRET, 56:76
reviewer of *Desirable and Undesirable Characteristics of Offshore Racing Yachts* (book), 79:95
reviewer of *Hand Tools—Their Ways and Workings* (book), 51:118
reviewer of *Practical Yacht Joinery* (book), 54:132
reviewer of *Preliminary Design of Boats and Ships* (book), 94:102
White, Joel, builder:
ketch DOVEKIE, 5:55, 7:31
on cold-molded hull repairs, 52:92
steam-bending techniques, 44:86
White, Joel, designer:
Martha's Tender skiff, 45:92, 46:94, 47:58

Nutshell pram, 60:100
WoodenBoat School/Miskito (Honduras)
  Indians project, 88:76
See also Designs, White, Joel
White, Joel, designer and builder:
  Catspaw dinghy (Herreshoff Columbia
    model), 26:48, 27:63, 28:64
  power cruiser LADY JEANNE, 37:72
White, Laurie, photographer:
  "A Luders-16 Rejuvenation," 55:102
White, Mark, author and photographer:
  "Ed Opheim's Dories," 43:40
White, Steve, author and builder:
  "A Luders-16 Rejuvenation," 55:102
  "New Life for Old Decks," 66:64
White, Steve, builder:
  Swede 55 VORTEX, 100:84, 100:88
White ash:
  for boatbuilding, 9:31
WHITE CAP (Herreshoff 12½):
  refinishing techniques for, 40:56
WHITECAP (power cruiser):
  comments, plan, 52:40
White cedar:
  comments, 33:72
  for birchbark canoe, 87:80
  for planking, 16:39, 28:64
  letter on properties, 32:9
WHITE CLOUD (troller):
  comments, photo, 38:78
White cypress pine:
  for boatbuilding, 47:123
WHITEFIN (sloop):
  cover photo/Jennifer Cannell, 57:0
  design and construction commentary,
    performance, photos, plans, 57:80
  letter on, 58:7
Whitehall (pulling boat):
  construction methods of Shew & Burn-
    ham, photos, 77:76
  plans for Howard I. Chapelle design, 84:76
  Whitehall Jr./comments, photo, 77:70
Whitehall, built by Haynes:
  comments, photos, 16:15
Whitehall, built by Shew & Burnham:
  centerboard design, photos, 24:58
  construction methods, photos, 77:76
  cover photo, 45:0
Whitehall, built by Southworth:
  construction commentary, photos, 5:12
Whitehall, LILY:
  cover photo, 53:0
  design and construction commentary,
    photos, 53:86
Whitehall, San Francisco:
  history, photos, 40:16
WHITEHAWK (ketch):
  compared to sloop WHITEFIN, 57:80
  cover photo, 25:0
  design and construction commentary,
    photos, plans, 25:56
  letter on, 29:8
Whitehead, Jack, woodcarver:
  profile, 56:68
WHITE HEATHER (cutter):
  comments, photo, 90:84
White lead:
  in repair of fantail launch, 63:48
  comments on use, 49:97
White oak:
  decay resistance, strength properties, 65:112
  decay resistance and identification, 1:48
  identification of, 64:108

White pine: (*See* Pine, Southern yellow; Pine,
  Northern white)
WHITE RABBIT (power cruiser):
  owner's comments, photo, 13:26
WHITE WINGS (sloop):
  reframing, photos, 23:50
  replanking and refastening, photos, 24:72
WHITE WINGS II (model):
  comments, photos, 88:70
Whitford, Wallace D., author:
  "A Different Kind of Restoration," 80:14
  letter on boatyard hazards, 84:8
Whiticar Boat Works, builder:
  sportfishing boats, 76:44
Whitman, Leslie, author:
  "ALOHA: Launched Anew," 95:82
Whitney, Albert, builder:
  for Huckins Yacht Corp., 56:48
Wianno Senior class:
  cover photo/Benjamin Mendlowitz, 91:0
  history, photos, plans, 91:58
  racing tactics/Jack Fallon, 91:67
Wickerwork boat: (*See* River Boyne coracle)
Wilbur, Jack, builder:
  profile, photo, 69:48
WILD ROSE (Itchen boat):
  comments, plans, 48:58
WILD SPIRIT (cutter):
  comments, 26:70
Wiley, John P., Jr., author:
  "In My View: A Rowboat for Our Times,"
    85:95
Wiley, Ralph, builder:
  Comet class, 31:90
Wiley, Walter, author:
  "Small and Simple," 27:47
Wilkins, Isaac P., builder:
  cutter SCHEMER, 37:42
Wilkinson, Chuck, illustrator:
  "The Boatbuilders of Alexandria Bay,
    Part II," 49:58
Willauer, Peter:
  comments about, 71:44
Williams, Earle, author:
  "8,000 Wedges and 4,000 Trunnels," 3:44
Williams, Fenwick C., designer:
  yawl ANNIE, 41:78
  See also Designs, Williams, Fenwick C.
Williams, Hugh, author:
  "A Fine Heritage: Boatbuilding Report,"
    20:58
Williams, Rory:
  letter on boatbuilding course, 75:7
Williamson, James, builder (England):
  smack BOADICEA, 36:20
Willis, E.A. (Neet), builder:
  comments, 37:42
Willits, Earl, Floyd, and Lon, builders:
  canoes, 55:82
Willits canoe:
  construction commentary, history,
    photos, 55:82
Willits Canoe Factory, builder:
  history, 55:82
WILLOW (power cruiser):
  owner's comments, photos, 18:26
Willow canoe:
  comments, photo, 96:80
  cover photo/Thomas R. Stewart, 96:0
Wills, Gail, photographer:
  "How to Build PICCOLO, Part I," 36:44
  "How to Build PICCOLO, Part II," 37:57

Wilmington Boat Works, builder:
  Eight-Meter sloop ANGELITA, 59:40
Wilmot, Douglas, author:
  "Norway's Mellemværftet Shipyard," 84:58
Wilson, Dale, author and photographer:
  "Boatbuilder Clark Mills," 36:73
Wilson, Jon:
  profile, 60:44
Wilson, Jon, author:
  "A New Cabin Top," 20:52
  "Aesthetics and the Craftsman," 28:62
  "Are We Doing Enough?", 19:62
  "Ask the Pros: Alaskan Yellow Cedar,"
    24:100
  "Ask the Pros: Cabin Trunk Repair," 24:100
  "Ask the Pros: Finishes for Teak," 21:90
  "Ask the Pros: Live Oak," 19:98
  "Cold-Molding: Perfecting the Art and
    the Science," 26:70
  "Concordia's Beetle Cat Shop," 21:72
  "Deck Canvasing: The State of the Art,"
    22:72
  "Designs: 24' Gaff Yawl by Fenwick
    Williams," 28:96
  "Designs: 26' Marconi-Rigged Plywood
    SEA BIRD," 50:132
  "Designs: 28' Power Scow," 30:98
  "In the Classic Spirit," 29:33
  "Interior Arrangements," 93:52
  "Keeping the Water Out from Under,"
    28:76
  "Making a Choice, Part I: The Domestic
    Woods," 9:31
  "Making a Choice, Part II:
    The Imported Woods," 10:35
  "Our Thanks to John Gardner," 90:36
  "Product Review: Parallel Rules and
    Dividers: Choose Them Well," 100:124
  "The Boatshed: Small Craft Warnings,"
    6:65
  "The Elements of Craftsmanship," 26:53,
    27:57, 28:59, 29:89, 30:89, 31:79, 32:88
  "The Elements of Saw Cuts," 14:52
  "The History of Small Yacht Design,
    40-Footers, Part I," 48:58
  "The History of Small Yacht Design,
    40-Footers, Part II," 49:66
  "The Proper Boathook," 71:25
  "The Remarkable Sloop SHADOW,
    Part I," 43:64
  "The Remarkable Sloop SHADOW,
    Part II," 44:24
  "The Sano Shop," 80:54
  "The Wertenbaker Proposition," 83:86
  "Tool Critic: Brushes," 18:98
  "Tool Critic: Planking Clamps," 12:42
  "Tool Critic: Sandpaper," 15:82
  "Tool Critic: Sharpenset Whetstone,"
    20:98
  "Tool Critic: Sharpening Systems," 21:94
  "Transom Replacement," 99:28
  "Vic Carpenter, A Study in Superior
    Craftsmanship," 46:82
  "Winter Covers," 13:33
  comments on Howard I. Chapelle, 84:76
  comments on outboard runabout
    Downeaster 18, 73:67
  comments on schooner AMERICA, 54:67
  comments on sharpie EGRET, 56:2, 56:76
  comments on Thiokol compounds, 2:64
  editorial on Ned Ackerman, 33:2
  editorial on apprenticeship programs, 42:2
  editorial on articles in issue 91, 91:2

Wilson, Jon, author (*continued*)
editorial on articles in issue 93, 93:2
editorial on boatbuilding industry, 75:2, 85:2
editorial on boatbuilding wood, 40:2
editorial on boat design and copyrights, 32:2, 47:2, 47:46
editorial on boatyard hazards, 79:1
editorial on BOC Challenger AIRFORCE, 73:2
editorial on Malcolm Brewer, 37:2
editorial on Vic Carpenter, 45:2
editorial on Coast Guard regulations, 3:1
editorial on concept of tradition, 61:2
editorial on Concordia yawls, 80:2
editorial on William F. Crosby, 89:2
editorial on Ed Cutts, 78:2
editorial on Dudley Davidson, 39:2
editorial on design standards, 35:2
editorial on diversity of wooden boat construction, 63:2
editorial on Terry Driscoll, 45:2
editorial on fitting-out fever, 51:2
editorial on folding kayaks, 53:2
editorial on foundering of schooner JOHN F. LEAVITT, 33:2
editorial on good judgment in racing, 59:2
editorial on insurance for wooden boats, 68:2
editorial on loss of PRIDE OF BALTI-MORE, 71:2
editorial on maintenance, 65:2
editorial on marine industry, 97:2
editorial on maritime preservation, 38:2, 86:2
editorial on Eric McKee, 57:2
editorial on Ralph Munroe and sharpie EGRET, 56:2
editorial on noise pollution, 81:2
editorial on offshore raceboat JESSE JAMES, 73:2
editorial on Seth Persson, 37:2
editorial on plywood boatbuilding, 41:2
editorial on PRIDE OF BALTIMORE II, 96:2
editorial on Steve Redmond, 58:2
editorial on sail plan efficiency, 92:2
editorial on signal flags, 67:2
editorial on sloop FREE SPIRIT, 58:2
editorial on Charlie Sylvester, 37:2
editorial on taking sabbatical, 83:2, 87:2
editorial on traditionalists, 88:2
editorial on winter layup afloat, 20:2
editorial on *WoodenBoat*/advertising in, 43:2, 44:2
editorial on *WoodenBoat*/development, 16:1, 18:2, 60:44
editorial on *WoodenBoat*/editorial approach, 4:2, 44:2, 49:2, 52:2, 62:2, 74:2, 98:2
editorial on WoodenBoat Publications, 90:1, 100:2
editorial on *WoodenBoat*/purpose of, 1:2
editorial on wooden boat building conference, 17:3
editorial on wooden boat ownership, 58:2, 64:2, 66:2, 69:2, 95:2
editorial on wooden boats, 82:2
eulogy for Alan Bemis, 99:2
eulogy for Bob Baker, 55:2
eulogy for Pete Culler, 23:2
eulogy for Lois Darling, 94:2

eulogy for Capt. Irving Johnson, 99:2
eulogy for Darrell McClure, 76:2
eulogy for Bob Sloan, 70:2
letter on Redningskoites, 50:5
letter on Albert Strange, 50:5
reviewer of *AMERICA's Cup Yacht Designs 1851–1986* (book), 82:97
reviewer of *Building the SPRAY* (book), 26:98
reviewer of *Concordia—A Classic Wooden Yacht* (video), 94:101
reviewer of *Dictionary of Tools Used in the Woodworking and Allied Trades* (book), 13:18
reviewer of *Modern Wooden Yacht Construction* (book), 31:94
reviewer of *Nautical Quarterly #1* (periodical), 20:96
reviewer of *Plant a Tree* (book), 27:108
reviewer of *Some Books About Wood* (book), 2:65
reviewer of *The Catboat Book* (book), 3:72
reviewer of *The Gougeon Brothers on Boat Construction* (book), 31:94
reviewer of *The Marine Photography of Peter Barlow* (book), 6:72
reviewer of *The North American Yacht Register, 1978* (book), 26:98
reviewer of *Traditions and Memories of American Yachting* (book, 50th–anniversary edition), 91:92
reviewer of *Woodwork Joints* (book), 14:76
Wilson, Jon, builder:
sailing peapod, 1:42
Wilson, Jon, photographer:
"A Boatbuilding Shop," 85:27
"Building a Dinghy for Oar and Sail, Part I," 26:48
cover photo/schooner JOHN F. LEAVITT, 31:0
Wilson, Ken:
letter on keelbolts, 90:6
Wilson, Nathaniel S., author:
"Ask the Pros: Cuprinol," 22:94
on boat covers, 54:92
Wilson, Rodney, builder (Barbados),
comments, 9:52
WINCHESTER IV (commuter):
comments, photo, 94:74
WINDANCE (sloop):
comments, photo, plans, 89:44
Windermere Steamboat Museum (England):
comments, 46:54
cover photo/Christian Février, 98:0
history, profile of George Pattinson, photos, 98:66
Windmill class:
design commentary, 36:73
design commentary, history, photos, 26:88
Windmill design:
for research vessel, NISMIME, 30:20
Windmill-propelled boat:
comments by Havilah Hawkins, photos, plans, 88:60, 88:66
Windshield construction:
outboard runabout Downeaster 18, 75:53
Windsurfer:
design comments by Llewellyn Howland III, 60:52
Windswept yawl:
designs/Ted Brewer Yacht Designs, 63:116
Wingerath, Charles, builder:
St. Lawrence skiffs, 11:58

Wingsails:
catamaran TAULUA, 72:70
commentary by Iain Oughtred, 78:66
Winslow, Ralph, designer:
comments on by Bud McIntosh, 51:40
Winter Harbor 21 class:
comments, 73:32
repair/illustrations, photos, 93:76
Winter layup:
haulout using a float, 36:96
methods/Maynard Bray, 54:88
methods/Hilda Marvin, 13:30
methods/Riverside Boat Yard, 48:91
options, 12:59
schedule for wooden boats, 75:30
See also Boat cradles, Boat covers, Boathouse, Painting techniques, Storage
Winter layup afloat:
in Maine/methods of Maynard Bray, 30:54
in the Chesapeake/methods of Jim Emmett, 32:62
Winter Wren (sloop):
comments, plans, 85:52
Wire:
service technique/Brion Toss, 59:106
Wire grommet:
making of, 55:114
Wire splice:
technique for 1x19 splice/Brion Toss, 81:45
Wiser, William, builder:
sailing canoe, 20:89
Wishbone rig:
commentary by Iain Oughtred, 78:66
Wisniewski, Roger, builder:
Au Sable River boats, 5:6
Witt, Glen L., designer:
designs/plywood sneakbox, 61:124
letter on plywood sneakbox, 62:7
recommendations for finishing fir plywood, 81:75
See also Designs, Glen-L Marine
Wittholz, Charles, designer:
comments on Downeaster 18, 73:77
See also Designs, Wittholz, Charles
Wittman, Rebecca, author:
"The Art of Brightwork, Part I," 81:88
"The Art of Brightwork, Part II," 82:88
"The Art of Brightwork, Part III," 83:66
Woas, Lee, author:
"Cordage: Camel Hitch," 30:18
WONDER (Itchen Ferry smack):
design and construction commentary, photo, plans, 14:22
Wood, bending: (*See* Steam-bending)
Wood, for boatbuilding:
air drying, 9:31
air-drying techniques, 67:76
air-drying theory and technique for stacking, 66:92
analysis by U.S. Forest Products Laboratory, 1:4
Australian and New Zealand species, 47:123
Australian species, 96:104
Australian species/annotated list, 95:102
availability, 28:46, 29:82, 32:90
availability, characteristics, 35:45
availability, comments by George Putz, 59:56
botanical nomenclature, 36:89
characteristics of wood (plank curvature)/Ed McClave, 100:31

commentary on pines/Richard Jagels, 83:107

comments, 10:43, 40:2, 53:119

comments by George Buehler, 5:32

comments by George Luzier, 66:56

comments by Olin F. Stephens II, 98:50

compression wood in Northern white pine, 88:100

crook timber, 40:120

decay resistance of, 72:105

dimensional instability, 33:72

domestic species, 9:31

drying properties and drying techniques, 10:39, 23:22

durability ratings/comments by Richard Jagels, 54:120

ecology, 44:50

ecology, growth rate analysis, 39:115

for colonial shipbuilding, 58:120

forest decline, 80:108

grading/comments by Richard Jagels, 22:20

guide to compiling a boatbuilding lumber list, 87:46

imported species, 10:35

kiln drying comments, 79:103

letter about old-growth timber management, 85:5

list of European and North American species, 71:111

list of hardwoods, softwoods, imported woods, 37:108

native vs. imported, 70:38

naturalization of new tree species, 86:105

New Zealand alternatives, 97:104

Philippine species, 40:78

pressure-treated/comments by Richard Jagels, 28:94, 76:115, 77:116, 85:121, 89:106

prevention of checks while seasoning, 63:14

producing and marketing advice for tropical woods, 69:35

purchasing advice/Richard Jagels, 41:123

review of Flounder Bay Boat Lumber, 99:107

scrounging for, 43:13

secondhand lumber, 76:29

selection, 53:119

sources/Forest Service, 45:46

terms "long-grained," "short-grained" defined, 67:109

tropical deforestation/letter on, 93:4

tropical forest exploitation, 78:100, 87:125, 90:128, 99:125

tropical forest exploitation/alternatives to boycotting imports, 92:112

tropical forest management, 94:114

tropical woods/importing procedures, 69:35

underutilized species discussed/Richard Jagels, 42:123, 43:120

using recycled timber, 93:134

utilization of local woods, 35:45

utilization systems, 25:20

water curing of/comments by Richard Jagels, 69:119

Western species, 68:103

See also Alaska yellow cedar, Ash, Black walnut, Canadian pine, Cedar, Cypress, Douglas-fir, Eucalyptus, Hackmatack, Iroko, Kauri, Mahogany, Maple, Melaleuca, Pitch pine, Plane tree, Plywood, Port Orford cedar, Red oak, Sassafras, Silverballi, Sitka spruce, Southern yellow pines, Teak, Veneers, Western larch, Western white pine, Western yew, White cedar, White oak, Yellowbark oak

Wood, Gar, builder: (See Gar Wood, Inc., builder)

Wood, harvesting:
comments by boatbuilders, 29:82

letters on, 11:4, 30:7

technique and equipment/Charles Page, 9:36

technique and equipment for teak/India, 32:42

See also Chainsaw milling, Hackmatack, Live oak, Sawmill operation

Wood, identification:
Australian and New Zealand species, 47:123

of mahogany, by hand-lens method, 55:120

of red and white oaks, 1:48, 64:108

Wood-and-canvas canoe: (See E.H. Gerrish canoe, E.M. White canoe)

Wood boat, St. John River: (See BRUNSWICK LION)

Wood Brothers, builder:
NYSSA, 37:42

Wood dust:
health hazards/OSHA regulations, 93:86

Wooden Boat Center (CA):
boatbuilding program, 42:100

WoodenBoat Design Competition:
results, 29:20, 30:20

WoodenBoat Design Group, designers:
Yankee Tender skiff, 30:74, 31:71

WoodenBoat Editors, authors:
"Building Martha's Tender, Part I," 45:92

"Building Martha's Tender, Part II," 46:94

"Building Martha's Tender, Part III," 47:58

"Building a Dinghy for Oar and Sail, Part I," 26:48

"Building a Dinghy for Oar and Sail, Part II," 27:63

"Building a Dinghy for Oar and Sail, Part III," 28:64

"Building a Flat-Bottomed Skiff, Part I," 30:74

"Building a Flat-Bottomed Skiff, Part II," 31:71

"DOVEKIE: A Saga Begins," 5:55

"Maintenance with Meaning: An Interview with Giffy Full," 27:40

"Pete Culler's Workshop, Part I," 27:81

"Pete Culler's Workshop, Part II," 28:83

"Sharpie Update," 2:32

"The Drascombe Boats," 26:73

"The Great Ones Gather," 38:71

"The Preservation Forum," 41:36

"The Wake of the Vikings," 28:33

"The Westport Skiff," 32:29

"The Winners! WoodenBoat Design Competition Results, Part I," 29:20

"The Winners! WoodenBoat Design Competition Results, Part II," 30:20

Wooden Boat Festival (WA):
1977/photos and commentary, 19:56

WoodenBoat magazine:
advertisements, suitability of, 43:2, 44:2

editorial approach, 4:2, 44:2, 49:2, 52:2, 62:2, 74:2, 98:2

history, 16:1, 18:2, 60:44

purpose, 1:2, 90:1, 100:2

setting maintenance standards/comments by David Kasanof, 59:13

staff photos, 3:1, 14:97, 34:2, 60:44

WoodenBoat School (ME):
boatbuilding program, 42:100

Martha's Tender skiff, 45:92, 46:94, 47:58

profile of instructor Arno Day, 63:38

project/Miskito (Honduras) Indians, 88:76

projects, 44:86, 45:92, 46:94, 47:58

seamanship course, 58:82

Wooden Boat Shop (Seattle, WA):
product review by Peter H. Spectre, 93:115

Wooden Boat Show (RI):
letter by Stephen R. Prime, 76:4

1981/photos and commentary, 43:84

Wooden boat shows:
1980, gatherings in the U.S./photos and commentary, 34:60

Woodin, Russ, designer:
comments, 95:60

Woodlot management:
by pulp and paper companies, 28:46, 29:82

comments by boatbuilders, 29:82

comments by George Putz, 44:50, 45:36

live oak, 46:76

methods described, 35:50

methods of Elzeard Bouffier, 27:22

WOODPECKER (power cruiser):
photos, plans, 24:24

Wood preservatives: (See Preservatives, wood)

Wood screws:
compared to rivets, 51:72

compared to rivets, composition and corrosion of, removal from planking, 55:43

corrosion of, 3:18, 23:30, 24:78, 29:77, 41:84

defined and illustrated, 81:82

installation, characteristics, 54:47

removal from lapstrake planking, 92:90

removal from planking, 53:109, 55:43, 70:23

removal from planking and refastening, 12:30, 14:9, 16:9

use in teak deck overlay repair, 72:53

Woods, Richard and Lilian, designers:
letter on catamaran STRIDER, 74:7

review of plans catalog, 96:98

See also Designs, Woods, Richard and Lilian

Woodstoves:
for boats, 25:27, 31:25

Woodward, James, author:
"Nuts and Bolts Solutions," 17:20

letter on building cradles, 22:5

Woodward, Stanley, author:
"MOCCASIN—Whose Time Has Come," 18:20

Woodworkers Alliance for Rainforest Protection (WARP):
comments, 99:125

Wootton, Michael, photographer:
"A DOVE for Saint Mary's," 26:30

Workshops: (See Boatshops)

Woycke, Steve, author:
reviewer of navigational videos, 77:109, 81:100

WRAITH (sportfishing boat):
comments, photo, 76:44

WREN (launch):
comments, photo, 62:74

Wright, Alan, designer (New Zealand):
Quintet 6 kit boat, 39:69

Wright, Michael Henry, author:
"Stalking the Western Yew," 82:72
Wright, Roger, author:
"Fleamarket Tools," 20:65
Wrought-iron bolts:
making of, 50:59
Wycoff, Arthur, designer: (*See* Designs, Wycoff, Arthur R.)
Wylie, Thomas, designer:
cutter WILD SPIRIT, 26:70
profile, photos, 63:56
Wylie, Thomas, Design Group, builder:
cold-molded boats, 12:24, 17:48
Wylie 42, NO GO VIII:
design and construction commentary, photos, 17:48

XANTHO (steam launch):
comments, photo, 84:34
XARA (40′ class):
history, photo, 48:58

Yachting history:
commuters/C. Philip Moore, 94:74
correspondence/N.G. Herreshoff and W.P. Stephens, 100:70
influence of Edward Burgess, 71:52
influence of W. Starling Burgess, 71:52, 72:44, 73:32, 74:42
modern multihulls/James W. Brown, 91:38
profile of Charles Francis Adams III, 85:74
profile of the Fifes of Fairlie, Scotland, 90:84
schooner PEGGY, 70:17
12-Meter class, 68:40
YAKABOO (sailing canoe):
letter by John Martsolf, 82:5
YANKEE (J-boat):
comments, photos, 85:74

YANKEE (R-class sloop):
comments, 46:30
design commentary, photos, 55:32
YANKEE GIRL III (sloop):
comments, plans, 75:34
Yankee Tender skiff:
compared to Westport skiff, photos, 32:29
how to build, performance, photos, plans, 31:71
how to build, photos, plans, 30:74
YARANA (cutter):
comments, photo, 91:92
Yates, Herb, and John Erikson, authors:
"The Columbia River Gillnetter," 22:27
Yawls: (*See* Advanced Sharpie, AÏDA, AMIGO, ANNIE, ARBELLA, AYESHA, Bar Harbor 31′ class, BELISARIUS, BLOOD-HOUND, BLUE MOON, BRENDA, CHERUB II [canoe yawl], CHESAPEAKE, CIRRUS [Fishers Island 31], CLOUD [canoe yawl], Concordia yawl, COTTON BLOSSOM IV, DAKINI, DANCING DRAG-ON, Designs appearing in *WoodenBoat* design section, DEUCE, DORADE, Drascombe lugger, EEL [canoe yawl], ESCAPADE, EVENING STAR, FINIS-TERRE, Forest Belle yawl, HOB NOB, Iota, ISLA TROTHE, ISOBEL [canoe yawl], Keyhaven yawl, LA MOUETTE [canoe yawl], Malabar Jr. [sloop and yawl], MANX-MAN, MERIDIAN, MOCCASIN, MOON-GLOW II, NIRVANA, PACIFICA, PETREL, PLEASURE, PUFFIN, ROB ROY, ROY-ONO, SAGA, St. Lawrence yawl, SAN-TANA, SASSOON [knockabout yawl], SCUD, Sea Bird yawl, SHEILA [canoe yawl], SHEILA II, SNIKERSNEE [canoe yawl], SPARTAN [New York 50], SPRAY, STORMY WEATHER, Story 20, TEVA, THISTLE, TIGRIS, TREKKA, UNICORN, Wanderer yawl, WENDA [canoe yawl], Windswept yawl)
YAZOO (power cruiser):
cold-molded hull repair, photo, 60:76
Yellowbark oak:
for repair of fantail launch, 63:48
Yeomans, Edward, author:
"Downeast Traditions," 13:82
letter on Gustav Erikson, 73:10
Yew, Western:
comments, 68:103
YOLANDE (cutter):
comments, plan, 41:26
Yonkin, Roger:
letter on bungs, 82:6
YOREL (power cruiser):
design and construction commentary, photos, plans, 95:60
detail photos, comments, 71:92
transom construction details, photos, 95:67
Young, Orvil:
on woodlot management, 35:50
YP-class patrol boat:
comments, photo, 58:90
YUCCA (Eight-Meter class):
comments, photo, 83:38
Yuloh (sculling oar):
comments, illustrations, sculling technique, 100:60
history, 42:38

ZACA (schooner):
history, photos, 50:31
Zahniser's Marina and Boatyard, builder:
method of building ketch CARRIE L, 42:75
ZANDER (Waterwag class):
comments, photos, plans, 19:67
Zeusche, Paul, author:
"Colin Archer: His Life and Times," 20:35
Zimmer, Nelson, author and designer:
"Designs: 18′8″Mackinaw Boat," 23:90
"Designs: 21′3″ Utility Boat," 43:124
"Designs: 45′ Cutter," 51:133
See also Designs, Zimmer, Nelson
Zimmerly, David W., author and photographer:
"The Hooper Bay Kayak," 58:74
on Kodiak kayak construction, 58:68
Zimmerman, Peter S.:
letter on bungs, 81:5
Zimmermann, Jan, author:
"Building the Banks Dory," 19:32
"Dick Pulsifer and the Strip-Planked Hampton," 57:50
Zimmermann, Jan, author and photographer:
"Ancient Curraghs," 50:80
ZIO (12-Meter):
cover photo, 68:0
Zuteck, Mike, designer:
comments, 87:66
Zydler, Tom, author:
"Boats of the Polish Coast," 89:74
"Kuna Canoe," 97:62
Zysk, Ed:
on boat covers, 54:92

If you've been admiring the boat silhouettes through-
out this Index and would like to examine them in
detail, they can be found in *Fifty Wooden Boats: A
Catalog of Building Plans* and in *Thirty Wooden Boats,
A Second Catalog of Building Plan*s. To order these call
The WoodenBoat Store 1–800–273–SHIP (7447).

CONTENTS PAGES
VOLUME I: ISSUES 1–6

1 SEPTEMBER/OCTOBER 1974

ROYONO Gets Some New Planking 4
R. Bruce MacAdam
Building a Traditional Sharpie Today 8
James M. Curry
Traditional Boatbuilders' Tools 14
John Gardner
Bill Page's Homebuilder's Project 20
NELLIE
L.D. Bailey
A Tribute to Murray Peterson 29
William M. Peterson
Murray Peterson: A Brief Biography 30
John F. Leavitt
SILVER HEELS 32
Howland B. Jones, Jr.
The Return of the Sailing Peapod 42
Grace B. Carter
A Technical Comparison of Red and 48
White Oaks
T.C. Scheffer, G.H. Englerth, and
C.G. Duncan
Searching for EDNA's Past, Part I 58
James P. Foley
The Plymouth Lobster Boats 65
William Lambert Barnard
Designs:
A Modified Friendship Sloop/John 72
Atkin

2 NOVEMBER/DECEMBER 1974

For a Keg of Rum 8
Jill Bobrow
The Maine Sloop 15
William Lambert Barnard
Friendship Sloop Days 22
William M. Peterson
Electrical Installations in Wood Yachts, 24
Part I
Lloyd's Register of Shipping
When the Keel Drops Off 28
William Payne
Sharpie Update 32
WoodenBoat Editors
The Decay of Wood in Boats 36
Carl Hartley and Curtis May
The Lincolnville Wherry 44
Walter J. Simmons
IOLAIRE: 1905 to ? 48
Donald M. Street
A Smoky Mountains (?) Dory 52
Brooks Townes
Winter 57
John N. Cole
Designs:
BLUE MOON Revisited/Tom Gillmer 58
The Antique Boat Show 66
Robert Pittaway

3 JANUARY/FEBRUARY 1975

San Francisco's ALMA 8
Barbara Fetesoff
Degradation of Wood by Products of 18
Metal Corrosion
A.J. Baker
The Traditional Sharpie: Performance 24
Aspects
James M. Curry
Electrical Installations in Wood Yachts, 31
Part II
Lloyd's Register of Shipping
The Oysterman's Race 34
Randall S. Peffer
RESTLESS 41
William C. Payne
8000 Wedges & 4000 Trunnels 44
Earle Williams
The Cape Cod Catboat 51
William Lambert Barnard
Check the Bilge 59
Donald M. Street, Jr.
Designs:
SUNRISE/Jay Benford 61
The Pilot's Pinky DOVE/Edward 65
Brewer

4 MARCH/APRIL 1975

Boatbuilding—The Philosophy of an 4
Approach
R.D. Culler
The Fish and the Bird 14
Joe Richards
Cold-Molded Construction 17
Thomas MacNaughton
Searching for EDNA's Past, Part II 25
Sturgis Haskins
The Apprenticeshop: A Discussion 31
Lance Lee
Adhesives and the Boatbuilder 47
Gerald Schindler
Scottish Fishing Boat Conversions 50
Ian Nicolson
Designs:
LA TROPICANA/Winthrop Warner 66

5 MAY/JUNE 1975

Howard I. Chapelle 1
Thomas C. Gillmer
Au Sable River Boats 6
Frank Starkweather
An Amateur-Built Boat 12
William B. Southworth
Mystic: Small Craft Workshop 24
Peter Barlow
Designs:
NOBLE 41/Robert Perry 33
My Ultimate Cruiser/Eva Hollman 38
Antique Nautical Instruments 41
John and Vicki Hanson
The Building of a Tancook Whaler, 44
Part I
John Nation
DOVEKIE: A Saga Begins 55
WoodenBoat Editors
Designs:
VOYAGER 30/Tom MacNaughton 64

6 JULY/AUGUST 1975

Unemployed—But Happy 6
Charles R. McNeill
From Knockabout to Yawl 14
William Lambert Barnard
An Apprentice in England 20
David Leather
Cut and Look: Building a Chesapeake 26
Bay Sailing Log Canoe
Randall Peffer
Marine Museums: Obligations and 34
Objectives
John Gardner
L.A. DUNTON: A Brief Encounter 44
Michael Moss
A New Life for HIPPOCAMPUS JR 54
Milanne Rehor
MARY CELESTE: The Story of a 60
Mystery Ship
Stanley T. Spicer
Designs:
Great Pacific Boat Works/George 68
Buehler

VOLUME II: ISSUES 7–12

7 SEPTEMBER/OCTOBER 1975

Henderson's Boatyard: Mallaig's 5
  Traditionalists
    Charles Holzhauer
Cousin Sam's Friendship Sloop 8
    Earle Wescott
VOLSUNGA II: Thimble Island's 14
  Ferryboat
    Alyssa A. Lappen
ASPENET 17
    Sturgis Haskins
ACTIVE to England 20
    John Marsland
The Bancroft Tapes 31
    Margie and Dennison Bancroft
Estimating Construction Costs 36
    Thomas MacNaughton
Cold-Molded Construction (a Critique) 45
    John W. Shortall III
A Non-Professional's Working 52
  Perspective
    Spence F. Maier
The Building of a Tancook Whaler, 56
  Part II
    John Nation
Instant Boats 64
    Harold Payson
Designs:
  "510" Class Sloop/C. Raymond Hunt 69

[NOTE: No Nov./Dec. 1975 issue.]

8 JANUARY/FEBRUARY 1976

How I Almost Used My Kayak As 5
  Firewood
    Ben Luberoff
Taken Easy 7
    Richard F. Caruzzi
PILGRIM's People Get Ready 12
    Randall Peffer
RHIANNON 18
    E.H. Chamberlin
Small Craft Restoration in Search of 30
  Professionalism
    John O. Sands
Voyaging in the Trade Winds: 36
  To Tahiti on JOSEPHA
    George Day
Documentation Primer 44
    Robert deGast
HIPPOCAMPUS JR: Adventure 46
  Challenges the Will
    Milanne Rehor
Ashcroft Construction Using Flat Strips 50
  and Epoxy
    R.R. Richardson
California Friendships 53
    Bill Payne
St. Lawrence Yawls 58
    Lewis Evans
The Original Knockabouts NANCY 62
  & JANE
    William A. Baker
The Deben Four-Tonner 67
    Don Goodsell

9 MARCH/APRIL 1976

MAYA 16
    George Day
Old John's Kicker 22
    Joe Richards
The Same after 75 Years 24
    W. Lyman Phillips
Making a Choice: The Domestic Woods, 31
  Part I
    Jon Wilson
Wood Harvest 36
    Charles Page
Rediscovering Hackmatack 44
    Edward A. Ackerman
The Old Building 47
    John Garber
A 20-Minute Job 50
    W.A. Phair
Barbados Boatbuilding 52
    Gerald Ingersoll
Manson Boat Works 56
    W. Lyman Phillips
Designs:
  EAST HUE & CRY/William Baker 60
  25-Year 25-Footer/David Beach 62
  HIPPOCAMPUS JR: Back to Virginia 66
    Milanne Rehor

10 MAY/JUNE 1976

The Creation of SIOLA TAU 16
    Robert Hobman
Working Boats of Connemara 25
    K.E. Sanders
Folkboats Revisited 30
    Lloyd Bergeson
Making a Choice: The Imported Woods, 35
  Part II
    Jon Wilson
Seasoning Science 39
    Charles Page
What Good is Wood? 43
    David Keith
The Rowboat 48
    John Garber
The Real Runabouts 53
    Robert Speltz
A Pro Speaks on Painting 56
    W. Lyman Phillips and Jim Walker
WELCOME Once Again 60
    J.F. Schroeger
Designs:
  LYRA/Tom Tucker 65
  Forget the Alehouses 70
    Gordon P. Jones

11 JULY/AUGUST 1976

Viking Replica 15
    Lance Lee
Wooden Tallship: GAZELA PRIMEIRO 24
    R.B. Benson and F. Hopkinson, Jr.
Understanding, Appreciating, Pre- 36
  venting Rot
    Lin and Larry Pardey
The Liveaboard Experience: A Trawler 40
  Yacht
    Al and Alma Jones
Some Thoughts on Lofting 43
    Sam Manning
On Laying Down and Taking Off 48
    Bud McIntosh
The Nearly Forgotten Art 52
  of Making Planes
    James Curry
St. Lawrence Skiffs 58
    Bolling W. Haxall
The KATY G 62
    John Garber
Friendship Charter 65
    Tom Moffat
The Care and Feeding of Teak Decks 70
    Jim Emmett
Designs:
  GIRL FRIDAY/A.G. Skidmore 73
  Peterson 33/Douglas Peterson 76

12 SEPTEMBER/OCTOBER 1976

A Quest for Perfection 14
    Stephen L. Davis
The Perfect Material 24
    Alex Monson
An Introduction to Refastening 30
    L.E. Nicholson
Out of My Class 40
    Ken Abbott
The Essence of Lofting 43
    Jack Ehrhorn
Lofting the Lubec Boat 44
    Sam Manning
Something of My Own 54
    Gifford Jackson
A Winter Storage Primer 59
    Jon Wilson
Clamps & Cleverness 62
    Walter J. Simmons
McQueen's Boat Yard 66
    Peter Vassilopoulos
Designs:
  The Bass Boat/Alan McInnis 68
  Three Views of the SAANICH 70
    BEAGLE/Alex Bavelas

VOLUME III: ISSUES 13–18

13 NOVEMBER/DECEMBER 1976

The Longboats of Pitcairn Island 22
Tad Donnan
Two Elcos 26
Walter Hadley and Donald Rose
Winter Lay-Up: Doing It Now 30
Hilda Marvin
Winter Covers 33
Jon Wilson
High Standards 34
John K. Hanson
Elusive GYPSY 40
Sturgis Haskins
Ships Such as Those: MATILDA D, 45
Part I
William Gilkerson
Bevels 50
Sam Manning
The Making of Molds 53
Bud McIntosh
Spiling the Garboard 56
Pemberton Drinker
Leaks are Lousy 60
Barbara Cochran
A Peapod for Passage 61
Tom Rubino
Keeping the Structure Together 65
Donald Street
Sailing the Carolina Sharpie IDIE 68
Charles McNeill and Michael Alford
The Return of the Steam Launch 76
John F. Leather
West Coast Traditions 79
Kimball Livingston
Downeast Traditions 82
Edward Yeomans

14 JANUARY/FEBRUARY 1977

The Emergence of PRIDE, A Baltimore 16
Clipper
Thomas Gillmer
Exploring the Smacks of Itchen Ferry 22
J.W. Holness
The Hudson's Hardwater Heritage 26
Peter A. Burckmyer
An Exceptional Man 31
Bert Smith
A Boatbuilder's Trade School 34
Randall Peffer
Setting Up 38
Fred Ajootian
The Rabbet 42
Sam Manning
Ships Such as Those: MATILDA D, 45
Part II
William Gilkerson
Saw Cuts 52
Jon Wilson
The Incredible Herreshoff Dugout 54
Maynard Bray
Designs:
A Diesel Cruiser/William Garden 59
No Wrinkles: Canvasing the Deck 64
Howard Rosenfeld
The Makassar Ketch 66
Jim Rooney
The Ship's Wheel: A New Turn 70
John Marsland
Boatbuilding Report: The Lafitte Skiff 73
David Snyder

15 MARCH/APRIL 1977

The Venetian Gondola 21
Leslie Bruning
Watertight: A Simple Teak Deck 26
Seth Emmer
Machin Knight & Sons, Ltd.: Boat- 29
building Report
Nicholas Knight
Cold Molding: Opinion 33
Allan Vaitses
BRUNSWICK LION 34
Gerald D. Ingersoll
The Sounding Pole 40
Edwin Frost
The Blue Jay 42
Pamela Detels and Janet Harris
Colorado Dories 47
Rich Turner
The Fine Art of Stripping Paint 55
Dan MacNaughton
Mast Making: Start From Scratch 58
Jim Emmett
Mast Making: The Hollow Spar 60
John Marsland
Mast Making: Build a Practical 64
Wooden Spar
Lin and Larry Pardey
Pouring the Lead Keel 70
Fred Ajootian
Designs:
34′ Trawler Yacht/Charles Wittholz 72
Ribbands 74
Bud McIntosh
Timbering Out 76
Bud McIntosh

16 MAY/JUNE 1977

Whitehall Pulling Boats 15
J.R. Wheeler
When Boats Are Proud 17
David Roper
Transom Repair 20
George Clapp
The Flatness Issue 26
Charles Minor Blackford
A Modern Composite 27
Frank Starkweather
GOLDEN DAZY: Revolution in Wood 29
Meade Gougeon
The Americanization of a Fuukien Junk 35
Joe Maggio
Planking the Maine Lobster Boat 39
Royal Lowell
Caulking 47
Sam Manning
With Feeling: Varnishing, Music & Love 56
Rae Sutcliffe
Better with Age 63
Michael Crowley
To Each His Own 66
George Day

17 JULY/AUGUST 1977

Northwest Passage 14
Tim Snider
Nuts & Bolts Solutions 20
Jim Woodward
A Flair for Raging Inlets 23
Phil Bowie
Docking a Schooner Under Sail 26
Nicholas Benton
Surfing: Sea Bright Style 29
Gerald Bouchal
Conversation with a Master Caulker 32
George Emlen
On Knots 38
Spike Africa and Jan Adkins
Save a Cotton Plant 40
Jim Emmett
Ever Try Finishing Off From a Float? 41
Jim Emmett
A Tempered Boat 42
Lafayette Stuch
Designs:
30′ Sailing Dory/Jay Benford Assoc. 45
34′ Displacement Cruiser/A.G. 46
Skidmore
From Rags to Riches 48
Matthew Walker
Sheathing—What We Know 54
Gerald Schindler
Consider the Peapod 61
Clinton Trowbridge
They Never Stopped Working: 63
British Sail
John Mellor
Money to Spare 66
Julius Johnson
Joy Is a Wooden Boat 69
Dayna Adamson
Riva 70
John Watney

18 SEPTEMBER/OCTOBER 1977

MOCCASIN—Whose Time Has Come 20
Stanley Woodward
Hankins Heritage 26
Kevin Sheehan
The Monterey Clipper 28
Jim Douthit
ENDLESS SUMMER 32
Tony Latimer
Skill of Hand, Part I 38
Bud McIntosh
RELIANCE, A Pinky Schooner 46
Linda Krotenko
Cradles for Storage and Shipping 51
Dan MacNaughton
Building the Adirondack Guideboat 55
Howard Ford
The Once In 3-Year Refit 65
Lin and Larry Pardey
As Old as the Dory 71
Bob Atkinson
Basic Plywood Scarfing 77
Harold Payson
A Lucky Break 82
Clifton Andrews
Designs:
FRANCES/C.W. Paine Yacht Design 84
8′ Pram/Gougeon Brothers 86
HERCULES/Glen-L Marine Designs 88
26′ Eastport Pinky/Brewer, Wallstrom 89
& Associates

VOLUME IV: ISSUES 19–24

19 NOVEMBER/DECEMBER 1977

The Timeless Tumlarens	18
John Pazereskis	
Polynesia's Honored Beings	25
Barbara Robinson	
Building the Banks Dory	32
Jan Zimmermann	
Taking the Lines	42
David Littleton-Taylor	
Icky, Sticky, Goo	46
John Pazereskis	
Skill of Hand, Part II	50
Bud McIntosh	
The Great Wooden Boat Festival	56
Tim Snider	
Are We Doing Enough?	62
Jon Wilson	
The Winsome Waterwag	67
J.W. Holness	
A Little Ship: LAZY JACK	70
Edwin Frost	
The Herreshoff Connection	72
Donald Street	
Going It Alone in Comox	76
Tony Gregson	
Designs:	
18′ LWL Cruising Sloop/Roger Long	80
28′ Skipjack/Charles Coad	82
Double-Paddle Canoe/L.F. Herreshoff	83
25′ 9″ Weekender/Robert MacNeill	84

20 JANUARY/FEBRUARY 1978

Wood Technology: Lumber Grading	20
Richard Jagels	
Sneakbox	23
Pemberton H. Drinker	
Liberating the UNICORN	27
Edie and Bruce King	
Boatbuilders by Degrees	33
Fred Bonavita	
Colin Archer—His Life and Times	35
Paul Zeusche	
The Archer Poised	38
Peter Leth	
PASSIONELLA, A Ten-Dollar Skiff	44
Bulkeley Smith, Jr.	
Native to the Thousand Islands, Part I	48
Andrew Steever	
A New Cabin Top	52
Jon Wilson	
A Fine Heritage	58
Hugh Williams	
One Mahogany Log	61
Douglas Elliott	
Flea Market Tools	65
Roger Wright	
Lofting Aids	68
Jim Emmett	
Building a Rudder	70
Philip Teuscher	
POOR RICHARD	76
Weston Farmer	
Something of a Legend	80
Kevin Kelley and Susan Kelman	
How the Legend Began	82
Bo Colomby	
Building the BRUCE	87
Erik Morch	
Designs:	
14′ 6″ Sailing Canoe/Ned Costello	89
21′ 7″ Cape Cod Catboat/Brewer,	91
Wallstrom & Associates	
29′ 6″ Cutter HOBO/A.G. Skidmore	92
25′ 9″ Motor Yacht/Arthur Wycoff	94

21 MARCH/APRIL 1978

Wood Technology: Modern Chemistry	18
Richard Jagels	
The Return of a Classic	21
Gail Shelton	
Native to the Thousand Islands, Part II	26
Andrew Steever	
Understanding a Boat Plan	30
Weston Farmer	
George Pocock Racing Shells, Inc.	36
T.M. Green	
Water Spider: The Shells of Garofalo	40
George Day	
The Aegean Tradition	42
Nicholas J. Lee	
I Didn't Know I Couldn't Do It	49
Robert J. Campbell	
For Her Name's Sake	50
Karl MacKeeman	
Built to Portage	54
Scott Landis	
Sailing Together Around the World	58
Mary Maynard	
Butt Blocks: As They Should Be	66
W. Lyman Phillips	
Where Do I Start?	69
Dan MacNaughton	
Concordia's Beetle Cat Shop	72
Jon Wilson	
Mock TURTLE	74
Joseph Leary	
Topsides Never Lie	79
Dan MacNaughton	
Designs:	
24′ Cat-Ketch/C.W. Paine Yacht Design	82
23′ Cutter/Kaufman & Ladd	84
15′ & 20′ Outboards/Dow & Dias	86

22 MAY/JUNE 1978

Wood Technology: Lumber Grading	20
Richard Jagels	
The Block Island Cowhorn	22
Beverley Holle	
The Columbia River Gillnetter	27
Herb Yates and John Erickson	
Easy Does It	30
Lindsay A. Fowler	
Sticks & String	33
Sam Manning	
The Most Notable of all Distinctions	42
Roger Marshall	
Eye-Sweet & Spacious	46
Jill Sanderson	
LIGHTFOOT	53
Robert K. Johnson	
A Taste of the '20s	57
Greg Wenger and Darien Murray	
Rebuilding a Basket Case	61
George A. Hill, Jr.	
Battle Below the Waterline	64
Dan MacNaughton	
Leeboards	71
Allan Bayless	
Deck Canvasing: The State of the Art	72
Jon Wilson	
Confidence	74
Benjamin Mendlowitz	
TLC at East Bay Boat Works	77
L.E. Nicholson	
Designs:	
24′ 6″ Sloop/Warwick & Associates	86
26′ Runabout/William Baber	88
20′ 3″ Sloop/John Atkin	89
34′ 6″ Schooner/Herve Gloux	90

23 JULY/AUGUST 1978

Wood Technology: Drying Out	22
Richard Jagels	
The Tradition of Burnside St.	25
L.E. Nicholson	
Electrolysis and Corrosion, Part I	30
Jerry Kirschenbaum	
PEGGOTTY	39
Jennifer Buckley Gilmore, Bob	
Baker, and Kevin Dwyer	
A Wooden Bilge Pump	44
Ed Frost	
Oars by Aylings	47
Dag Pike	
Because They're the Best	48
Peter Barmonde	
The Restoration of WHITE WINGS,	50
Part I	
Garth F. Graves	
SIMPLICITY for the Amateur Builder,	53
Part I	
Thomas MacNaughton	
The Lure of the Multihull: Introduction	63
Dan MacNaughton	
The Catamaran Chronicle	64
Nathanael Herreshoff	
A Second Tri	69
Meade Gougeon	
A Dynamic Tradition	77
Dan MacNaughton	
A Norwegian Boatbuilding School	80
Gunnar Eldjarn and Bjorn Skauge	
Designs:	
18′ 8″ Mackinaw Boat/Nelson Zimmer	90
26′ 9″ Sloop/Roger Marshall	92
17′ Cruiser/David Beach	93
30′ 8″ Ketch/Philip Rhodes	94

24 SEPTEMBER/OCTOBER 1978

Wood Technology: Lumber Grading	22
Richard Jagels	
Extending the Limits: The Gift of	24
Laurent Giles	
Andrew Pool	
The VERTUE and Her Achievements	32
Andrew Pool	
More Than Boats for Hire	36
Marty Loken	
Getting the Feel of Caulking	40
Clarence Dirks	
The Better Canvas Cover	44
Maynard Bray	
Mr. Souter's New Boat	47
Roland Paxton	
Gentleman Jim	53
Randall Peffer	
Whitehall to Windward, a Centerboard	58
Saga	
Pat Cahill	
Roque Island	64
Clinton W. Trowbridge	
SIMPLICITY For the Amateur Builder,	68
Part II	
Thomas MacNaughton	
The Restoration of WHITE WINGS,	72
Part II	
Garth F. Graves	
Electrolysis & Corrosion, Part II	78
Jerry Kirschenbaum	
Designs:	
42′ 3″ Cutter/Edward S. Brewer	93
31′ 2″ Half-Tonner/Yves Tanton	94
26′ Sportfisherman/David Martin	95
17′ Skiff/R.D. Culler	96

VOLUME V: ISSUES 25–30

25 NOVEMBER/DECEMBER 1978

Wood Technology: Acronym Update in Wood Products   20
Richard Jagels
New Life for an Old Canoe   22
Jim Emmett
Calling a Cruiser Home   24
Lea Malmquist
Keeping Warm   27
Richard J. Wetstone
Pilot Gigs of Cornwall and the Scilly Islands   28
Simon Watts
The Sharpie: Flat Is Back   36
Dan MacNaughton
Ferdinand Nimphius   42
Joe Caravello
Ruby's Bloom   48
Joe Caravello
Matter of Detail: Stems and Breasthooks   52
Maynard Bray
WHITEHAWK Flies!   57
Jane Day
Electrolysis & Corrosion, Part III   61
Jerry Kirschenbaum
Black Magic: Carbon Fiber Comes to Wooden Boatbuilding   76
Matthew Walker
Pelican Harbour   80
Brooks Townes
Leaking Decks: Watertight Solutions   89
Donald Street
Designs:
49' Batwing Schooner/George Buehler   94
12' Dinghy/Frederick Goeller   95
43' 11" Cutter/Bob Wallstrom   96
49' Cruiser/Tom Beard   97

26 JANUARY/FEBRUARY 1979

Wood Technology: Clear Boat Finishes   22
Richard Jagels
Don't Give Up the Ship   24
Irving Sheldon
Clench Nailing for Planks and Frames   28
Barry Thomas
A Dove for St. Mary's   30
Maynard Bray
Mr. Herreshoff's Wonderful Rozinante   40
Roger Taylor
Building a Dinghy for Oar and Sail, Part I   48
WoodenBoat Editors
The Elements of Craftsmanship   53
Jon Wilson
Giffy's Hammer: Surveying Wooden Boats   57
Jerry Kirschenbaum
Cold Molding: Perfecting the Art and the Science   70
Jon Wilson
The Drascombe Boats   73
WoodenBoat Editors
The Trap Skiff's Delicate Daughter   76
Walter J. Simmons
Matter of Detail: Seat Knees and Quarter Knees   80
Maynard Bray
Bayou Lumberman   83
Richard Jagels
Designs:
37' Cat-Ketch/Phil Bolger   94
18' 7" Hardangersjekte/John Atkin   95
39' 6" Sloop/Ted Brewer   96
30' 6" Power Cruiser/Colin Mudie   97

27 MARCH/APRIL 1979

Wood Technology: Teak   20
Richard Jagels
The Man Who Planted Hope   22
Jean Giono
Lowell's Boat Shop   26
Jane Day
The Dutch Boeier   32
E.H. Bon
Maintenance with Meaning: An Interview with Giffy Full   40
WoodenBoat Editors
Small & Simple   47
Walter Wiley
Peapods Are for Sailing   52
Joel White
The Elements of Craftsmanship   57
Jon Wilson
Building a Dinghy for Oar and Sail, Part II   63
WoodenBoat Editors
Before You Set Sail   74
Dan MacNaughton
Ashcroft's Simplex System   78
J.W. Holness
Pete Culler's Workshop, Part I   81
WoodenBoat Editors
Matter of Detail: Stern Sheets   86
Maynard Bray
Designs:
36' 7" Power Cruiser/William Garden   89
20' Sloop/Bruce King   90
51' 9" Cutter/Norman Boettcher   91
19' Sailing Dory/Frank Davis   92

28 MAY/JUNE 1979

William Hand: The Evolution of an Architect, Part I   20
Jerry Kirschenbaum
ENDEAVOUR: A Motorsailer Lifestyle   29
Jerry Kirschenbaum
Shavings on the North Wall   34
Lance Lee
Timber, Sail & Oar   36
Greg Owen
Sure Eye and Steady Hand   39
Arne Emil Christensen, Jr.
The Wake in the Fjord   42
Scott Danielson
Will It Last? A Lumber Forecast   46
Scott Traxler
The George Kirby, Jr., Paint Co.   50
Jane Day
Matter of Detail: Keels   56
Maynard Bray
The Elements of Craftsmanship   59
Jon Wilson
Building a Dinghy for Oar and Sail, Part III   64
WoodenBoat Editors
Keeping the Water Out from Under   76
Jon Wilson
Fitting the Bottom Plywood Panel   80
Percy Blandford
Pete Culler's Workshop, Part II   83
WoodenBoat Editors
Wood Technology: Pressure-Treated Timber   94
Richard Jagels
Designs:
24' Gaff Yawl/Fenwick Williams   96
17' "Rover" Class Sloop/Philip Rhodes   97
6' 8" Pram/Peterson Associates   98
27' Power Cruiser/John Atkin   99

29 JULY/AUGUST 1979

Wood Technology: Bending Wood   14
Richard Jagels
The Winners! WoodenBoat Design Competition Results, Part I   20
In the Classic Spirit   33
Jon Wilson
William Hand: The Evolution of an Architect, Part II   38
Maynard Bray, Jerry Kirschenbaum, and Jon Wilson
Asa Thomson's Elegant Skiffs   50
Dan Phalen
SAM WISE: A Skiff for All Seasons   56
John Erickson
Friendship Sloop Days   61
Gunnar Hansen
A Crewman's View of a Sloop Race   64
Roger Taylor
The Brenne Clamp   67
Bjorn Skauge
Rebuilding the Wood & Canvas Canoe   68
Jerry Stelmok
Bleeding Fastenings   77
Robert Gardner
Forest Timber: Who Has It? Who Gets It?   82
Jane Day
The Elements of Craftsmanship   89
Jon Wilson
Matter of Detail: Toe Rails   94
Maynard Bray
The Concordia Sloop Boat   98
Waldo Howland
Places to Go: Museums with Small Boats to See   102
Maynard Bray

30 SEPTEMBER/OCTOBER 1979

The Winners! WoodenBoat Design Competition Results, Part II   20
The San Francisco Pelican   29
Richard Conrad
English River Skiffs   36
Percy Blandford
CAPT. R.D. CULLER: A Scow Schooner Dream   42
Bob Servais
Before You Let Her Go   46
C.H. Andrews
BROWN SUGAR: 7,600 Pounds of Power   50
J.B. Carey
Winter Layup Afloat   54
Maynard Bray
The Reliable One-Lunger   59
Peter H. Spectre
Harvesting Hackmatack Knees: A Conversation with Frank Morse   66
Jane Day
Building a Flat-Bottomed Skiff, Part I   74
WoodenBoat Editors
Matter of Detail: Bow Chocks   84
Maynard Bray
A Thwartships Double Berth   86
Jim Emmett
The Elements of Craftsmanship   89
Jon Wilson
The Borneo Adze   93
Paul Butler
Wood Technology: Paint Adhesion   94
Richard Jagels
Designs:
28' Power Scow/Roger Haddock   98
25' 8" Cutter/John Atkin   100

VOLUME VI: ISSUES 31–36

31 NOVEMBER/DECEMBER 1979

The Return of Working Sail 18
Jane Day
Using the Rest of the Tree: Heating a 25
Wooden Boat with Wood
Richard Jagels
A Ditty Bag Apprenticeship, Part I 30
Malcolm Wehncke
Falmouth Oyster Boats 36
Pete Greenfield
They Go Like the Wind 42
Pemberton Drinker
ISH-TY-IQUE 48
Heidi Landecker
The Building of RANDOM SCOOT 50
David Kendall
The Building of Lightning No. 13219 56
Karl Vermandois
The Bear Mountain Canoes 58
Merilyn Mohr
Saving Time in the Mold Loft: 64
Pick 'Em Up Fast
Dave Porter
Saving Time in the Mold Loft: 66
Pick 'Em Up with Precision
Richard Lagner
Building a Flat-Bottomed Skiff, Part II 71
WoodenBoat Editors
The Elements of Craftsmanship 79
Jon Wilson
Matter of Detail: Rudders and Tillers, 84
Part I
Maynard Bray
Wood Technology: Improving Wood's 88
Natural Durability
Richard Jagels
Designs:
LYRA II/Tom Tucker 97
30' Cargo Sloop/Frederic Fenger 98

32 JANUARY/FEBRUARY 1980

CORONET: Whither Away? 20
Timothy F. Murray
The Westport Skiff 29
WoodenBoat Editors
Keep It Simple 32
Bob Baker
Roy Blaney Knows What's Right 36
Jane Day
Clear Morning 40
Heidi Landecker
India's Teak Harvest 42
J. Garrett Glover
A Ditty Bag Apprenticeship, Part II 49
Malcolm Wehncke
Extending the Life of a Skiff 57
Keith Quarrier
Wintering on the Chesapeake 62
Jim Emmett
The Alden Era 66
Waldo Howland
Matter of Detail: Rudders, Part II 76
Maynard Bray
Marine Electrical Systems 79
Jerry Kirschenbaum
The Elements of Craftsmanship 88
Jon Wilson
Wood Technology: Clear Stock 90
Richard Jagels
Designs:
18' O-Boat/John Alden 102
37' Gaff Ketch/Tom Gillmer 103

33 MARCH/APRIL 1980

North Atlantic Shakedown: The Aban- 20
donment of the JOHN F. LEAVITT
Peter H. Spectre
The Vineyard Triangle 30
Jan Adkins
Before the Dream Fades 33
Ray Hamburgh
SQUAW: A Sharpie Schooner 36
Steve Pagels and Philip Shelton
Sonny Hodgdon's Half Models 41
Maynard Bray
The Genius of Nathanael Herreshoff, 50
Part I
Maynard Bray
The Vanishing Craft of the Nile 61
Mary C. Dungan
The Backbone, Part I 66
Bud McIntosh
Wood Technology: Dimensional 72
Instability
Richard Jagels
Bending Rangeley Stems at Mystic 74
Seaport
Edward McClave
Spring Fitting Out: Finding A Boatyard 81
in the Northwest
George Kuchenbecker
A Boat Worth Keeping 90
Peter Phillipps
Designs:
26' Dory Cruiser/Tom Beard 102
15' 3" Sailing Peapod/H.I. Chapelle 104

34 MAY/JUNE 1980

Another REALITY 20
Bent Jespersen
The Stevens Family 26
Simon Watts
On the Road to Quality 32
Paul Lipke
The Shipwrights' Co-op: A Look 36
from Outside
Peter H. Spectre
The Shipwrights' Co-op: A Report 38
from Inside
Jon Bielinski
CIRRUS: A Treasure from Herreshoff 42
Alan Bemis
Good Sense and Seamanship 51
Michael Badham
Gatherings 60
Jennifer Buckley
The Backbone, Part II 66
Bud McIntosh
Marine Batteries, Part I 72
Jerry Kirschenbaum
Eddie Crosby's Last Boat 82
John Burke
Other Ways: Small Craft Accessories, 86
Conveniences
Ben Fuller
Wood Technology: Wood—A Source of 91
Food
Richard Jagels
Designs:
34' Canoe Sloop/Paul Kotzebue 102
35' Canoe-Sterned Sloop/Sparkman 104
& Stephens

35 JULY/AUGUST 1980

The New York Thirties 20
David Kiremidjian
At 25, One of the Best Classes Built 25
William H. Taylor
A Salute to the First One-Design 25
Yachts to Reach the Half-Century Mark
William H. Taylor
Recollections Under Sail 27
Roger C. Taylor
The Restoration of Number 14 30
William T. Okie, Jr.
How It All Began 32
Gherardi Davis
Richardson Boat Owners' Association 37
David Eastman
EMME 41
Bruce McMillan
Alternative to the Lumberyard 45
Robert Darr
Putting Down Roots 50
Jane Day
The Backbone, Part III 56
Bud McIntosh
Restoration of the STANLEY NORMAN 62
Christopher Hall
Marine Batteries, Part II 69
Jerry Kirschenbaum
A Core Sound Sharpie 76
Susan Schmidt-Fonseca
Seizing Hanks 80
Malcolm Wehncke
California's Ancient Canoe 82
Peter C. Howorth
Stretching Canoe Canvas 94
George D. Orr, Jr.
Picking Up Through Plastic 95
Ed and Dave Minch
Wood Technology: Preventing Decay 96
Richard Jagels
Designs:
30' Cat Ketch/William Garden 98

36 SEPTEMBER/OCTOBER 1980

BOADICEA 20
Roger Taylor
Marine Insurance 29
Peter H. Spectre
Birchbark Canoes 36
Jeff Dean
How to Build PICCOLO, Part I 44
Bob Baker
How Firm a Foundation? 53
Bud McIntosh
The Old Man's Sharpie 62
Stanley O. Davis
Alaska Packers 66
Joe Upton
Boatbuilder Clark Mills 73
Dale Wilson
Swampscott Dories: Work or Pleasure 78
John Carter, Lance Lee, and
Evers Burtner
Sewing A Patch 86
Malcolm Wehncke
Wood Technology: A Rosewood by 89
Any Other Name
Richard Jagels
Designs:
Oysterman 22/Paul Gartside 92
71' Ketch/Arthur Wycoff 93
Bob Cat/Winthrop Warner 94
Planking the MORGAN 98
Maynard Bray

VOLUME VII: ISSUES 37–42

37 NOVEMBER/DECEMBER 1980

Alaska Limit Seiners 31
Joe Upton
Bill Grunwald: 26 Different Boats 36
Leon Fletcher
Clean Tools 40
Dustin W. Leavitt
The History of Small Yacht Design, 42
Part I
Russell Clark
Winter Reading: An Editor's Choice 50
Peter H. Spectre
How to Build PICCOLO, Part II 57
Bob Baker
How to Build a Double Paddle 67
Peter H. Spectre
LADY JEANNE 73
Jeanne St. Andre Merkel
The Biloxi Schooners 80
Connie Toops
Other Ways: Liberated Caulking 86
Joel White
The Backbone, Part IV 89
Bud McIntosh
Herringboning 95
Malcolm Wehncke
Milling Your Own 98
Bob Darr
Wood Technology: Scientific Names 108
Richard Jagels
Designs:
Dark Harbor 17½/B.B. Crowninshield 116
Dark Harbor 12½/B.B. Crowninshield 117
Camden Class/B.B. Crowninshield 117

38 JANUARY/FEBRUARY 1981

An Ancient Masterpiece 28
Nancy Jenkins
The Issues of Maritime Preservation 36
Peter H. Spectre
Acquisition is Just the Beginning 40
Maynard Bray
The Testimony of the Thing Itself 45
Peter Stanford
The Case for the Restoration of 48
Skillfulness
Lance Lee
The JOLIE BRISE 54
Simon Watts
A Bird for Thin Water 58
Thomas McGuane
The History and Development of the 64
Iceboat, Part I: 1600-1930
Raymond A. Ruge
The Great Ones Gather 71
Photos by Benjamin Mendlowitz
Northwest Trollers and Gillnetters 78
Joe Upton
Kit Boats for the Eighties, Part I 84
John K. Hanson, Jr.
Spritsail Barges 88
Martin Hazell
The Backbone, Part V 95
Bud McIntosh
Other Ways: Shifting Leeboards 98
Ben Fuller
Sewing Reef Nettles 100
Malcolm Wehncke
Wood Technology: Sawmill Objectives 108
Richard Jagels
Designs:
25' Ice Yacht/L.F. Herreshoff 119
33' Lobsterboat Cruiser/Glen-L 120
Marine

39 MARCH/APRIL 1981

The Rangeley Tradition 26
Paul McGuire
The Maine Schooners 32
Peter H. Spectre
The Uncompromised Craftsmanship 44
of L'Estérel
Matthew Walker
Dudley Davidson's Secrets 50
Michael Broom
Patternmaking for Custom Hardware 58
Michael Podmaniczky
Kit Boats for the Eighties, Part II 69
John K. Hanson, Jr.
Lest We Forget 76
L.E. Nicholson
On Making a Beryllium-Copper Knife 84
Richard Golden
The History and Development of the 88
Iceboat, Part II: 1930–1980
Raymond A. Ruge
The Repair and Replacement of Stems 97
Willits Ansel
Hitches 102
Brion Toss and Malcolm Wehncke
Other Ways: Jogglestick 106
Roger C.E. Simpson
Wood Technology: Growth Rate and 115
Wood Properties
Richard Jagels
Designs:
37' Troller/William Garden 128
44' Motorsailer/James Krogen 130
24'4" Sloop/Chuck Paine 132

40 MAY/JUNE 1981

John Gardner, In His Own Words 31
Peter H. Spectre
The Elements of Seamanship, Part I 38
Roger C. Taylor
San Francisco's Two Oldest 46
Rowing Clubs
Jon Bielinski
Basque Racing Sculls 52
Scotty Sapiro
Voga Is Again in Vogue 54
Rob van Mesdag
Looking Good Again 56
Maynard Bray
PASTIME 68
Robert Stowell
Singlehanding an Old Gaffer 72
Frank Mulville
Knock On Wood, Part I 78
James W. Brown
Ray Speck and the Sid Skiff 88
Larry Sturhahn
Sons of Hitches 92
Brion Toss and Malcolm Wehncke
The Last Boom 94
Bill Durham
Other Ways: Leaky Shaft Log 102
Irving Sheldon
Wood Technology: Crook Timber 120
Richard Jagels
Designs:
21' Double-Ended Sloop/John Alden 126
25' Keel/Centerboard Sloop/John 128
Alden

41 JULY/AUGUST 1981

The History of Small Yacht Design, 26
Part II
Russell Clark
The Preservation Forum 36
WoodenBoat Editors
The Elements of Seamanship, Part II 42
Roger C. Taylor
Knock on Wood, Part II 50
James W. Brown
The Handy Billy 58
Brion Toss
A Classic in Plywood, Part I 63
Harold Payson
Runabout Renaissance 72
Philip Thorneycroft Teuscher
ANNIE 78
Art Brendze
GAUNTLET 84
George Cadwalader
Fitting the Deck Framing 91
Bud McIntosh
The Narrowboats of Great Britain 98
Kenneth Abel
Wood Technology: Ignorance or 123
Deception?
Richard Jagels
Designs:
41' Schooner MALABAR II/John Alden 127
30' Malabar Jr./John Alden 128

42 SEPTEMBER/OCTOBER 1981

Other Ways: Mast Protection 27
Dan Conner
Welcome to Hard Times 30
Peter H. Spectre
The Elements of Seamanship, Part III 38
Roger C. Taylor
A Classic in Plywood, Part II 44
Harold Payson
Building the House 53
Bud McIntosh
Knock on Wood, Part III 66
James W. Brown
Zahniser's 74
Dan MacNaughton
Wooden Yachts Earning Their Keep 82
Jennifer Buckley
Keeping Up with LINDØ 92
G. Francis Birra
The International Boatbuilding 96
Training Center
Michael Badham
Learning to Build in Wood 100
Peter Anderheggen
Wood Technology: Under-Utilized 123
Boatbuilding Woods, Part I
Richard Jagels
Designs:
21' Indian Class/John Alden 126
30' Keel/Centerboard Sloop/John 127
Alden
18' O-Boat/John Alden 128

VOLUME VIII: ISSUES 43–48

43 NOVEMBER/DECEMBER 1981

Tom Day and the SEA BIRD Yawl   26
  Thomas Fleming Day
How to Build SEA BIRD   38
  C.D. Mower
Ed Opheim's Dories   40
  Mark White
Plywood Lapstrake Construction   44
  Kenneth C. Mobert
The Elements of Seamanship, Part IV   50
  Roger C. Taylor
Self Apprenticing   56
  Barry C. Nelson
To Fit a Bulkhead   61
  Bud McIntosh
The Remarkable Sloop SHADOW   64
  Jon Wilson
A Ship's Boat for the CONRAD   72
  Willits Ansel
Boatbuilding in Morocco   76
  Ingrid Holm
Newport's Wooden Boat Show   84
  Peter H. Spectre
The Classic Yacht Regatta   92
  L.E. Nicholson
The Herreshoff Rendezvous   94
  Peggy C. Nicholson
A Classic in Plywood, Part III   96
  Harold Payson
Northwest Crannies   104
  Brion Toss
Wood Technology: Under-Utilized   120
  Boatbuilding Woods, Part II
  Richard Jagels
Designs:
  21′3″ Utility Launch/Nelson Zimmer   124
  24′ Tug and Utility Boat/S. Sprague   126
  49′ Cruising Sloop/Paul Kotzebue   128

44 JANUARY/FEBRUARY 1982

The Remarkable Sloop SHADOW,   24
  Part II
  Jon Wilson
Across the Atlantic in SEA BIRD   32
  Thomas Fleming Day
Floor Timbers   43
  Bud McIntosh
A Boatbuilder's Garden, Part I   50
  George Putz
The Politics of Maritime Preservation   62
  Peter H. Spectre
Unity in Maritime Preservation   70
  David A. Hull
Sailing the PRIDE   72
  Armin E. Elsaesser III
Donald C. Rosencrantz and William   78
  Avery Baker—Remembered
  Jon Persson and Maynard Bray
Grand Craft   80
  Robin McAlear
Steaming an Oak Coaming   86
  WoodenBoat Editors
Cutting an Apple Knee   88
  WoodenBoat Editors
Tale of Two Sisters   90
  W. Tay Vaughan III
Backyard Vacuum Bagging   99
  John Marples
Fire Bending   104
  David Moodie
Out of the Ashes: A Prospecting Tale   108
  Waldo Howland
Wood Technology: Wood Adhesives   133
  Richard Jagels

45 MARCH/APRIL 1982

Other Ways: Let There Be Bandsaws   33
  Bob Hollingsworth
A Boatbuilder's Garden, Part II   36
  George Putz
The People's Timber   46
  Jon Bielinski
Vic Carpenter, A Superior Craftsman,   50
  Part I
  David Lees
Pungy Boats of the Chesapeake   56
  Eric J. Steinlein
The Elements of Seamanship, Part V   62
  Roger C. Taylor
The Bar Harbor 31s   68
  Maynard Bray
ACE Speedboat   77
  Peter H. Spectre
The Lobsterboats of Grand Manan   82
  Bill Mayher
Understanding a Novi Boat   88
  Maynard Bray
Building Martha's Tender, Part I   92
  WoodenBoat Editors
EDITH JANE   100
  Rodger C. Swanson
A Whitehall Backbone   108
  Maynard Bray
Designs:
  10′6″ Rowing and Sailing Tender/   110
    Robert P. Beebe
Wood Technology: Tacks to Trunnels   115
  Richard Jagels

46 MAY/JUNE 1982

A Farewell to Bror Tamm   30
  Llewellyn Howland III
An Evolution from Sail to Power   42
  Simon Watts
Why Aren't Heads Called Tails?   49
  Bob Leve
A Shortcut to Casting   52
  Stephen Olsen
Knocking on Boat Heaven's Door   54
  Peter H. Spectre
The Finishing Touch   66
  Jennifer Buckley
The Mighty Maritime Oak   76
  Connie Toops
Live Oaking Today   80
  Maynard Bray
Vic Carpenter, Part II   82
  Jon Wilson
No Passage to Zanzibar   88
  Douglas Knapp
Building Martha's Tender, Part II   94
  WoodenBoat Editors
To Lay a Deck   103
  Bud McIntosh
Designs:
  42′ Trawler Yacht/Glen-L Marine   113
  36′ Schooner/William Garden   114
Wood Technology: Woods of Australia   131
  and New Zealand, Part I
  Richard Jagels

47 JULY/AUGUST 1982

The BOWDOIN Project   30
  Peter H. Spectre
Common Sense and the Energy 48   40
  Madeline Lee
Whose Right? Boat Plans and the   46
  Public Domain
  John Gardner
Rowing the Maine Coast   52
  Henry W. Taft
Building Martha's Tender, Part III   58
  WoodenBoat Editors
Ceilings   69
  Bud McIntosh
On Deck   74
  Matthew Walker
Coming of Age   80
  Mike Baird
The Vineyard Haven 15   87
  Brian Dowley
Keeping a Cutting Edge: Handsaws   91
  Harold Payson
The Barnegat Bay Sneakbox   102
  Eric L. Stark
Getting the Old Girl Back In Shape   109
  Ulf Henrikson
Wood Technology: Woods of Australia   123
  and New Zealand, Part II
  Richard Jagels
Designs:
  15′8″ Dory Skiff/King & Davis   126
  11′8″ Sailing Skiff/King & Davis   127
  9′7″ Dinghy/King & Davis   127
  20′ Daysailer/Overnighter/George   128
    Stadel, Jr.

48 SEPTEMBER/OCTOBER 1982

The Unretired Frank Prothero   30
  Peter H. Spectre
Lindsay Lord's POT O'GOLD   38
  Michael Badham
Keeping A Cutting Edge: Power Saws   44
  Harold Payson
MOCKINGULL: A Wing in the Water,   50
  a Wing in the Wind
  Douglas Martin
The History of Small Yacht Design: 58
  The 40-Footers
  Jon Wilson
The Boatbuilders of Alexandria Bay: 66
  Skiff-Putts and Gold Cups
  D.W. Fostle
Building a Cheap Boat Shelter   74
  George Cadwalader
Delaware Duckers:
  A Brief History   78
  Ben Fuller
  The Ducker in Use   83
  Ben Fuller
  Why the Ducker Today?   86
  Lance Lee
Ways and Means at Riverside Boat Yard   91
  Maynard Bray
Spike Knots   100
  Brion Toss
Whose Right?   105
  WoodenBoat Editors
Wood Technology: Isocyanate Resins   123
  Richard Jagels
Designs:
  28′ Sloop/W.B. Harris, Concordia Co.   126
  31′ Sloop/W.B. Harris, Concordia Co.   127
  33′ Sloop/W.B. Harris, Concordia Co.   130

VOLUME IX: ISSUES 49–54

49 NOVEMBER/DECEMBER 1982

Building a Norwegian Pram	28
Arne Emil Christensen	
Building by Eye in America	36
Jane Day	
Poling a Canoe	40
Lynn Franklin	
The Masterful Work of Malcolm Brewer	44
Jane Day	
Always a Gentleman	51
William E. Peterson	
Always Right	53
William M. Peterson	
The Boatbuilders of Alexandria Bay, Part II	58
D.W. Fostle	
The History of Small Yacht Design: The Forty-Footers, Part II	66
Jon Wilson	
A SAGA	74
Virginia Biddle	
The Chincoteague Scow	81
Spencer Rowe	
A Real Charley Noble	86
Ed Frost	
Quick and...er...Dirty Boatbuilding	89
Peter H. Spectre	
Renewing TARNE's Keel, Part I	97
Maynard Bray	
A Look Inside China	108
J. Baldwin	
Designs:	
26′ Folding Multihull/J.R. Marples	112
36′8″ Cutter/Henry Scheel	114
Wood Technology: Mahoganies and Their Substitutes	124
Richard Jagels	

50 JANUARY/FEBRUARY 1983

Nunes Brothers' Boat and Ways Co.	31
Ann Lyn Sutter	
Bears on the Bay	34
Bill Jelliffe	
Chainsaw Lumbermaking: Natural Knees	38
Will Malloff	
The Shipsmith's Art	46
Alan Scott	
A New ERA	52
Peter H. Spectre	
Renewing TARNE's Keel, Part II	59
Maynard Bray	
Inside the Wood Block	67
Phil and Gerry Troy	
Ireland's Jack Tyrell	70
Paul Dunphy	
Irish Hookers	74
Bill Crampton	
The Galway Bay Púcan	78
Risteard MacAodha	
Ancient Curraghs	80
Jan Zimmermann	
Improving the Classic Dinghy	88
Donald M. Street, Jr.	
Hardtack's Running Moor	96
Lincoln Colcord	
Lashmanship	101
Brion Toss	
Boatbuilding in Grenada	106
Mark Baldwin	
Wood Technology: Huon Pine	116
Richard Jagels	
Designs:	
21′ Catboat/Paul Kotzebue	130
26′ Sea Bird Yawl/C.G. MacGregor	132

51 MARCH/APRIL 1983

Conversations with Bud McIntosh	40
Peter H. Spectre	
The Swampscott Dory—Hodgdon Style	50
Diana Eames Esterly	
RONDO's Recovery	59
Robert Vespa	
The Modified McInnis Bateau	66
John Gardner	
Bronze: The Non-Timber	72
Lin and Larry Pardy	
SKIDOO	80
Taylor M. Chambers	
Swift and Sensitive	83
Taylor M. Chambers	
Designer's Comments	85
Chuck Burns	
Building the Wayfarer Kit	88
David Brooks	
Projection Lofting	94
Paul Haist	
Building the Beetle Cats, Part I	99
Peter Vermilya	
Custom Sawmilling	106
Doug Andersen	
Wood Technology: A Mangled Tale	121
Richard Jagels	
Designs:	
18′ Lapstrake Boat/Rob Pittaway	131
45′ Cutter/Nelson Zimmer	133

52 MAY/JUNE 1983

Walter McInnis, Part I: The Lawley Years	40
Llewellyn Howland III	
ALVIN CLARK: An Unfinished Voyage	52
C.T. McCutcheon, Jr.	
The Challenge of the Challenge	59
Peter H. Spectre	
The ALVIN CLARK Revisited	66
Sam Manning	
Lofting by Numbers	69
Ralph Morris	
The Ancient and Versatile Vlet	75
Bob Chandler	
The McKenzie River Drift Boat	80
John Babbs	
Motonautica	86
Carol Wagner-Martin	
A Cold-Molded Rejuvenation	92
Rick Kotalac	
The Australian Cadet Dinghy	100
Graeme Griggs	
Building the Beetle Cats, Part II	107
Peter Vermilya	
The End of Your Rope	112
Brion Toss	
Wood Technology: Decay Resistant Joints	118
Richard Jagels	
Designs:	
20′ Sliding-Seat Rowing Wherry/Joel White	122

53 JULY/AUGUST 1983

Walter McInnis, Part II: The Emergence of Eldredge-McInnis	38
Llewellyn Howland III	
The Weather Side of Gaff Rig	48
William S. Payne	
A New Coaster: The Schooner HERITAGE	52
Peter H. Spectre	
The Theft of RANDOM SCOOT	66
David Kendall	
Building the First Lightning	68
Susan Kenney	
The Folding Kayak	75
Larry Rice	
Folding Boats at Sea	80
John and Beatrice Dowd	
LILY—A Boat Lover's Dream	86
Bet Oliver	
ISKRA Sails Down East	90
Frank Mulville	
Seven Bends	96
Brion Toss	
Building the Beetle Cats, Part III	101
Peter T. Vermilya	
Damaged Planks—Their Repair and Replacement	109
Maynard Bray	
Wood Technology: Defects or Gems— A Knotty Problem	119
Richard Jagels	

54 SEPTEMBER/OCTOBER 1983

Walter McInnis, Part III: The Years of Achievement	34
Llewellyn Howland III	
A Close Look at Wood Screws, Part I	45
Ed McClave	
Chris White and His Multihulls	56
Dan Levin	
The Schooner AMERICA	67
Eric Dow	
Three Friends	74
Peter H. Spectre	
Just the Right Medium	80
Peter H. Spectre	
Keeping a Wooden Hull from Drying Out	88
Maynard Bray	
Canvas and Other Winter Cover Stories	92
Jennifer Buckley	
Auxiliary Power: Views from Experience	
A Preference for Gas	101
Fritz Seyfarth	
Living with a Diesel	106
George Cadwalader	
WoodenBoat Talks with Jimmy Archer, an Expert	108
WoodenBoat Editors	
STAR: A Designer's Own Boat	114
Frederick S. Ford, Jr.	
Wood Technology: How Reliable Are Wood Durability Ratings?	120
Richard Jagels	
Designs:	
26′ "Best Boat"/Uffa Fox	130
24′9″ LAZY JACK: A Keel Sharpie/Ed Frost	131

VOLUME X: ISSUES 55–60

55 NOVEMBER/DECEMBER 1983

L. Francis Herreshoff, Part I   32
Philip C. Bolger
A Close Look at Wood Screws, Part II   43
Ed McClave
The Rebirth of WANDER BIRD   56
Annie Sutter
The Greatest Little Motorboat Afloat   68
Paul Dodington, Joe Fossey, Paul
Gockel III, James Smith, and
Peter H. Spectre
Paddling Like an Ancient   79
Lynn Franklin
The Willits Brothers Canoes   82
Holly Hughes
The Education of a Young Boatbuilder   88
Lynn Darroch
Cold-Molded Repairs for Laminated   96
Boats
Jim Watson
Laminating at Luders   100
Bill Luders
A Luders-16 Rejuvenation   102
Steve White
A Smooth and Fair Hull   107
Bud McIntosh
Grommeting   114
Brion Toss
Wood Technology: Distinguishing   120
Mahogany from the Substitutes
Richard Jagels
Designs:
16′ V-Bottom Cat/R.D. Culler   122
45′ She Pungy/R.D. Culler   123

56 JANUARY/FEBRUARY 1984

L. Francis Herreshoff, Part II   38
Philip C. Bolger
The Huckins Yacht Corporation, Part I   48
Pembroke Huckins and Nick Stowe
A Plywood Lapstrake Classic   60
Maynard Bray
WARRIOR's Figurehead   68
Peter H. Spectre
What More Could the Commodore Ask?   76
Bill Schwicker
CHRISTINE   86
Victor Grandidier
Restoration of 12½-Footers, Part I   93
Maynard Bray
"The Race it Blew" and Others   102
Joseph E. Garland
Stopwaters   116
Ed McClave
In My View: Wooden Boat Immigrants   122
Bill Durham
Wood Technology: Plywood, an   125
Engineered Wood Product
Richard Jagels
Designs:
26′ Canoe-Sterned Sloop/Charles   130
Wittholz

57 MARCH/APRIL 1984

In My View: Avoiding Product   39
Liability Suits
Kevin Hart
The Bermuda Fitted Dinghy   42
Kevin M. Stevenson
Dick Pulsifer and the Strip-Planked   50
Hampton
Jan Zimmermann
Strip Planking: Where Did It Come   55
From?
Michael Badham
The Tale of a Strip-Planked Kayak   60
Curtis Rindlaub
Just an Overnighter   66
Nick Skeates
A Matter of Family Tradition   72
Peter H. Spectre
WHITEFIN   80
James W. Brown
Restoration of 12½-Footers, Part II   93
Maynard Bray
The Huckins Yacht Corporation,   102
Part II
A.T. Lyman
Making Your Boat Tight Again   112
Maynard Bray
Designs:
18¼′ Sail Skiff/R.D. Culler   118
14′ Flattie Skiff/S.S. Rabl   119
15½′ Pulling Boat/Joseph Dobler   120
Wood Technology: Plywood—   122
Applications to Boatbuilding
Richard Jagels

58 MAY/JUNE 1984

In My View: An Interview with Larry   34
Dahlmer
Myfanwy Phillips
ELLY: A Swedish Treasure in America   40
William Gilkerson
A New Kåg   48
Lars Johansson
Sardine Carriers, Part I   52
Michael Crowley
AMARETTO   60
Joe Upton
The Kodiak Kayak   68
Derrell Short
The Hooper Bay Kayak   74
David W. Zimmerly
Sailing a Tancook Whaler   82
Roger C. Taylor
The Modern Wooden Navy   90
Maynard Bray
The Wizard of Speed   100
Peter H. Spectre
Bending SPARTAN's Frames   107
Ed McClave
Designs:
21′ Sloop/Nelson Zimmer   114
25′ Cat Yawl/Philip C. Bolger   116
Wood Technology: Summer-Built   120
Vessels of New England
Richard Jagels

59 JULY/AUGUST 1984

In My View: Sharpie Points and   36
Counterpoints
J. Rodger Martin and Bill
Schwicker
The Return of an Olympic 8-Meter   40
Timothy F. O'Neill
SHEARWATER   48
Anne Lawrence
The Outlook for World Timber   56
George Putz
Guideboats: From the Ground Up   64
Barbara M. Hale
Sardine Carriers, Part II   70
Michael Crowley
The Koa Canoe   80
Mark Osmun
Holding Fast: Sonny Hodgdon on   88
Glues
Jennifer Buckley
The Case for Simple Edge-Gluing   93
Michael Podmaniczky
The Once and Future FOXY   96
R.W.V. Board
The Right Jaws for Your Gaff and   100
Boom
William Garden
The Art of Finding Your Way   102
Douglas McClennen
The Comforts of Service   106
Brion Toss
Wood Technology: Health Hazards of   111
Wood Additives
Richard Jagels
Designs:
Ensenada 25/Ken Hankinson   114
20′ Cutter/John Atkin   116
21′ Itchen Ferry Punt/Uffa Fox   117

60 SEPTEMBER/OCTOBER 1984

In My View: To Err is Human,   41
To Admit Divine
Fritz Seyfarth
Ten Years After   44
Peter H. Spectre
The Singular Beauty of Wooden Boats   52
Llewellyn Howland III
Buying a Wooden Boat   62
George Putz
TELKKÄ   68
Basil Greenhill
Save It! Part I   76
Jim P. Brown
BABY BOOTLEGGER   84
Mason Smith
Toad's Landing   96
William Garden
Building the Nutshell Pram   100
Maynard Bray
The Anatomy of a Wooden Boat   115
Samuel F. Manning
Shovels and Pails   120
Ross Norgrove
Spars   125
Bud McIntosh
Designs:
32′ Cutter/William Garden   134
27′ Sloop/Murray Peterson   135
16′ Double-Paddle Canoe/L. Francis   140
Herreshoff
Wood Technology: Can the Pace be   145
Sustained?
Richard Jagels

VOLUME XI: ISSUES 61–66

61 NOVEMBER/DECEMBER 1984

The Storys of Essex 32
Elizabeth Story
Brad Story: The New Generation 38
Philip C. Bolger
The Light-Displacement Controversy 42
Dan MacNaughton
Substance to the Legend, Mystery 52
to the Man
Joseph E. Garland
Building the KINGFISHER, Part I 60
Graeme King
A RIVERKEEPER for the Hudson 72
Andre Mele
The Time Warp of a Topsail Cutter 80
W.M. Nixon
Give 'Em Hell, Harry 88
Peter Spectre
CHEROKEE: The Several Lives of 100
a Launch
Annie Sutter
Cold-Molded Overlay: A Close Look 104
at One Technique
Maynard Bray
Wood Technology: Questions and 123
Answers on Preservatives
Richard Jagels
Designs:
The Versatile Sneakbox 124
Steve Redmond
60′ 6″ Sportfisherman PORPOISE/ 127
Geerd Hendel

62 JANUARY/FEBRUARY 1985

Henry Scheel 36
Jim P. Brown
The Caddo Lake Bateau 44
James H. Conrad and Thad Sitton
Traditional Teak Grates 53
Maynard Bray
Barnagat Bay's A-Cat 60
George Petty
The Scottish Fishing Fleet 68
Jeremy Cresswell
Concourse d'Élégance…and Hang 74
the Expense!
Peter Spectre
Not Just Boats, But Craftsmen, Too 82
Kitty Reithel
The Weather's Every Caprice 88
S.G.W. Benjamin
Designs:
20′ 10″ Catboat FRANCES/Wilton 96
Crosby
19′ 9″ Pocket Cruiser/S.S. Crocker 100
Building the KINGFISHER, Part II 103
Graeme King
The Bandmill 110
Christian Becksvoort
Wood Technology: Questions and 113
Answers on Epoxy
Richard Jagels

63 MARCH/APRIL 1985

Arno Day: From Master Builder to 38
Master Teacher
Mason Smith
New Life at Ninety 48
Gary Weisenburger
Hot Ideas for Cold-Molded Boats 56
Taylor Chambers
Building the KINGFISHER, Part III 63
Graeme King
The Hackmatack Schooner JANET 74
MAY
Mary R. Maynard
The Hands of August Crabtree 80
Peter H. Spectre
Quick Steps to Spring Painting, Part I 87
Anne and Maynard Bray
Manhattan's Mystery Merchant Ship: 96
Her Discovery Today
Nicholas Dean
Her Probable Past
Ralph L. Snow
The Careful Creation of MELE KAI, 106
Part I
James L. Meriam
Designs:
An Antique-Shop Sandbagger 112
Steve Redmond
A Modern Quay Punt/Lyle Hess 116
Wood Technology: On PEG 113
Richard Jagels

64 MAY/JUNE 1985

DYON 40
George Carey
Albert Strange and the CanoeYawl 49
SHEILA
Michael Burn
Quick Steps to Spring Painting, Part II 58
Anne and Maynard Bray
Building the Belles of the Western 64
Rivers
Jack Custer
TROUT UNLIMITED: The Compleat 70
Fly-Fisherman
Peter Lentini
PILGRIM's Progress 76
Pete Johnson
Bagging the GULL, Part I 83
James W. Brown, John Marples, and
Dick Newick
The Careful Creation of MELE KAI, 92
Part II
James L. Meriam
Designs:
Cutters/William Garden 98
An Antique-Shop Sandbagger, Part II 102
Steve Redmond
Wood Technology: The Yeoman Oak, 108
Part I
Richard Jagels

65 JULY/AUGUST 1985

JENNY NORMAN Comes Alive 32
Lila Line
Pert Lowell and the Art of the Mast 40
Hoop
Curtis Rindlaub
VARUA: Soul of the Southern Sea 44
Timothy Mickleburgh
A Matter of Detail 52
Maynard Bray
A Story of Priorities 56
Reuel Parker
My Brother Everett 66
Mason Smith
Up to the Mark 76
Meg Davis
A Conversation with Dick Clarke 90
Peter H. Spectre
Bagging the GULL, Part II 97
James W. Brown, John Marples,
and Dick Newick
Designs:
36′ Shoal-Draft Sloop/Joseph H. 104
Hack
13′ 8″ Duckboat MERGANSER/Daniel 108
Marcus
Wood Technology: The Yeoman Oak, 112
Part II
Richard Jagels

66 SEPTEMBER/OCTOBER 1985

Three Men in a Boat 23
R. Mark Neyman
The Beauty of Construction Models 29
Jay Hanna
"Do You Have A Moment?' He Asked 35
Peter H. Spectre
Forest Belle 38
Philip C. Bolger
The Butt Block in Its Place 45
Michael Podmaniczky
Simplicity, Skiffs, and Sharpies 48
Jennifer Buckley and A.W. Baker
Craftsmanship in Sarasota 56
Ricki Lindsay
Renewing the Deck 64
J. Steven White
Dragonquest: In Search of the 76
Chinese Junk
Randy Thomas
From the Brink of Extinction: 84
Mediterranean Molding
John Sarsfield
Matter of Detail 90
Maynard Bray
Perfectly Seasoned: Air-Drying 92
Your Lumber, Part I
Doug Andersen
Wood Technology: On Pines 109
Richard Jagels
Designs:
30′ 9″ Gentleman's Launch/William 120
Garden
25′ Daysailer SHEARWATER/Henry A. 124
Scheel

VOLUME XII: ISSUES 67–72

67 NOVEMBER/DECEMBER 1985

The Boat As a Way of Life 19
Jane DeRidder
Butt...The Butt-Block Chronicle 23
Continues
Ed McClave
Resheathing a Copper Bottom 35
Frank Mulville
A Mentor Would Appear: Mick Fahey 38
and the North Woods Way
Jerry Stelmok
The North Woods Paddle 44
Rick Waters
Every Inch a Riverman 54
Jane Day
A Three-Fathom Sharpie 60
Bill Schwicker
Steam Power, Fantail Stern 70
Albert W. Giles
Perfectly Seasoned: Air-Drying 76
Your Lumber, Part II
Doug Andersen
In a New Light: The Creation of 82
LA FILLE D'OR
James Luxton
Hatches and Other Deck Joinery 91
Bud McIntosh
A Matter of Detail: The Concordia 100
Yawl
Maynard Bray
Wood Technology: On Teak 109
Richard Jagels
Designs:
  Cyrus Hamlin's Wanderer 112
  Joel White
  A Chesapeake Skiff and a British 117
  Dinghy
  Steve Redmond

68 JANUARY/FEBRUARY 1986

A Viking Ship to Sail the World 19
Arne Emil Christensen
The Boats of Autumn 25
Peter H. Spectre
Bequia Beauty 29
Fritz Seyfarth
The Professional Difference 35
Clay Furtaw
A Decade of Legendary 12s 40
Michael Adams
Pieces of Eight 56
Bill Schwicker
Dubbin' the Latigo 64
Larry Montgomery
A Matter of Detail 70
Maynard Bray
AIRFORCE 72
Tod Cheney
A Proper Lady 80
Virginia Biddle
Bent Frames: Why They Break, 87
and How to Fix Them
Ed McClave
Wood Technology: Woods of the West 103
Richard Jagels
Designs:
  Eye-Pleasing Pungy: Bruce Northrup's 110
  RUBEN DE CLOUX
  Joel White
  Hooked on Schooners 114
  William Garden

69 MARCH/APRIL 1986

Engine Systems Checkup 22
Larry Montgomery
A Shark with Teeth 29
John Rogers
Importing Tropical Wood 35
Lynn Darroch
From Sail to Power: The Evolution 42
of the Noank Lobsterboat
Paul Stubing, Maynard Bray, and
Meg Maiden
Jack Wilbur and the Return of the 48
Noank Boats
Mary Maynard Drake
Sons of the Fleet 54
Morry Edwards
With Adze and Steam 64
James Tirrul-Jones
A Simple Wooden Plane 70
Bud McIntosh
Trimaran Jim 76
Peter H. Spectre
Trailers and Cradles, Planks and 86
Rollers
Maynard Bray
Two Weeks on the Ways 94
Peter Phillipps
A Matter of Detail 104
Maynard Bray
Designs:
  Chesapeake Crabbing Skiffs 100
  Steve Redmond
  Wood Technology: Water-Curing 119
  of Timber
  Richard Jagels

70 MAY/JUNE 1986

Meetings with Mature Ladies 17
W.M. Nixon
A Cautionary Tale Continued 23
George Cadwalader
Buying Used Tools 31
Harold ("Dynamite") Payson
In My View: Native vs. Imported 38
Lumber
Doug Andersen
California Schoonerman 42
Maynard Bray
Legs for Boats 52
Paul Lipke
Building the DK 13 Kayak 56
Dennis Davis
Open-Boat Cruising 68
Billy Ray Sims
In Search of the British Wooden 74
Boat Revival
Peter H. Spectre
A Matter of Detail 82
Maynard Bray
Carroll Lowell Comes in from the Cold 84
David R. Getchell, Sr.
Living Aloft 92
Brion Toss
Wood Technology: A Call for Accurate 101
Names
Richard Jagels
Designs:
  Open-Boat Cruisers Compared 104
  Steve Redmond
  39' 2" Ultralight Double-Ender/Scott 110
  Sprague and Nathan Smith

71 JULY/AUGUST 1986

The Proper Boathook 25
Jon Wilson
The Long Oars of Pete Culler 28
Rick Cahoon
Lapstrake Plank Repair 38
Michael Crowley
Less Is More! 44
Lance Lee
The Burgess Legacy: The Early 52
Years, Part I
Llewellyn Howland III
Sailing a Bristol Channel Pilot Cutter 60
Tom Cunliffe
An Open and Shut Case for Seacocks 69
Larry Montgomery
Shpountz: A French Designer's Vision 74
Nick Nicholson
Speedboats from the Golden Era 82
Peter H. Spectre
A Matter of Detail 92
Maynard Bray
As She Was Meant to Be 94
Robert Jones
Designs:
  Open-Boat Cruisers, Part II 105
  Steve Redmond
  MYRA, a Punt 105
  Steve Redmond
  Wood Technology: A Common 111
  Ancestry
  Richard Jagels

72 SEPTEMBER/OCTOBER 1986

The Japanese Edge 21
Harold ("Dynamite")Payson
Fitting Out in the Fall 25
Jennifer Buckley
Inside the Insurance Business 28
A.T. Lyman
The Search for Insurance 35
Matthew Spaulding
Binds that Tie 40
Brion Toss
The Burgess Legacy: Part II 44
Llewellyn Howland III
Teak on Teak 53
Allan Vaitses
Between a Rock and a Hard Place 60
Peter H. Spectre
All for a Horse 70
Wayland Combewright
The Fishing Boats of Portugal 80
Nathanael and Maynard Bray
Against the Flow 84
Jim Boone
Out of the Delta 90
Morry Edwards
Designs:
  Two Multi-Purpose Skiffs/Steve 98
  Redmond
  Wood Technology: Questions and 105
  Answers on Black Walnut and
  Plywood Grading
  Richard Jagels

VOLUME XIII: ISSUES 73–78

73 NOVEMBER/DECEMBER 1986

Oarlocks on Your Own 21
Jack McKee
The Burgess Legacy, Part III 32
Llewellyn Howland III
The New York 32s 42
Maynard Bray
Modelmaker Lloyd McCaffery 52
Mary Maynard Drake
The Itinerant Teacher of Boatbuilding 60
Strikes Again
Peter H. Spectre
Building the Downeaster 18, Part I 67
Graham Ero
Variations on the Lugsail 80
Iain Oughtred
Good Guys in Outlaw Boats 86
Tim Cahill
Preserving Norway's Sailing Freighters 96
Michael Crowley
Designs:
24' Catamaran STRIDER/Richard and 106
Lilian Woods
Wood Technology: Saving a Pilot 108
Cutter and Defining Silverballi
Richard Jagels

74 JANUARY/FEBRUARY 1987

Ways that Work: That's Right, Roofing 17
Tar
Ed McClave
Coppering GAZELA 19
Steve Masone
In My View: The Dream Business 25
Kenneth C. Mobert
The Indian's Apprentice 27
Lincoln Stoller
Financing Your Boat 35
Steve Henkel
The Burgess Legacy, Part IV 42
Llewellyn Howland III
A Week Along the Thames 54
Peter H. Spectre
Jack Holt: A Brilliant Career in 64
Dinghies
Timothy Mickleburgh
NORDSØ 74
Christian W. Dahl
A Matter of Detail 80
Maynard Bray
Building the Downeaster 18, Part II 87
Graham Ero
Designs:
26' 3" Norwalk Island Sharpie/Bruce 96
Kirby
22' 6" Beach-Cruiser Sharpie/Daniel 96
Bombigher
The Gunter Rig 100
Iain Oughtred

75 MARCH/APRIL 1987

In the Wake of a High: The Creation 22
and Demise of AIRFORCE
Tod Cheney
A Schedule for Maintaining Your 30
Wooden Boat
Maynard Bray
Winthrop Warner 34
Kathleen Grobe
Three of What? The Reconstruction of 44
an Ancient Athenian Trireme
Peter H. Spectre
Building the Downeaster18, Part III 53
Graham Ero
Pocket Cruisers from the Past:
West Coast: LA MOUETTE 62
Ray Speck
Lapstrake Planking, English Style 68
Ray Speck
Sailing LA MOUETTE 69
Jack Weingand
East Coast: PETREL 70
Jay Oker
A Ghost That Only We Could See 72
Philip C. Bolger
Sailing PETREL 73
Roger C. Taylor
A Matter of Detail 76
Maynard Bray
The Gaff Rig 80
Iain Oughtred
Ways That Work: Recanvasing Decks 89
Ed McClave
Wood Technology: Going to the Source 99
Richard Jagels
Designs:
Looking at Boat Plans 111
Joel White

76 MAY/JUNE 1987

Ways that Work: Shellac— the 18
Neglected Helper
Ed McClave
Hot-Weather Varnishing 22
Ian Bruce
The Scavenger's Art 29
Tom Duggleby
Off to Far Places 36
Mary Maynard Drake
On the Hunt 44
Pete Smyth and Maynard Bray
Dream-Boat Man 60
Morry Edwards
A Matter of Detail 70
Maynard Bray
The Geodesic Airolites 72
Jane Day
Snowshoe for Two 77
Richard P. Talbot
Sprit Rigs 80
Iain Oughtred
A Locker for the Main Cabin 89
Aldren Watson
Designs:
22' 7" Powerboat Bartender/George 101
Calkins
Wood Technology: Adapting New 115
Strategies for Pine
Richard Jagels

77 JULY/AUGUST 1987

The National Watercraft Collection, 21
Whither Away?
Peter H. Spectre
Port Townsend's Bob Lange 34
Stephen L. Davis
The Bermudian Rig 44
Iain Oughtred
The Janggolans of Madura 52
Bryan Kaiser
Deck Care 60
Maynard Bray
A Living from Small Boats? 70
David R. Getchell, Sr.
Buying a Runabout 79
Don Benjamin
A Locker for the Main Cabin, Part II 87
Aldren Watson
Designs:
28' Lobsterboat/Philip C. Bolger
Wood Technology: Wood Preser- 116
vation Update
Richard Jagels

78 SEPTEMBER/OCTOBER 1987

Linear Polyurethanes 21
Doug Templin
A Lineage of Craftsmanship 30
Winston Groom
Centerboards and Trunks 41
Bud McIntosh
Spidsgatters 50
Robert Moss
Wood-and-Canvas Canoe Restoration, 56
Part I
Rollin Thurlow
Exotic Rigs 66
Iain Oughtred
Melbourne Smith and the Art of 76
the Possible
Peter H. Spectre
A Matter of Detail: Fitting a Dutchman 84
Maynard Bray
Ways that Work: Proper Poppets 93
Ed McClave
Wood Technology: Tropical Forest 100
Exploitation
Richard Jagels
Designs:
A Contemporary Cutter Designed by 106
Charles Wittholz
Joel White

VOLUME XIV: ISSUES 79–84

79 NOVEMBER/DECEMBER 1987

The Basket Boat of Halifax Harbour 17
  Joleen Gordon
Lucy's Launch 22
  Jane Day
The Shipwright's Toolbox 29
  Larry Montgomery
Boatyard Hazards 34
  Peter H. Spectre
The Fisherman's Sea Tractor 48
  Morry Edwards
A Look at JUNO After 12 Years 64
  George Buehler
Wood-and-Canvas Canoe Restoration, 72
  Part II
  Rollin Thurlow and Jerry Stelmok
A Byte at Tradition 84
  Richard Webster
Wood Technology: Rapid Lumber 103
Drying for the Boatshop
  Richard Jagels
Designs:
  CALICO JACK—A Chesapeake Bay 106
  Skipjack
  Mike O'Brien

80 JANUARY/FEBRUARY 1988

A Different Kind of Restoration 14
  Wallace Whitford
Driving for Speed 24
  Ted Hugger
Float Like a Butterfly, Sting 32
Like a Bee
  Peter H. Spectre
Two Contemporary Centerboard 44
Schooners
  Reuel B. Parker
Sano Magic 50
  Ken Szymkowiak
The Sano Shop 54
  Jon Wilson
Replacing Planks 56
  Allen Taube
Bungs 63
  Maynard and Kathy Bray
The Concordia Yawls 64
  Maynard Bray
JAVA, Father, and Capt. Hardy 72
  Waldo Howland
Sassafras 82
  D.W. Blake
Designs:
  WENDA and MARTHA JANE: 102
  Shoal-Draft Yawls
  Mike O'Brien
Wood Technology: Airborne Pollution 108
and Forest Decline
  Richard Jagels

81 MARCH/APRIL 1988

Rags to Riches 21
  Annie Sutter
A Niche in the Insurance Market 29
  Steve Henkel
Alfred Bain and UNITY B 34
  Maynard Bray
The 1 x 19 Splice Made Possible 45
  Brion Toss
DIABLESSE and Her Disputed Rig 52
  Martin Rudy Haase
Building the Cabin Sole, Part I 65
  Aldren Watson
Spring Fitting Out:
  Tips from the Professionals 75
  Rolling and Tipping 78
  Dan MacNaughton
  Screws, Tubes & Doohickeys 82
  George Cadwalader
The Art of Brightwork, Part I 88
  Rebecca Wittman
Designs:
  OCEANUS, Old and New: Canoe- 106
  Sterned Sloops
  Joel White
  Wood Technology: Growing Trees 117
  for Tomorrow's Boats
  Richard Jagels

82 MAY/JUNE 1988

A Well-Used Boat 19
  Jack Tuberville
Heavy Metal 27
  Larry Montgomery
Championships for Struer 44
  Fletcher Anderson
Double-Sawn Framing 48
  Andy Davis
The Lyman Legend 60
  Peter H. Spectre
Lyman: A Sleeping Assembly Line 68
  Gary Weisenburger
Stalking the Western Yew 72
  Michael Henry Wright
Building the Cabin Sole, Part II 75
  Aldren Watson
The Art of Brightwork, Part II 88
  Rebecca Wittman
Designs:
  Outboard Cruisers by Farmer and 108
  Chapelle
  Mike O'Brien
Wood Technology: Stabilizing and 117
Preserving Wood
  Richard Jagels

83 JULY/AUGUST 1988

The Self-Survey 22
  Paul Lipke
Aboard "Old Ironsides" 32
  Commander Tyrone G. Martin
Nick Potter 38
  Thomas G. Skahill
Surviving the Tropics 48
  Allen Taube
Russell Brown and His Proven Proas 58
  Mike O'Brien
The Art of Brightwork, Part III 66
  Rebecca Wittman
Wreck at Cape Ann: The Last Cruise of the
  Schooner TYEHEE 74
  John H. Gilchrist
The Wertenbaker Proposition 86
  Jon Wilson
  What Went Wrong 88
  R. Dana Gibson
  Parting Thoughts 90
  William Wertenbaker
Wood Technology: A Trade Deficit in 107
Pines
  Richard Jagels
Designs:
  SASKIANNA, A Contemporary Cutter 112
  with Traditional Flavor
  Joel White

84 SEPTEMBER/OCTOBER 1988

NIMBLE 21
  Ted Jones
Mock It Up 29
  Val Haigh
Heydays at Herreshoff's 34
  Maynard Bray
To Stop a Leak 44
  Bud McIntosh
Epoxy 48
  Aimé Ontario Fraser
Norway's Mellemværftet Shipyard 58
  Douglas Wilmot
Able to Go: The Boats and Freedom of
  Jon Guzzwell 64
  James W. Brown
The Legacy of Howard Chapelle 76
  Peter H. Spectre
Building a Classic Yacht Boarding 91
Ladder
  Sam Manning
Designs:
  Wee Rob and MacGregor, Double- 106
  Paddle Sailing Canoes
  Mike O'Brien

VOLUME XV: ISSUES 85–90

85 NOVEMBER/DECEMBER 1988

A Cutter's Story 21
  Clark Poston
A Boatbuilding Shop 27
  Harold Payson
Build a Construction Model, Build 36
  a Boat, Part I
  Harold Payson
FRAM: The Ultimate Ice Ship 44
  James Carr
Sam Devlin 52
  Tom Brown
Bienvenue à Douarnenez 88 64
  Maynard Bray
Charles Francis Adams:
  Sailing with Uncle Charlie 74
  George C. Homans
  America's Greatest Amateur Helmsman 74
  Llewellyn Howland III
Set Work 99
  Bud McIntosh
Designs:
  A St. Lawrence Yawl by Tim Evans 117
  Joel White
Wood Technology: Pressure-Treated 121
  Lumber Revisited
  Richard Jagels

86 JANUARY/FEBRUARY 1989

Adventures in the Marine Arts Game 21
  Llewellyn Howland III
Build a Construction Model, Build 29
  a Boat, Part II
  Harold Payson
Three of a Kind 36
  Morry Edwards
Forest E. Johnson 44
  C. Philip Moore
Hardwater and Splinters 52
  Gifford Gibson
The English Coble 58
  George Featherston
A Conversation with C.A. Goodall, 70
  Coblebuilder
  Peter H. Spectre
Six Cruising Scenarios 76
  Philip C. Bolger
Designs
  Schooner and Flashboat 94
  Mike O'Brien
Wood Technology: Tree Immigration 105
  Quotas?
  Richard Jagels

87 MARCH/APRIL 1989

The Passing of a New England 27
  Boatbuilder
  Paula Darois Verlicco
Build a Construction Model, Build 29
  a Boat, Part III
  Harold Payson
FRI: Taking Care of a Ship—and 36
  the World
  David Moodie
Ordering Lumber 46
  Joel White
Memories of a T-Wharfer 56
  Art Hansen
Warp Speed 66
  Ted Hugger
Henri Vaillancourt and the Bark 80
  Canoe
  Jerry Stelmok
Flat-Bottomed Skiffs 90
  Mike O'Brien
Designs:
  A Cogge Cruiser by William 119
  Garden
  Joel White
Wood Technology: Forest Survival, 125
  Human Needs
  Richard Jagels

88 MAY/JUNE 1989

Build a Construction Model, Build 31
  a Boat, Part IV
  Harold Payson
Danish Seiners 40
  Jeremy Cresswell
Steamboxes:
  A Low-Pressure Approach 50
  Ed McClave
  A Steambox Scrapbook 51
  WoodenBoat Readers
  A Steambox Primer 58
  Simon Watts
Havilah Hawkins 60
  Jim P. Brown
WHITE WINGS 70
  Anne Lawrence Greer
Plank-on-Frame Dugouts 76
  James W. Brown
Wood Technology: Compression 100
  Wood in White Pine Planking
  Richard Jagels
Designs:
  Simple Daysailers—Chesapeake Style 114
  Mike O'Brien

89 JULY/AUGUST 1989

Sprit Rig Basics 30
  Ernie Cassidy
William Crosby's Snipe 36
  Paul Lazarus
Joe Trumbly 44
  Joseph A. Jacobson
Casting Lead Keels 52
  Richard Remsen
The Gilkersonian Imperative 64
  Peter H. Spectre
Boats of the Polish Coast 74
  Tom Zydler
  The Smaller Boats of Kaszuby 80
  Aleksander Celarek
  Traditional Boats in Poland Today 84
  Aleksander Celarek
The DISCOVERY's Launch 86
  Roger C. Taylor
Repair Strategies for Cold-Molded 92
  Construction
  Reuel Parker
Wood Technology: Fungus and Worms 106
  Richard Jagels
Designs:
  LONE STAR and BOUNTY 114
  Joel White

90 SEPTEMBER/OCTOBER 1989

Our Thanks to John Gardner 36
  Cast of Thousands!
Looking for the One Shot 46
  John Rousmaniere
Double-Paddle Canoes 56
  Mike O'Brien
Building the Cardboard Dory 63
  Sam Manning
A Matter of Detail 66
  Maynard Bray
Seattle's Center for Wooden Boats 72
  Bob Allen
An Adventure in Antiques 78
  Polly Brown
The Fifes of Fairlie 84
  Iain McAllister
The ADVENTURESS and Mrs. B. 94
  Brion Toss
The Steam Yacht ENA 102
  Laurie Stubbs
Structure of a Winner 108
  George Kuchenbecker
Scrapers 113
  Sam Manning
Designs:
  A 29' Joel White Double-Ender 122
  William Garden
Wood Technology: Soothing the 128
  Conscience vs. Saving the
  Environment
  Richard Jagels

VOLUME XVI: ISSUES 91–96

91 NOVEMBER/DECEMBER 1989

Building a Hollow Mast	25
Arch Davis	
Yukon Practicalities	34
Jim Borisenko	
Modern Multihulls, Part I	38
James W. Brown	
Classics for Charter	50
Jolyon Byerley and John K.	
Hanson, Jr.	
The Wianno Senior:	
75 Years of Serious Sailing	58
Malcolm Howes	
Tuning Up	67
Jack Fallon	
Unleaded Gas	70
Gordon H. Millar	
Maurice Griffiths	78
Peter H. Spectre	
Rough Water Over the Sands	89
Maurice Griffiths	
Traditions and Memories of American	92
Yachting: Introduction to the	
50th Anniversary Edition	
Jon Wilson	
Designs:	
Outboard-Powered Garveys by Devlin	96
and Stephens	
Mike O'Brien	
Wood Technology: Correspondence	118
from Down Under	
Richard Jagels	

92 JANUARY/FEBRUARY 1990

Goops and Goos	23
Aimé Ontario Fraser	
Building a Skylight	28
Paul Lazarus	
Modern Multihulls, Part II	34
James W. Brown	
Philip C. Bolger, Boat Designer	42
Dan Segal	
The Great South Bay Scooters	52
David Seidman	
The Restoration of the Trader Ketch	62
DEFENDER	
David Murphy	
Sail and Hull Performance	76
Colin Palmer	
Repairing Lapstrake Planking	90
Walter J. Simmons	
Designs:	
One Man's "Shorey"	96
Mait Edey	
Wood Technology: Alternatives to	112
Boycotting	
Richard Jagels	

93 MARCH/APRIL 1990

Quick & Dirty Repairs	29
Peter H. Spectre	
Fitting Out	36
Paul Bryant	
Painting for Decoration	42
Maynard Bray	
Interior Arrangements	52
Jon Wilson	
Surveying Your Sails	60
Robin Lincoln	
Painting for Longevity	70
Ed McClave	
Whipping WHIPPET Into Shape	76
Maynard Bray	
A New Twist on Bending Frames	84
Doug Hylan	
Boatbuilder, Beware	86
Paul Lazarus	
Corrosion-Related Problems	94
Ed McClave	
Designs:	
Seagoing Powerboats by Beebe and	128
Eldredge-McInnis	
Joel White	
Wood Technology: Recycling a	134
Renewable Resource	
Richard Jagels	

94 MAY/JUNE 1990

Fairing	29
Arch Davis	
Final Fairing	35
Ted Hugger	
Ratty's Boat	44
Lois Darling	
The Blanchard Boat Company	54
Neil Rabinowitz	
MER-NA	62
Marty Loken	
The Marine Industries of Lunenburg,	64
Nova Scotia	
Peter H. Spectre	
The Commuters	74
C. Philip Moore	
Building Louvered Doors	84
Tim Allen	
Designs:	
Iota and Gray Seal, Designs by	110
Benford and Oughtred	
Mike O'Brien	
Wood Technology: Tropical Forests	114
Revisited	
Richard Jagels	

95 JULY/AUGUST 1990

Railboat	34
Bill Vaughn	
Chip Stulen, Boatbuilder	38
Owen Cecil	
The Moliceiros of Aveiro Lagoon	48
John Eide	
Racing Gently	55
Art Paine	
Class Without Flash	60
Maynard Bray	
Gannon & Benjamin	70
Katherine Scott	
ALOHA	82
Leslie Whitman	
VARIN, the Lestabåt	90
Roger C. Taylor	
Wood Technology: Woods of Australia	102
Richard Jagels	
Designs:	
PATIENCE, a Shoal-Draft Ketch/Ed	110
Frost	

96 SEPTEMBER/OCTOBER 1990

Building the Biscayne Bay 14, Part I	24
Maynard Bray with Eric Dow	
DREOILIN: Tale of a Galway Hooker	36
John Seymour	
A New PRIDE for Baltimore	50
Andy Davis	
Thomas Gillmer and the PRIDEs	56
Andy Davis	
Professional Sailors, Traditional	58
Vessels	
Peter H. Spectre	
Olde Tyme Shyppes	64
Peter H. Spectre	
The Heaving Deck of History	72
Peter H. Spectre	
A Brighter Future	73
Maynard Bray	
First Aid: A Primer for the Boatshop	74
Mitchell K. Ross, M.D.	
The North Woods Canoe	80
Garrett Conover	
A Contemporary Planking Technique	87
Ken Bassett	
Wood Technology: Comparing Wood	104
Species	
Richard Jagels	
Designs:	
TLINGIT and CZARINNA, Power-	112
boats by William Garden	
Joel White	

VOLUME XVII: ISSUES 97–102

97 NOVEMBER/DECEMBER 1990

Building the Biscayne Bay 14, Part II 33
Maynard Bray with Eric Dow
Making Laminated Frames 44
Arch Davis
Two Modelmakers 52
Peter H. Spectre
A Kuna Canoe 62
Tom Zydler
A Strange Reincarnation 70
David Hardy
R.O. Davis 76
Michael McMenemy and
Debbie Pointer
ALICE 92
Philip C. Bolger
Wood Technology: Plantation Exotics; 104
Considering the Alternatives
Richard Jagels
Designs:
Touring Kayaks by Alford and 108
Wahlman
Mike O'Brien
The Three Davis-Nevins 86
Motorsailers
Michael McMenemy and
Debbie Pointer

98 JANUARY/FEBRUARY 1991

Building the Biscayne Bay 14, Part III 28
Maynard Bray with Eric Dow
Lofting Curved, Raked Transoms 41
Arno Day
Designer Olin J. Stephens II 50
Robby Robinson
Windermere Steamboat Museum 66
Peter H. Spectre
GIPSY JAC 74
Craig Walters
Wedge-Seam Construction 82
Simon Watts
Crooked Drawers 89
James W. Brown
Designs:
STING RAY V by C. Raymond 104
Hunt Assoc.
Joel White
Wood Technology: The Wood/Paint 113
Interface: Will it Stick?
Richard Jagels

99 MARCH/APRIL 1991

Transom Replacement 28
Jon Wilson
A Trouble-Free DC System 41
Nigel Calder
The Artist's Eye 48
Art Paine
Name in Gold, Hail in Black 54
Maynard Bray
Healing the Break 63
Daniel MacNaughton
A Lasting Finish 66
David L. Jackson
Building a Proper Icebox 74
James W. Brown
Raised Panels 86
Arch Davis
Singlehanded Boatbuilding 94
Sam Manning
Paintbrush Care 104
E. Barton Chapin III
Designs:
Nesting Dinghies 116
Mike O'Brien
Wood Technology: Woodworkers' 125
Alliance for Rainforest Protection
Richard Jagels

100 MAY/JUNE 1991

Plank Curvature 31
Ed McClave
'Glass vs. Wood 38
Ben Ellison
Damned by Faint Praise 46
David Seidman
A New Sea Sled from Mystic 58
David Seidman
How to Scull a Boat 60
Sam Manning
Letters from the Masters 70
John Streeter, Editor
VORTEX 84
Mark Malone
Redesigning the Swede 55 88
Art Paine
Strip-Building a Double-Paddle 92
Canoe
Henry ("Mac") McCarthy
The Cosine Wherry 100
John A. Hartsock
Designs:
AERIEL, a Design by McCurdy 108
& Rhodes
Joel White
Wood Technology: Mildew, and 128
Lots of It!
Richard Jagels

101* JULY/AUGUST 1991

A Small Schooner 36
Christian Dahl
Holding a Delicate Balance 42
Peter H. Spectre
Repowering with a Diesel, Part I 52
Nigel Calder
A Postcard Album of Early Great Lakes 64
Small Craft
Owen Cecil
WANDERER III 74
Thies Matzen
The Buckboard Trailer 82
Richard Jagels
Lining Off 88
Arno Day
Wood Technology: Growth Rate and 91
Durability
Richard Jagels
Designs:
Caledonia Yawl and Hitia: Superb 93
Beach Cruisers
Mike O'Brien

102* SEPTEMBER/OCTOBER 1991

Build a Molded Coach Roof 31
Arch Davis
More Clamps 38
Craig Walsh
The Elco Cruisette 40
William C. Swanson
Hvalsoe's Hacker 48
Chas. Dowd
WYNFALL 56
Mark Smaalders
The Tragedy of DEFIANCE 62
Lloyd Bergeson
Making the Perfect Dash 82
Robert Simper
A Boat for Troubled Waters 88
Edward McCabe
Repowering with a Diesel, Part II 92
Nigel Calder
Designs:
Cold-Molded Pilothouse Cutter by 104
Paul Gartside
Joel White
Wood Technology: Dangers of Mildew- 123
cides
Richard Jagels

* *Please note that although the contents pages for Issues 101 and 102 are listed here to complete Volume 17, author and subject referencing are not included in this index.*

* VOLUME XVIII: ISSUES 103–108

103 NOVEMBER/DECEMBER 1991

The Deadeye Tool	30
Harry Bryan	
SCAMPER and EVALENA	36
Steve Bunnell	
Mogano	44
Peter H. Spectre	
In Search of the Perfect Skiff	54
Mike O'Brien	
Boatbuilder as Shaman	64
John Emery	
Patternmaking with Acrylic Plastic	72
Franz Amussen	
Passage to Wind'ard	76
Maurice Griffiths	
A Drying Rack for Cedar Planking Stock	80
Harry Bryan	
Wood Technolgy: Surface Rot	93
Richard Jagels	
Designs:	
Plywood Composite Outboard Boats	100
Mike O'Brien	

104 JANUARY/FEBRUARY 1992

Kayaking at Chewonki	30
David D. Platt	
Old World Craftsmanship—Modern Boatbuilding Technology	38
Ted Hugger	
Capt. Adrian Raynaud	48
Peter H. Spectre	
Draw Me a Dream	56
Rupert Lyle	
KHAYA: The Designer's Own Boat	62
Rupert Lyle	
The Family Island Regatta	66
Art Paine	
Building Sweet Pea, Part I	82
Harold H. Payson	
Wood Technology: Good Intentions/ Bad Solutions	102
Richard Jagels	
Designs:	
NORTHERN CROWN: A Tough, Graceful Cutter	108
Joel White	

105 MARCH/APRIL 1992

A Simple Outboard Rudder	33
Brion Rieff	
Out, Out, Damned Keelbolt!	38
Simon Watts	
Repairing an Iron-Sick Bilge	42
Samuel E. Slaymaker	
Skiff Repairs	46
Skip Green	
Building BLIXTEN	48
Lars Johansson	
Tables: Strong and Stowable	58
Kendall Williams	
A Fold-Up Table and Shelves	60
Joel White	
A Stowable Gimbaled Table	63
Michael Kortchmar	
High Tech Meets Tradition	68
Art Paine	
Building Sweet Pea, Part II	78
Harold H. Payson	
Traditional Rope Fenders	91
Barbara Merry	
Wood & Epoxy	94
Jim Brown	
Wood Technology: When Decay Is Not Rot	112
Richard Jagels	
Designs:	
A Pair of Elegant Double-Enders	128
Maynard Bray	

106 MAY/JUNE 1992

A Scarfing Jig for Plywood	31
Robert Kozak	
Plywood: Making the Right Choices	35
David D. Platt	
The CONSTELLATION Meets Her Match	42
Peter H. Spectre	
Wooden Boat Building in New Zealand	54
Arch Davis	
RONA: The Story of a Classic Yacht Restoration	62
Shane Kelly	
Rowing Against the Tide	72
Kim Keister	
Converting to Stitch-and-Glue	80
Sam Devlin	
Wood Technology: Some Thoughts on Wood Chemistry	95
Richard Jagels	
Designs:	
Packet and Tramp, Plywood Cruising Houseboats	105
Joel White	

107 JULY/AUGUST 1992

Build a Traditional Ship's Wheel, Part I	29
Michael Podmaniczky	
Rite of Passage	36
Jon Wilson	
The Shipyard in a Box	50
Peter H. Spectre	
Rybovich	58
Paul Lazarus	
Taking Lines Off Small Craft	70
D.W. Dillion	
Chebacco 20	80
Dan Segal	
Designs:	
Plywood Pocket Cruisers	97
Mike O'Brien	
Wood Technology: Using a Local Wood Supply	102
Richard Jagels	

108 SEPTEMBER/OCTOBER 1992

Strip Planking a New Garboard	31
Daniel MacNaughton	
Build a Traditional Ship's Wheel, Part II	33
Michael Podmaniczky	
Willem Vos and the BATAVIA	40
Peter H. Spectre	
A Double-Paddle Canoe by Moonlight	50
Robert A. Miller	
A. Mason	54
Michael and Debbie McMenemy	
Building a Double-Bladed Paddle	67
Donald MacKenzie	
ELIZABETH MUIR: A Masterpiece	74
Annie Sutter	
Balancing the Rig of a Small Sailboat	80
John Gardner	
Wood Technology: New Regs, New Products, New Headaches, Pt I: VOCs	97
Richard Jagels	
Designs:	
CANDLE IN THE WIND, A New Yawl in the Old Tradition	105
Joel White	

* *Author and subject referencing not included in this index.*

The WoodenBoat Store

Providing Access to Experience

On the following pages you'll find information on back issues of *WoodenBoat*, plus hardbound editions of *WoodenBoat*, Binders and Slipcases to store *WoodenBoat*, and full photocopy versions of the out-of-print issues of *WoodenBoat*. That's a bunch of ways to collect all the great information we've ever published.

If you turn past the back issues listings, you will find out how to contact us, so you can order these great items.

Buy Five Back Issues Pay Only $20.00— Save $5.00!

Issues Available: 16-24, 36-40, 42-80, 82 through current
Five Issues: #210-000 Ship Wt. 2½ lbs $20.00 *(specify issues)*
Single Issues: #200–000 Ship Wt. 1/2 lb each $5.00 *(specify issues)*

16 — The Construction of GOLDEN DAZY... Repairing a Cruiser Transom... An Expert's Views on Varnishing... Planking the Maine Lobsterboat.

17 — New Frontiers: The Pacific Northwest... Evaluating Sheathing Materials... Italy's Premier Boatbuilders... Surfboating on the Jersey Shore.

18 — Building the Adirondack Guideboat... Another Bolger Triumph... New England's Lowells and Their Dories... ENDLESS SUMMER.

19 — Sailing Canoes of Polynesia... The Banks Dory... Taking Off Lines... The Wooden Boat Festival.

20 — Make Your Own Rudder... Repairing the Cabintop... St. Lawrence Rowing Skiffs... The Life and Times of Colin Archer.

21 — Maintaining the Seams and Topsides... How to Understand Boat Plans... A Wooden Submarine... Building Racing Shells.

22 — Deck Canvasing: The State of the Art... Practical Bottom Maintenance... Classic Cruisers: Power & Sail... The Versatile Leeboard.

23 — A Norwegian Boatbuilding School... Electrolysis—Debunking the Myths... The Classic Speedboats of Lake Tahoe... Multihulls.

24 — A Sailing Whitehall... The Genius of Laurent Giles... Getting the Feel of Caulking... Cold Molding: A Powerboat for Today.

36 — Understanding Marine Insurance... The Birchbark Canoe Lives On... How to Build a Seaworthy Sailing Canoe... The Versatile Swampscott Dory.

37 — The Alaska Limit Seiner... The History of Small Yacht Design, Part I... Finishing of the Seaworthy Sailing Canoe... Milling Your Own Lumber.

38 — The Oldest Known Boat in the World... The Preservation of Ships and Skills... The Remarkable Herreshoff MEADOW LARK... Boats to Build from a Kit.

39 — The Maine Schooner... Making Patterns for Castings... More Boats from Kits... Stem Repairs and Replacements.

40 — An Interview with John Gardner... Spring Outfitting with a Pro... Singlehanding an Old Gaffer... The Last Wooden Shipbuilding Boom.

42 — Planking the Plywood Dory... Sailing Workboats for the Future... Wooden Yachts That Earn Their Keep... A Survey of Boatbuilding Schools.

43 — The Sea Bird Yawl Revisited... Teaching Yourself to Build Boats... Newport's First Wooden Boat Show... Finishing Off the Plywood Dory.

44 — A New Classic Runabout... SEA BIRD's Atlantic Crossing... Maritime Preservation... Comparing Carvel and Cold-Molded Construction.

45 — Classics in Sail and Power... Boatbuilding Woods... Vic Carpenter... A Seaworthy Plywood Tender.

46 — Laying a Tight Deck... Details of Outstanding Craftsmanship... English Maritime Museums... Planking a Plywood Tender.

47 — Saw Sharpening... Tough Competition from Wooden Daysailers... A Penny-Pinching Power Cruiser... Craftsmanship on Deck.

48 — Early Runabouts... The Northwest's Frank Prothero... An Inexpensive Boat Shelter You Can Build... Keeping Power Saws Sharp.

49 — The Masterful Work of Malcolm Brewer... Small Boatbuilding, Norwegian Style... Quick & Dirty Boatbuilding... Replacing the Keel.

50 — San Francisco's Nunes Brothers... Cutting Your Own Natural Crooks... Boats and Builders in Ireland... Improving a Classic Dinghy.

51 — Conversations with Bud McIntosh... Restoring a Burned-Out Yacht... John Gardner's Plywood Bateau... Building the Wayfarer Dinghy Kit.

52 — Lesson from a Great Lakes Schooner... A Cold-Molded Rejuvenation... Elegant Launches from Venice... Building the Concordia Beetle Cats.

53 — Making Gaff Rig Work to Windward... Folding Boats at Sea... An Elegant Classic... Plank Repair and Replacement.

54 — Build AMERICA's Half Model... Plywood Boats for Oar & Paddle... Winter Covers... Auxiliary Engines: Diesel & Gas.

55 — L. Francis Herreshoff... The Schooner WANDER BIRD... Restoring Molded Wooden Boats... The Greatest Little Motorboat.

56 — The First Planing Power Cruisers... A Classic in Lapstrake Plywood... The Sharpie for All Seasons... Restoring a Herreshoff 12½.

57 — One Ultimate Wooden Yacht... Sailing the Bermuda Dinghy... Restoration to the Highest Standards... Making Your Boat Tight Again.

58 — Getting Into Kayaks... Sailing the Tancook Schooner... Steam-Bending as a Science... Modern Wooden Shipbuilding.

59 — An Amphibious Cat-Ketch... Outlook for World Timber... Hawaii's Koa Canoes... On Glues and Gluing.

60 — How to Buy a Wooden Boat... The Perfect Pram... Cold-Molded Sheathing... Celebration of Wooden Boats.

61 — Build a Fast Plywood Single Shell... A High-Performance River Boat... Step-by-Step Cold-Molded Sheathing... A Legacy of Ship Preservation.

62 — Step-by-Step Traditional Teak Grates... Lake Tahoe's Elegant Classics... The Forward Thinking of Henry Scheel.

63 — Hot Ideas for Cold-Molded Boats... How to Row a Single Scull... Spring Commissioning in Just Two Weekends... Restoring a Fantail Launch.

64 — Albert Strange and the Canoe Yawl... The Arts of the Riverboat Builders... Spring Painting and Varnishing... Unusual Backyard Boats.

65 — Keeper of Classic Speedboats... The Boatbuilder as Artist... Making Traditional Mast Hoops... The Wooden Boat Regattas.

66 — In Praise of the Junk... Seasoning Your Lumber... Skiffs and Sharpies... Renewing the Deck.

67 — Make a Canoe Paddle... A Classic Steam Yacht, Part I... Hatches and Deck Joinery... A Plywood Sharpie.

68 — Celebration of Early 12-Meters... State-of-the-Art Singlehander... Renewing a Classic Outboard Launch... Leatherwork for the Sailor.

69 — Trimaran Jim Brown... Make Your Own Wooden Plane... Trailers and Cradles... Powerboat Systems.

70 — California Schoonerman... Build a Plywood Kayak... The British Wooden Boat Revival... Buying Used Tools.

71 — Make Your Own Oars... Speedboats from the Golden Era... Repairing Lapstrake Planks... Sailing a Gaff Cutter.

72 — Gulf Coast Outboards... Starling Burgess... Wooden Boat Insurance... Recovering a Teak Deck.

73 — Offshore Powerboats... Casting Bronze Hardware... Rod Stephens & the N.Y. 32s... How to Build a Plywood Runabout.

74 — Rowing the River Thames... Jack Holt's Sailing Dinghies... North Sea Trawler-Yacht... The Gunter Rig.

75 — Building a Pocket Cruiser... Maintenance Schedules... The Designs of Winthrop Warner... Looking at Boat Plans.

76 — High-Speed Sportfishing Yachts... Build a Locker for the Main Cabin... The Safe and Able Boats of Lyle Hess... Hot-Weather Varnishing.

77 — A Modern Northwest Classic... Deck Care... Production-Built Small Boats... Buying a Runabout.

78 — Canoe Restoration... Centerboards and Trunks... Exotic Rigs... Danish Spidsgatters.

79 — The New England Dragger... Tool Storage and Transport... Boatyard Hazards... A Woven Coracle.

80 — Grass Roots Outboard Racing... Celebrating Concordia Yawls... Replacing Planks... Sano Magic.

82 — Summer Festivals... Lyman Boatworks... Galvanizing Hardware... The Reelfoot Stumpjumper.

83 — Proven Proas... The Designs of Nick Potter... Wreck at Cape Ann... The Self Survey.

84 — Stopping Leaks... Howard Chapelle... Herreshoffs Revealed... Epoxy-Wood Connection.

85 — Douarnenez Festival... Tack-and-Tape Construction... Charles Francis Adams... A Cutter's Story.

86 — The English Coble... Scarfing Plywood... The Legendary Prowler... Collecting Marine Art.

87 — Warp Speed... Fishing Schooners... Leakproof Hatches... Good Skiffs.

88 — Steam Boxes... Windmill Boat... Plank-on-Frame Dugouts... Chesapeake Daysailers.

89 — Snipes... Repair Strategies... Sprit Rig Basics... Art of Wm. Gilkerson.

90 — Double-Paddle Canoes... The Steam Yacht ENA... Build a Dory Model... Simple Boat Details.

91 — Mast Building... Charter Classics... Wianno Seniors... Unleaded Gas Controversy.

92 — Multihull Safety... Build a Skylight... Lapstrake Repairs... Rig and Hull Performance.

93 — Special Hands-On Issue... Fitting Out... Painting... Quick Repairs.

94 — Fast Commuters... Louvered Doors... Blanchard Boats... Pocket Cruisers.

95 — Class without Flash... Gannon & Benjamin... Building by Eye... Squaresail Sailing.

96 — Building the Biscayne Bay 14... PRIDE OF BALTIMORE... Replanking a Runabout... North Woods Canoe.

97 — Building a Canoe Yawl... Kayak Designs... Laminated Frames.

98 — Olin J. Stephens II... Steamboats at Windermere... Building Crooked Drawers... A New MOBJACK.

99 — Raised-Panel Joinerwork... A Trouble-Free DC System... Build a Proper Icebox.

100 — Maintenance Costs: Glass vs Wood... The Hickman Sea Sled... How to Scull... Build WEE LASSIE.

101 — Winning Shells in Wood... Installing a New Diesel... Great Lakes Small Craft... The Buckboard Trailer.

102 — Affordable Boat Design... Build a Molded Coach Roof... The Elco Cruisette.

103 — The Perfect Skiff... Mahogany Classics in Italy... Patternmaking with Acrylic Plastic.

104 — Kayak Camp... Designing a Dream... Build Sweet Pea... Van Dam Craftsmanship... Capt. Adrian Raynaud.

105 — Cabin Tables... Epoxy & Wood... Making a New Rudder... Rope Fenders... Sweet Pea, Part II.

106 — The Constellation Controversy... Buying the Right Plywood... Coverting to Stitch & Glue... Lowell's Boat Shop.

107 — Build a Ship's Wheel... Rybovich... Civilized Daysailers... A Shipyard in a Box.

108 — Building a Double Paddle... Designer Al Mason... An Innovative Garboard Repair... The Batavia Replica.

109 — The Sea Bright Skiff... Knowing the Ropes... The Stone Boat Yard.

110 — Wave-Piercing Catamarans... Lofting Demystified, Part I... Curved Spars & Halyard Hooks.

111 — Build a Perfect Skiff, Part I... Varnishing... Mast Repair... Shipworms & Gribbles... Bottom Paints... Copper Sheathing... Lofting Demystified, Part II.

112 — Skiff Craft... The Strip-Diagonal Combination... The McManuses of Boston... An Invisible Motor... Finishing the Perfect Skiff.

113 — Building the Cape Charles Kayak, Part I... Restoration of VIOLET... Edson Schock... Riva!

114 — An Elegant Sea Kayak, Part II... Carlo Riva... Refastening with Rivets... Sharpies... Square Meters.

115 — Double-Paddle Cruising... Homemade Hardware... Yacht Yards of the North Shore... The Bonding Debate.

116 — Shellback Dinghy, Part I... Extraordinary Launches from Minett... An Ideal Tender... Transom Repairs... Kettenburg of California.

117 — Deck Seams... Shellback II... Oars... A Grady-White Makeover... Accurate Joinerwork... Moorings.

118 — Sandbaggers... Shellback III... A Stealth Dinghy... Norway's Maritime Traditions... Tugs on San Francisco Bay.

119 — Canoe called YAKABOO... Putting a Shaper to Work... Building DOLLY... Sheathing Fabrics for Wooden Boats... Inner-City Boatbuilding.

120 — Schooner Stories... A Railbird Skiff... Finishing Off a Sportfisherman... TENACITY, A Woman's Work of Art... WoodenBoat Heroes: Where are They Now?

121 — Grand Lake Canoes... TILIKUM: A World-Roaming Log Canoe... A Fast and Simple Garvey... Designing TAMARA... Future of Maritime History.

122 — Schooner BRILLIANT... Boats of the Yangtze River... Catamaran Designer James Wharram... A Retractable Skeg.

123 — PRINCIPIA Recycled... The Canoe Yawl RED HEAD... Clamps in the Boatshop... A Folding Dinghy.

124 — Boatbuilding Methods... Dragon Boats... Replacing a Keel and Centerboard Trunk... Building CHANTY.

Internet: http://www.woodenboat.com **Email:** wbstore@woodenboat.com

Organize Your Back Issues with Our Slipcases and Binders

Slipcase
#250-002
Ship Wt. 1 lb $10.95

Binder
#250-001
Ship Wt. 1 lb $11.95

125 — Understanding Hull Stress, Part I... A Modern French Fishing Lugger... Paul E. Luke and ROSA II... The 6-Hour Canoe.

126 — Building the Dory Skiff, Part I... Hurricane Island Boats... The Purdys of Port Washington... Whitehalls...Double-ended Daysailer LALA... Repowering CHEWINK.

127 — Chesapeake Bay Log Canoes... North Carolina Sportfishing Boats... Re-decking a Philip Rhodes Yawl... Making Oars and Leathers... Beach Cruisers... Dory Skiff, Part II.

128 — BLOODHOUND... Drilling Long Holes... Grey Seal, Part I...Potomac River Dory-Boats... Ideal Trainer.

129 — ZULU... Bending Wood with Dry Heat... PT Boat Design and Development... Trollers of the Pacific Northwest... The Schooner BOWDOIN... Building Grey Seal, Part II.

130 — Adirondack Guideboats... Casting Bronze... Alton Wallace... The Knarr Class... Grey Seal, Part III.

131 — Build the Osprey Triple-Cockpit Kayak, Part I... Sailing Rigs for Kayaks... Claud Worth... Tale of Two Sonders... Simple Patterns... Huris, Sunbuqs, and Boatbuilders of Yemen... Tops'l to Trys'l.

132 — The Trumpy Story... Widgeon... Manhasset Bay One Designs... Harvesting Hackmatack Knees... Harry Bryan... McGruer's... A Triple-Cockpit Kayak, Part II.

The WoodenBoat Index
Issues 1-100

The *WoodenBoat Index* is the most comprehensive guide to information on design, construction, use, history, care, and repair of wooden boats of all types and sizes. It's organized alphabetically, with extensive cross references with directions to related information. Spiralbound for easy, constant use.
115 pp., softcover
#325-023 Ship Wt. 1 lb $12.95

The WoodenBoat Index Supplement
Issues 101-126

32 pp., softcover
#325-024 Ship Wt. 1/2 lb $6.95

Hardbound Volumes of *WoodenBoat*

Handsome library-style volumes, contain six issues, and have *WoodenBoat* and the volume numbers embossed in gold.

#220-000 (specify volumes) Ship Wt. 5 lbs each $35.00

Vol. 4 Issues 19 – 24
Vol. 8 Issues 43 – 48
Vol. 9 Issues 49 – 54
Vol. 10 Issues 55 – 60
Vol. 11 Issues 61 – 66
Vol 12 Issues 67 – 72
Vol. 13 Issues 73 – 78
Vol. 14 Issues 79 – 84

Vol. 15 Issues 85 – 90
Vol. 16 Issues 91 – 96
Vol. 17 Issues 97 – 102
Vol. 18 Issues 103 – 108
Vol. 19 Issues 109 – 114
Vol. 20 Issues 115 – 120
Vol. 21 Issues 121 – 126
Vol. 22 Issues 127 – 132

Out-of-Print Issues of *WoodenBoat* Available as Complete Photocopies

Reader demand for the timeless information from out-of-print issues of *WoodenBoat* has resulted in complete photocopies of each of these issues. Now available: 1–15, 25–35, 41 & 81.

#205-000 Ship Wt. 1 lb each $10.95 (specify issues)

1 – Traditional Boatbuilder's Tools... Building a Sharpie... Red & White Oaks... A Modified Friendship.

2 – The Lincolnville Wherry... A Smoky Mountains Dory... Electrical Installations... The Decay of Wood in Boats... The Maine Sloop.

3 – Racing Skipjacks on the Chesapeake... Inspecting the Bilge... The Cape Cod Catboat... ALMA, a San Francisco Scow Schooner.

4 – The Bath Marine Museum Apprenticeshop... Scottish Fishing Boat Conversions... Cold-Molded Construction... Pete Culler on Boatbuilding.

5 – The Mystic Seaport Small Craft... Building a Whitehall from Lofting through Finishing... Au Sable River Boats... Building a Tancook Whaler, Part I.

6 – Chesapeake Bay Log Canoe... John Gardner on Marine Museums... The Great Pacific Boatworks.

7 – Estimating Construction Costs... Cold-Molded Construction... The Building of a Tancook Whaler... Instant Boats... ACTIVE to England.

8 – The Original Knockabouts... Documentation Primer... Ashcroft Construction... Small Craft Restoration... St. Lawrence Yawls.

9 – Rediscovering Hackmatack... Mason Boat Works... Barbados Boatbuilding... Domestic Woods, Part I...

10 – Imported Woods, Part II: ... A Pro on Painting... Folkboats Revisited... Runabouts... Seasoning Science.

11 – Understanding, Appreciating, Preventing Rot... Some Thoughts on Lofting... The Nearly Forgotten Art of Making Planes... On Laying Down and Taking Off... The Care and Feeding of Teak Decks.

12 – An Intro to Refastening... The Essence of Lofting... A Winter Storage Primer... Clamps & Cleverness... The Bass Boat.

13 – Winter Layup... Making Molds... Leaks Are Lousy... Keeping the Structure Together... West Coast Traditions.

14 – The Rabbet... Saw Cuts... No Wrinkles: Canvasing the Deck... The Incredible Herreshoff Dugout... Setting Up.

15 – Watertight: A Simple Teak Deck... The Fine Art of Stripping Paint... Ribbands... Timbering Out... The Venetian Gondola... Pouring the Lead Keel.

25 – Living Aboard... Cornish Gigs... WHITE-HAWK Under Sail... Leaking Decks.

26 – Herreshoff's Rozinante... How to Build a Classic Dinghy... Surveying... Cold-Molding in the West.

27 – New England's Oldest Dory Shop... Professional Quality Maintenance... Sailing Peapods... Pete Culler's Workshop.

28 – William Hand's Motorsailers... Norwegian Boatbuilding... Lumber Forecast... Bedding Compounds.

29 – Design Competition Results... Classic Runabouts Today... Rebuilding the Wood & Canvas Canoe... Friendship Sloops Under Sail.

30 – Winter Layup... The San Francisco Pelican... Bow Chocks... The Reliable One-Lunger.

31 – Working Sail Returns... Heating Your Boat with Wood... Falmouth Oyster Boats... Finish Off a Flat-Bottomed Skiff.

32 – Simple Tools for Simple Boats... Restoring a St. Lawrence Skiff... John Alden's Yachts... Understanding Marine Electrical Systems.

33—Making Half Models... Nathanael Herreshoff... The JOHN F. LEAVITT.

34—An Exquisite Yacht Tender... Festival Season... Cold-Molded Metamorphosis.

35 – Herreshoff's New York Thirties... St. Pierre Dory... Restoring a Working Skipjack.

41 – Yachting's Cutter Craze... Build a Classic Plywood Dory... Restoring a Runabout... Narrowboats of Great Britain.

81 – Sailing a Bahamian Smack... The Art of Brightwork... Building a Cabin Sole... 50 Years with *Diablesse*.

For <u>Future</u> Issues of *WoodenBoat* — SUBSCRIBE
1 year – $27.00   *2 years* – $51.00   *3 years* – $75.00
In Canada add $5.00, overseas add $12.00

The WoodenBoat Store

P.O. Box 78, Naskeag Road, Brooklin, Maine 04616-0078

EMail: wbstore@woodenboat.com

Toll-Free U.S. & Canada:
1-800-273-SHIP (7447)

Hours: 8am–6pm EST, Mon.–Fri. (9–5 Sats. Oct.–Dec.)
24-Hour Fax: 207-359-8920 **Overseas:** Call 207-359-4647
Internet Address: http://www.woodenboat.com

Ordered by _____

Address _____

_____

City/State/Zip _____

Day Phone# _____

Catalog Code **WBP**

SHIP TO — only if different than "ORDERED BY"

Name _____

Address _____

_____

City/State/Zip _____

Product #	Qty.	Item, Size, Color	Ship Wt.	Total
		WoodenBoat Magazine—US Subscriptions: One-year $27.00, Two-years $51.00, Three-years $75.00		

SUB TOTAL

Maine Residents Add 6% Tax

❏ Standard
❏ Priority Mail

❏ Two Day
❏ Next Day

❏ Int'l Surface
❏ Int'l Air

TOTAL

Our Guarantee... Satisfaction or Your Money Back!

Pre-payment is required. Payment MUST be in U.S. funds payable on a U.S. bank,

VISA *VISA* MasterCard *MasterCard* Discover *DISCOVER* Check, or Money Orders.

CARD NUMBER

EXPIRES Month/Year (required)

SIGNATURE OF CARDHOLDER

U.S. Shipping Charges

	Standard Delivery		Priority Mail		Rush Delivery	
	Zip Codes up to 49999	50000+	49999	50000	Two Day	Next Day
Minimum	$2.00	$2.00	$3.00	$3.00	$7.50	$12.00
½ to 1 lb.	3.00	3.00	3.00	3.00	7.50	13.50
up to 2 lbs.	3.00	3.00	3.00	3.00	8.50	14.50
up to 5 lbs.	4.50	6.00	6.50	6.50	9.50	18.50
up to 10 lbs	5.00	8.00	10.00	14.50	15.50	26.00
up to 15 lbs	6.00	10.00	14.00	20.00	21.50	31.50
Add for each additional 5 lbs.	+1.00	+2.00	+5.00	+5.00	+5.00	+5.00

Alaska and Hawaii ADD $10.00 to Two Day and Next Day Charges (No PO Boxes.)

International Shipping

CANADIAN CHARGES	OVERSEAS SURFACE	OVERSEAS PRIORITY/AIR
Up to ½ lb. $3.00	Up to ½ lb. $4.00	Up to ½ lb. $7.00
Up to 2 lbs. 5.00	Up to 2 lbs. 9.00	Up to 1 lbs. 13.00
Up to 3 lbs. 6.50	Up to 3 lbs. 11.00	Up to 2 lbs. 22.00
Up to 4 lbs. 8.00	Up to 4 lbs. 13.00	Up to 3 lbs. 28.00
		Up to 4 lbs. 34.00
ADD $1.50 for each additional lb. PRIORITY/AIR: ADD $2.00 to Total	ADD $2.00 for each additional lb. (Allow 2-4 months for delivery)	ADD $6.00 for each additional lb. (Allow 2-4 weeks)

The WoodenBoat Store

P.O. Box 78, Naskeag Road, Brooklin, Maine 04616-0078

EMail: wbstore@woodenboat.com

Ordered by _____

Address _____

_____

City/State/Zip _____

Day Phone # _____

Catalog Code **WBP**

SHIP TO — only if different than "ORDERED BY"

Name _____

Address _____

_____

City/State/Zip _____

Product #	Qty.	Item, Size, Color	Ship Wt.	Total

WoodenBoat Magazine—US Subscriptions: One-year $27.00, Two-years $51.00, Three-years $75.00

SUB TOTAL

Maine Residents Add 6% Tax

❑ Standard
❑ Priority Mail

❑ Two Day
❑ Next Day

❑ Int'l Surface
❑ Int'l Air

TOTAL

Our Guarantee... Satisfaction or Your Money Back!

Pre-payment is required. Payment MUST be in U.S. funds payable on a U.S. bank,

VISA **VISA**   MasterCard **MasterCard**   Discover **DISCOVER**   Check, or Money Orders.

CARD NUMBER										EXPIRES Month/Year (required)	

SIGNATURE OF CARDHOLDER

U.S. Shipping Charges

	Standard Delivery		Priority Mail		Rush Delivery	
Zip Codes	up to 49999	50000+	49999	50000	Two Day	Next Day
Minimum	$2.00	$2.00	$3.00	$3.00	$7.50	$12.00
½ to 1 lb.	3.00	3.00	3.00	3.00	7.50	13.50
up to 2 lbs.	3.00	3.00	3.00	3.00	8.50	14.50
up to 5 lbs.	4.50	6.00	6.50	6.50	9.50	18.50
up to 10 lbs	5.00	8.00	10.00	14.50	15.50	26.00
up to 15 lbs	6.00	10.00	14.00	20.00	21.50	31.50
Add for each additional 5 lbs.	+1.00	+2.00	+5.00	+5.00	+5.00	+5.00

Alaska and Hawaii ADD $10.00 to Two Day and Next Day Charges (No PO Boxes.)

International Shipping

CANADIAN CHARGES	OVERSEAS SURFACE	OVERSEAS PRIORITY/AIR
Up to ½ lb. $3.00	Up to ½ lb. $4.00	Up to ½ lb. $7.00
Up to 2 lbs. 5.00	Up to 2 lbs. 9.00	Up to 1 lbs. 13.00
Up to 3 lbs. 6.50	Up to 3 lbs. 11.00	Up to 2 lbs. 22.00
Up to 4 lbs. 8.00	Up to 4 lbs. 13.00	Up to 3 lbs. 28.00
		Up to 4 lbs. 34.00
ADD $1.50 for each additional lb. PRIORITY/AIR: ADD $2.00 to Total	ADD $2.00 for each additional lb. (Allow 2-4 months for delivery)	ADD $6.00 for each additional lb. (Allow 2-4 weeks)